A COMPANION GUIDE TO MENTALLY DISORDERED OFFENDERS

2ND EDITION

NIGEL STONE

Shaw & Sons

A Companion Guide to
Mentally Disordered Offenders
Second Edition

Published by
Shaw & Sons Limited
Shaway House
21 Bourne Park
Bourne Road
Crayford
Kent DA1 4BZ

www.shaws.co.uk

© Shaw & Sons Limited 2003

Published May 2003
(First Edition published 1995 by Owen Wells Publisher)

ISBN 0 7219 1621 X

A CIP catalogue record for this book is
available from the British Library

Printed in Great Britain by
Bell & Bain Limited, Glasgow

SUMMARY OF CONTENTS

TABLE OF CONTENTS

FOREWORD

Completion of the first edition of this book left a feeling of incompleteness, a sense that the whole ought to be greater than the sum of the parts, offering an all-encompassing 'big picture' vista, weaving law, policy and practice into a one-stop sourcebook. Regrettably, take two does not go any further in achieving that prospect. However, in so far as it pulls together and illuminates the content and use of the somewhat complex criminal law provisions affecting mentally disordered offenders, it appears to offer more specific detail along the criminal justice pathway, from police station to absolute discharge of the restricted patient, than anything else currently on the market, even if it will not provide ready answers and psychiatric solutions to every sentencing dilemma or management problem. Not that ready answers necessarily lie elsewhere, of course, given the reality that the problems and needs of many mentally disordered offenders do not lend themselves to ready solutions within criminal justice or any other form of intervention. For a considerable number, the penal system will have to continue absorbing them, perhaps because the needs of public protection must take precedence or because the offender is not ready to respond to help. The meeting points (or collision sites) of health, social, legal and ethical demands are notoriously fraught crossroads but the contents here may provide a serviceable route map. I am fully conscious, of course, that many of the relevant legal provisions remain characterised by considerable under-use, to the point of virtual desuetude.

In concluding a book of this kind there is always a fear that the text will be overtaken by a surge of new legislation, rendering much of the contents obsolete. The legislative tide in mental health has been slow moving, compared to the dizzying pace of criminal justice changes, despite prolonged serious criticism of the 1983 Act. In this instance it can be said with complete confidence that fundamental change is in sight. The Government is committed to mental health law reform and, in the wake of the White Paper of 2000, has published its draft *Mental Health Bill* (2002). However, finalising, passing and implementing the controversial new law is likely to take some while, justifying a new edition of this guide within the existing framework. It has been tempting to try to include extensive details both of the arguments for change and the essentials of the new framework but that would be outside the scope and practical purpose of the text. Instead, brief reference has been made to some of the proposals in the Bill and also to the mental health aspects of the Criminal Justice Bill, currently before Parliament. Though the latter is enjoying a smoother passage, the cost and resource implications suggest there will be no rush to implement the new sentencing framework.

The term 'mentally disordered offenders' is not to everyone's liking. NACRO (1994) has preferred 'mentally disturbed offenders' to avoid the appearance of addressing only those persons who come within the criteria of the 1983 Act. The publisher and I have opted to continue use of the more familiar and generally used handle, without intending to confine the focus so narrowly and without wishing to enter a protracted preliminary debate about terminology.

There are bound to be errors and omissions and I would be grateful for constructive criticism and comments of readers so that these can be rectified in any future editions. Thanks as before to the probation officers and psychiatrists who contributed case material, to Erica Barr who cheerfully and skilfully processed the manuscript of the first edition, thus providing the core of this update and expansion, even though the author has now had to become self-servicing at the typeface, and to Sue Massey who endured its preparation at no small cost to quality time.

Nigel Stone

GLOSSARY

AA	appropriate adult
ACR	automatic conditional release
ADSS	Association of Directors of Social Services
ASW	approved social worker
BA	Bail Act 1976
BASW	British Association of Social Workers
CAA	Criminal Appeal Act 1968
CJA	Criminal Justice Act 1991
CJPOA	Criminal Justice and Public Order Act 1994
CPA	Care Programme Approach
CP(I)A	Criminal Procedure (Insanity) Act 1964
CP(IUP)A	Criminal Procedure (Insanity and Unfitness to Plead) Act 1991
CPN	community psychiatric nurse
CPS	Crown Prosecution Service
Cr App R(S)	Criminal Appeal Reports (Sentencing)
Crim LR	Criminal Law Review
CRO	community rehabilitation order
C(S)A	Crime (Sentences) Act 1997
DoH	Department of Health
ECHR	European Convention on Human Rights
ECT	electro-convulsant therapy
EHRR	European Human Rights Reports
FME	forensic medical examiner (police surgeon)
HA	Homicide Act 1957
HMIP	HM Inspectorate of Probation
HOC	Home Office Circular
HSG	Health Service Guideline
J	Justice of the High Court
LASSL	Local Authority Social Services Letter
LJ	Lord Justice of Appeal
MCA	Magistrates' Courts Act 1980
MCR	Magistrates' Courts Rules 1981
MDO	mentally disordered offender
MHA	Mental Health Act 1983

MHA(COP)	Mental Health Act Code of Practice 1999
MH(PC)A	Mental Health (Patients in the Community) Act 1995
MHRTR	Mental Health Review Tribunal Rules
MH(S)A	Mental Health (Scotland) Act 1984
NHSA	National Health Service Act 1977
PACE	Police and Criminal Evidence Act 1984
PCC(S)A	Powers of Criminal Courts (Sentencing) Act 2000
POA	Prosecution of Offences Act 1985
RMO	Responsible Medical Officer
RSU	Regional Secure Unit
SSI	Social Services Inspectorate
TLA	Trial of Lunatics Act 1883

1
INTRODUCTION

Mentally disordered offenders (MDOs) can no longer be considered the marginalised, disenfranchised group they were in the relatively recent past, 'the people nobody owns' (Prins, 1993). The thrust of official reports and guidance from the Home Office and the Department of Health, from HOC 66/1990 onwards and particularly the Reed Report (1992), the analytical attentions of powerful Committees of Inquiry (*eg* Ritchie *et al*, 1994 on the events leading up to the killing of Jonathan Zito by Christopher Clunis; Blom-Cooper *et al*, 1995 on the management of Andrew Robinson at Torbay) and a flurry of recent publications (*eg* Staite *et al*, 1994; Children's Legal Centre, 1994; Vaughan and Badger, 1995; Laing, 1999) all contribute to a concerted focus on MDOs as a special challenge within the criminal justice system and a particular priority within mainstream health service provision. The NHS planning and priorities guidance since 1994-95 has identified services for MDOs as a 'first order' ministerial priority.

Probation staff have had an unprecedented opportunity to get to grips with the new social care market to address the needs of mentally disturbed defendants and appropriate phrasebooks (*eg* ACOP, 1994) have been prepared to guide them through the bureaucratic maze. Diversion opportunities are being explored and developed in a rapidly developing evolution of partnership and innovative practice. Speedier and more accurate recognition, earlier intervention, avoidance of unnecessary and counter-productive prosecution and concentrated focus upon care in the community seem to be the new orthodoxy of compassionate good sense.

This optimism has to be balanced with more downbeat realism. In somewhat cursory and summary form, the inhibiting factors worth bearing in mind can be cited as follows:

The legislative base: As Blom-Cooper *et al* (1995) pointed out, there are fundamental flaws in the 1983 Act which now make it somewhat obsolete. It assumes that 'care and treatment for people with mental disorder of a certain severity require hospital treatment' and it removes 'medical treatment from the social context in which care must be delivered to be therapeutic', focusing 'not on patients but on doctors'. The radical transformation of mental health services from hospital base to community focus has not been reflected adequately in legislation. The Act does not address the wide range of seriously mentally disordered people who do not necessarily require compulsory admission. The limited legislation which is designed to support mentally disprdered offenders in the community (*eg* psychiatric community rehabilitation orders and guardianship orders) has been little used.

High security hospital care: The level of patient care in the Special Hospital system has been subject to a searing critique by the Committee of Inquiry into Ashworth Hospital (Blom-Cooper, 1992), finding disquieting evidence of a regime 'hostile to therapeutic aims' and presenting a 'profoundly depressing' picture of life in a 'brutalising, stagnant, closed institution'. See also Fallon *et al* (1999).

1

'The all-pervading nature of an oppressive sub-culture which persistently undermines the therapeutic approach and places constraints on those who do not conform to it, was made clear.'

Covert and overt racial discrimination and homophobic attitudes were evident. Social workers had been obliged to play a marginal role in patient care and 'were outside the mainstream of patient-care decisions'. They were also professionally isolated from social work colleagues and weakened in their capacity to form an effective bridge between the hospital, the patient's home and the wider community. The hospital has since committed itself to a programme of urgent reformation.

Medium secure provision: Though the Government has pledged to increase the provision of medium secure beds, the shortfall remains a major block to meeting the needs of offender-patients, despite the growth in private sector provision which has exploited a niche in the market, albeit locating patients at considerably greater distance from their home communities. The Lord Chief Justice of the day added his voice to judicial concern about the 'alarming' shortage of hospital beds for mentally disordered offenders for whom retribution and deterrence is inappropriate (*Guardian*, 1 April 1995):

'It is no more acceptable for the Government to deny the courts the ability to order the detention of disturbed and dangerous offenders in secure hospitals than it would be to deny them the ability to send ruthless criminals to prison.'

Facilities in the Community: While the psychiatric population has benefited from the avoidance of unnecessary, long-term institutional care, community facilities have yet to catch up with deinstitutionalisation. 'Court diversion schemes are in danger of diverting offenders into a care in the community system that does not exist' (Haynes and Henfrey, 1995).

Obstacles to inter-agency collaboration: The Mental Health Foundation (1994) summarised the obstacles and difficulties as follows:

(i)   the unco-ordinated nature of existing management and operational structures within parallel organisations;

(ii) uncertainty over future developments;

(iii) different definitions of what constitutes a 'mentally disordered offender';

(iv) lack of familiarity with the financial systems which operate under the new purchaser/ provider relationships in the NHS and local authorities;

(v)   lack of effective systems for monitoring the provision and quality of services;

(vi) the unwillingness of agencies, and some Government departments in particular, to accept that they have responsibility for mentally disordered offenders;

(vii) the difficulty in achieving early intervention, due to the lack of inter-agency co-operation;

(viii)the fact that existing structures are underdeveloped and responsibilities for funding are not clarified, needs are undefined and unquantified, and providers not clearly identified nor contracts agreed;

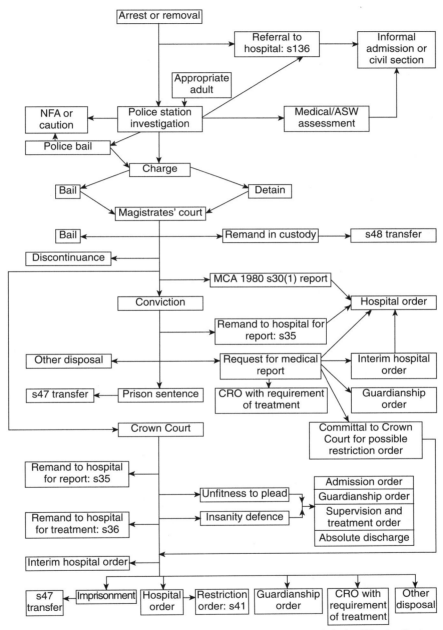

Simplified Flow Chart of Mentally Disordered Offenders in the Criminal Justice System

(ix) uncertainty about the availability of funding and the lack of long-term funding for new projects;

(x) the absence of any statutory obligation for agencies to provide care;

(xi) the fact that care provision is often dependent on the services of committed individuals;

(xii) the fact that the problem of the mentally disordered offender is one of low incidence but high cost.

The Home Office and the Department of Health (1995) have since emphasised the importance of inter-agency working, including 'full and timely sharing of information', 'active co-operation between all agencies in securing access to resources and facilities' and 'monitoring success'. Among key elements which it has recommended should be reflected in inter-agency arrangements are the following:

(i) local services to be planned on the basis of clearly assessed local needs;

(ii) a nominated lead agency to provide a vital co-ordinating role;

(iii) joint training initiatives;

(iv) a system of recording information both within and between agencies to be established to monitor the effectiveness of arrangements.

Haynes and Henfrey (1995) identified that the social care market has many hidden pitfalls for the unwary, with agencies in unhealthy competition for funding and juggling limited resources. For example, they cautioned that probation involvement in a case can offer an excuse for low priority and they suggest that probation officers should be reluctant to offer themselves as key workers in any care plan as this may have the unintended consequence of 'closing the door to future health and social services expenditure on their clients'.

'Criminal justice agencies do not have large-scale purchasing resources and their clients depend on retaining their existing rights to non-criminal justice purchasing.'

They argued that there is thus more mileage for probation staff in pursuing an advocacy role and in supporting multi-agency forms or 'broker' agencies which can create lines of communication between criminal justice and social care agencies, ensuring that purchasers are properly aware of the social care needs of offenders.

On the basis of inspections in eight local authorities of Social Services' contribution to inter-agency work and services for MDOs, the Social Services Inspectorate (1997) concluded that 'users of mental health services, and particularly those who offend, are faced by a bewildering number of agencies and professional workers with a part to play in their health, social care and supervision'. Though locating evidence of joint work on mental health policy in all the authorities inspected, the SSI noted that 'sometimes the needs of MDOs were low priority or were overlooked altogether'.

'The policy initiative to divert people into more appropriate social and health care was well understood but resources were sometimes limited to support this in practice. Although all health authorities are reporting full implementation of the CPA, there is some concern about the quality of implementation.'

To explore further the capacity to support MDOs in the community, Vaughan *et al* (2000) surveyed community mental health teams in Wessex. All teams reported having considerable problems in working with this group (who represented on average 7% of each team's caseload). 'In particular, they had difficulty in balancing the needs of a small group of mobile, non-compliant and difficult-to-engage clients with the very large numbers of "more routine" referrals', and proficiency levels did not match the demands of this client group. One of the biggest difficulties was in obtaining appropriate support from other services: specialist forensic services being seen as remote, difficult to access and slow to respond to requests for advice and assessments, coupled with a shortage of secure beds. Among other common deficiencies, teams lacked access to appropriate day services and accommodation resources. Learning disability teams had the highest levels of MDOs on their caseloads, with clients who posed the greatest challenge in terms of violence, self-harm and sexual offences.

Equal opportunities: A disproportionately high number of women and black people enter the mental health system and secure units in particular. Though the factors of race, culture and gender remain insufficiently analysed, there is a real basis of concern that black people are misdiagnosed and that women have been over-exposed to forensic psychiatric intervention (Allen, 1987) and, in particular, have been selected for maximum security far too readily (Mental Health Foundation, 1994).

Mentally disordered offenders remain a complex, unpredictable and multi-problem sector and the rhetoric of 'diversion', a term now in ministerial disfavour at the Home Office, is no substitute for staff-intensive, sustained collaborative initiatives such as the multidisciplinary case management system described by Cooke *et al* (1994) fostering longer-term relationships with small numbers of offenders requiring sustained special care. This type of intensive teamwork was advocated in the Christopher Clunis Inquiry Report (Ritchie *et al*, 1994) and may be provided for within the revitalised Care Programme Approach (see Chapter 15), following the failure of the Supervision Register initiative of 1994 to strengthen community oversight and overcome the pattern of failure and missed opportunity that Ritchie *et al* identified so tellingly.

The text that follows aims to cover comprehensively but compactly the stage-by-stage scope for discretion and intervention, stating the law as understood on 31 January 2003.

2
POLICE INVESTIGATION AND DISCRETION

As the most common first point of contact between mentally disordered people and the criminal justice system, the police play a key role: intervening when a person is presenting a risk to themselves or others in public; identifying that a suspected person may be mentally disordered; arranging for the suspect to be examined by a doctor (FME); calling for the services of an appropriate adult; contacting an approved social worker (ASW) to arrange an assessment of the suspect. Thereafter, the police may decide to take no further action or to caution, thus diverting the offender from prosecution, or, if it is considered right to charge the suspect, the police may notify the court, where appropriate, of any mental health concerns. It is thus important that the police 'establish close working relationships with local health, probation and social services to assist them in exercising their powers' (HOC 66/1990 para. 4(I)). The Circular (para. 26(i)) asked Chief Constables:

> '... to ensure that, taking account of the public interest, consideration is always given to alternatives to prosecuting mentally disordered offenders, including taking no further action where appropriate, and that effective arrangements are established with local health and social services authorities to ensure their speedy involvement when mentally disordered persons are taken into police custody.'

This message has since been augmented by Section 3 of *Inter-Agency Working* (Home Office/DoH, 1995), giving examples of training, liaison and monitoring initiatives.

This chapter outlines police powers and responsibilities, and summarises recent research which suggests that these objectives are as yet unrealised in many respects. Ritchie *et al* (1994), in the light of the Christopher Clunis Enquiry, recommended that the police should be given proper training in mental illness, and that an officer should be appointed at every police station to deal with mental health issues and liaise with local community mental health services. From March 1995, this advice became part of Metropolitan Police policy, which pledges 'to treat mentally disordered people in a compassionate, skilful and informed way', seeking 'the most appropriate course of action for any individual coming to police attention, in consultation and co-operation with carers and other relevant agencies'. For a general review of the issues, see Laing (1995).

Reference will be made at various points to two Home Office Research Studies, so the foundation for these can be conveniently outlined here:

(a) Bucke and Brown's (1997) study of suspects in police custody is based on observation in the custody areas of 13 police stations in ten police areas from August 1995 to February 1996, during which 3,950 suspects passed through. In addition, some 12,500 custody records were analysed from mid-1995, drawn from 25 police stations (the 13 observed plus another 12 stations in the same areas). Just 2% of the custody record sample were treated as being mentally disordered or mentally handicapped, tending to be older in comparison to other detainees (43%

being over 30 compared to 27% under that age) and more likely to be female (24% being women compared to 15% of the whole sample). The researchers acknowledged that custody officers probably failed to identify the full extent of mental disorder, given studies reporting higher proportions using independent assessments (see page 14).

(b) Phillips and Brown's (1998) survey of arrests made between late 1993 and early 1994, based on ten police stations in seven police areas (some being the same as featured in the Bucke and Brown study), collecting information about 4,250 detainees, proceeding to examine prosecution and court outcomes.

'PLACE OF SAFETY' DETENTION UNDER SECTION 136

This provision applies to anyone who appears to be 'mentally disordered' as defined by MHA 1983 s1 (see page 84).

MHA 1983 s136

(1) If a constable finds in a place to which the public have access a person who appears to him to be suffering from mental disorder and to be in immediate need of care or control, the constable may, if he thinks it necessary to do so in the interests of that person or for the protection of other persons, remove that person to a place of safety within the meaning of section 135 above.

(2) A person removed to a place of safety under this section may be detained there for a period not exceeding 72 hours for the purpose of enabling him to be examined by a registered medical practitioner and to be interviewed by an approved social worker and of making any necessary arrangements for his treatment or care.

The police are often placed under considerable pressure from the public to intervene in incidents of bizarre, abnormal or disordered behaviour in circumstances where a nuisance is being caused, even though it may not be clear whether an offence has been committed. The power of this provision, available whether or not the person has or is suspected of having committed an offence, may thus provide a useful interventive discretion but also raises obvious civil liberties issues. By far the greatest use of this provision has been in the Thames area. Research by Bean *et al* for MIND (1991) of 100 cases in the Metropolitan Police Area 1985-87 provides the fullest recent evidence of the use and abuse of s136. Guidance on the use of s136 is contained in the Department of Health's *Code of Practice* on Implementation of MHA 1983 (1999, Chapter 10), which may have served to improve local practice and thus have superseded this research.

MIND's study of an admittedly unrepresentative sample showed a group young in proportion to other psychiatric populations, with a high level of unemployment, the majority having local addresses, only 18% being regarded as 'no fixed abode' or 'drifting'. A disproportionately high number were of an African-Caribbean ethnicity, suggesting a pattern of police differentiation. Audini and Lelliott's (1999) analysis of Metropolitan Police data indicated that over a quarter of s136 detainees were black, with over a tenth from an 'other' ethnic minority group, and that over a third were born outside the United Kingdom. However, while Churchill *et al* (1999) note that s136 detentions are more common in the black population, they add that 'several authors have found no evidence of differences in the behaviour of the police implementing s136 in different ethnic groups'.

The majority of cases were referred by the public, including neighbours or relatives, only 9% of cases being police-initiated. The Metropolitan Police's Standing Orders advise officers that there is no reason to interfere with the liberty of those who may be suffering delusions but who are not in other respects mentally disordered or presenting any risk. Nevertheless, in a small number of sample cases, s136 was used despite the absence of any evidence of serious mental disturbance or of danger.

Public Place

A 'place to which the public have access' is not defined but clearly extends beyond the public highway and open spaces to include areas to which the public are admitted as 'the public', *eg* shops, bus and railway stations, pubs, sports centres, etc. This will also extend to Probation and Social Services offices. Most difficulty will arise in practice in regard to landings, staircases and walkways serving flats and other communal living units, though the issue is likely to be interpreted permissively by courts. In the MIND study, subjects were arrested from 'private premises' in approximately one-fifth of the cases, either because the police officer misunderstood s136 or the police felt they had 'no option', in the face of difficulty in securing the assistance of Social Services. For power of entry onto private premises under s135, see page 12.

Arrest

Though a person detained under s136 is not arrested for an offence, the reality of the situation may well mean that the police officer reacts pragmatically to 'deal' with the situation. In Bean's study, the officer intended: to use s136 from the outset in 38% of the sample cases; to charge with an offence (17%); to remove the subject from the incident and take to the police station for consultation (39%).

Charge, Detain or Refer?

Most of the MIND sample 'could have been charged with an offence, generally of a minor nature' but normally no prosecution will be pursued following s136 detentions.

> 'Section 136 was likely to be invoked in preference to charging when the disorder was of an apparently serious nature and the offence of a relatively minor nature. A grey area existed where the implementation of s136 depended on the exigencies of the case and where charges might have been preferred if the practical arrangements for s136 had not materialised. Officers regarded s136 and charging as alternative and not concurrent disposals.'

Section 136 thus can be used as a form of diversion from prosecution. It may, of course, be possible to resolve the matter by referral to a community mental health service or agency.

In a number of MIND's sample cases, an informal referral for psychiatric assessment might have been preferable but police officers held a general presumption favouring s136 powers, believing that this was 'the standard procedure', or that this placed the hospital under a greater obligation to admit the subject.

Place of Detention

A 'place of safety' includes a hospital, a police station, local authority residential accommodation, private or voluntary residential or nursing homes for the mentally disordered, and 'any other suitable place where the occupier is willing temporarily to receive the person ' (s135(6)).

Though the DoH suggests that, ideally, a police station should be used only in exceptional circumstances and, even then, only temporarily while an approved social worker makes arrangements for removal elsewhere, in practice the police station may prove a convenient first destination, prior to removal to hospital. Robertson (1992) found that at only two of the 14 police stations studied were officers able to take a person considered in need of psychiatric help directly to hospital. Hoggett (1996) suggested that the subject may well prefer to sort things out there rather than be taken direct to a psychiatric hospital. Hospitals are under no legal duty to accept a s136 detainee and may well be some distance away. Churchill *et al* (1999) noted that hospitals have been refusing s136 referrals on the basis of bed shortages. MIND suggest that a community-based health or local authority facility should be designated as the preferred place of safety, especially given genuine concern about detaining mentally disordered people in police custody for any length of time and poor relations between sections of the black community and the police.

HOC 66/90 indicated the desirability of ensuring that, wherever possible, police stations are not used as places of safety as they will not have the facilities necessary for the welfare of mentally disordered persons. The Reed Committee (1992, para. 11.2) recommended that effective local agreement between police and mental health services should seek to ensure that, wherever possible, mentally disordered people can receive supportive care without first being taken to a police station. This was echoed by *Inter-Agency Working* (Home Office/DoH, 1995) which suggested that where use of police stations cannot be avoided, for example in the investigation of serious offences, it may be advantageous to identify designated stations and officers with specialist training, either on duty or on call.

At the Police Station

The s136 subject is not a suspect but is in 'legal custody' (s137(1)) and is subject to PACE Code C (see the later part of this chapter in the context of mentally disordered suspects), other than in regard to reviews and extensions of detention (para. 1.10). Care should thus be taken to withhold where necessary any personal property which the subject may use to cause harm to self or others (para. 4.2).

Code C para. 3.10 specifies:

'It is imperative that a mentally disordered or mentally handicapped person who has been detained under section 136 of the Mental Health Act 1983 should be assessed as soon as possible. If that assessment is to take place at the police station, an approved social worker and a registered medical practitioner shall be called to the police station as soon as possible in order to interview and examine the person. Once the person has been interviewed and examined and suitable arrangements have been made for his treatment or care, he can no longer be detained under

9

section 136. The person shall not be released until he has been seen by both the approved social worker and the registered medical practitioner.'

MHA (COP) 1999 para. 10.6(b) also advises that the local Social Services and an appropriately qualified doctor should be contacted immediately and that local police should have specified procedures for establishing such contact. If an assessment by a doctor can be undertaken 'without undue delay', the custody officer has discretion not to call for a police surgeon as would otherwise be necessary (Code C para. 9.2). Once the subject has been assessed and a decision made about their care, s136 has served its purpose, detention ceases and there is no power to detain the person further even though 72 hours have not yet elapsed.

As the MIND study indicated, the length of time spent at the police station is normally quite short, the average time for their sample being 234 minutes, a figure 'probably biased by the two incidents in which people spent over 15 hours in the police station'.

Phillips and Brown (1998) reported that of 67 detainees treated as mentally disordered or handicapped, 22 had been detained under s136. Bucke and Brown (1997) reported that four in ten of detainees with mental problems were in custody under s136.

Assessment
Police officers have to act as initial psychiatric diagnosticians and tend to make common-sense, behaviourally-based diagnoses. The MIND study demonstrated that police and psychiatrists did not collaborate readily together. The police were often frustrated by difficulties in obtaining an assessment because of catchment area disputes, inadequate facilities for violent detainees, insufficient beds or a psychiatric view that the subject was untreatable. Doctors were sometimes unhappy with the lack of information supplied by the police, and their reluctance to remain at the hospital with the subject. Nevertheless, the psychiatrists thought that most referrals were appropriate (in 69 out of 82 cases).

Social workers were involved comparatively infrequently in the MIND study. This is at odds with s136(2) and appeared to reflect a common psychiatric perception that s136 provides direct statutory authority to admit to hospital, by-passing social worker involvement, whereas its purpose is actually to obtain an assessment with a view to possible admission as an informal patient or under a civil power to detention. MHA (COP) paras. 10.8 and 10.14 make clear that s136 is not an emergency admissions section and that the person must be seen by both the doctor and the approved social worker, preferably in a joint assessment. 'If the doctor sees the person first and concludes that admission to hospital is unnecessary, or the person agrees to informal admission, the individual must still be seen by an ASW, who must consult with the doctor about any other necessary arrangements that might need to be made for (the person's) treatment and care' (10.14).

Of the 22 s136 detainees noted in Phillips and Brown's (1998) study, the full assessment procedure under MHA 1983 was conducted on just five occasions.

Compulsory Admission
MHA (COP) 1999 para. 10.18 states that, where compulsory admission is indicated, the following principles should apply:

(i) Where the hospital is the 'place of safety', the person should be admitted under MHA 1983 s2 or s3, whichever is appropriate.

(ii) Where the police station is the 'place of safety', compulsory admission should normally be under s2 or s3 but s4 may be used if there is an urgent need to move the person to hospital.

(iii) Persons detained in hospital under s136 pending completion of their assessment should not have their detention extended under s5(2) or (4) (see page 232).

MHA statistics (DoH Bulletin 2002/26) record 3,075 (men accounting for 1,861 or 61%) detentions under s136 in the 12 months to 31 March 2002 where the place of safety was a hospital, comparable with only 829 in 1991-92 and 1,833 in 1997-98. The Bulletin does not indicate the numbers that led to use of ss2-4 powers.

Personality Disorder and Section 136

In a retrospective analysis of all those detained under s136 in Westminster in the six month period June to November 1991, Spence and McPhillips (1995) reported 57 individuals who were assessed in 65 instances. Whereas, schizophrenia was the most common diagnosis (38.5%), personality disordered individuals (29.8%) received the most assessments. They were less likely to be admitted to hospital or to be detained under further MHA section but were more likely to come to repeat s136 attention. The mental health system appeared unable to address their needs.

Section 136 in 'Rural' England

Churchill *et al* (1999) have noted that s136 detentions are more common in urban areas and in London in particular. They have suggested that London may be over-represented because the Metropolitan Police maintain better records and 'other areas rarely record its use unless the patient is admitted'. Seeking to establish the application of s136 in 'rural areas', Greenberg *et al* (2002) surveyed its use in six custody centres in Devon and Cornwall between October and December 2000. Over that period 178 (116 male) persons were detained (47 in Plymouth, which is not typically rural), most from the street (with only four from private dwellings). The most common behaviour leading to detention was suicidal or self-harming conduct (in 62 – 35% – cases), followed by bizarre behaviour, apparently drunken/intoxicated behaviour and passive behaviour. Detention occurred in the daytime period 9am – 5pm in only a quarter of cases. The mean total time in custody was just over 7 hours, the longest delay being to await the ASW's arrival. Overall, 57 of the 178 detainees were admitted to hospital, a conversion rate of 32%, nearly half (28) as informal patients, with 27 subject to s2 and two as s3 admissions. This rate was noticeably lower than reported in previous studies, located predominantly in inner city areas.

The researchers note that health services were concerned that use of s136 was increasing and might be deployed where other courses of action, such as arrest for drunkenness, would have been more appropriate. Social Services had the greater difficulty in providing timely response to requests for assessment. The police were worried most by self-harming and bizarre behaviour. The report concludes by suggesting that a rural area is not well served by a rigid and polarised view that a place of safety should be either a police station or a hospital and advocating a more collaborative and flexible approach in meeting the mental health and security needs of a rural community. The same researchers (Greenberg and Haines, 2003) have since compared use of s136 in Devon and Cornwall with such detentions in other provincial police areas with similar characteristics, discovering considerable variation in detention rate per 10,000 population – Devon and Cornwall using the section over 30 times more often than Lincolnshire. They speculate that the reason for such wide variation may include lack of sufficient mental health training, causing less well trained officers to make inappropriate use of this power.

POWERS OF ENTRY AND 'PLACE OF SAFETY' DETENTION UNDER SECTION 135

MHA 1983 s135 may prove appropriate where the individual causing concern is not in a public place and access to private property is denied. The section applies to a person believed to be suffering from mental disorder who has been, or is being, ill-treated, neglected or not kept under proper control, or who is living alone and is unable to care for themselves. Acting upon information on oath laid by an ASW, a magistrate is empowered to issue a warrant authorising a police officer to enter specified premises to remove the individual to a 'place of safety', normally a hospital. The warrant authorises the person's detention for up to 72 hours.

MHA (COP) 1999 paras. 2.12 and 2.24 suggest that s135 powers may be helpful where either an ASW or a doctor is seeking access to a person for assessment purposes to avoid either communication through a closed door or delay while access is negotiated.

MHA statistics (DoH Bulletin 2002/26) record 318 (men accounting for 166 or 52%) detentions under s135 in the 12 months to 31 March 2002 where the place of safety was a hospital, comparable with only 99 in 1991-92 and 204 in 1997-98. The Bulletin does not indicate the numbers that led to use of ss2-4 powers.

TREATMENT AND QUESTIONING OF MENTALLY DISORDERED SUSPECTS

PACE 1984 Code C (revised 1995 as part of the 'green' Codes), governing the detention, treatment and questioning of persons, recognises mental disorder as a special category of vulnerability requiring additional provisions and safeguards, in particular the involvement of an appropriate adult (AA), usefully summarised in Annex E of the Code.

A number of reported cases over the past decade, where the defence has appealed on the grounds that admissions obtained from the suspect are unreliable, illustrate the problems that can arise in police interviews and the potential importance of the safeguard of involving an independent adult. Reported cases have largely concerned suspects with learning difficulties.

In *R v Delaney* (1989) 88 Cr App R 338, the appellant, after initial denial, had eventually admitted indecently assaulting a girl aged three. He was described as educationally subnormal with an IQ of 80. 'His personality was such that when being interviewed as a suspect, he would be subject to quick and unpleasant emotional arousal which might lead him to wish to rid himself of the interview by bringing it to an end as rapidly as possible'. The police officers in their questioning had sought to minimise the gravity of the offence and to emphasise that 'the real requirement of the offender was psychiatric help ... that this was a case more for the attention of doctors than judges'. The officers said that they 'did not want to frighten the appellant away from confessing his guilt', overlooking that this might be encouraging a false confession. The appellant's conviction was thus quashed as 'unsafe and unsatisfactory'. He was 'poorly equipped to cope with sustained interrogation and the longer the pressure was imposed upon him the more confused he was likely to be in his own mind'.

R v MacKenzie (1992) 96 Cr App R 98 illustrates a suspect, again with a limited IQ of 73-76, who confessed to offences, some of which he could not possibly have done, because of his propensity to be 'the centre of attention' and to 'manipulate the system' because of his wish to be in a psychiatric hospital.

The well-known case of *R v Judith Ward* (1993) 96 Cr App R 1 concerned a suspect who, though not subject to any improper pressure or inducement to confess, was said to suffer from a mental disorder which caused her to make claims which, in the words of one psychiatrist, 'brought interest and excitement to an otherwise lonely, friendless person'. The Court of Appeal noted two terms used by the clinical psychologist in evidence: 'suggestibility' ('the extent to which a person can be persuaded to adopt a leading question or give an answer which is affected by verbal pressure') and 'confabulation' ('the extent to which a memory of an event or statement can have added to it some other material which is conscious or unconscious invention'). Appropriate adults should thus be alert to suspects' tendencies to accept too readily suggestions offered or to confabulate.

In a study of the interviewing of suspects with intellectual disabilities, Tully and Cahill (1984), noted by Brown (1997), identified their varying response to questioning:

> 'In some cases they may be extremely resistant but in others they perceive the situation as one demanding obedience and be over-ready to answer questions in a way which they believe will please the interviewer, irrespective of the truth. ... Questioning designed to portray the suspect in a bad light may lead the interviewee to respond in ways that avoid him or her looking foolish rather than representing the truth. Pressure to respond may also reduce the accuracy of replies. ... Police officers consistently over-estimated the reliability of information provided by them. Furthermore, officers took suspects' co-operativeness and confidence to imply reliability, probably because in normal cases these qualities are linked.'

Initial Recognition

Code C para. 1.4 specifies:

> 'If an officer has any suspicion, or is told in good faith, that a person of any age may be mentally disordered or mentally handicapped, or mentally incapable of understanding the significance of questions put to him or his replies, then that person shall be treated as mentally disordered or mentally handicapped for the purposes of this Code.'

'Mental disorder' is defined in accordance with MHA 1983 s1(2) (see page 84) whereas 'mental handicap' means that a person 'is in a state of arrested or incomplete development of mind which includes significant impairment of intelligence and social functioning' (PACE 1984 s77(3)).

The police officer is thus expected to make a lay diagnosis, and the suspect's use of alcohol or drugs could mask a mental disability. Some evidence of the police's competence and accuracy is provided by Gudjonsson's study (1993) of 156 adult suspects being interviewed at two police stations in the Metropolitan Police Area. On the basis of a clinical assessment prior to interview, 7% of suspects were judged to be suffering from mental illness and 3% from mental handicap, but an appropriate adult (AA) was summonsed in just four of the 12 cases of identified mental illness and in two of the four cases of intellectual impairment. Between 15 and 20% of suspects might have been entitled to the additional safeguard of an AA, allowing for the ambiguity of the guidelines. The police were considered to be 'very good at identifying the most disabled and vulnerable'. Suspects suffering from schizophrenia were most readily identified, while those suffering clinical depression were least often identified. It was also clear that proper identification of mild mental handicap is a very difficult task, often being masked by a reasonable level of social functioning. Even significantly impaired social functioning may not be identifiable on brief acquaintance and suspects may regard their disability as a private matter which they do not wish to raise with police officers. The report recommends that clear operational criteria for identifying mental disorder and vulnerability should be laid down, supported by proper training in recognising defined conditions.

Medical Assessment

If a person brought to or detained at a police station appears to be suffering from mental disorder or fails to respond normally to questions or conversation other than through drunkenness alone, the custody officer must immediately call a forensic medical examiner (FME, formerly known as a police surgeon) (Code C para. 3.10) or, in urgent cases, send the person to hospital or call the nearest available medical practitioner (Code C para. 9.2). Bucke and Brown (1997) found that a doctor attended in 76% of cases in their custody record sample fulfilling the criteria.

Where the FME thinks admission to hospital may be appropriate, he may advise the custody officer to contact an ASW to arrange a MHA assessment which could lead to the suspect's admission to hospital under MHA 1983 Part II or to voluntary admission. Though the FME might be expected to take a central role in the assessment of mental disorder at the police station, in reality pressures of time and circumstance preclude this in most instances. Most FMEs are busy GPs undertaking police work part-time. Only some 10% are approved under MHA 1983 s12(2) 'and most of these are in rural areas where approval may depend on availability rather than training' (James, 2000). Their examinations tend to be brief – a London study (Revolving Doors, 1994) recorded an average of 15 minutes spent with the subject. The FME's role 'tends to be narrowed to making judgement as to fitness to be detained and fitness to be interviewed. Unfortunately, many custody sergeants misinterpret the FME's findings as to fitness to be interviewed as indicating the presence or absence of mental illness' (James, 1995). FMEs are often not well equipped to make judgements about mental disorder (Laing, 1996).

It is certainly clear that the FME is highly influential in determining the police response and the use made of appropriate adults. Robertson's study (1992) of the increased prominence of police surgeons (by examining their work at 15 police stations in eight force areas) noted a significant difference in the assessment of mentally disordered suspects and in willingness to use appropriate adults between London police stations and those in the provinces. In London, few suspects were deemed unfit to be interviewed but in nearly a quarter of cases they were said to require an appropriate adult to be present at interview. Outside London, around one in eight of those referred because of concern about their mental health was assessed as being unfit for interview and very little use was made of appropriate adults. These issues were explored further by Bean and Nemitz (page 24). More recently, in a sample of 33 cases where AAs were used, Phillips and Brown (1998) reported that this occurred only after examination by a doctor in 20 cases. See also page 25.

Requirement for 'Appropriate Adult' to be Present
Code C para. 11.14 specifies:

> '... a person who is mentally disordered or mentally handicapped, whether suspected or not, must not be interviewed or asked to provide or sign a written statement in the absence of the appropriate adult.'

'Appropriate Adult' Defined
Para. 1.7(b) specifies:

(a)   a relative, guardian or some other person responsible for his care or custody;

(b)   someone who has experience of dealing with mentally disordered or mentally handicapped people but is not a police officer or employed by the police; or

(c)   failing either of the above, some other responsible adult aged 18 or over who is not a police officer or employed by the police.

Note 1E adds:

> 'In the case of mentally disordered or mentally handicapped people, it may in certain circumstances be more satisfactory for all concerned if the appropriate adult is someone who has experience or training in their care rather than a relative lacking such qualifications. But if the person himself prefers a relative to a better qualified stranger or objects to a particular person as the appropriate adult, his wishes should if practicable be respected.'

Estranged Relatives
Case law arising from challenges in respect of adult relatives acting as appropriate adult for juvenile detainees indicates that a relative from whom the suspect is estranged and whom the suspect does not wish to attend is not an appropriate person to exercise the role since this puts at risk the objective of ensuring fairness. This was well demonstrated in *DPP v Blake* [1989] 1 WLR 432 where an estranged father had purported to act, even though the suspect (arrested following a fire at the hostel where she had been resident) had made clear that she did not want her parents contacted. She had eventually agreed to inform police of her father's whereabouts because Social Services

had advised police that they would not attend unless it proved impossible to contact any other suitable person and she was told that her continuing refusal to divulge information about her father would prolong her detention. When he arrived, she had ignored him. The Divisional Court was satisfied that the estranged parent in this instance 'did not come within the spirit of the code of guidance' – 'An AA cannot be a person with whom the (suspect) has no empathy.' (The Court indicated that it hoped social workers would attend promptly to act as AA when requested to do so.)

AA's Capacity to Exercise Authority

If the person who is asked to act as AA lacks credible authority to exercise this function, this factor may flaw their selection for the task (*R v Palmer* (1991) *Legal Action* September 1991 – where the juvenile suspect's brother was considered to be too close in age to him and thus unable to exercise authority over him).

AA's Mental Incapacity

Where the AA is of significantly limited intelligence, he will not be able to fulfil the role, being someone who would need attendance by an AA if he himself had been the suspect (*R v Morse* [1991] Crim LR 195 – father with very low IQ). However, where the AA has another form of mental disorder, this will not necessarily cause his fulfilment of the AA role to be flawed in law. In the somewhat unconvincing case of *R v W* [1994] Crim LR 130, the suspect's mother had undertaken the role. The defence sought to challenge the trial judge's decision to admit the suspect's confession on the ground that this should have been excluded under PACE 1984 s76(2)(b) (see page 28) because of the mother's mental health problems. Dismissing the appeal, the Court of Appeal noted the finding at Crown Court that though the mother was psychotic at the relevant time and therefore suffering from some intellectual deficit, 'her paranoid delusions were confined to her neighbours and her thought processes were rational in discussing her family. Although her memory for past events was defective and confused, she was perfectly capable of dealing rationally with current events.' Though it seems that the mother would have required an AA if she had been a suspect, the Appeal Court concluded that she had been able to give appropriate support to her daughter and there was nothing in the conduct of the interview or in the circumstances of the case likely to have made the admission of interview unfair.

Solicitor

A solicitor (or 'lay visitor') who is present at the police station in that capacity may not act as the appropriate adult (Note 1F). Further, the fact that the suspect has a legal advisor acting for him at the police station does not affect the application of AA requirements. There is, nevertheless, a clear overlap between the roles of solicitor and AA, and the presence and assistance of a solicitor may cause a court to consider that a confession obtained without an AA is nevertheless admissible. The similarity in function was recognised by the Court of Appeal in *R v Lewis* [1996] Crim LR 260, dealing with an instance of a suspect who had been interviewed without an AA but who was later assessed by a clinical psychologist to have an IQ of 69, strongly suggestive of brain damage:

> 'An appropriate adult may have a greater insight into the disabilities of a mentally handicapped person who is suffering from a low IQ. Nevertheless, the functions of

such an AA and a solicitor are largely the same, namely to see that the accused fully understands his rights, fully understands that he does not have to say anything unless he wishes to do so, to see that the interview is conducted correctly and that the police do not abuse their position, and that the accused is able to make himself clearly understood and clearly understands what is being put to him.'

Noting that, in retrospect, the suspect should have had an AA present but that, at the time, neither the police nor the lawyer had appreciated that he was mentally handicapped, the Court concluded that neither s76 nor s78 of PACE (see pages 28 and 29) required rejection of the interview with the suspect as evidence. He had had the benefit of a consultation before the interview with a solicitor who had remained present throughout. There was nothing to suggest that his admissions were unreliable.

Legal representatives can play an important role as regards mentally disordered persons at the police station, as acknowledged by *Inter-Agency Working* (Home Office/DoH, 1995) which identified that the solicitor should:

- where an AA is called in, see the client alone at first, to explain in simple terms the role of the AA and how that differs from the solicitor's own role, including explanation that an AA has no duty of confidentiality and may be asked to pass information to the police (see below);

- spend time with the client before interview to make an assessment of their ability to understand the caution and questions put to him or her. It may be helpful to discuss this with the AA;

- during interview, ensure that questions are put in simple language, using understandable terms, and be alert to use of words or phrases that can be misunderstood;

- watch for signs that the client may be getting distressed or anxious and ask for regular breaks to relieve stress or to use private consultation to check their understanding.

Conflict of Interest or Role

In some instances the person undertaking the role of AA may not be suitable for the purpose because they have a role in relation to the suspect or the investigation that is not compatible with the AA task. In *R v O'Neill* (1990, unreported) where the suspect had severe learning difficulties and an IQ of just over 50, Hodgson J expressed doubt whether a probation officer should be asked to act as AA, 'in the absence of any indication that that is what the suspect wants', save in 'very exceptional circumstances', because a probation officer, 'particularly in relation to a mentally handicapped person, is a person in some sort of authority over him'. Additionally, if the officer has on-going supervisory responsibility for the suspected person, this might cause the jury in any subsequent trial to learn that the suspect has previous convictions. *Inter-Agency Working* (Home Office/DoH, 1995) stated that it is undesirable for the person's own probation officer to undertake the role.

In *DPP v Morris* (1990, unreported), where the manager of a residential home had called the police because of suspicions that residents had committed theft, the manager had subsequently acted as AA when the three suspected residents were questioned. He had not spoken to them individually and had told all three that 'it would be much easier for everyone to say what happened, get it right first time and not give anyone a hard time'. The magistrates had refused to admit the ensuing confessions as evidence. While of the view that the case was 'very near the borderline', with no suggestion of impropriety on the part of the police or manager, the Divisional Court upheld the justices' decision, in light of a defence submission that the manager would have been perceived as on the side of the police.

As regards ASWs, *Inter-Agency Working* (Home Office/DoH, 1995) indicated that where an ASW has been called to assess a suspect, that person should not also be asked to undertake the AA function, to avoid potential conflict.

Police Selection of AA and 'Duty of Care'

The case of *Leach v Chief Constable of Gloucestershire* [1999] 1 All ER 215 arose from a request from the police to the plaintiff, a voluntary worker with a Young Homeless Project, to act as AA in interviews with Frederick West, who was suspected of numerous murders. She sought damages for negligence, claiming that as an unqualified/untrained volunteer with experience limited to the young and homeless, she had been placed in that role with insufficient consideration to fulfil the task without risk of mental or psychological harm and without counselling to help her cope with the trauma of exposure to harrowing detail. The Court of Appeal, while dealing with preliminary issues rather than the substantive case, noted the potential beneficiaries of such a duty of care constitute a very wide class of people, including relatives who are likely to be in an anxious, nervous state, and pointed out that the AA could have stopped her participation at any time if she found the interviews distressing. Henry LJ stated that 'where the AA retains such a power, there is little point in a rigorous selection procedure for an unpredictable outcome'. He considered that 'public policy militates against there being pressure on the police to act defensively and to restrict their approaches to act as AAs to the hardened and cynical'.

General Considerations and a Critique of the Role

The term 'appropriate adult' and the relevant provisions of PACE 1984 link suspects who are vulnerable on grounds of mental disorder or disability with juveniles. Robertson *et al* (1996) have argued that 'it is demeaning for people who are themselves adult to be said to require another adult when they are being dealt with by the police' and suggest that the term 'independent third person', as used in several Australian jurisdictions, would be more appropriate. Pearse and Gudjonsson (1996) go further and suggest that the role was introduced 'without sufficient thought for exactly what an AA is supposed to do or how the AA is going to do it ... It has been introduced completely devoid of resources, thus creating a vacuum in terms of who would be an AA.' They question whether the role of AA represents a realistic and workable safeguard or is 'merely a cosmetic and superficial exercise designed to satisfy legal etiquette'. A parent or family member is less likely to feel confident enough to participate in proceedings or, alternatively, may be unsupportive or act collusively with the police in seeking to obtain a confession. If the aim is truly to ensure safeguards for vulnerable suspects, 'we should move away from using the (often) ill-informed amateur and develop a professionalised service' (Williams, 2000), akin to that adopted in Scotland (Scottish Office, 1998). For a useful recent review of the challenges posed to AAs in fulfilling a clearer, more confident role, particularly in respect of vulnerable adults, see White (2002) who argues for clearer, more detailed guidance and better training for social workers.

In some areas (see, for example, Staite *et al* (1994)) it has proved possible to develop training courses for AAs who are then registered so that the police can have ready access to a suitable, knowledgeable person at any time. Nemitz and Bean (1998) have evaluated one of the developing number of volunteer schemes, that run by Southampton MIND, reporting that volunteers were well regarded by the police who viewed them as useful in facilitating communication and sought their advice about suspects' mental states. However, volunteers noted that 'it will always be an uphill task to get the police to understand the value of the AA and the legal requirement to use one'. *Inter-Agency Working* (Home Office/DoH, 1995) proposed that Chief Police Officers should discuss with other relevant agencies the development of resources providing the police with ready access to persons suitable and trained to act as AAs.

Police Duty to Inform Appropriate Adult
If the custody officer authorises the detention of a person who is mentally handicapped or appears to be suffering from a mental disorder, s/he 'must, as soon as practicable, inform the AA of the grounds of the person's detention and his whereabouts, and ask the adult to come to the police station to see the person' (para. 3.9).

Role of Appropriate Adult
The Codes of Practice do not require that AAs should be informed about their role on their arrival at the police station. However, custody officers are required to outline the role of the AA to the detained person, *ie* that the person is there to assist and advise them while they remain in custody and may be seen in private (Code C para. 3.12). Commentators (*eg* Pearse and Gudjonsson, 1996) have frequently observed how confusing the task can be and the lack of advice from the police that might aid the inexperienced. Dixon *et al* (1990) cite a police officer giving informal, robust advice to a social worker AA: 'You are wallpaper, pal.'

The following list seeks to summarise the role as currently identified and contained in PACE Codes and may serve to assist AAs minded to play a fuller part in proceedings. AAs should note that they are entitled to ask for a copy of the PACE Codes to consult while undertaking their role. This recitation of functions and tasks leaves open several questions on which case law provides few, if any, answers. As Palmer (1996) asks:

'What are AAs meant to advise the suspect about – welfare issues or legal rights? Should they advise whether to answer questions? How can they assess whether an interview is being conducted properly and fairly without knowing what kind of behaviour has been held to be improper or unfair? What are they meant to do if they consider an interview to be biased? Does the term "facilitating communication" mean ensuring that questions are put simply and clearly and that replies reflect what the suspect intended to say, or is an AA required to encourage an otherwise silent suspect to answer police questions?'

1. To witness the preliminary procedures

These procedures, specified by paras. 3.1-3.5, require the custody officer:

(i) to tell the detained person of their continuing rights (to have someone informed of their detention, to consult privately with a solicitor, to consult a copy of the Codes of Practice) and to give them a written notice setting out these rights;

(ii) to inform the person of the grounds for their detention as soon as practicable and before that person is questioned about any offence;

(iii) to ask the detained person if s/he would like legal advice;

(iv) in the case of a foreign national (including those from the Republic of Ireland), to inform the person of their right of communication with their High Commission, Embassy or Consulate.

If the AA is not at the police station when these provisions are complied with, they must be complied with again in the adult's presence after their arrival (para. 3.11). Robertson *et al* (1996, see page 25) suggest that this 'can be an embarrassing experience for all concerned as it is often the case that the detainee has understood his rights perfectly well and will probably have exercised them on arrival at the police station'.

2. To seek legal advice

If the AA, having been informed of the right to legal advice, considers that legal advice should be taken, the provisions of Code C section 6 (right to legal advice) apply as if the detained person had requested access to legal advice (para. 3.13), even though the detainee has chosen not to exercise this option. The purpose is to protect the rights of a detained person who may not understand the significance of what is being said to them. If the detained person wishes to exercise the right to legal advice before the AA arrives, appropriate action should be taken immediately and not delayed until the adult arrives (Note 3G). A detained person should always be given the opportunity to consult privately with a solicitor in the absence of the adult if they wish to do so (Note 1EE). Robertson *et al* did not observe any AA to exercise this right and 'no one in the custody suite seemed to be aware that it was possible for an AA to act in this way'.

3. To hear cautioning

If the detained person is cautioned in the absence of the adult, the caution must be repeated in the AA's presence (para. 10.6). If it appears that a person does not understand what the caution means, the cautioning officer should go on to explain it in his or her own words (Note 10C). The AA should ensure that the detainee understands its meaning. As a result of changes introduced by CJPOA 1994 allowing inferences to be drawn in contested trials in certain circumstances if a suspect chose to remain silent during interview, the caution as regards 'right to silence' was reworded to state:

'You do not have to say anything. But it may harm your defence if you do not mention when questioned something which you later rely on in court. Anything you do say may be given in evidence.'

Vulnerable suspects may find it difficult to grasp the implications of this statutory change and AAs may also find it helpful to be familiar with the provisions of Code C paras. 10.5A-C relating to failure to account for presence at place of arrest or items found.

4. To be present during interview

A detained person, whether suspected or not, must not be interviewed or asked to provide or sign a written statement in the absence of the AA, unless either para. 11.1 or Annex C apply (para. 11.14). Annex C permits urgent interviews at police stations where an officer of superintendent rank or above considers that delay would be likely to:

(i) lead to interference with or harm to evidence connected with an offence or interference with or physical harm to other people; or

(ii) lead to the alerting of other people suspected of having committed an offence but not yet arrested for it; or

(iii) hinder the recovery of property obtained in consequence of the commission of an offence.

Para. 11.1 permits an interview outside of a police station where delay would be likely to cause any of (i), (ii) or (iii) above. In both instances interviewing shall cease once the relevant risk has been averted or the necessary questions have been put in order to attempt to avert that risk. Note C1 adds that these provisions:

'which override safeguards designed to protect (vulnerable persons) and to minimise the risk of interviews producing unreliable evidence, should be applied only in exceptional cases of need'.

5. To be informed of their role during an interview

Though the Codes do not identify who should give this information, para. 11.16 specifies that where the AA is present at an interview s/he shall be informed that s/he is not expected to act simply as an observer; and also that the purposes of their presence are:

(i) to advise the person being questioned;

(ii) to observe whether or not the interview is being conducted properly and fairly;

(iii) to facilitate communication with the person being interviewed.

Note 11B comments:

'It is important to bear in mind that although mentally disordered or mentally handicapped are people often capable of providing reliable evidence, they may, without knowing or wishing to do so, be particularly prone in certain circumstances to provide information which is unreliable, misleading or self-incriminating. Special care should therefore always be exercised in questioning such a person, and the appropriate adult involved, if there is any doubt about a person's mental state or capacity. Because of the risk of unreliable evidence, it is important to obtain corroboration of any facts admitted whenever possible.'

If the briefing is provided by the investigating officer as the interview commences, this is rather late for the AA to initiate a private discussion with the suspect, but this will nevertheless be a legitimate request. If the AA is unhappy with the conduct of the interview or the responses of the interviewing police officer, s/he should request to see the custody officer and has a right to do so. In reality an AA is likely to be uncertain as to their function during interview and hesitant to intervene. As Robertson *et al* (1996) have commented in respect of their role as AAs:

> 'Despite our professional backgrounds and our familiarity with police stations and police procedures, we all felt that we had little idea what was required of us or what we were allowed to do in terms of intervention. ... We imagine that very few people who act as AAs know when it would be appropriate to object and that even fewer would have the courage to interrupt the police in their business of questioning someone.'

Nemitz and Bean (1994) could not find a single instance in their sample (outlined below) where a custody officer had recorded that the AA was informed of his or her responsibilities. Pearse and Gudjonsson (1996) note that this provision is the only explicit instance where the police are required to advise the AA about their role and that, though it implies an active role, it is far from clear what kind of advice is within the AA's remit.

> 'Should an AA provide legal advice? Or indeed advice that overrides legal advice? ... the words of the Codes can be interpreted as designed to propel the roles of the solicitor and AA into direct conflict.'

They cite instances of such conflict, for example: where the solicitor as the more authoritative professional had succeeded in having the AA removed from the interview room to prevent advice being given that conflicted with defence guidance; where the solicitor had advised the suspect by telephone to say nothing, following which the AA encouraged him to give his version of events, leading to his elimination from inquiries.

The Court of Appeal has stated that an AA is not under any duty to protect the suspect from 'fair and proper questioning, for example by advising him to remain silent or by refraining from intervening to encourage him to be truthful'. The issue arose in *R v Jefferson and others* (1994) 99 Cr App R 13. A juvenile's father had joined in the questioning of his son, challenging his exculpatory account of certain events. The Court dismissed the boy's claim that his father had not fulfilled the role of AA envisaged for him in the PACE Code and thus evidence from the interview should not be admissible. The Court concluded that the father's interventions had had little effect on the account given but stated that 'encouragement by an AA of a juvenile who is being fairly interviewed to tell the truth should not normally be stigmatised as a failure to fulfil the first of his duties (to advise the suspect) nor should it have the consequence of turning him from an appropriate adult to an inappropriate adult'. For a useful illustration of the role that an AA may play in interview, see *Ali* at page 29.

H and M v DPP [1998] Crim LR 655, though concerned with juvenile suspects, nicely illustrates the pragmatic arrangements that can arise in regard to the practice and interpretation of PACE provisions for AAs. Two suspects were interviewed in the presence of their fathers, one of whom spoke no English and the other only limited English. A third man who had acted as taxi driver to bring them to the police station was asked to stay by one of the fathers, as he spoke fluent English. The suspects were interviewed in the presence of all three adults who were told that they were there to assist the suspects, though without a proper explanation of the AA role. No particular adult was identified as the AA and the taxi driver was not aware of the legal term. He had nevertheless played a positive and active role. Dismissing the defence claim that the suspects' confession evidence should be excluded, the Court of Appeal acknowledged that Code C had not been strictly complied with but stated that it is important in such instances not to lose sight of the fact that the whole purpose of the provisions is to provide protection for vulnerable suspects. There was here an abundant basis for concluding that such protection had been provided. The Court noted that it will usually be inappropriate for more than one person to be designated as AA, the language of the Code being singular and that, if there were more than one designated AA, this could cause confusion so that neither could perform the function properly.

6. To make representations to review officer
Where the detained person's detention is reviewed to determine whether that detention continues to be necessary, the AA must, if available at the time, be given an opportunity to make representations to the reviewing officer about the need for continuing detention (para. 15.1).

7. To be present when the detained person is charged
If the custody officer charges a detained person with an offence or takes such other action as is appropriate when there is sufficient evidence for a prosecution, this must be done in the presence of the AA. The written notice showing particulars of the offence (and containing the caution about the consequences of making or not making any statement in response) must be given to the AA (paras. 16.1-16.3).

8. To be present during intimate or strip search
An 'intimate' (physical examination of body orifices other than the mouth) or a 'strip' (removal of more than outer clothing) search of a detained person may take place only in the presence of an AA of the same sex, unless the person specifically requests the presence of a particular adult of the opposite sex. A strip search may take place in the absence of an AA only in cases of urgency where there is a risk of serious harm to the person detained or to others (Annex A paras. 5 and 11(c)). The ADSS suggests that AAs in these circumstances should be 'sensitive to the issue of race' as 'additional distress may be caused if the detainee feels alienated from the appropriate adult in addition to the officers'.

Identification Procedures
PACE 1984 Code D, *Code of Practice for the Identification of Persons by Police Officers*, also provides safeguards for mentally disordered and mentally handicapped persons akin to Code C, requiring the participation of an appropriate adult.

- In the case of any procedure requiring a person's consent, their consent is only valid if given in the presence of the AA (para. 1.11).

- In the case of any procedure requiring information to be given to or sought from a suspect, it must be given or sought in the presence of the AA. If the AA is not present when the information is first given or sought, the procedure must be repeated in their presence on their arrival (para. 1.13).

- Any procedure involving the participation (whether as a suspect or a witness) of a person who is mentally disordered or handicapped must take place in the presence of the AA, but the adult must not be allowed to prompt any identification of a suspect by a witness (para. 1.14).

Research on the Use of Appropriate Adults

No research has been reported fully on the behaviour and contribution of AAs but several studies have thrown light on the extent to which AAs are present when they should be. Brown *et al* (1992) noted that only 106 suspects (1%) out of a total of 10,048 cases observed had the benefit of an AA. Bean and Nemitz (1994), on behalf of MENCAP, were able to examine the custody records of four police stations (Skegness, Grantham, Derby and Sheffield). Out of 20,805 records compiled in 1992 (plus six months of Derby's 1990 records), only 38 (less than 0.2%) recorded the attendance of an AA on grounds of mental disorder or vulnerability. If Gudjonsson's estimate (that some 10% of all detained persons are mentally disordered, disabled or vulnerable) was correct, the records could be expected to indicate around 2,080 persons, a startling shortfall. In fact, information on record showed only 197 suspects to be regarded as mentally disordered, with a further 251 cases where the record was more ambiguous (*eg* 'depressed' or 'suicidal') but nevertheless indicative of the need for an AA.

Even in the 38 positive cases it was not always clear if the person called was recognised as acting in the role of AA or, if mental health professionals were called, whether they were actually conducting a mental health assessment, such as for the purposes of s136. In only 19 cases did the custody officer formally use the term 'appropriate adult', signifying implementation of AA procedures. Out of the 38 AAs, 19 were either social workers, probation officers or CPNs (mental health or criminal justice professionals), ten were relatives and nine were 'others', *eg* a hostel warden, nurse or interpreter (for deaf suspects without speech). Of the 19 formal AAs, ten were 'professionals' (including three probation officers), five were relatives, with four 'others'.

Among the research findings are the following:

- Custody officers seem to be able to identify mental disorder well enough. The problem primarily lies in what they think should happen to the mentally disordered once detected.

- Custody officers commonly believe that AA procedures are for juveniles only.

- Many custody officers assume that the need for an AA is a medical decision to be taken by the FME, not a question for their independent judgement. When the FME concluded that the detained suspect was 'fit to be detained and/or interviewed', the assumption seemed to follow predominantly that an AA was not required, though if the suspect was 'unfit' there would be no need for an AA.

- All custody officers complained of the additional demands and pressures that AA procedures create; social workers were considered to be particularly elusive, delaying proceedings. Police surgeons, on the other hand, were seen as being both readily available and helpfully 'on the side of the police'. Officers favoured use of local victim support volunteers as they were felt to be 'on our side – the side of the victim'.

- Custody officers were often confused or ambivalent about the role of the AA, believing that the AA was there for 'welfare' reasons, *eg* the need for food/drink or the lavatory, and should not interrupt an interview (something considered the prerogative only of a solicitor).

Nemitz and Bean (1994) illustrate a typical case: a woman aged 32 suspected of criminal damage. The custody officer noted that it was 'difficult to make her understand what was being said to her' and believed she had been drinking. On her mother's arrival at the police station, she indicated that her daughter had a psychiatric problem and had recently spent five months in a psychiatric hospital. The FME obtained a history of the suspect's mental condition, noted that she was to see a psychiatrist the following week with a view to re-admission to hospital, and stated: 'not certifiable at present; fit to be detained and interviewed'. The record gave no indication that the suspect's mother remained at the station or acted in the role of AA.

In a study not suggestive of major failure to adhere to PACE expectations, Robertson *et al* (1996) observed practice at seven Metropolitan Police Stations for 21 days at each station, during which time 2,947 custody records were opened, though only three in 10 suspects were interviewed. Some 37 persons were assessed by the researchers to be mentally disordered, of whom only two were interviewed, one with an AA, the FME assessing the other detainee as not requiring this facility despite indications of disturbed behaviour at the time of the alleged offence, 'strange' demeanour at the police station and apparent inability to recall her children's ages. A further 16 were known to have been psychiatric patients in the past, all being judged to be currently well. Eight of these were interviewed, half of them without an AA. Of a further three persons whom the researchers categorised as of 'uncertain' mental status, two were approved for interview by the FME and one was the only instance where the arresting officer had considered that the suspect might be ill (but this advice was ignored by the custody sergeant, who did not seek an FME's opinion).

Of 752 adults interviewed in the research period, 13 had an appropriate adult present (2%; 0.4% of the total detainee population), of whom 10 required an AA on the basis of mental disorder of some kind, as assessed by the police. In some instances the researchers acted as AA so it was not certain whether an AA would have been present if they had not been available on the spot. Of these 10, three were of low intelligence; a further five told police that they had been psychiatric patients but appeared well. One factor that appeared to determine whether an AA was asked for was the seriousness of the alleged offence. Overall, the researchers were impressed by the quality of the custody sergeants who had considerable experience and common-sense. In situations where they called an AA despite the advice of a FME to the contrary, the researchers shared the opinion of the officer rather than the doctor.

As further indication of recent practice, Phillips and Brown (1998) found that of 67 detainees identified by the police as mentally disordered or mentally handicapped (around 2% of the full sample), AAs were used in only 33 instances. In 20 of those instances, an approved social worker attended (and in a further six instances, the police sought an ASW without success). Bucke and Brown (1997) noted that AAs were used in 66% of cases involving mentally disordered detainees. As to why no AA was involved in the remaining third of cases, they identified that in the majority of cases a doctor had attended and recommended that an AA was not required. They point out that the requirement to summon an AA is independent of that requiring a doctor and that the police should not delay requesting an AA whilst awaiting a doctor's assessment. In 60% of instances where an AA attended, the role was undertaken by a social worker, either a duty team member or a specialist. A friend/neighbour of the suspect acted as AA in 16% of cases.

Bean and Nemitz (1994) note the possibility of a conflict of interest when a professional, especially one who is already involved with the detainee, takes on the AA role:

> 'The conflict arises when issues about the care and control of the client must be decided. Confusion is created because of the advocate supportive role of the Appropriate Adult and the demands of the social worker/client relationship. What for example should be the professional's duties or responsibilities if the suspect disclosed or confessed his/her guilt to the social worker/Appropriate Adult? Should disclosure or confession to the Appropriate Adult remain confidential? No one seems to know.'

This issue is considered further below. In the context of juvenile suspects, Bucke and Brown (1997) found that while family members are less likely to be supportive towards the suspect than social workers, social workers are also more likely to be co-operative towards the police than family members.

Admissions to the Appropriate Adult

The suspected person may make an admission of guilt either to or in the presence of the appropriate adult, other than in the course of a police interview attended by the adult. An AA has no protection of professional legal privilege enjoyed by legal advisers. This can place social workers acting as appropriate adults in difficulty as they may feel justified in giving information to the police as part of their duty to assist in the prevention and detection of crime and to protect the public. The British Association of Social Workers' Code of Ethics (Littlechild, 1995) states that a social worker should respect the privacy of clients and will divulge confidential information only with the consent of the client, 'except where there is clear evidence of serious danger to the client, worker, other person or the community'. Littlechild, a BASW adviser, indicates that 'this proviso would seem to relate, for example, to actions or threats of serious violence or issues of child abuse, but could clearly relate to admissions of guilt which the social worker may feel obliged to pass on to the police'.

PACE 1984 Code C Note 1D acknowledges the problem for social workers who hear an admission from a juvenile suspect, stating that 'another social worker should be the appropriate adult in the interests of fairness'. If this requires the social worker to request to be relieved of their AA role, the police may draw the inference that the first worker has been compromised by an admission and will simply proceed to question that worker.

BASW Advice BASW's guidelines for social workers acting as AA, advise that the AA should:

(i) ensure that the detained person is seen separately from their solicitor in order to recognise the distinct difference in roles;

(ii) advise the detained person of their role, before any discussions take place, in particular drawing the person's attention to what could happen to any information given to the AA, and informing them that the social worker acting as AA would have to change if s/he receives an admission of guilt;

(iii) advise the police and the detained person that s/he may refuse to act as AA for a number of reasons and that it cannot be presumed that such a refusal is because an admission of guilt has been made.

Littlechild adds that social workers 'are also advised to draw the attention of the suspect to the possible lack of confidentiality as a result of hearing what could be construed as admissions. Suspects need to know this before any joint interviews with solicitors.'

Law Society's Advice

The Criminal Law Committee of the Law Society (1993) has given the following guidance to solicitors:

● To ensure that a suspect has the opportunity of confidential consultations with their solicitor, it is recommended that the suspect is at first advised, in the appropriate adult's absence, about the risk of disclosure.

● A problem may arise with a mentally disordered or mentally handicapped person who may not be able to understand the risk of disclosure. The appropriate adult may be of help to the solicitor in clarifying whether the person is able to comprehend this.

● The question of whether the appropriate adult's presence is desirable or not during any further consultations between the suspect and the solicitor can then be considered, in consultation with the appropriate adult, taking into account any risk of disclosure and the wishes of the client, who may find reassurance in the presence of an appropriate adult whom they know.

The Association of Directors of Social Services (ADSS) has suggested that it be made clear that appropriate adults should not be present during interviews between solicitor and client unless requested.

Calling for a complete overhaul of the role of the AA, the Royal Commission on Criminal Justice (1993) recommended that clear rules should be formulated governing the status of information passed by a suspect to an AA but this call has not to date led to such an outcome. The Home Office Appropriate Adults Review Group (1995) recommended that meeting between suspects and AAs should be both confidential and privileged. White (2002) points out that failure to communicate information about an arrestable offence is not a criminal offence unless done for profit or gain (CLA 1967 s5). He argues that the Scottish guidelines' assertion (Scottish Office, 1998, para. 3.8), that an AA 'cannot withhold from the police information divulged by an interviewee', lacks authority and could confuse a suspect who is seeking a rapport with their AA. He proposes extension of legal professional privilege to AAs. For an account of the predicament faced by the AA who acted in respect of Frederick West and who was called by the prosecution in the trial of Rosemary West to give evidence as to what Frederick West had said in the course of their private meetings, see Palmer (1996) (and page 18).

Legal Consequences of Not Having an Appropriate Adult

A prosecution founded, at least in part, on an interview conducted without the presence of an appropriate adult may be challenged at trial (in what is known as a *voire dire* hearing), as illustrated by *R v Cox* [1991] Crim LR 276 where the police had interviewed a man with an IQ of 58 without an AA being present, in breach of the Code of Practice, gaining his admission that he had been party to two burglaries. At trial the judge ruled that his interview should be admitted in evidence because, in the judge's view, it was likely to be true, despite evidence that he was suggestible and had an IQ lower than 99.6% of the adult population. Allowing his appeal, the Court of Appeal ruled that the judge should have applied the test specified by PACE 1984 s76(2)(b):

> If, in any proceedings where the prosecution proposes to give in evidence a confession made by an accused person, it is represented in court that the confession may have been obtained –
>
> ...
>
> (b)   in consequence of anything said or done which was likely, in the circumstances existing at the time, to render unreliable any confession which might have been made by him in consequence thereof,
>
> the court shall not allow the confession to be given in evidence against him except insofar as the prosecution proves to the court beyond reasonable doubt that the confession (notwithstanding that it may be true) was not obtained as aforesaid.

The essential question at stake was whether the breach of the Code made it likely that the confession was unreliable, not whether it was true.

R v Aspinall [1999] Crim LR 741 illustrates application of another PACE safeguard in this context. When arrested in the early hours for conspiracy to supply heroin, the suspect had informed the custody officer at the police station that he suffered from schizophrenia. A FME found him to be adhering to his medication and lucid and this was confirmed by a second FME who considered him probably fit to be interviewed. He was eventually interviewed in that afternoon, 13 hours after arrest, without either an AA or a solicitor being present, the police having made a mistake as to his legal representation so that attendance was delayed, and eventually he indicated that he would rather proceed so that he could go home to his partner and six week old baby. At trial, the defendant's consultant psychiatrist gave evidence that the defendant would probably have been tired, under stress and worried and might have been less able to cope with questions, possibly giving answers that he thought likely to lead to his early release from custody. Upholding his appeal against the trial judge's decision that evidence from his interview was admissible, the Court of Appeal stated that though he appeared lucid, this did not negate the requirement for the safeguard of an AA.

> 'A vulnerable person who has been in custody for some 13 hours and who is more likely to be stressed than a normal person cannot be equated with a person lacking any disability ... A significant part of the duty of an AA is to advise about the presence of a solicitor at interview and this appellant was deprived of such advice which in all likelihood would have urged him to have legal representation .... The interview

contained some lies, as subsequently admitted by the appellant, and in various respects the answers given did not accord with the evidence of the appellant at trial. Assuming the account given at trial was the truth, the AA or legal advisor could have been expected to advise him to tell the truth at interview. If he had done that, his answers would have assisted the defence and not the police ... He thought he was assisting his case but the AA or legal advisor would have urged him to tell the truth because patent lies could only harm his defence. The appellant's credibility was undermined by his lies, which was essentially unfair, not by reason of malice or pressure, but by lack of safeguards to which he was entitled by reason of his disability.'

The interview evidence was thus excluded, under PACE 1984 s78, which provides that in any proceedings:

The court may refuse to allow evidence on which the prosecution proposes to rely to be given if it appears to the court that, having regard to all the circumstances in which the evidence was obtained, the admission of the evidence would have such an adverse effect on the fairness of the proceedings that the court ought not to admit it.

As the Court in *Aspinall* made clear, though the breaches there were 'so fundamental' that they could not be countenanced, not every breach of the AA safeguards will lead to exclusion. *R v Law-Thompson* [1997] Crim LR 674 illustrates circumstances where the failure to involve an AA was not fatal to the fairness of the case. The appellant, who had faced trial for attempted murder of his mother, was of high intelligence but suffered autistic psychopathy, Asberger's Syndrome, marked by extreme rigidity of thought, in this instance causing him to believe that his mother was evil. Though the police had in mind to involve an AA (a family friend), a psychiatric social worker advised that this was not necessary, so the interview proceeded in the presence of a solicitor and led to his admission that he had intended to kill her. The Appeal Court determined that there was no basis for believing that the confession was unreliable and thus to be excluded under PACE 1984 s76(2). The Court also rejected the appellant's 'startling' argument that any evidence obtained in interview with a mentally disordered suspect should be excluded under s78, regardless of the circumstances.

R v Ali [1999] 2 *Archbold News* 2 provides a further illustration of where exclusion of admissions was considered justified under s78. The suspect, then aged 18, was interviewed without presence of either an AA or a solicitor about allegations of drug dealing, having been found in possession of 11 £10 wraps of heroin. He quickly made admissions of dealing in heroin for a couple of years, about the considerable amount of money he had made and how he had spent this. Evidence was received at trial that his IQ was between 66 and 72 and that he functioned at the level of a 12/13 year old, though he was not assessed as particularly suggestible. The trial judge concluded that he was 'mentally handicapped' and ruled that the latter part of the interview should be excluded from evidence on the basis that:

'had an AA been present, there would have come a point in the interview where such a person could and probably should have intervened to establish from the defendant privately whether he really meant what he was saying, whether he was boasting, whether he wanted to suspend the interview so that a solicitor could give him further advice or, if he wished to continue with the interview, such a person could have established that he appreciated the need to stick closely to the truth and not to exaggerate.'

On his appeal against conviction, the Court of Appeal concluded that as the accused's admissions and assertions, the sole basis for counts of supplying drugs, were obviously exaggerated and likely to be unreliable (albeit that some information given was apparently sensible and reliable), the convictions should be quashed. For an instance where the presence of a solicitor aided a decision that confession evidence was admissible, see *Lewis* at page 16.

Citing Parker's (1992) analysis of the basis on which a confession may be excluded on the basis that no AA was present during interview, Brown (1997) suggests that for a verdict based on such evidence to be considered unsafe and unsatisfactory, the following requirements will need to be met:

(i)   the prosecution must depend wholly on the confessions;

(ii)   the defendant must suffer from a significant degree of mental disability;

(iii) the confessions must be unconvincing to a point where a jury, properly directed, could not properly convict upon them.

In *Director of Public Prosecutions v Cornish* (1997) *The Times* 27 January, the Divisional Court gave guidance on the approach that should be adopted by a court where the defence seek to exclude evidence arising from interview with a suspect in the absence of an AA. The magistrates had evidence from a psychologist that the defendant was someone for whom an AA should have been in attendance. When the defence had belatedly made submissions that the interview evidence should be excluded under PACE 1984 s76(2)(b), the justices had agreed and dismissed the case without having received prosecution evidence about the interviews. The Divisional Court determined that this had not been the proper approach. The magistrates should have received 'relevant evidence which the Crown would wish the court to receive':

'... such evidence I would expect to be evidence of who was there at the time of the interview and how the interview went, so that the court could form some impression of the effect of the absence of the AA upon the conduct of the interview and other matters of that kind.' (per Kennedy LJ)

Confessions by Mentally Handicapped Persons: PACE 1984 s77
Though not directly related to the conduct of police investigation and AAs, it is worth noting the special provision of s77 of the 1984 Act relating to trial of an accused person who is 'mentally handicapped', where the case is based wholly or substantially on his confession which was not made 'in the presence of an independent person' (not a police officer or person employed for or engaged on police business). In such instances, 'the court shall warn the jury that there is a special need for caution before convicting the accused in reliance on the confession and shall explain that the need arises because of the circumstances mentioned' above.

CHARGE, CAUTION AND 'NO FURTHER ACTION'

Where there is sufficient evidence that mentally disordered persons have committed an offence, the police have to consider whether prosecution is in the public interest having regard to the scope for such persons to be dealt with instead by health and social services. Though Phillips and Brown (1998) give little specific attention to the mentally disordered, their research broadly suggested that 'the police do indeed give serious attention to alternatives to prosecution' in such cases.

'The proportion charged was below average, while NFA, sometimes in conjunction with admission to hospital, was much more common. It would seem that the main filter in cases involving the mentally disordered is at the police decision-making stage.'

Inter-Agency Working (Home Office/DoH, 1995) indicated that 'determining when prosecution is the proper course can be a finely balanced judgement' that should be taken after establishing whether the person has any history of mental disorder or has had any previous contact with the criminal justice system' and obtaining advice from local psychiatric and social services. The police will need to consider:

- Is the incident an isolated event?

- The gravity of the offending.

- The potential risk to others if the behaviour recurs.

- Whether the incident represents the latest in a developing pattern of dangerous behaviour which requires intervention by the criminal justice system.

- Any options offered by health and social services.

'In cases where prosecution is not necessary in the public interest, Chief Police Officers will wish to ensure that adequate alternative forms of response are available.' The guide also urges solicitors at the police station to be aware of all possible alternatives to charges in order to assess whether access to health or care services at that stage might be the appropriate option, or whether the matter can be dealt with through caution or other quick disposal.

'If charges are made, the solicitor should try to avoid the client being kept in police cells, as confinement of mentally vulnerable people can lead to swift deterioration, and should press for the client to be cared for in the least stressful environment. ... The solicitor should also press for an early court date, to avoid long delays after charging.'

Cautioning

The non-statutory practice of cautioning adults has not been affected by the introduction of reprimands and warnings for juveniles under CDA 1998 ss65-66. A formal caution allows 'less serious' offenders to be dealt with quickly and simply, avoiding an unnecessary court prosecution, provided that the following conditions are met:

(i) there must be evidence of the offender's guilt sufficient to give a realistic prospect of conviction;

(ii) the offender must admit the offence;

(iii) the offender must understand the significance of a caution (*ie* that a record of the caution will be kept, that this may influence the decision whether or not to prosecute if the person offends again, and that it may be cited if the person should subsequently be found guilty of an offence) and give informed consent to being cautioned.

The *National Standards for Cautioning* in *HOC 18/1994* specify that if (i) and (ii) above are satisfied, consideration should be given to whether a caution is in the public interest. Note 3A adds:

> 'There should be a presumption in favour of not prosecuting certain categories of offender such as elderly people or those suffering from some sort of mental illness or impairment, or a severe physical illness. Membership of these groups does not, however, afford absolute protection against prosecution, which may be justified by the seriousness of the offence'.

There are still wide variations in cautioning practice across the country and the scope for diverting mentally disordered offenders from the court by this means is still arguably under-utilised. Health and social work professionals attending the police station can advise the custody officer about the appropriateness of the cautioning option, and in particular whether the offender is able to understand what a caution means and can give informed consent to such a course.

NACRO (1993b) suggested that it could be helpful to establish cautioning panels like those already operating to advise on the prosecution or diversion of young offenders, so that agencies delivering community mental health services can both contribute consistently to police decision-making and ensure proper commitment of support and services, thus increasing police confidence in cautioning as an effective rather than a merely 'negative' choice.

Oral Warning

HOC 18/1994 para. 13 made clear that 'there is no intention of inhibiting the practice of taking action short of a formal caution by giving an oral warning', which is neither recorded nor to be cited in any subsequent court proceedings. This form of NFA (no further action) is distinguishable from other NFA situations where the police determine that there are insufficient grounds for accepting an offence. As in respect of cautioning, the police may be reluctant to take this course, particularly if the individual appears distressed, confused or liable to come to some harm, unless resources or intervention are forthcoming to provide a measure of care.

SCREENING AND DIVERSION SCHEMES

The Royal Commission on Criminal Justice (1993, para. 92) proposed initiatives to determine whether duty psychiatrist schemes, as operated in magistrates' courts (see Chapter 4), could be extended to larger, busier police stations to ensure an opportunity for earlier identification and potential filtering out of mentally disordered persons, particularly those who had committed more minor offences. Staite and Martin (1993) reported an initiative in North Humberside enabling a team combining a CPN, an ASW and a probation officer to visit stations each weekday morning to assess cell detainees for mental health problems.

One early initiative of this kind began at Bournville Lane police station in inner city Birmingham, involving a CPN screening system (NACRO, 1994; Wix, 1994; Laing, 1995; Home Office/DoH, 1995). In a recent review of the first four years of the scheme, November 1993 to October 1997, Riordan *et al* (2000) note 492 referrals of 420 persons. Only 16 individuals disclosed a criminal history. Following assessment, the following interventions were recommended: admission to a forensic unit in four cases (resulting in three admissions), compulsory admission to a local psychiatric hospital in 59 cases (54 admissions), informal admission in 110 cases (97 admissions). Voluntary out-patient treatment was suggested in 127 instances, being achieved in 94 cases. All outcomes were achieved direct from the police station. Not all those assessed to be mentally disordered were diverted from custody:

> 'In some cases it was deemed appropriate that they remain in custody but that their presence should be brought to the notice of appropriate services. In a few cases it was recommended that the only appropriate course of action was remand to prison where there would be a more prolonged period of observation and assessment. This was particularly the case where the individual concerned had been charged with a more serious offence, where the diagnosis was in question or where it was unclear what the most appropriate ultimate disposal might be.'

In London, a CPN screening scheme was established covering three West End police stations in Westminster (James, 2000). In the first 31 months of operation, 712 cases were assessed (1.1% of all custody cases), 85% on referral by custody sergeants, psychotic illnesses being diagnosed in nearly half of the subjects. The CPNs were more effective in identifying mental health problems than the FMEs also concerned. The CPNs identified a need for admission to hospital in 34% of referrals. Following CPN intervention, 223 cases (31%) were admitted to psychiatric hospital, 172 under civil orders, 30 as voluntary admissions and 21 under Part III (criminal orders) after referral to the linked court-based diversion team. Of all admissions, 91% were accomplished on the day of assessment. The number of admissions to hospital from the three police stations increased by 400% as a result of the scheme. Of those not admitted, 44% were referred to community agencies (*eg* the local community mental health team or Social Services). As for formal criminal justice outcomes, no further action was taken in 39% of cases while 12% were cautioned and 3% were given a formal warning. In some 44% of cases, suspects were charged with an offence. James suggests that while referrals from police station and court share common characteristics – being predominantly young, unemployed men with social instability, previous psychiatric problems and a history of prior convictions – the police station cases appeared to have travelled less far down the road of offending and were more likely to be under the care of psychiatric services, at least nominally. He tentatively concludes that early intervention at this stage 'might be able to prevent a progression to further offending before eventual inception into psychiatric care'.

The police may be able to refer persons to panel assessment schemes (page 62) where available, prior to a decision whether or not to prosecute, though not all schemes have been able to accept police referrals.

Vaughan *et al* (2001) compared police practice at four stations within one provincial police area (Hampshire), surveying the processing of 1,191 persons detained in three stations where diversion schemes were well established and one which had no such scheme. Of this total sample, 67 persons were recorded by police as having a mental disorder. The project workers conducting the research undertook a sample screening and concluded that about 96 of the 1,124 persons not so identified would warrant referral for diversion. In stations with schemes, an average of about 7% of detained individuals had mental disorder but were not detected, while that figure was 14% in the remaining station. Suspects with schizophrenia proved most readily identifiable, while those with clinical depression were often missed. The effects of alcohol and drugs could mask the presence of mental illness. Conversely, many individuals without a formal mental disorder were inappropriately referred to the diversion schemes on the basis of disturbed behaviour unrelated to mental disorder.

The study identified the considerable variation between custodial officers. Officers at two stations were much more diligent and sophisticated in asking relevant questions that could elicit evidence of mental health problems. In contrast, officers at the station without a diversion scheme were much more likely to restrict themselves to a more superficial approach of the 'are you fit and healthy?' kind.

There was clearly some difficulty in obtaining speedy assessments, particularly in out-of-office hours, the diversion schemes operating only in such conventional times, Monday to Friday. ASWs were widely considered to be extremely difficult to contact and police believed that many ASWs may take the view that as suspect individuals are in a safe place, they are less of a priority. In consequence, disordered and vulnerable individuals were often detained in cells for unsatisfactory lengths of time.

The Police Complaints Authority (1996) has suggested that as a basic screening practice each prisoner should be asked at point of being booked into custody:

- Are you currently under treatment by a doctor or psychiatrist?

- When did you last see your doctor/psychiatrist?

- Have you ever attempted suicide or self-harm?

Inappropriate Diversion from Prosecution
Noting that Christopher Clunis was not charged but was instead dealt with by removal under s136 powers and subsequently detained under MHA 1983 s2, following an incident when he had rushed at police officers brandishing a knife, requiring three officers to disarm him, Ritchie *et al* (1994, para. 11.2.1) noted that, though there is 'a quite proper desire to divert the mentally ill from the criminal justice system', the decision not to charge was inappropriate in the circumstances.

> 'Detention under s136 was quite correct in the circumstances to deal with the immediate danger but no thought seems subsequently to have been given whether to charge him, despite his use of serious violence. Since there was no conviction, the event tended thereafter to be brushed aside or trivialised.'

Noting a subsequent incident when police were called to deal with Christopher Clunis who had been threatening co-residents at a hostel with a carving knife, leading to his arrest and subsequent binding over to keep the peace, Ritchie *et al* commented (para. 15.2.1):

'It seems wrong that a person who is mentally ill should not be prosecuted for committing a serious offence and should thereby be deprived of the real help he might otherwise receive under a hospital order or via the Probation Service. We consider that the police should encourage the victim to prosecute in such a case.'

However, in the context of a later occasion when Christopher Clunis was found outside a shop sucking a dummy, having stolen sweets, Ritchie *et al* felt that the use of s136 powers was entirely proper to provide him with immediate access to health care.

The appropriateness of prosecution was also noted by Smith and Donovan (1990) in the context of offending by psychiatric in-patients:

'Excusing offending may not always be in the patient's interests. The formal legal process can be a valuable exercise in reality testing. The patient can measure his or her own perceptions against those of society. This can be a useful preparation for life outside hospital. The knowledge that prosecution is routine rather than exceptional may deter further assaults and help aggressive patients to accept responsibility for their behaviour. (Non prosecution) can reinforce the patient's belief that he or she need not control his or her behaviour.'

Inter-Agency Working (Home Office/DoH, 1995) indicated that:

'the existence of mental disorder should never be the only factor considered in reaching a decision about charging. The need to protect the safety of the public may indicate that formal action is needed. It is important to recognise that prosecution does not prevent the individual having access to the health and social care services. ... If the person's current or previous behaviour appears to put others at risk, it will be preferable to charge so that the court can consider whether a (MHA) disposal is required for the longer-term protection of the public as well as enabling the person's needs to be met.'

3
DISCONTINUANCE BY THE
CROWN PROSECUTION SERVICE

Once the police have made the initial decision to prosecute and have referred a case to the Crown Prosecution Service, the CPS must decide whether to proceed or not, on the basis of the sufficiency of the evidence and an assessment of the public interest. The Crown must also consider the adverse effect that criminal proceedings may have on the accused's mental health. *Inter-Agency Working* (Home Office/DoH, 1995) identified that 'while the existence of mental disorder is a factor against prosecution, it must be weighed against the seriousness of the offence and the possibility that it may be repeated'.

OBTAINING INFORMATION

The CPS will rely strongly on the police for relevant information and *Inter-Agency Working* indicates that 'any information the police may have about the accused's psychiatric condition should be recorded in the police file which is passed to the prosecutor', including a note of any assessment and advice from a medical practitioner or nurse who has examined the person under PACE provisions or local arrangements with the health authority. In addition:

'there may be some rare circumstances when the CPS wishes to have its own report on the defendant's mental condition. In such circumstances it is open to the CPS to approach the defence to obtain agreement to the defendant being seen by another doctor so that a further medical report may be prepared.'

PUBLIC INTEREST ASSESSMENT

Among public interest factors against prosecution, the Code for Crown Prosecutors (2000, para. 6.5(f) and (g)) specifies that a prosecution is less likely to be needed if:

(f) a prosecution is likely to have a very bad effect on the victim's physical or mental health, always bearing in mind the seriousness of the offence;

(g) the defendant is elderly or is, or was at the time of the offence, suffering from significant mental or physical ill health, unless the offence is serious or there is a real possibility that it may be repeated. The Crown Prosecution Service, where necessary, applies Home Office guidelines about how to deal with mentally disordered offenders. Crown Prosecutors must balance the desirability of diverting a defendant who is suffering from significant mental or physical ill health with the need to safeguard the general public.

The 1992 version of the Code (para. 8(v)(b)) was more expansive on the possibility that 'the strain of criminal proceedings may lead to a considerable worsening of the accused's mental health', advising that:

'an independent medical report may be sought but should generally be reserved for cases of such gravity as plainly to require prosecution unless the examination provides clear evidence that such a course would be likely to result in a permanent worsening of the accused's condition.'

TERMINATION OF PROCEEDINGS

Proceedings can be terminated in one of the following ways:

1. *Withdrawal of Charge or Summons* Where the defendant has not entered a plea, the prosecution can seek the court's leave to withdraw the proceedings.

2. *Offering No Evidence* After the defendant has entered a plea of not guilty, the prosecution can 'offer no evidence', thus inviting the court to acquit or discharge the defendant.

3. *Discontinuance under POA 1985 s23* Power to give notice of discontinuance is exercisable only at a 'preliminary stage' of proceedings, *ie*:

   Summary Trial: before the court has begun to hear evidence for the prosecution;

   Crown Court Trial: before the defendant has been committed for trial or, under CJPOA 1994, the case has been transferred to Crown Court.

When giving notice to the magistrates' clerk, the CPS must give reasons for not wanting proceedings to continue (s23(5)). The defendant must be informed but is not entitled to receive any indication of the reasons for the decision (s23(6)). If, however, the accused has been charged at the police station and the CPS wish to discontinue before there has yet been a court appearance, it is merely necessary to serve notice to that effect on the accused (s23(4)).

A further possibility, for example if the CPS is represented by an agent without power to discontinue or withdraw, is for the court to adjourn the case *sine die*, which in practice means that the case ceases active life without proceeding to conviction.

Discontinuance in action is illustrated in the discussion of psychiatric liaison services at court (page 54). Phillips and Brown (1998) reported that the CPS terminated proceedings on the basis of the defendant's mental condition in only three cases within their research sample (see Chapter 2).

PUBLIC INTEREST CASE ASSESSMENT (PICA)

As an initiative in contributing information to assist the CPS in weighing whether a prosecution is in the public interest, a number of Probation Areas, starting with Inner London pilot scheme in 1988 and extending to Greater Manchester, Northumbria and the West Midlands in 1991, established PICA projects. Project staff wrote to defendants inviting their participation. If consent was received, verified information was obtained about the accused's circumstances and a report supplied to the CPS, if possible prior to the accused's first court appearance. Though not aimed exclusively at mentally disordered subjects, the investigation included any history of involvement with mental health services and potentially adverse consequences of conviction. Brown and Crisp (1992) reported that concern about mental health was the second most frequently used criterion for discontinuance in the Inner London area. The CPS decided that it was not in the public interest to prosecute a third of the cases in which reports had been submitted.

The Home Office undertook an evaluation of PICA (Crisp *et al*, 1995), reporting that:

(i)   schemes were able to target offenders successfully;

(ii) discontinuance rates for those on whom a report was prepared were more than double the rate for those who did not respond to an invitation to participate;

(iii) the Probation Service was able to meet a need for support for people finding it difficult to cope with the stress of the criminal process.

Nevertheless, the probation resources required outweighed the savings made by diverting schemes from court. As a consequence, *Probation Circular 21/1995* instructed that all PICA schemes should be discontinued at the earliest opportunity. The Circular expressed the view that gaps in information provided to the CPS may be filled by more comprehensive details supplied by the police, backed by more comprehensive CPS training and improved pre-trial probation work.

NACRO (1994) had already suggested that PICA schemes 'are unlikely to be appropriate in many areas and/or they are likely to be seen as an excessive demand on scarce resources. It also remains the case that the CPS has primary responsibility for ensuring that information about offences and offenders is obtained and considered as early as possible'.

4
REMANDS AND REPORTS

This chapter addresses the liberty of the defendant prior to sentencing, the circumstances in which a court may remand a defendant, either for inquiries to be made about their mental or physical health or for them to receive treatment, and the scope for early psychiatric intervention at court, together with multi-agency assessment initiatives, to increase the identification rate of mental disorder and to facilitate more speedy transfer to hospital care, with the potential for diversion. An obvious concern is to avoid the unnecessary, inappropriate, inhumane or counter-productive use of remands in custody, convenient as the local prison may seem as a holding unit. As James *et al* (2002: 4) have noted, conventional mechanisms for assessment and admission have proved cumbersome and inefficient.

Some indication of the rate of psychiatric disorder among defendants appearing at magistrates' court (and the effectiveness of detection even in courts with a 'diversion' programme) is provided by Shaw *et al* (1999), who screened defendants appearing before Manchester Magistrates' Court, using a self-administered questionnaire with subsequent psychiatric interview of those with high scores. The first stage of study, involving all defendants (229) attending court from the community on 33 days, revealed only three with serious psychiatric disorder, so the second phase concentrated on those held in custody overnight. Such defendants may be detained because of unusual behaviour, lack of reliable address, or other factors associated with mental disorder. Of 1,460 persons screened after overnight custody, 96 had serious psychiatric disorder. Of the total of 99 persons assessed as having such disorder, 34 had schizophrenia or other psychoses, five had hypomania, 55 had depressive disorder and five had generalised anxiety disorder. Some 42 of those with depressive disorder and 16 of those with schizophrenia reported some form of suicidal ideation. All 99 were judged to require diversion to mental health facilities.

During the 113 days that the research was conducted and court diversion staff also attended, the researchers identified 96 seriously disordered individuals of whom 11 were referred to the diversion programme by court staff. The researchers themselves referred a further three because they caused such immediate pressing concern. Twelve of the 14 referred had schizophrenia. Of the 48 assessed to have the most severe psychiatric disorder, only eight were referred to the diversion programme. Of 56 indicating some form of suicidal ideation, only six were referred. The 82 not referred had disorders of similar severity to those referred but were less likely to have a history of previous psychiatric treatment.

BAIL OR CUSTODY?
Mentally disturbed offenders have the same right to be considered for bail as any other offenders and the broad presumption in favour of bail under BA 1976 s4(1) applies equally to them. However, among exceptions to the general right to bail, the court has a discretion to refuse bail in respect of any offence, whether imprisonable or otherwise,

if the court 'is satisfied that the defendant should be kept in custody for his own protection' (BA 1976 sch 1 Part I para. 3 and Part II para. 3).

HOC 66/1990 (para. 7) was firm that:

> 'a mentally disordered person should never be remanded to prison simply to receive medical treatment or assessment'

and the Reed Committee (1992, 9.6(iii)) has suggested that current powers to remand to prison for the primary purpose of medical assessment should be removed or at least restricted. The limitations of custodial remand for assessment and report have been well described by James *et al* (2002: 4):

> 'If there is thought to be any possibility of the need for admission, the Prison Medical Service asks for a second opinion from the catchment area consultant psychiatrist. The latter must first be identified. There is then a wait until the consultant has time to visit the prison in question, which is often distant and where the access hours are restricted. There is usually little information available at the prison about the person's medical or psychiatric history or about the details of the alleged offence, so obliging the visiting consultant to assess "blind". If the consultant deems admission appropriate, in many cases he/she will not have access to beds in the level of security required, and the whole process must start again. If it is possible for the consultant to offer a bed in his/her own service, there is then a further delay until the prisoner returns to court. Assuming that there are no complications thrown up by the legal process (often an unrealistic assumption), an order for admission can then be made; but the immediate result is that the person is returned to the remand prison for a period of up to 28 days to await transfer to hospital.'

Bail information officers (if in post) or court team members may be able to help to generate a set of arrangements which can enhance the prospects of bail.

Remand to Hospital

There is no general power to remand the defendant to a hospital, though MHA 1983 ss35 and 36 provide a more limited power of this nature, as detailed below. If the defendant has been admitted to hospital prior to their court appearance, this is clearly compatible with a remand on unconditional bail, subject to consideration of their fitness to attend court on the next occasion. If the court considers that requirements of bail are justified, the defendant may be made subject to a condition of residence which can include residence at a hospital. However, unless the defendant has been admitted or detained under 'section', s/he is simply an informal patient who cannot be detained, albeit that leaving hospital without appropriate amendment of their bail condition may place the defendant at risk of arrest, return to court and re-consideration of their remand status. The Christopher Clunis Inquiry Report (Ritchie *et al* 1995) recommended:

> 'When a mentally disordered person charged with an offence is remanded to hospital, ... the Consultant Psychiatrist should consider whether it is appropriate for the patient to be detained under MHA 1983, irrespective of the charge and the ultimate disposal of the case. Hence if a patient needs to be detained under s3 for his own health or safety, or for the protection of others, then he should be detained in hospital irrespective of the charge against him. Then if the case is dropped at any

stage, or if he is found not guilty of the offence, he will not be discharged into the community unless and until those treating him consider that he is fit to be discharged from the MHA 1983 section under which he is detained.'

Hostel Placement and Support on Bail

To gain some estimate of the need and scope for specialist psychiatric bail provision, Kennedy *et al* (1997) studied the numbers, nature and outcome of mentally vulnerable defendants appearing before the main Inner London magistrates' courts between April and September 1993, using a wider definitional ambit than that of MHA 1983 to extend to 'people with multiple social and emotional problems about whom there is some concern for their mental health'. A total of 495 cases were identified in which there was clear evidence that a defendant had a mental health problem. Of these 312 were remanded in custody. Of these 105 were identified to be potentially 'bailable', excluding serious alleged offences, and were characterised by a large proportion of public order and criminal damage charges. This 'bailable' group were mostly male, in their early 30s, poorly housed and often with an unclear or changing mental health diagnosis. Most had a lower tariff criminal record which frequently included Bail Act offences. Their custodial remand was often on the basis of concern about their lack of stable accommodation and their reliability in returning to court. Around 65% of the group were referred to a court diversion scheme. Some 28% received hospital orders. Many were given the diagnosis of 'personality disorder' and deemed not to require treatment under MHA 1983.

The researchers concluded that on the basis of an estimated average hostel stay of six weeks the bailable group would require approximately 25-30 permanent bed spaces that could be provided by specialist units or by psychiatric support to existing hostels. They suggest that use of hostels or a combination of other services has potential to connect such defendants with appropriate services, as well as avoiding unnecessary use of remand for defendants where so few ultimately received custodial sentences.

Staff of approved probation and bail hostels may be wary of accepting mentally disturbed defendants, feeling inexperienced in dealing with their needs and conscious that there may be little support from local mental health services. West Midlands Probation Service responded by establishing a specialised hostel for mentally disordered offenders with a national catchment area (Elliott House, Moseley, Birmingham – see Geelan *et al* 2000, noted at page 125). The Reed Committee (1992, para. 11.6) encouraged further such development but NACRO (1994) identified doubts about this kind of resource, arguing that:

(i)   it is a temporary measure, often leaving offenders to fend for themselves afterwards;

(ii) there would be insufficient demand to justify specialist hostels other than in major urban centres, so that many persons would be placed at long distance from their local community.

'Many argue that rather than establish specialist bail hostels it would be more helpful to find ways to improve access to mainstream mental health services (including accommodation). Ideally an assessment of the immediate care and accommodation needs of mentally disturbed people who are prosecuted should be made at the earliest possible point and matched against local health and social services provision. This implies that local authority community care plans and health purchasing/business plans need to make provision for mentally disturbed offenders on bail.'

It is noteworthy that Ritchie *et al* (1994:14) found it regrettable that Christopher Clunis was bailed to a hostel away from the environment with which he was familiar and from his family. However, the Elliott House project has been commended by the Chief Inspector of Prisons (1999) as a model that should be widely replicated as a means of preventing or shortening custodial remands for mentally disordered defendants.

MEDICAL REPORTS: A GENERAL NOTE

A court's duty to obtain a psychiatric report prior to imposing a custodial sentence is detailed in Chapter 12. Medical evidence, usually secured via a psychiatric report, is required before a court may make a hospital order or interim hospital order (see Chapter 7); a guardianship order (see Chapter 11); or a community rehabilitation or supervision order with a requirement of mental treatment (see Chapters 8 and 9). Evidence is also required in determining unfitness to plead (see Chapter 5). Reports have traditionally been prepared routinely in all cases of homicide (but see below). The Court of Appeal has in the past also indicated the desirability of receiving a medical report in cases of arson (*R v Calladine* (1975) *The Times* 3 December), though this may be unduly pathologising or stereotyping this kind of offence. Reports will almost certainly be secured prior to passing a discretionary life sentence (see Chapter 12). Assessment and reports can also be initiated at the request of the defence (see page 50), in very rare instances by the Crown, and also by the Prison Health Care Service, either in-house or from an outside psychiatrist.

Where a report has been requested by the court, in relation to a possible admission to hospital under MHA 1983, the doctor undertaking the report should explain to the subject the source of the request for the report and the limits of confidentiality in relation to the report, including that the data and the opinion could be relevant not only to medical disposal but also to the imposition of a custodial sentence or its length. Further, the doctor:

'should request relevant pre-sentence reports, the Inmate Medical Record, if there is one, previous psychiatric treatment records as well as relevant documentation regarding the alleged offence. If any of this information is not available, the doctor's reports should say so clearly.' (MHA(COP) 1999 para. 3.7)

The Code (para. 3.11) further specifies that the report should set out clearly:

(i)   the data on which the report is based;

(ii)   how this relates to the opinion given;

(iii) where relevant, how the opinion may relate to any medical condition defence, or other trial issue;

(iv)   factors relating to the presence of mental disorder that may affect the risk that the patient poses to himself, including risk of re-offending;

(v)   if admission to hospital is recommended, what, if any, special treatment or security is required and how this would be addressed.

The report should not comment on guilt or innocence.

Where a report has been prepared at the request of the court for the purpose of any provision of MHA 1983:

(i)   a copy of the report shall be given to the defendant's counsel or solicitor;

(ii)   if the defendant is unrepresented, the substance of the report shall be disclosed to him or her (or to the parent or guardian in the case of a child or young person);

(iii) the doctor may be required to attend to give oral evidence, either at the request of the court or (unless the report relates only to arrangements for the defendant's admission to hospital) the defence;

(iv) the defence may call evidence to rebut the evidence contained in the report (MHA 1983 s54(2) and (3)).

Most psychiatric remands result in a diagnosis of at least mild mental disorder (Salem, 1982) but not necessarily in a psychiatric disposal, particularly for non-psychotic defendants (Dell *et al*, 1993b). The value of the report may then be simply of a mitigatory nature.

As James and Hamilton (1991) note, the traditional system for acquiring psychiatric reports is cumbersome and unsatisfactory, involving a triple delay, especially where the defendant is remanded in custody:

'Once a mental disorder is suspected by the prison or the court a request is made by the prison medical service for a second opinion from the catchment area psychiatric service. A period elapses before the psychiatrist is able to attend the prison to make an assessment. There is then a further delay until the case next comes to court. If the court makes a hospital order under the Mental Health Act a further period in custody follows until the receiving hospital offers a bed.'

As Austin *et al* (2003) note, providing medical reports to the courts is not a mandatory duty of consultant psychiatrists and their response is reliant on goodwill rather than a matter of obligation. Another ground for criticism is the conventional content of such reports, often unnecessarily re-addressing matters of a non-medical nature already covered in the pre-sentence report, as remarked upon by Robertson *et al* (page 53). The scope for new strategies in delivering expert assessment and proposals speedily to courts via psychiatric liaison services based in the court building is addressed later in this chapter.

Pre-Trial Reports and the Prosecution
In some Crown Court Centres it has been practice for the CPS to obtain psychiatric reports for the Court. The Court of Appeal in *R v Reid and Others* [2002] 1 Cr App R(S) 234 has stated that this practice is 'manifestly unsatisfactory because the prosecution should not properly be required to act as an agent of the court'. In *Reid*, a case involving the trial of several defendants for murder, the prosecution, having obtained reports on

them, mistakenly distributed the report on one to the solicitors acting for another. At trial, defendants were cross-examined on what they had stated to the reporting psychiatrist who had interviewed them. In *R v Godfrey and Hardiman* (1994, unreported) the Appeal Court had stated that, where there is a single defendant:

> 'the practice is that neither the Crown nor the court refers to the contents of such a report unless a medical issue arises during the trial to which the report is relevant ... A defendant will not anticipate that what he says to the doctor may be used in evidence at his trial. There is a clear public interest in our opinion that such reports are prepared on the basis of frank disclosure of facts material to the accused's fitness to plead and to stand his trial so that the conclusions in the report advising the court on the accused's mental competence are reliable.'

The Court left open the question as to the proper principles that should apply where there are several defendants but noted that a report 'is not brought into existence by the prosecution for the purposes of preparing a case against the defendant'. Though noting the absence of clear guidelines governing these situations and concluding that disclosure of the reports in suitably edited form was compatible with the disclosure requirements of CPIA 1996 and that the defendants had been properly subject to a limited degree of cross-examination based on what they had told the psychiatrist but incompatible with their evidence, the Court's view in *Reid* (see below), that reports should not be routinely prepared in murder cases, should reduce the scope for this kind of conflict and uncertainty.

Murder Cases

Bail

In the uncommon instances where bail is granted in the case of a defendant accused of murder, the court is required by BA 1976 s3(6A) to impose as a condition of bail a requirement that the accused 'shall undergo medical examination by two medical practitioners', one of whom must be approved under MHA 1983 s12 (see page 233), so that reports on their mental condition can be prepared, with the allied requirement that the accused 'shall attend such an institution or place as the court direct and comply with any other directions which may be given to him for that purpose' by either doctor. This requirement does not apply if 'satisfactory reports on (the defendant's) mental condition have already been obtained'.

Note that under CJPOA 1994 s25, a person charged with or convicted of murder shall not be granted bail if the defendant has a previous conviction in the United Kingdom for murder, attempted murder, manslaughter, culpable homicide (a Scottish offence), rape or attempted rape, and (in the case of manslaughter or culpable homicide only) has received a custodial sentence upon that conviction.

Other Instances

In *R v Reid and Others* [2002] 1 Cr App R(S) 234, the Court of Appeal indicated that the long-standing general practice in murder cases for a court to require a psychiatrist's report before trial is no longer necessary. The Court considered that in exceptional cases, where issues of mental state are at stake, an appropriate order can be made at the plea and directions hearing. It was noted that the absence of such reports serves to avoid the complications that can arise when reports are circulating, as illustrated by *Reid* itself (see above).

REPORTS FOR MAGISTRATES' COURTS: AFTER CONVICTION

The court has a general power to adjourn after conviction and prior to sentence or otherwise dealing with the defendant, to enable enquiries (including medical assessment) to be made or to determine the most suitable method of dealing with the case, even in regard to non-imprisonable offences (MCA 1980 s10(3)). The maximum period for adjournment is four weeks, or three weeks if the defendant is remanded in custody. The general presumption in favour of bail applies to such remands (BA 1976 s4(4)) but the defendant need not be granted bail in the case of an imprisonable offence if it appears to the court that it would be impracticable to complete the enquiries or make the report without keeping the defendant in custody (BA 1976 sch 1 part 1 para. 7). The court can impose conditional bail requiring the defendant 'to make himself available for the purpose of enabling enquiries or a report to be made to assist the court', if such a requirement is considered necessary to secure compliance (BA 1976 s3(6)(d)).

REPORTS FOR MAGISTRATES' COURTS: BEFORE OR AFTER CONVICTION

PCC(S)A 2000 s11 gives magistrates' courts a flexible power to obtain a medical report in any instance where the court determines that the accused's physical or mental condition should be investigated, provided that the case is being dealt with by summary trial and the offence is imprisonable.

PCC(S)A 2000 s11

(1) If, on the trial by a magistrates' court of an offence punishable on summary conviction with imprisonment, the court –

  (a) is satisfied that the accused did the act or made the omission charged but

  (b) is of the opinion that an inquiry ought to be made into his physical or mental condition before the method of dealing with him is determined,

  the court shall adjourn the case to enable a medical examination and report to be made and shall remand him; but the adjournment shall not be for more than three weeks at a time where the court remands him in custody nor for more than four weeks at a time where it remands him on bail.

(2) Where on an adjournment under subsection (1) above the accused is remanded on bail, the court shall impose conditions under BA 1976 s3(6)(d) and the requirements imposed as conditions under that paragraph shall be or shall include requirements that the accused –

  (a) undergo medical examination by a duly qualified medical practitioner or, where the inquiry is into his mental condition and the court so directs, two such practitioners; and

  (b) for that purpose attend such an institution or place, or on such practitioner as the court directs and, where the inquiry is into his mental condition, comply with any other directions which may be given to him for that purpose by any person specified by the court or by a person of any class so specified.

This power has primary use prior to conviction, provided that the court is satisfied that the accused 'did the act or made the omission', allowing a psychiatric assessment to proceed prior to plea, either with a view to possible discontinuance of prosecution, or simply to promote early medical intervention and to avoid delay. It can also pave the way to the unusual step of a hospital order under MHA 1983 s37(3) without convicting the accused (see page 89). The defence may indicate that the facts of the allegation are not disputed; alternatively, a not guilty plea may have to be entered, allowing the prosecution evidence to be heard so that the court can reach the necessary judgment.

Remand on Bail
The usual presumption in favour of bail applies (BA 1976 s4(2)) but, if bail is granted, the court must impose conditions of bail under BA 1976 s3(6)(d) (see above) as amplified by s30(2). The option to require assessment by two doctors allows the court to anticipate a hospital or guardianship order under MHA 1983 s37 or an interim hospital order under s38, which procedurally require two medical opinions (see Chapter 7).

Documentation of Reasons and Information
A statement of the reasons why the court is of opinion that an enquiry should be made into the defendant's physical or mental condition, and of any information before the court about his or her condition, should be sent either to the institution to which s/he is remanded in custody or to the institution or place at which s/he is to be examined (or to the doctor who is to conduct the examination): MCR 1981 r24.

Enhancing Alternative Access to Psychiatric Information
A familiar problem has been the difficulty experienced by consultant psychiatrists in meeting courts' requests for reports within the timescale of prosecution and sentencing procedures, causing no little frustration for magistrates. For example, about 250 requests each year for a formal psychiatric opinion have been received within Hampshire and the Isle of Wight, yet only a handful prove necessary in law for the action taken by the courts. To assist and guide magistrates through different routes to obtaining timely and appropriate information and advice in dealing with mentally disordered offenders, a protocol has been developed in Hampshire (Austin *et al*, 2003) with effect from January 2003 that aims to expand courts' access to useful information beyond the traditional source of a consultant psychiatrist. The protocol addresses the approach to be followed at various stages: remand on bail (whether a court diversion scheme operates or not); remand in custody (using the services of the prison mental health team); and in securing more readily a formal psychiatric opinion where required for a MHA 1983 disposal or for a psychiatric community rehabilitation order. The protocol can be accessed at: www.hants.gov.uk/wessexconsortium.

REPORTS FOR THE CROWN COURT
With the exception of MHA 1983 s35, detailed below, no specific statutory provisions provide for the Crown Court to obtain a medical report; however, the court has an inherent power to adjourn so that a report can be prepared.

REMAND TO HOSPITAL FOR REPORT: MHA 1983 SECTION 35

Either the Crown Court or magistrates' courts may remand a defendant to a specified hospital for a report on their mental condition, under this provision, as follows.

Availability of Power by Tier of Court

Crown Court

Where the defendant is awaiting trial for an imprisonable offence or has been arraigned before the court for such an offence (except murder) but has not yet been sentenced or dealt with.

Magistrates' Courts

Where the offence is punishable on summary conviction with imprisonment and:

(i)   the defendant has been convicted of the offence; or

(ii) the court is satisfied that the defendant 'did the act or made the omission charged'; or

(iii) the defendant has consented to the court's exercise of this power.

Procedural Requirements

The following procedural pre-requirements apply (s35(3) and (4)):

(i)   the court must be satisfied, on the written or oral evidence of a doctor, that 'there is reason to suspect that the accused is suffering from mental illness, psychopathic disorder, severe mental impairment or mental impairment';

(ii) the court must be of the opinion that 'it would be impracticable for a report on (the accused's) mental condition to be made if (s/he) were remanded on bail';

(iii) there must be written or oral evidence, from either the doctor who will prepare the report or a representative of the hospital managers, that arrangements have been made for the defendant's admission to hospital, within seven days of the remand date.

The defendant may be detained in 'a place of safety' (normally a prison establishment but alternatively a police station or another hospital) pending admission.

It is the court's responsibility to organise transport from the court to the receiving hospital (MHA(COP) 1999 para. 7.3).

Use of s35 is clearly facilitated if a psychiatrist has been able to assess the defendant quickly as part of a court-based psychiatric assessment or screening scheme (see page 54). If the defendant is already in custody, s35 may prove less helpful as the psychiatrist may prefer to assess the defendant at the prison and arrange for their transfer to hospital under the broader ambit of MHA 1983 s48 (see Chapter 13). Some hospitals are reluctant to take patients under s35 because it does not give the right to treat or discharge.

Period of Remand

A period of remand cannot exceed 28 days but the defendant may be re-remanded 'if it appears to the court on the written or oral evidence of the doctor responsible for the report that a further remand is necessary' to complete the assessment, but the total period spent on remand shall not exceed 12 weeks. It is not necessary for the defendant to be present in court for a re-remand to be ordered, provided that s/he is legally represented and the advocate has the opportunity to address the court. The court may terminate the remand at any time if it appears appropriate to do so (s35(7)).

Treatment

The defendant is not legally obliged to receive treatment during their assessment (MHA 1983 s56(1)(b)). Section 35 has been criticised because it allows only assessment and not treatment, *eg* by the Reed Committee (1992, para. 9.6(ii)). However, NACRO (1994) noted:

> 'in practice many psychiatrists admit people under s35 and then arrange for treatment under a civil section such as MHA 1983 s3. Although cumbersome, this arrangement probably strikes a reasonable balance between the court's view that an offender should be detained in hospital and the need to ensure that treatment is given with consent.'

Detention

The defendant is 'detained' at the hospital during their remand. In the event of abscondment, s/he may be arrested without warrant and must then be brought as soon as practicable before the remanding court, which may then terminate the remand and deal with the defendant in any way that would have been open to the court if s/he had not been remanded (s35(9) and (10)). Responsible Medical Officers (RMOs) are not entitled to grant leave of absence to patients so detained.

Assessment and Report

MHA(COP) 1999 para. 17.3 specifies:

> 'Where a patient remanded under s35 is thought to be in need of medical treatment for mental disorder under Part IV of the Act, the patient should be referred back to court as soon as possible with an appropriate recommendation, and with an assessment of whether the patient is in a fit state to attend court. If there is a delay in securing a court date consideration should be given to whether the patient meets the criteria for detention under MHA 1983 s3.'

A report prepared in pursuit of a s35 remand order should contain:

(i)   a statement as to whether a patient is suffering from a specified form of mental disorder as required by the section, identifying its relevance to the alleged offence. The report should not comment on guilt or innocence. It may be appropriate to suggest that a further report be submitted to the court between conviction and sentence;

(ii) relevant social factors;

(iii) any recommendations on care and treatment, including where and when it should take place and who should be responsible. (para. 17.4)

Independent Report

The defendant is entitled to obtain an independent medical report from a doctor of their own choice and at their own expense and to apply to the court for the remand to be terminated on the basis of that report (s35(8)). The hospital managers should help in the exercise of this right by enabling the patient to contact a suitably qualified and experienced solicitor or other adviser: MHA(COP) 1999 para. 17.1.

Crediting Time on Remand

PCC(S)A 2000 s87, replacing C(S)A 1997 ss9 and 9A (as amended by CDA 1998 s107(5)) but awaiting implementation, governs the credit to be given for any period spent on remand in custody when the defendant subsequently receives a term of imprisonment. The court passing sentence 'shall direct that the number of days for which the offender was remanded in custody ... shall count as time served by him as part of the sentence' (s87(3)), unless 'it is in the opinion of the court just in all the circumstances not to give a direction' (s87(4)(b)). The meaning of 'remand in custody' is amplified by s88 which specifies in s88(1)(d) that this includes time when the offender was remanded, admitted or removed to hospital under MHA 1983 ss35, 36, 38 or 48. Implementation of this provision giving courts a discretionary power in this respect will trigger the repeal under C(S)A 1997 of the current provisions governing time served prior to imposition of sentence under CJA 1967 s67 which affords automatic credit in the computation of sentences but does not incorporate MHA provisions within time to be counted as served prior to sentence.

Use of Section 35

MHA statistics (DoH Bulletin 2002/26) record 137 admissions under s135 in the 12 months ending 31 March 2002, of which 126 were to NHS facilities. That number indicates reduced use of this option since 1991-92 (419 admissions), with 269 admissions in 1997-98. Of the 126 admissions, 100 were categorised as mentally ill and only one as psychopathically disordered, with a further 22 being unspecified.

REMAND TO HOSPITAL FOR TREATMENT: MHA 1983 SECTION 36

The Crown Court, but not a magistrates' court, has a limited power to remand a defendant to hospital for treatment as an alternative to a remand in custody. To be eligible, the defendant must be in custody either awaiting trial or be in the pre-sentence stage of an ongoing trial at Crown Court for an imprisonable offence (except murder). The provisions of s36 are very similar to s35 but do not apply to psychopathic disorder or mental impairment.

Procedural Requirements

The court must be satisfied on the written or oral evidence of two doctors that the defendant 'is suffering from mental illness or severe mental impairment of a nature or degree which makes it appropriate for him or her to be detained in a hospital for mental treatment'. The court must also be satisfied, on the evidence of the doctor who would be responsible for treatment or a representative of the hospital managers, that arrangements have been made for the defendant's admission to hospital within seven days of the remand date. The court may direct the defendant's detention in a 'place of safety' (see page 47) pending admission.

Period of Remand

The effect of the order as regards duration, renewal, absconding and obtaining an independent report of the period of remand are specified in exactly the same way as for s35 (above). The detained patient is, however, subject to the provisions of the 1983 Act authorising compulsory treatment. As regards credit for time spent on remand, see above.

The Reed Report (1992, para. 9.6(ii)(b)) suggested that this power should be extended to magistrates' courts. Dell *et al* (1993a) noted the infrequent use of s36 in respect of psychotic women on remand in HMP Holloway:

> 'Prison psychiatrists believed that it involved difficulties in cases where the defendant intended to deny the charges or to oppose hospital disposals. Moreover, it only allows the patient to remain in hospital for 12 weeks, an unrealistically short period, given current delays in the Crown Court'.

Use of Section 36

MHA statistics (DoH Bulletin 2002/26) record only 25 admissions under s36 in the 12 months ending 31 March 2002, of which 21 were to NHS facilities. That number indicates little variation in use of this option in the decade since 1991-92 (48 admissions), with 25 admissions in 1997-98. Of the 21 admissions, 17 were categorised as mentally ill, with a further four being unspecified.

REPORTS OBTAINED BY THE DEFENCE

The defence is at liberty to obtain a medical report at any stage of proceedings. This capacity is specifically recognised in MHA 1983 ss35 and 36 (above) and, in addition, MHA 1983 s54(3)(c) provides that the defence may call evidence to rebut the evidence contained in any report obtained upon the direction of the court in furtherance of the 1983 Act.

If the defence does not feel that the report obtained is helpful to the defence case, it is not under an obligation to submit it to the court. However, it does not 'own' its expert's opinion or have a right to veto its use. Thus in *R v Crozier* [1991] Crim LR 138, a psychiatrist commissioned by the defence to assess the defendant, learning that his report recommending the defendant's detention in a Special Hospital had not been submitted to the court, disclosed his opinion to the prosecution. The Crown passed this information to the court. On the defence's appeal, the Court of Appeal held that the strong public interest in disclosure of the psychiatrist's opinion overrode his duty of confidence to the defendant. This decision appears to leave it somewhat to chance whether the psychiatrist becomes aware of their report's fate and chooses to intervene or not.

'Legal Aid' Funding

For most defendants, their opportunity to secure a medical report will depend on whether public funding can be secured to pay for the exercise and in reality this is unlikely to be approved. Though each case is looked at on its merits, to secure financial approval for a report to be obtained before one is ordered by the court, the defence will need to convince the Legal Services Commission (LSC) that a report is necessary for the proper conduct of proceedings, *eg* in determining fitness to plead. The LSC is likely to advise that the matter should be left to the court's discretion and if the court subsequently chooses not to order a report, the Board will almost certainly feel justified in declining authorisation. As a matter of general principle the LSC has determined in relation to Criminal Defence Service work (*Criminal Bills Assessment Manual* (2002) para. 4.3, citing CRIMLA 3):

> 'Where it appears that a court may be considering a disposal under MHA 1983, only in exceptional cases will costs of medical or psychiatric reports be allowed for use in mitigation on conviction where no request has been made by the court. ... The Board's first position would be to say that the court should order the cost of the report and an application should be made to the court. If in an exceptional case the application has been refused a prior authority may be considered by the Board. If it has never been made then it will be exceptional for the Board to consider granting a prior authority. In considering any application by a solicitor for prior authority to cover the commissioning of a medial report, area offices should assume judges will not normally order medical or psychiatric reports except where there is likely to be a MHA disposal or community rehabilitation order requiring medical treatment for a mental condition.'

RESEARCHING CUSTODIAL REMANDS OF MENTALLY DISORDERED OFFENDERS

Unnecessary Use of Custodial Remand

A number of research studies have drawn attention to the excessive or unnecessary use of remands in custody to secure psychiatric assessment. Salem's (1982) study of 600 cases in 14 magistrates' courts found that bail was granted during the assessment period to little more than half of the sample. This seems partly to arise from the defendant's social circumstances, especially homelessness. Thus Coid's (1988) study of 334 mentally abnormal men remanded to HMP Winchester for psychiatric reports 1979-83 showed that 197 were of no fixed abode on arrival in prison and, in 136 cases, the prison doctors considered the men to be incapable of caring for themselves independently in the community at the time of their arrest. Dell *et al* (1993a) found that 43% of 95 psychotic women remanded to HMP Holloway in 1989 'had no place they could call home, living in squats, bed and breakfast accommodation, hostels and so on'. Their offences were of a comparatively less serious nature, the most common offence being criminal damage (30%) and only 17% being eventually dealt with by the Crown Court. Major violence was not common (5%). Among Coid's sample, the most prevalent charges were burglary and theft (31%), often involving minor stealing of food, followed by criminal damage (22%). 'Violent' offences usually consisted of minor assaults, often on the police who had attempted to move the man on.

Further evidence of the unnecessary nature of custodial remand was provided by the sentencing outcomes. Robertson *et al* (1992) report that the great majority of psychotic remanded prisoners in Holloway, Brixton and Risley Prisons who did not obtain psychiatric beds were released with nominal or non-custodial penalties. Only 15% received custodial sentences that were longer than the period spent on remand. All the women in the Holloway sample who did not receive hospital orders were returned to the community at point of sentence, either because of a non-custodial disposal or because they had already served their custodial sentence on remand. Dell and her colleagues conclude that the reason for prison remand:

'was not because of the seriousness of their offences but because of their apparent need for help. The courts were using remand prisons as social and psychiatric assessment and referral centres.'

Black Defendants

Browne's small-scale study (1990) of 70 defendants remanded for a psychiatric report in one magistrates' court found that ten (37%) of 27 white defendants were granted bail compared with three (13%) of black defendants, a difference which could only partly be accounted for by their number of previous convictions or the seriousness of the present offence. Browne suggests that 'decision makers seemed more likely to err on the side of caution with black mentally vulnerable defendants and to be affected by a heightened perception of (their) dangerousness'.

Assessment and Referral

Coid's study looked at men remanded for reports who were classified as suffering mental illness or sub-normality. The majority (72%) had schizophrenia, while 10% were of sub-normal intelligence. One in five of the sample were rejected for treatment by a NHS consultant psychiatrist.

'Those with mental handicaps, organic brain damage or a chronic psychotic illness rendering them unable to cope independently in the community were the most likely to be rejected. They posed the least threat to the community in terms of their criminal behaviour yet were more likely to be sentenced to imprisonment. Such subjects were commonly described by consultants as too disturbed or potentially dangerous to be admitted to hospital or as criminals and unsuitable for treatment. Consultants in mental hospitals were most likely and those in district general hospitals and academic units were least likely to accept prisoners.'

The study by Robertson *et al* (1992) of 952 cases of remand in Brixton, Risley and Holloway Prisons in 1991 looked not just at those remanded for reports but all mentally disordered remand prisoners who came to the attention of prison doctors for psychiatric reasons, whether because reports had been ordered (the majority source) or because of concern within the prison for their mental health. (The study was not designed to ascertain how many remand prisoners were mentally disordered). Among the findings were the following:

- Just over half of the sample (53%) were thought to be suffering from psychotic illnesses (primarily schizophrenia).

- The majority of those assessed as psychotic were referred to outside psychiatrists in the hope of an offer of a psychiatric bed (this ranged from 66% at Risley to 85% at Holloway). Reasons for non-referral included the prisoner's improvement on medication or the shortness of the remand but in some instances represented an unacceptable failure to take appropriate action.

- Referral to an outside psychiatrist substantially lengthens the time that a mentally disordered person spends in prison. Thus 14 non-referred psychotic women in Holloway spent 17 days in prison on average, while their referred counterparts averaged 42 days. The average remand time for those referred to only one consultant was 28 days; for those referred to more than one it was 63 days.

- Outside psychiatrists offered beds to over half of those referred. When they declined to accept patients, security was rarely the issue: those thought to require secure beds were usually accepted in secure units or special hospitals. Beds were most commonly refused for one of two reasons:

  (i) the person was not thought to be suffering from a psychotic illness; or

  (ii) the illness was not thought severe enough to warrant hospitalisation, sometimes because it had improved since admission.

    Though a consultant's unwillingness to accept a patient had sometimes influenced their diagnostic formulation, usually a disagreement with the prison doctor reflected a genuine diagnostic difference of perspective.

- When the outside doctor offered to provide a bed, it was nearly always under MHA 1983 s37. Almost without exception, courts made hospital orders when they were given the option but the procedures were slow and cumbersome in contrast to admission to hospital under civil procedures (this aspect of the research is detailed further in Chapter 7).

- Most psychotic offenders who were not offered beds were soon picked up again by the police and then once more remanded in custody by concerned magistrates looking for psychiatric solutions. 'The courts are in a bind: if they cannot make a hospital order they cannot as a rule deliver social or psychiatric help to the mentally disordered'.

- *Quality of Court Reports:* 'The lengthy catalogue of social and criminal histories which some doctors supplied was of questionable value to the courts, especially when probation reports were also provided; yet the production of such reports was extremely expensive in terms of doctors' time'.

- *Unnecessary Delay for Crown Court Trial:* In almost half of the cases where Holloway prisoners went to Crown Court on indictable only offences, necessitating additional weeks in custody before eventual admission to (unrestricted) hospital beds which had long been available, the CPS might well have laid alternative charges triable by magistrates, thus achieving an identical outcome more quickly.

- Given the need for less cumbersome, swifter access to hospital, far greater use should be made of MHA 1983 s48 transfer of remand prisoners to hospital if they are in urgent need of treatment (this aspect is detailed further in Chapter 13).

Robertson and his colleagues concluded:

'As a method of obtaining psychiatric help for mentally disordered offenders, the custodial remand has nothing to commend it: it is inhumane, expensive and ineffective. It exposes mentally disordered people to conditions and regimes which are cruelly harsh and inappropriate. It brings into prison thousands of defendants who do not need to be there and for whom penal disposals are never contemplated. The establishment of alternative arrangements – local liaison and assessment schemes as recommended by the Home Office – is urgently required. If this cannot rapidly be achieved then we believe that it may be necessary to consider setting up special NHS units in the large population centres, to which the police could send disturbed people as a place of safety, and to which the courts would also have access. Such units would have the function of providing a rapid assessment and treatment service with a view to moving the patients as soon as possible to their own catchment areas. In one way or another the time has come to put an end to the extraordinary system under which people are sent to prison not because of their crimes, but because of their need to be referred to the health and social services.'

ACCELERATED ASSESSMENT AND REPORTS VIA COURT DIVERSION SCHEMES

HOC 66/1990 (para. 7) pointed out that 'it is desirable for the court to receive professional advice at as early a stage as possible on facilities which may be available to assist it with mentally disordered offenders' and referred approvingly to pioneering assessment schemes. These had been initiated primarily by scheduled weekly attendance at busy London courts, as detailed below, but one of the earliest initiatives began at Peterborough Magistrates' Court in 1986, using the following procedure.

As soon as the police or a duty solicitor identify a person who has been charged and is in custody as likely to need psychiatric assistance, the court is informed by telephone. The court then contacts the district hospital to arrange for the duty consultant psychiatrist to assess the accused in the cells and report either that day or the following day on the accused's fitness to plead, whether a hospital bed is urgently required or whether a full assessment via a prison remand is appropriate. The Peterborough scheme proved successful despite limited local psychiatric facilities and problems in placing persons considered to be dangerous. For an account of an alternative scheme, commenced in Reading Magistrates' Court in 1991, and a general review, see Wickham (1994). Two further schemes are now reported in detail.

In essence, a scheme operates by placing psychiatric staff in magistrates' courts where they can assess cases where there is any concern about mental health and then arrange appropriate interventions. Admission to hospital may be arranged at court, often on the same day and direct from court, using civil powers under MHA 1983 Part II as well as the criminal provisions of the Act. Schemes vary in their staff composition, from a single community forensic nurse visiting court, to multi-disciplinary teams with administration staff, computerised records and a permanent base in the court building. Diversity of practice was welcomed by the Reed Report (1992, para. 11.207) which felt that 'any national view of preferred models for court-based assessment and diversion schemes should be taken only after the growing range of such schemes and outcomes for patients, have been fully evaluated'.

A register of schemes held by the National Schizophrenia Fellowship (2000) listed 118 court schemes as at April 2000, while James et al (2002) reported approximately 150 schemes understood to be functioning in courts in England and Wales. From April 1993 the Home Office made funding available to meet the sessional costs or fees of psychiatrists or CPNs attending magistrates' courts but this does not extend to financing whole posts, administrative costs or schemes as a whole. This pump-priming initiative was very successful in encouraging the development of new initiatives but has now ended. James et al (Appendix B) offer guidance to setting up schemes.

The Clerkenwell Scheme

As described by James and Hamilton (1991, 1992), two psychiatrists attended a London magistrates' court one day a week to examine defendants held in custody for whom psychiatric reports had been requested. Those appearing in court on days when the psychiatrists were not present were remanded to the date of their next visit, occasionally being bailed overnight for the purpose. With the benefit of information about the case from the CPS, defence solicitors and the Probation Service, the doctors assessed defendants in the cell area and gave brief oral reports to the court on the same day. Recommendations were completed for hospital admission under both civil and criminal powers of MHA 1983.

Of 80 referrals over nine months (25% being women), hospital admission was recommended in 39 cases (21% of whom were women) and accepted by the court in every instance: 20 s2 assessment orders, five s3 treatment orders and 14 s37 hospital orders. Hospital orders were used where the CPS or the psychiatrists felt that it was in the public interest for a conviction to be recorded, though in three cases the decision was made because no ASW could be found to make an application for a civil order, Social Services departments showing mixed interest and co-operation. Where a civil admission was secured, charges were discontinued in all but four cases. Sometimes a civil admission was preferable because the receiving hospital was willing to receive a patient on that basis, whereas a s37 admission would have required a review by the hospital's own nursing and medical teams. When faced with serious offences which could not be dealt with summarily, it was possible to divert cases to medium secure units to await trial, by arranging a bed and completing recommendations under MHA 1983 s48, which were then faxed to the Home Office for immediate approval via the local remand prison.

The effectiveness of the scheme was demonstrated by two comparison measures. First, the scheme achieved a hospital admission rate of 4.3 a month, four times higher than that for the 12 months before the scheme began, after adjusting for a 9% increase in the numbers appearing before the court. Orders for crimes not involving personal violence increased fivefold, suggesting that 'readier access to psychiatrists encouraged the referral of mentally disordered people who might previously have not been referred as their outward behaviour was not severely disturbed'.

Secondly, the throughput of defendants under the scheme was compared with 50 defendants admitted to hospital after being remanded to Brixton Prison for the preparation of reports. Whereas the mean time from arrest to hospital admission for the Brixton sample was 50.8 days (of which 15.1 days were spent waiting for the case to be dealt with after assessment and 16.9 days waiting for hospital admission after a hospital order had been made), for defendants reaching hospital through the scheme, the mean time from arrest to admission was 8.7 days. For those assessed under the scheme but not sent to hospital, the mean time from arrest to appearance in court with a report was 5.4 days, compared with 33.7 days for those receiving second opinion assessment in prison.

Bow Street and Marlborough Street

Joseph and Potter (1993) report a pilot scheme, operating in two central London magistrates' courts where a high number of homeless mentally disordered defendants appeared, February 1989 to September 1990. A psychiatrist was available at court two mornings a week with a wider remit than the preparation of reports, assessing 'defendants perceived by any court official as requiring a psychiatric assessment who might be or had already been, remanded into custody for a medical report'. Defendants were seen either on the day of their first court appearance or after a remand in custody to the next designated morning and 92% were thus assessed before conviction. Most referrals (68%) were made by magistrates but referrals were also accepted from probation officers, police gaolers and duty solicitors. CPS and court files were made available. The psychiatrist gave oral evidence to the court in regard to fitness to plead, diagnosis and medical recommendation. If hospital admission was indicated, an ASW from the local Social Services department attended court and a second psychiatrist was also available.

Over 18 months of the study, 201 referrals were received in respect of 185 defendants, of whom 84% were men. The majority were of no fixed abode and socially isolated, 37% being on the streets at time of arrest and 28% in unsettled, temporary accommodation such as night shelters, hostels or squats. Only one-third were living in stable accommodation. One hundred and fifty seven defendants (85%) had been in previous contact with psychiatric services, 130 (70%) as in-patients (of whom three-quarters had been subject to civil or criminal detention). Only 25% of those with previous admissions were currently receiving psychiatric support, mainly out-patient appointments. Over three-quarters (77%) of defendants had a criminal record. The most common diagnosis was schizophrenia (39%), a further 21% suffering other forms of psychosis; 38 of psychiatric defendants were considered unfit to plead (though this issue was never tested in court).

The mean time from arrest to assessment was six days, 50% being seen within three days. Psychiatric recommendations were as follows: 26% no recommendation; 38% out-patient treatment; 10% informal admission to hospital; 12% detention under MHA 1983 civil powers; 9% detention under MHA 1983 criminal powers; 5% further assessment. The court followed 90% of these recommendations, outcomes being: 29% discontinuance or withdrawal of charge, of whom 60% were admitted to hospital; 49% non-custodial disposal; 12% s37 hospital order; 6.5% custodial sentence. Of 65 cases admitted to hospital by one route or another, 51 (78%) were admitted direct from court and 14 via custodial remand. All of these admissions, except one, were to general psychiatry beds.

One obvious advantage of the system was the scope for direct communication so that the psychiatrist was able to gain immediate assistance from the Probation Service and discuss the issues face to face with the CPS and defence advocate, thus allowing the doctor a direct voice in the issue of discontinuance in the public interest, something virtually unknown for psychiatrists at prison.

Comparing Court Assessment and Diversion via Conventional Section 48 Transfer

Pierzchniak *et al* (1997) studied men transferred to hospital following court appearance in the area served by HMP Pentonville: 114 being admitted during 1994, 103 following remand to prison and 11 direct from court following assessment by court-based diversion schemes. Of the 114, 41 had been seen by a diversion scheme and these were transferred to hospital much more quickly. Factors such as ethnicity, diagnosis and offence type did not make a significant difference to the delays but time taken to transfer was significantly greater for those who required secure beds.

Of the 45 who transferred to open wards, the mean number of days to transfer was 8 for those who went via court diversion and prison, compared with 47 via prison only. Of 36 who transferred to closed wards, the mean number of days to transfer was 9 for those who went via court diversion and prison, compared with 57 via prison only. Of 31 who went to medium/maximum security, the mean number of days to transfer was 25 for those who went via court diversion and prison, compared with 58 via prison only.

Comparing Assessments by Doctors and Nurses

In an initiative both to assess the effectiveness of a provincial assessment and diversion scheme and to compare outcomes according to whether psychiatrists or CPNs undertook the assessment (each professional group was responsible for a phase of the study period, with a 'control' phase when neither undertook screening and defendants were seen by bail information officers who could refer on), Chambers and Rix (1999) studied practice at Leeds Magistrates' Court and compared their findings with London-based studies and that of research conducted at Rotherham Magistrates' Court (Rowlands *et al*, 1996) and at Leeds by Greenhalgh *et al* (1996).

- Only 2.5% of the offenders referred to the diversion scheme were found to be suffering from schizophrenia or a related psychosis, a much lower rate than found in London studies, particularly in the central area. Compare 12% (including substance-induced psychotic disorders) in Rotherham and 7% in Leeds earlier.

- The discontinuence rate was 6% during the phase of doctor assessment and 4% during the nurse phase (and during the control phase). Compare an overall 11% rate in Rotherham.

- When magistrates had reports available from doctors they released more prisoners on bail than during the control period but when they had reports from nurses the proportion did not differ from the control period.

- The rate of admission to hospital was 12% (compare 26% in Rotherham). The difference from admission rates in other studies seems explicable, at least in part, by diagnosis.

- Although doctors and nurses recommended out-patient treatment in many cases, the attendance rate was low.

- Doctors were more likely than nurses to identify persons with medical needs that needed to be brought to the attention of the prison healthcare service, to recommend out-patient psychiatric treatment and to identify relevant medico-legal issues.

- Assessment by doctors was associated with prisoners spending less time remanded in custody.

The researchers concluded on the basis of this survey that models of service which have proved effective in London have not been shown to be necessarily appropriate in the provinces, nor have schemes yet been shown to reduce or delay re-offending, or to improve the mental health of the bulk of MDOs who are not psychotic.

A General Overview

In a national survey of the availability of court-based psychiatric assessment schemes conducted in December 1991, Blumenthal and Wessely (1992) gained the impression that the existence of schemes 'is often associated more with the availability of local forensic services (and interested staff) than local need'. Particular problems identified included: lack of adequate transport arrangements to take defendants to hospital; difficulties in securing hospital places for offenders because of reluctance to expose hospital staff to the risk of violence; over-dependence on a 'key person' with a personal commitment to the scheme (probation respondents indicated that just over half of schemes would not continue if the key person left). Overall, few health authorities had included regular attendance at a police station, court or prison as part of any mental health professional's job description. Regular meetings between members of health services and other agencies participating in diversion were sparsely reported. Some 34% of mental health services' purchasers had no current or future plans to develop a policy dealing with mentally disordered offenders and over a half did not regard the setting up of diversion schemes as a priority. The researchers concluded:

> 'Many of the schemes currently operating have adequate provisions for psychiatric assessment but inadequate arrangements for follow-up treatment and care of the offender once diverted from custody. Of particular note are the inner city schemes in London. A further gap is the provision of medium secure beds presently provided by RSUs. Diversion schemes mean increases in admissions and greater demand on already limited resources. Resistance to the setting up of schemes reflects concern not only for the cost of the scheme itself but also for the cost of treating and housing mentally ill offenders.'

NACRO (1994) pointed out that schemes are open to criticism 'on grounds that they may encourage the police and CPS to bring cases to court in the knowledge that assessment will be made', thus undermining the scope for diversion at earlier points in the criminal justice system.

A decade on, James *et al* (2002) surveyed the current state of court diversion services (see their Appendix A) and summed up the effectiveness of court schemes as follows:

Identification of Mental Illness

Schemes can improve identification fourfold. In one scheme (Hudson *et al*, 1995), 39% of those compulsorily admitted to hospital *via* the court after a period spent on custodial remand had not been recognised as mentally ill at their remand prison. Use of questionnaires as a screening device may help to improve identification rates (Shaw *et al*, 1999).

Achievement of Hospital Admission

The evidence is consistently encouraging. In one particularly successful initiative reported by James and Harlow (2000), 0.28% of all arrests in one year in a large area of central London were admitted to hospital through the local court scheme. Some 60% of all referrals to hospital were admitted, with 56% of all admissions going to locked beds. In one year the scheme was responsible for one in eight of all the unrestricted s37 orders in England and Wales, as well as one in 16 of all s48 admissions and one in 24 of all s35 admissions.

Acceleration of Admission

Studies indicate very similar results, with time from arrest to admission being reduced from around seven weeks to one week. However, the greater the level of security required, the longer the time interval (Hudson *et al*, 1995).

Serious Offences

Though it might be assumed that only less serious offenders can be dealt with by court schemes, there is persuasive evidence that they can deal effectively with graver offences. In a survey of 106 criminal justice admissions in one area in the course of a year, James *et al* (1997) found that there was no significant difference in seriousness of offending between those processed at court and those processed elsewhere.

Non-Urban Areas

Though published reports of court schemes deal predominantly with metropolitan areas that have the most established schemes as well as higher rates of psychiatric morbidity, unpublished accounts from elsewhere show that it is possible to adapt the court-based model to semi-rural or small-town environments by combining on-call CPN services with consultant back-up offering protected assessment time, as part of a wider integrated strategy in responding to MDOs.

Factors Associated with Ineffective Practice

The effectiveness of schemes appears inhibited by: poor planning; inadequate case identification and referral procedures; lack of commitment from local psychiatric services, where concerns may remain that those referred are criminals, not patients, and are likely to be disruptive in hospital and unlikely to benefit from admission; inadequate staffing and resources; lack of access to beds. The researchers suggest that diversion schemes will not be effective as part of an overall strategy in delivering psychiatric services within the criminal justice system unless they are integrated into mainstream general psychiatry services and incorporated into community mental health team structures.

Outcome of Admissions

Noting the dearth of research into the outcome of admissions via court schemes, James *et al* (2000) undertook an outcome study, comparing admissions through the courts with admissions from the community. A sample of 214 admissions through two court schemes in central London (Horseferry Road and Clerkenwell) were identified prospectively between 1992 and 1996. These were compared with 214 compulsory admissions from the community, matched for admitting hospital, month of admission and compulsory status. Follow-up was for a minimum of two years. Admissions and convictions in the two years before admission were compared with the two years after discharge.

Court and community admissions were not distinguishable in terms of previous admissions to hospital. Some 75% of court admissions had previously been admitted to psychiatric hospital, almost half of them in the previous two years. Only 23% had previously been admitted through the criminal justice system while 44% had undergone previous compulsory admission from the community. Some 67% of court admissions had a prior criminal record, compared with 44% of community admissions. However, the majority of those admitted from court were not career criminals who had become mentally ill. 'Most appeared to have offended in the context of mental illness and social exclusion, having fallen through gaps in community care.' More court admissions had a history of substance misuse.

Comparing court and community admissions in terms of hospital stay, the research found no differences between the two samples in terms of: failure to reach planned discharge; length of stay; clinical outcome; drug-use in hospital; proportion involved in violence; discharge planning; compliance with out-patient follow-up. Community patients: were responsible for more incidents of violence; made more use of seclusion; required more intensive nursing; were more likely to be offered follow-up.

Re-Admission
There were no differences between court and community admissions in terms of rate of re-admission, numbers or length of re-admission in the two years after discharge, and differences between the two years before admission and the two years after discharge. Only 12% of court admissions were re-admitted through the courts within two years and there was a significant decrease in the number of admissions in the two years after the admission episode compared to the two preceding years. However, this did not translate into a reduction in the total number of nights in hospital, as admissions were for longer periods after discharge. Re-admission in both groups was associated with clinical, not criminological variables.

Re-offending
Only 28% of the court admissions were convicted in the two years after discharge (though the rate for the community admission group was only 5%), a rate which is half the equivalent general population rate for those given non-medical disposals at court. Comparing offending in the two years before and after admission, there was a highly significant reduction in number of cases convicted, number of overall convictions and number of sentencing occasions. The most significant decreases were in property offences. Reconviction was associated most significantly with a history of substance misuse and use of illicit substances during period of admission.

In conclusion, the study showed:

(i)   most court admissions resulted in a successful clinical outcome;

(ii) outcome was as good for court admissions as compulsory community admissions;

(iii) perceptions that court-originating patients gain little benefit, are more disruptive, fail to engage in follow-up and rapidly re-offend are almost entirely false.

Outcomes and Loss of Contact
The question has often been posed 'Diversion to where?' (Exworthy and Parrott, 1993; Rowlands *et* al, 1996; Chambers and Rix, 1999), indicating the need to determine how

effectively psychiatric interventions are delivered, with what effect and with what outcome. Seeking to find out more about the consequences for defendants referred to court diversion schemes and diverted to psychiatric care from magistrates' courts in provincial centres, given doubts whether results from London can be generalised to the rest of the country, Shaw *et al* (2001) followed up all persons referred to/diverted from Manchester Magistrates' Court between October 1993 and October 1995 to establish outcomes and reasons for any subsequent loss of contact. In that period, 235 defendants were referred to the court diversion scheme. Nearly a quarter had schizophrenia and just over a quarter had a primary diagnosis of drug or alcohol dependence.

Recommendations

In 34 instances (14%) in-patient treatment was recommended by scheme doctors, with beds being organised in local psychiatric units. In a further 34 instances reports were submitted recommending out-patient or day hospital treatment, with appointments being made in each instance. No recommendations were made in 90 cases (38%) and remand in custody for further psychiatric assessment was proposed in 24 cases (10%), being instances of serious charges or where no bed could be found.

Court Decisions and Immediate Outcomes

In 25 of the 34 instances of in-patient recommendations, the magistrates agreed, 20 patients being admitted under MHA 1983 Part II (civil powers) and the remainder under Part III (criminal powers). In the other nine instances, either the court felt unable to agree because of the seriousness of the offence (six cases) or voluntary admission was arranged but the person did not attend. In respect of the 34 proposals for out-patient contact, the court dealt with all the cases in ways that would allow the proposal to proceed but without being linked to the court's decision (*eg* a psychiatric probation order or deferment of sentence expectation). Ten of the 34 attended their first appointment, five being admitted as in-patients at that appointment, four under MHA 1983 Part II. This rate of attendance compared unfavourably with the rate following GP referral (74%). Of the 24 who were remanded in custody in hope of further assessment, four were eventually admitted to hospital and two were referred for out-patient follow-up (one not attending). The remaining 18 were either not assessed (seven instances) or were not considered to require treatment (11). Persons with schizophrenia and hypomania/manic depressive psychosis were more likely to attend hospital appointments than those with depression and anxiety. Defendants with a past psychiatric history were significantly more likely to attend than those with no past history.

Twelve-Month Follow-Up

Of a total of 34 persons admitted to in-patient care, either directly from court or subsequently, 20 were still in contact with psychiatric services at follow-up, two remaining as in-patients under Part II orders and the rest as out-patients. Of the five referred to out-patient care who were not admitted to in-patient care, four were still in contact a the 12-month point, one having been discharged. Those who were in contact with psychiatric services at the time of their offence were more likely to remain in contact at 12 months. As regards the low rate of out-patient appointment attendance, the researchers suggest that attendance could be improved by offering an outreach service from the courts, including financial assistance for travel and accompaniment by healthcare staff for first appointment.

In an earlier study of offenders' well-being, after-care and quality of life following diversion via a court-based scheme, Chung *et al* (1999) sought to follow up those who had been screened and diverted from a court in the West Midlands. It proved possible to assess 65 out of 189 persons after six months and only 22 after 12 months. The report does not make clear what was the outcome at court but indicates that only 38% had been able to go home after diversion, the remainder having to rely on family, friends, hostels, etc. Their transient living patterns were thus not surprising and their quality of life, as measured by various assessment checklists and reflected in unemployment and lack of other avenues of fulfilment, was found to be correspondingly poor. Twelve of the 22 were still in regular contact with their GPs after a year but only one was still in contact with a hospital doctor (compared with eight at the six-month point), despite the fact that their psychiatric conditions had not changed over the year. Only three were in contact with Social Services. The researchers advocated a multi-agency outreach programme that would aim to improve quality of life as well as provide effective monitoring of mental health.

Youth Courts
Accounts of the court-based schemes above have addressed the challenge in adult magistrates' courts. However, it is apparent that adolescent offenders appearing before youth courts also have psychiatric needs. Dolan *et al* (1999) screened juveniles appearing before Manchester City juvenile court during August 1992. Of the 192 subjects interviewed (74% of those listed), 7% were assessed to have psychiatric problems requiring further treatment. Three subjects showed psychotic illness requiring hospital admission. The researchers describe a girl aged 16 revealed to be suffering a psychotic illness that had been undetected by the court or staff at the court detention facility. Her social worker, GP and psychiatrist were unaware of her court appearance. The assessment team recommended hospital admission but were unable to find a suitable bed in either adolescent or adult psychiatric facilities in the region. The Adolescent Forensic Service now operates regular psychiatric clinics in the youth court, in liaison with other court-based agencies.

PANEL ASSESSMENT SCHEMES
Under panel assessment schemes (PAS) formal arrangements were set up from the late 1980s so that probation officers, social workers, psychiatrists and other health professionals could consider how best to provide for mentally disordered offenders, whether by diversion from the criminal justice system or by community intervention, and make co-ordinated treatment proposals to the court or agency which had referred a case for assessment.

The first scheme was set up by the Probation Service in Hertfordshire in 1985 to provide information and advice to magistrates' courts, becoming an inspiration and model for other Probation Areas, and specifically commended by HOC 66/1990 (para. 21) and the Lord Chancellor's Department Best Practice Advisory Group (1992). A telephone survey of Probation Areas by the Home Office in late 1992 (Gordon and Hedderman, 1993) showed that eight areas had PAS in operation, with several more schemes in the planning stage. Probation has clearly become the co-ordinating agency for PAS (providing the co-ordinator for six of the eight schemes), though 'this seems to be a reflection of the origins of the panel idea rather than an essential feature'. The mode of operation varied: in three areas panel assessment meetings were held to deal with most cases, whilst in four areas a mixture of panel meetings and telephone/letter liaison operated; one panel area operated almost entirely by telephone links.

The Home Office's evaluation of 187 cases processed by three PAS areas, Bolton, Reading and Hertfordshire (Hedderman, 1993) concluded that 'it is not possible to construct a blue print for the ideal PAS, as the particular form a scheme takes is determined by local problems, facilities and working practices'. Among the findings:

- Only 7% (14) of cases were referred before charges were brought but the panel's recommendations were accepted in every case, so that six ended in a caution or 'no further action' and eight were prosecuted.

- The number of prosecuted (163) cases remanded for psychiatric reports increased at both Bolton and Reading once PAS had been introduced, while the proportion remanded for reports in Hertfordshire where PAS had been available longest was higher than at either Bolton or Reading. This suggests that magistrates welcomed and made use of formal arrangements for assessing MDOs and that confidence in such arrangements increases with time.

- Approximately a fifth of defendants assessed received a discharge or bind over, probation order, or some form of medical disposal (in the clear majority of cases a psychiatric probation order).

The Reading PAS, where panel meetings were held least frequently, was least likely to have its recommendations to court rejected (7%, compared to 17% in Hertfordshire and 28% in Bolton).

NACRO (1994) suggested that PAS work best in areas where the number of relevant cases is relatively small and where the court process allows time for panel assessments to be made.

'In areas where the volume of cases involving mentally disturbed people is higher, and in cases where there is little time, it may be that the model is too elaborate or time-consuming. Less formalised liaison and co-operation may be more appropriate, an approach which reflects local need and circumstances. Even in areas where case panel assessment schemes operate it is important that arrangements for diversion earlier in the criminal justice process are also pursued. Whether or not there is a case panel assessment scheme in operation it is important that magistrates can be confident that a community disposal is appropriate when they are dealing with mentally disturbed people.'

Mentally Disordered Offenders: Inter-Agency Working (Home Office/DoH, 1995) identified that though there is no single ideal model for PAS, the key elements for success include:

- All agencies involved must make an initial commitment, including a willingness to allocate resources needed to make the scheme work.

- A steering group is needed from the outset to give a sense of joint ownership of and common purpose to the project.

- Membership of the group must be at senior level in order to implement agreed policies.

- Arrangements must be set up to monitor and evaluate the scheme.

MENTAL HEALTH BILL

Chapter One of Part Three of the draft Bill sets out a new system of remands, on bail and to hospital, for mental health reports within the proposed new statutory framework, and remands and committal to hospital for medical treatment.

Remand on Bail

Clause 57 provides power (*in addition to* any other power the court has to order medical examinations and reports) for a court to order a mental health report, covering the subject's mental condition and/or the appropriate treatment for that condition, where the court is satisfied, on the evidence of a registered medical practitioner, that there is reason to suspect that the person is suffering from mental disorder. This power will operate as follows:

Crown Court

Where the defendant is awaiting trial for an offence punishable by imprisonment (unless the sentence is fixed by law), or has been arraigned before the court but has not been sentenced or otherwise dealt with, or has been committed for sentence, or has been committed to the court with a view to a restriction order being made (clause 85).

Magistrates' Court

Where the defendant is charged with or been convicted of an offence punishable on summary conviction with imprisonment.

Remand to Hospital for Report

Clauses 58-61 are intended to replace MHA 1983 s35. Clause 58(1)(a) extends the power to the Court of Appeal in respect of a person who is appealing against a custodial sentence, a mental health order or hospital/limitation directions. This permits an assessment without affecting their current disposal which will thus continue if the remand order terminates and their sentence is not quashed by the Appeal Court. The power is exercisable by the Crown Court or magistrates' courts in respect of those persons as stated above in respect of remand on bail. Three conditions must be satisfied, as specified currently in s35(3) and (4), save that the court must be satisfied 'that there is reason to suspect that the person is suffering from mental disorder'. The court may specify any particular matters to be dealt with in the report, including an assessment of risk posed to members of the public (clause 60(3)(a)).

Period of Remand

Clause 59(5) specifies a maximum period of remand of 28 days but under clause 59(6) the Court of Appeal may remand for a maximum period of 16 weeks (or until the person's release date, if that arises in less than 16 weeks). The Crown Court or a magistrates' court may further remand the person under clause 61 if it appears to the court on appropriate evidence (defined by sub-clause (8)) that this is necessary for completing the report and it would be impractical for that report to be completed if the person were remanded on bail. Further remands shall be for a maximum of 28 days and the total period must not exceed 16 weeks.

Temporary Leave

The court must state whether the approved clinician responsible for preparing the report may give the subject temporary leave from hospital or whether this decision is to be reserved to the court.

Treatment

Clause 60(3) empowers the court to authorise the clinical supervisor to provide medical treatment to the remanded person, where the criteria specified in clause 60(4) to (6) are met. As regards treatment for a period exceeding 28 days, see below.

Remand or Committal for Treatment

Clauses 62 to 66 provide for the Crown Court or a magistrates' court to remand a person to hospital for treatment where otherwise they would have been remanded in custody, or for a magistrates' court to commit a person to the Crown Court in hospital rather than custody. The conditions to be satisfied are that (clause 64):

(i)   the person is suffering from mental disorder;

(ii) that mental disorder is of such a nature or degree as to require the provision of medical treatment to the person;

(iii) appropriate medical treatment is available;

(iv) arrangements have been made for admission to hospital within seven days of the date of remand or committal.

This provision replaces MHA 1983 s36, extended to magistrates' courts and not subject to the 12 week limit of that provision, though subject to safeguards in respect of treatment periods exceeding 28 days.

Treatment Periods Exceeding 28 days

A court may not remand, further remand or commit a person for treatment, or authorise treatment for a person remanded for a report, if that would mean a treatment period exceeding 28 days, unless a care plan has been drawn up for that person by their clinical supervisor and authorised by the court (clause 70) (or by a Tribunal in the case of and acting for the Court of Appeal, before which reviews of remanded persons is not a practical proposition).

5
UNFITNESS TO PLEAD

Unfitness to plead to an indictment is not exclusively associated with mental disorder but almost invariably arises in that context. The challenge at stake is finding the means to treat an unfit accused person in a fair and humane way when they cannot be tried in the ordinary way, while protecting the public against the risk of danger they may pose. The issue only arises in Crown Court trial proceedings, though a magistrates' court has power under MHA 1983 s37(3) to make a hospital order without convicting the defendant (see page 89 and the decision in *Barking Youth Court* – below at page 68). For a more detailed account of unfitness, see Mackay (1995) and Grubin (1996).

THE TEST OF UNFITNESS
The test to be applied is drawn from common law rather than statute, the leading case remaining *R v Pritchard* (1836) 7 C&P 303 (a case that concerned a deaf man without speech) where the issue was posed thus:

'... whether he is of sufficient intellect to comprehend the course of proceedings on the trial, so as to make a proper defence, to challenge a juror to whom he might wish to object and to comprehend the details of the evidence.' (*per* Alderson B)

Pritchard has recently been approved by the Court of Appeal in *R v Friend* [1997] 2 All ER 1012, in which Otton LJ indicated:

'The test of unfitness is whether the accused will be able to comprehend the course of proceedings so as to make a proper defence. Whether he can understand and reply rationally to the indictment is obviously a relevant factor, but the jury must also consider whether he would be able to exercise his right to challenge jurors, understand the details of the evidence as it is given, instruct his legal advisers and give evidence himself if he so desires.'

Among relevant considerations: can the defendant understand and respond to the charge(s) and the evidence against him, enter a plea, instruct his legal advisers, challenge a juror and follow court proceedings? A defect in one such respect is enough to raise the issue of unfitness. The issue at stake is relatively narrow: the accused's cognitive capacity at time of trial, not his mental state at the time of the alleged offence nor the extent of his decision-making competence at trial (for a critique, see Grubin, 1993).

A defendant may be unfit to plead even though neither 'insane' within the *M'Naughten Rules* (see Chapter 6) nor suffering one of the four forms of mental disorder specified as a prerequisite for the making of a s37 hospital order (see page 84). However, the mere fact that the defendant is incapable of acting in their best interests because of their mental condition is insufficient to justify a finding of unfitness. Thus in *R v Robertson* [1968] 1 WLR 1767 the defendant on a murder charge had suffered persecution mania and believed that members of the crew of the ship on which he served, including the deceased, were putting noxious chemicals on his clothes. He stabbed the victim in an ensuing fight and claimed self-defence. Though his delusions might interfere with his capacity to conduct his defence in his best interests, this did not amount to disability enough to deprive him of the right to be tried. Similarly, a defendant who has amnesia in respect of the relevant events but who can understand the trial is not unfit to plead, despite the obvious difficulties posed in conducting their defence (*R v Podola* [1960] 1 QB 325).

Procedure

Procedure is laid down by CP(I)A 1964 as amended by CP(IUP) 1991, as outlined in HOC 93/1991. The issue of fitness to plead may be raised by either the prosecution or the defence and the question is determined by a jury, who must receive the written or oral evidence of two or more medical practitioners, at least one of whom must be approved under MHA 1983 s12. The defendant may well have been subject to a remand under MHA 1983 s35 for the preparation of reports on their mental condition or under s36 for treatment.

TRIAL OF THE FACTS

Where the defendant has been found unfit to be tried, a jury must then determine in a 'trial of the facts' whether the accused 'did the act or made the omission charged against him' (CP(I)A 1964 s4A). If the jury is not satisfied of this (beyond reasonable doubt), the defendant must be acquitted (s4A(4)). This procedure aims to avoid the possible compulsory detention of an innocent defendant in hospital, merely because of mental unfitness. As the House of Lords identified in *R v Antoine* [2001] 1AC 340, the purpose of s4A is to strike a fair balance between the need to protect an unfit defendant who has, in fact, done nothing wrong and the need to protect the public from a defendant who has committed an injurious/criminal act (*actus reus*) which would constitute a crime if done with the requisite mental intent (*mens rea*). This raises the question whether there is scope for the defence to raise possible defences in the course of the s4A hearing that might have been open to the defendant if a full trial had been possible.

In *R v Egan* [1998] 1 Cr App R 121, a case involving an allegation of robbery against a man who denied that he had snatched the victim's bag, the Court of Appeal held that the Crown had to prove not only the physical act but also the mental elements in the offence, but in this instance ruled that, as the defendant had simply asserted that it was not he who did the act, it was not necessary for the second limb relating to his capacity to form a dishonest intent to be considered by the jury, who had simply to consider whether he had acted in the way alleged.

However, *Egan* was reconsidered in *Antoine*, a case involving the killing of the victim, apparently as a sacrifice to the Devil. The defendant had been found unfit to plead in light of his paranoid schizophrenia. Prior to the s4A hearing, the defence argued that the defendant should be able to seek to prove his diminished responsibility (see Chapter 6) as this, if established by the jury, would constitute manslaughter and make him eligible for other disposals not available in respect of a murder offence (see below). Though rejecting this argument on the basis that the defence of diminished responsibility is available only in instances where the defendant would otherwise be liable to be convicted of murder (which is not clearly the case where the defendant is 'unfit'), the House of Lords concluded that the Crown does not have to establish *mens rea* and in a s4A hearing it is not open to the defence to argue the absence of *mens rea*. The Lords thus disapproved the *Egan* decision, citing the example of a defendant accused of rape – if the prosecution can establish that sexual intercourse took place without the consent of the victim, it is not open to the defence to argue that perpetrator's mental state caused him to believe that she was actually consenting. In using the word 'act' in s4A, Parliament had made clear that the jury is not to consider the mental ingredients of the offence.

The Lords concluded that there is residual scope for the defence to raise issues related to the *actus reus*: mistake, accident, self-defence or involuntariness. The Lords recognised that it can be difficult to distinguish precisely between issues relating to *actus reus* and *mens rea* and so left open the question whether provocation can be raised in s4A hearings involving homicide. This question has since been answered in the negative in *R v Grant* [2002] Crim LR 403, a case involving a woman who had killed her partner after he had allegedly hit her twice but who was 'unfit' by reason of her limited intellectual ability. The Court of Appeal determined that the defence of provocation is 'intimately bound up with the defendant's state of mind' and so related to *mens rea* rather than the determination of whether they 'did the act'.

Human Rights Act 1998

The question has understandably arisen whether a trial of the facts under s4A is incompatible with a right under ECHR Article 6 to a fair trial, in that a defendant's unfitness may render him unable to understand the proceedings, give instructions and defend himself. The Court of Appeal in *R v M, R v K, R v H* [2002] Crim LR 57 had ruled that Article 6 does not apply because a determination in a s4A hearing does not result in a finding of guilt or any punishment, available orders (see below) (save an absolute discharge which is non-punitive) being concerned with the treatment and care of the accused. The Appeal Court went on to conclude that, even if it was wrong in this ruling, proceedings under s4A comply with Article 6. A defendant with mental disabilities that do not amount to unfitness may well be under a disadvantage too. A court can only do its best to minimise that disadvantage. Sections 4 and 4A 'constitute a fair procedure, providing an opportunity for investigation of the facts on behalf of a disabled person, so far as possible', balancing the public interest in identifying persons who have committed criminal acts and the interests of those persons. The House of Lords in *R v H* [2003] UKHL 1 has since upheld the Appeal Court's view, applying the tests set by the European Court in *Engel v The Netherlands* (1976) 1 EHRR 647 in determining whether an issue should be regarded as criminal or civil/disciplinary. For a further human rights dimension of this procedure, in respect of compulsory detention, see below.

Fitness to Plead in a Youth Court

This issue of mentally impaired juveniles was posed in *R (on the application of P) v Barking Youth Court* [2002] Crim LR 657, 166 [2002] JP 641 where a youth court was dealing with a 16 year-old defendant charged with either way offences who was assessed to be severely intellectually impaired. At the initiative of the defence, the justices received evidence from an educational psychologist that the youth had incomplete development of mind which made him incapable of understanding the nature of the offence but they concluded that he was nevertheless fit to plead. The defence challenged their determination as perverse, allowing their own lay judgement to override expert opinion. The Administrative Court noted that the magistrates had purported to follow the procedure specified under CP(I)A 1964 (see above) and ruled that they had no power to adopt procedure designed to be followed by the Crown Court. As a 'magistrates' court' for these statutory purposes, the youth court should have relied instead on MHA 1983 s37(3) (see page 89) in conjunction with PCC(S)A 2000 s11(1) (see page 45). The matter was therefore remitted to the youth court for the case to be reconsidered in accordance with that machinery.

ORDERS AND DISPOSALS

Where the defendant is found to be unfit because of disability and also 'did the act or made the omission', the court now has a range of options and should exercise one of the following (CP(I)A 1964 s5 as replaced by CP(IUP)A 1991) (having previously been obliged to order the accused's detention in hospital as a restricted patient, with the prospect of returning to court for trial when fit enough to do so):

(i)   an admission order to such hospital as may be specified by the Secretary of State, in accordance with CP(IUP)A 1991 sch 1);

(ii) a guardianship order under MHA 1983 s37;

(iii) a supervision or treatment order, in accordance with CP(IUP)A 1991 sch 2;

(iv) an absolute discharge.

However, where the offence in question is one of murder, the court can only make an admission order. [In its Consultation Document (2002, para. 4.3) on the draft *Mental Health Bill*, the Government has acknowledged the inflexibility of this provision, recognising that 'in some cases such a disposal may not be justified by the person's medical condition, and the result is likely to be immediate discharge from hospital without any benefit to the person concerned, or added protection for others'. The Bill will thus include amendments to insanity and unfitness to plead legislation, giving courts more options in such cases. Compulsory treatment will only be possible where the person meets the conditions for compulsion as specified in the Bill.]

Options (ii)-(iv) may be used only if considered 'most suitable in all the circumstances of the case', a requirement which does not apply to the making of an admission order.

Admission Order

An admission order for compulsory hospital treatment has the same effect as a hospital order under MHA 1983 s37 (even though the accused would not have satisfied the criteria for the making of such an order) and, if the court so directs, a restriction order may be added, with or without limitation of time, having the same effect as a s41 order (CP(IUP)A 1991 sch 1 para. 2(1)(b)). Where the offence in question is one of murder, the court is required to direct restriction without limit of time (sch 1 para. 2(2)). The Secretary of State must specify the hospital in which the person will be detained within two calendar months of the date of the order, the person being detained in 'a place of safety' in the interim. Under provisions introduced by C(S)A 1997 s47, where a court makes a sch 1 para. 2(1)(b) order, the Secretary of State may specify not only the hospital at which the defendant will be detained but a 'unit' of the hospital (defined by s47(3) to mean 'any part of a hospital which is treated as a separate unit'). This refinement is designed to enable the Home Secretary to 'specify a level of security in which the patient needs to be detained' (MHA(COP) 1999 para. 3.15). In consequence, the Secretary of State's permission will be required for any transfer from the named unit, even to another part of the same hospital.

If, during the course of detention in pursuance of an admission order, the Secretary of State is satisfied that the patient can properly be tried, s/he may be remitted for trial, either direct to the court of trial or to a prison or remand centre in the meantime (sch 1 para. 4(1)). The admission order then ceases to have effect and the accused thus re-enters the normal pre-trial criminal justice system. At the time when the 1991 Act was implemented, about 60% of those found unfit to plead were being remitted subsequently for trial (White, 1992).

Only three restricted patients were admitted to hospital in 1992 as a consequence of unfitness to plead but the numbers have risen since 1993, with 22 and 44 respectively being so admitted in 2000 and 2001 (Johnson and Taylor, 2002).

Human Rights Act 1998

In *R v Grant* [2002] Crim LR 403 (see page 68), a case involving a charge of murder leading to a finding of unfitness to plead and an admission order, it was argued that the statutory provisions are incompatible with ECHR Article 5 (right to liberty). The Court of Appeal ruled that it was not unreasonable for Parliament to have decided to lay down a mandatory requirement of admission to hospital for a person charged with murder who had been found to have done the act charged. Detention in such circumstances is not arbitrary and the person affected has the right to make immediate application to a Mental Health Review Tribunal (MHRT), thus ensuring compliance with a right under Article 5(4) to take proceedings to test the continuing lawfulness of detention.

However, while ruling that in the case before it, there was ample medical evidence that the accused suffered mental impairment within MHA 1983, the Court raised concern whether procedure under CP(I)A 1964 s4 provides for it to be reliably shown in every instance that the person suffers from a mental disorder sufficiently serious to warrant their detention for the purposes of Article 5(1)(e) (which permits the 'detention of ... persons of unsound mind'). The issue addressed by s4 and s4A, fitness to be tried, does not relate to whether detention is justified on medical evidence relating to the severity of the defendant's mental condition. The statutory procedure under the 1964 Act does not require anyone to address the defendant's mental state more generally, beyond the issue of fitness. Accordingly, the Court was implicitly inviting a challenge to domestic law under Article 5(1)(e). As made clear by the European Court in *Winterwerp v The Netherlands* (1989-90) 2 EHRR 387 (see page 197), 'no one may be confined as being of unsound mind in the absence of medical evidence establishing that his mental state is such as to justify compulsory hospitalisation'.

Guardianship Order

This provision allows the offender to receive care and protection rather than medical treatment; the legal framework is as detailed in Chapter 11.

Supervision and Treatment Order
This order is detailed separately in Chapter 10.

Absolute Discharge
This option 'might be considered, for example, where the alleged offence was trivial and the accused clearly does not require treatment and supervision in the community' (HOC 93/1991 para. 17(d)(ix)).

USE OF UNFITNESS TO PLEAD BEFORE AND AFTER THE 1991 ACT
Mackay (1995) examined the files of all cases of unfitness from 1976 to 1988, a total of 302 findings. These concerned not simply very serious cases but also involved instances of less grave matters of theft/deception committed by destitute, mentally disordered persons. The most common basis for disability was schizophrenia (169 cases) followed by mental impairment (64 instances) and other psychoses (32 instances). The most frequently identified issue of incapacity addressed in psychiatric reports was ability to instruct a lawyer, followed closely by ability to understand proceedings. Mackay concluded that the reports demonstrated 'some ignorance and confusion about the criteria'.

Mackay and Kearns (2000) have reported the uptake of 'unfitness' in the first five years under the current legislation, 1992-96. After a slow start the number of findings of unfitness increased from around 13 annually to in excess of 30 in each year from 1994, a total of 123 cases. In nearly four in five cases there was no dispute between the defence and the prosecution, clear dispute being identified in only 8% of cases (the extent of dispute being uncertain in the remaining cases). The diagnostic basis for disability closely mirrored the basis of unfitness in the pre-1991 Act sample, as did the aspects of incapacity addressed in psychiatric reports. Additionally, the effect on the defendant's mental health of the trial process was also frequently commented on, 'to the extent that on a number of occasions the line between fitness to plead and fitness to stand trial was somewhat difficult to determine'. The outcome of the trial of the facts was predominantly that the accused person did the act, no formal defence being offered in 72 of 117 cases. The accused was acquitted in only seven instances. In the 110 cases where the defendant was found to have done the act, the offence range extended from murder to criminal damage, the largest single offence cluster being indecent assault (22 cases). Restriction orders followed in 50 of those 110 cases, with admission orders without restriction in a further 35 instances. Supervision and treatment orders were made in a total of 15 cases, the remaining 10 cases being either guardianship orders (six) or absolute discharge (four). Community-based disposals were thus less frequently imposed than resulted from insanity verdicts in the same period (see page 77), presumably because the accused's disability in unfitness cases relates to time of trial, not time of offence, and is thus more likely to be considered to indicate a need for hospital treatment.

It is likely that the issue of fitness, particularly in less serious cases, is often dealt with in a flexible, pragmatic way, in order to promote a desired psychiatric outcome, as illustrated by Joseph and Potter's study (1993) of a psychiatric assessment scheme at court (see page 55).

MENTAL CONDITION AND REMAINING SILENT

Though separate from the issue of fitness to plead, an allied aspect of mental condition may arise in the course of a trial of a defendant who is fit to plead but nevertheless under a mental disability. As a consequence of changes relating to the 'right to silence' introduced by CJPOA 1994, a court or jury may draw adverse inferences in respect of a defendant if he remains silent when questioned or charged by the police or questioned at trial, 'unless it appears to the court that the physical or mental condition of the accused makes it undesirable for him to give evidence' (s35(1)(b)). 'Mental condition' in this context is not confined to a mental disorder within the meaning of MHA 1983. The issue at stake is whether a jury or court is likely to misinterpret the defendant's responses and behaviour whilst he is giving evidence and whether, in consequence, this may prejudice his defence. Grubin (1996a) has described such a case, a man accused of rape who while not suffering from any illness or disorder within the scope of MHA 1983 was subject to agitation, mood swings, grandiosity, low frustration tolerance and irrational outbursts of anger.

Gray *et al* (2001) have subsequently identified a case (an allegation of s18 wounding where the accused was disabled as a consequence of a serious head injury, causing significant impairment of intellectual ability, orientation, memory and executive functioning) where the defendant's mental condition and consequent incapacity to give evidence without prejudice to his defence caused the issue of his fitness to plead to be considered afresh, even though the psychiatrists assessing him had previously advised that he was not under a disability in that respect. Their subsequent view was that if ability to give evidence in your own defence is vital to fitness to plead, he was indeed unfit. The judge instructed the jury to decide if he was capable of understanding the proceedings to the extent that he would be able to put forward any defence, including giving evidence on his own behalf. The jury found him unfit to plead. A second jury found that he committed the act and a guardianship order was made. Though this case is not a precedent, the authors speculate on the implications for a range of defendants, including those with learning disability, dementia, brain injury, etc.

6
INSANITY, DIMINISHED RESPONSIBILITY AND INFANTICIDE

This chapter addresses the three main instances where the offender's mental state at the time of the offence offers a defence, reduces their responsibility or changes the nature of the crime charged. These involve complex legal issues and so it is intended to offer only an outline here for the information of workers outside the legal profession. For a fuller account from a lawyer's perspective, see Mackay (1995).

DEFENCE OF INSANITY
The 'special verdict' of a jury of 'not guilty by reason of insanity' under TLA 1883 s2 (as amended) remains governed by the common law *M'Naughten Rules*, as first propounded by Tindal CJ in *M'Naughten's Case* (1843):

> '... the jurors ought to be told in all cases that every man is to be presumed to be sane, and to possess a sufficient degree of reason to be responsible for his crimes, until the contrary be proved to their satisfaction; and that to establish a defence on the ground of insanity, it must be clearly proved that, at the time of the committing of the act, the party accused was labouring under such a defect of reason, from disease of the mind, as not to know the nature and quality of the act he was doing; or, if he did know it, that he did not know he was doing what was wrong.'

The defence is not restricted to allegations of murder or offences of violence. The burden of proof is upon the defence, but the defence has to be established only on the balance of probabilities. A jury cannot reach this verdict without receiving the written or oral evidence of two or more medical practitioners, at least one of whom must be approved under MHA 1983 s12.

Prior to CP(IUP)A 1991, a Crown Court faced with this verdict was required (under CP(I)A 1964 in its original version) to make an order for the accused's admission to and compulsory detention in hospital but, since that Act, the court now has a number of alternative options, thus making the defence potentially more attractive to an accused. It nevertheless remains a somewhat archaic, restrictive and marginal concept, being used far more rarely than might seem justified by the number of mentally disordered persons appearing in court.

At Magistrates' Court
Though the special verdict under TLA 1883 s2 is available only upon trial on indictment, the availability of the defence of insanity in magistrates' courts had been uncertain and untested. The predominant view had been that it was not open to magistrates to reach this verdict (nor necessary, given their power to make a hospital order under MHA 1983 s37(3) – see page 89) but this was challenged (*eg* by White, 1991) on the basis that, though the legislation regulating the consequences of a successful offence applies only to trials on indictment, the common law defence itself can be raised in response to

any charge. However, in *R v Horseferry Road Magistrates' Court, ex p. K* [1996] 3 All ER 719, a case involving a defendant suffering paranoid schizophrenia who assaulted a police officer under the delusional belief that the officer had killed the defendant's girlfriend, the Divisional Court concluded that, though the issue was not at stake in the particular case under review, the common law defence had not been removed by legislation and is still available to a defendant in a summary trial where *mens rea* is at issue. *Ex p. K* was followed in *DPP v Harper* (1997) *The Times*, 2 May, a case involving driving with excess alcohol by a man with manic depressive psychosis, where the Divisional Court ruled that though it is open to a defendant to establish, on the balance of probabilities, their insanity at the time of commission of an offence, this was not relevant to the present offence as driving with excess alcohol is one of strict liability and does not require *mens rea*.

A successful defence at magistrates' court does not fall within the provisions of CP(I)A 1964 or CP(IUP)A 1991 and so leads to an unqualified acquittal. However, the court would still have scope to make a hospital order under MHA 1983 s37(3) (see page 89), provided that the criteria for such an order are met. As the Divisional Court identified in *ex p. K*, through a legislative lacuna, a magistrates' court has no power in such circumstances to commit the defendant to the Crown Court with a view to imposition of a s41 restriction order since that applies only on *conviction* of an imprisonable offence (MHA 1983 s43).

The view in *Harper* that the defence is not available on summary trial of a strict liability offence has been questioned by Ward (1997). Ward argues that the insanity defence has the following advantages at summary level: (a) the defendant does not incur the consequences of a 'conviction' and so should not be cited in court on any future occasion; (b) as many mentally disordered offenders do not gain access to mental health resources through the sentence of the court, it may be more legitimate simply to dismiss them or bind them over (an option that is available even after acquittal); (c) it may serve the interests of defendants who have acted as a consequence of epilepsy.

'Defect of Reason'

Rationality, rather than will, is the crucial consideration and, as *Blackstone's Criminal Practice* (2001, A 3.15) notes: 'Irresistible impulse and other emotional or volitional defects or disorders are not within the rules, since they are not defects of reason'.

'Disease of the Mind'

The meaning of this somewhat archaic language is as follows:

- The disease need not be located in the brain but the consequences it produces must impair the functioning of the mind.

- The disease may be of physical (*eg* arteriosclerosis) rather than mental origin.

- If the effect of a disease is to impair the mental faculties of reason, memory or understanding, 'it matters not whether the aetiology of the impairment is organic, as in epilepsy, or functional, or whether the impairment itself is permanent or is transient and intermittent, provided that it subsisted at the time of the commission of the act' (*R v Sullivan* [1984] AC 156). The question of epilepsy is addressed further below.

- The disease must be something 'internal' to the accused and not a malfunction arising from 'some external factor such as violence, drugs, including anaesthetics, alcohol and hypnotic influences' (*R v Quick* [1973] QB 910). This distinction can be illustrated with regard to diabetes. If the malfunctioning of the mind arose from the use of insulin then the factor would be 'external', but if it arose from the accused's condition in the absence of corrective medication the factor would be 'internal'.

The defence should be distinguished from the separate defence of 'non-insane automatism', where the person is not in control of his bodily functions for reasons other than 'disease of the mind', for example as a result of a sneezing fit or concussion resulting from a blow on the head or the medical administration of drugs. Hyperglycaemia as a consequence of a person with diabetes not taking their insulin has been held to be a disease of the mind (*R v Hennessey* [1989] 1 WLR 287). Sleepwalking, too, has been held to fall within the ambit of insane automatism, having 'an internal cause': *R v Burgess* [1991] 93 Cr App R 41.

Epilepsy

The question of epilepsy is a vexed one. The decision in *Sullivan* (above) that an epileptic seizure can constitute insanity is clearly an unfortunate and stigmatising misrepresentation of epilepsy, criticised by MIND and the British Epilepsy Association, even though the Home Office view (quoted in White, 1991) has been that the special verdict in such instances does not imply that the defendant is 'insane', even if the defendant's medical state ought to receive hospital investigation. White suggests that epileptic defendants who believe that they acted without awareness of their behaviour while suffering from or recovering from a seizure are frequently advised to plead guilty and to hope for a sympathetic disposal. It remains unclear whether a defendant can cite epilepsy as a defence without bringing this under the umbrella of the special verdict. The issue illustrates the need for the law relating to defences based on mental and neurological disorder to be reformed.

Two Kinds of Defence

The Rules allow for two different forms or limbs of defence: (a) not knowing the nature and quality of the act, and (b) not knowing it was wrong, perhaps best explained by reference to the illustrations given by Hoggett (1996: 111):

'An example of the first is assaulting someone with an axe believing him to be a block of wood. The disorder has negated the existence of the guilty mind, the element of intention or recklessness which would normally be required for a conviction. An example of the second is killing someone in the belief that one is God and thus entitled to do it. To that extent a person with a diseased mind is relieved from the presumption that we all know and understand the law and its relationship to our actions. Neither limb will excuse a man who knows what he is doing and knows it to be against the law, even though he is acting on the orders of his "voices", or under the delusion that his victim is persecuting him, or in the belief that he has a divine mission to exterminate prostitutes. Still less does it excuse a man whose perception, knowing and reasoning faculties are unaffected but whose capacity to resist his impulses or conform his behaviour to the law is substantially impaired by his disorder.'

'The Nature and Quality of the Act'
This has been interpreted to refer to the physical rather than the moral quality of the act and was reframed in *Sullivan* as: 'he did not know what he was doing'.

'Wrong'
In strict interpretation of the *M'Naughten Rules*, 'wrong' in 'did not know he was doing what was wrong' means legally, not morally wrong. However, the empirical evidence of the defence in practice (see below) indicates that the defence can be established where the accused knew that their act was wrong in either sense.

Consequences of Special Verdict
Under CP(I)A 1964 s5, as amended by CP(IUP)A 1991, the court has the following disposal options:

(i)   an order for admission to hospital for compulsory detention;

(ii) a guardianship order;

(iii) a supervision and treatment order;

(iv) an absolute discharge;

except that, for an offence of murder, the court is required to make an admission order backed by an indefinite restriction order. [In its Consultation Document (2002, para. 4.3) on the draft Mental Health Bill, the Government has acknowledged the inflexibility of this provision, recognising that 'in some cases such a disposal may not be justified by the person's medical condition, and the result is likely to be immediate discharge from hospital without any benefit to the person concerned, or added protection for others'. The Bill will thus include amendments to insanity and unfitness to plead legislation, giving courts more options in such cases. Compulsory treatment will only be possible where the person meets the conditions for compulsion as specified in the Bill.]

These powers are exactly the same as apply following a finding of unfitness to plead coupled with a determination of the facts (see page 69) and are thus detailed in Chapters 5, 10 and 11. Procedurally cumbersome as it may be, a 'special verdict' must returned by a jury, even though the prosecution does not dispute the psychiatric evidence: *R v Maidstone Crown Court, ex p. London Borough of Harrow* (1999) *The Times*, 14 May, where the judge had purported to deal with a defendant charged with arson by making a supervision and treatment order immediately following his plea of not guilty by reason of insanity.

Insanity Defence since the 1991 Act
As a consequence of the greater flexibility of disposal following a special verdict that would be introduced by the 1991 Act, the Law Commission (1989) anticipated that the insanity defence would assume greater practical importance. Mackay and Kearns (1999) have reported a modest increase in use, from a total of 20 in the five years 1987-91 to 44 in the first five years since implementation, 1992-96. Just over half (23 cases) involved ss18/20 GBH/wounding (13 cases), attempted murder (five cases) and ABH (five cases), a further four cases involving murder; the remaining instances involving a wide spread

of offending, from arson (three instances) to importing a Class A drug. In the clear majority of cases the defence was not disputed by the prosecution.

On examining the 88 psychiatric reports submitted in the 44 cases to see their use of the *M'Naughten Rules*, the researchers found that in 23 reports (20 cases) the psychiatrist made some reference to the limb relating to not knowing the 'nature and quality of the act' while in 25 reports (18 cases) indicated that the accused did not know that his act was 'wrong', and a further 10 reports (in seven additional cases) utilised the 'wrongness' limb without actually referring to it explicitly. However, 'the vast majority made no reference to knowledge of legal wrongness'. Rather, in most such reports:

> 'the wrongness limb was interpreted widely to cover whether the defendant thought his actions were morally justified, and/or whether the actions were in perceived self-defence of themselves or others, in the sense of protecting their physical or spiritual well-being and three resulted in supervision and treatment orders. ... In short, the overwhelming impression is that the question the majority of psychiatrists are addressing is: if the delusion that the defendant was experiencing at the time of the offence was in fact reality, then would the defendant's actions be morally justified? – rather than the narrow cognitive test of legal wrongness required by the *M'Naughten Rules*.'

Disposals
Some 21 of the 44 cases resulted in a hospital order, 17 involving a restriction order under s41 without limit of time. All 21 were already in hospital at time of their trial. Supervision and treatment orders were made in another 21 cases, with two absolute discharges. Thus the majority of cases did not result in hospital detention.

DIMINISHED RESPONSIBILITY
Though exposed to substantial criticism as an unsatisfactory muddling of moral and medical concepts which is also resented by the families of homicide victims (*eg* in the Report of the Committee on the Penalty for Homicide chaired by Lord Lane, 1993) this partial defence to murder remains as introduced by HA 1957 s2:

> Where a person kills or is party to the killing of another, he shall not be convicted of murder if he was suffering from such abnormality of mind (whether arising from a condition of arrested or retarded development of mind or any inherent causes or induced by disease or injury) as substantially impaired his mental responsibility for his acts or omissions in doing or being a party to the killing.

Where established, the defendant is convicted instead of manslaughter and thus has the benefit of the range of sentencing discretion. This defence has largely replaced the defence of insanity in cases of murder. The burden of proof rests with the defence on the balance of probabilities. This defence is sometimes run in tandem with that of provocation.

Note that the accused cannot initially be charged with manslaughter on the basis of diminished responsibility but that it is open to the prosecution to accept this plea to a charge of murder, where there is clear and convincing evidence in support. In exceptional cases (the trial of Peter Sutcliffe, the so-called Yorkshire Ripper, being an obvious instance), the judge may still require that the trial should proceed before a jury.

Medical evidence will almost certainly be received, albeit that psychiatrists are thus required to stray here into non-medical territory of moral responsibility, but is not conclusive because the question of 'substantial impairment' is a matter for the jury who can take into account the acts, statements and demeanour of the accused.

Abnormality of Mind

This was defined by Lord Parker CJ in *R v Byrne* [1960] 2QB 396 to mean:

> 'a state of mind so different from that of ordinary human beings that the reasonable man would term it abnormal. It appears to us to be wide enough to cover the mind's activities in all its aspects, not only the perception of physical acts and matters, and the ability to form a rational judgement as to whether an act is right or wrong, but also the ability to exercise willpower to control physical acts in accordance with that rational judgement'.

The accused person's mental abnormality must fall within the causes appearing in brackets in s2, raising potentially difficult issues of aetiology. Griew (1988) suggested that the wording was used to exclude 'the mere outburst of rage or jealousy'. Among causes of abnormality of mind, post-natal depression and pre-menstrual tension have been found to constitute a 'disease' for the purposes of the defence, as well as more clear-cut conditions or disorders such as clinical depression. Dell (1984) reported that a very wide range of conditions had successfully satisfied the section, including: 'At the mildest end of the spectrum of personality disorders those cases which would hardly have attracted the label had it not been for the offence.' Among milder forms of mental illness, she felt that doctors had been faced with a very difficult task in trying 'to determine where stress and strain ended and illness began'. Dell found that psychiatrists approached the classification of conditions in widely varying, imprecise and inconsistent ways, often omitting any reference in their opinions to the cause of the accused's abnormality. In *Byrne* the defendant had strangled his female victim as a result of an 'impulse' which he found very difficult, if not impossible, to control, as a feature of his sexual psychopathy.

'Alcoholism' presents a more difficult question (see Sullivan, 1994) but has been held to constitute the defence if the accused's brain has been 'injured by the repeated insult from intoxicants so that there was gross impairment of judgement and emotional responses' or if the accused was not voluntarily intoxicated because they are 'no longer able to resist the impulse to drink' (*R v Tandy* [1989] 1 WLR 350). While the 'diseases' to which drunkenness can lead may amount to diminished responsibility, it seems clear, if not entirely logical, that the mere transient effect of 'voluntary' drunkenness will not, even if it produced a toxic effect on the brain. In *R v O'Connell* [1997] Crim LR 683, where the accused had been taking sleeping tablets (Halcion) on prescription for some months prior to the killing, it was claimed that the drug could induce derangement of thought and mood. The Court of Appeal doubted whether the effects of Halcion could be considered an 'injury' leading to 'abnormality of mind', drawing a parallel with alcohol consumption. Perhaps, as Mackay (1995 and 1999) suggests, the cases that have stretched the idea of abnormality of mind the farthest have involved mercy killing, where it would appear that the psychiatric evidence can be stretched pragmatically to achieve a merciful outcome.

Substantial Impairment

The jury should be instructed that 'substantial' should be interpreted in a broad common-sense way or that the word means 'more than some trivial degree of impairment but less than total impairment' (*R v Egan* [1992] 4 All ER 470).

Sentencing

The proper approach to sentencing was propounded by Leonard J in *R v Chambers* (1983) 5 Cr App R(S) 190:

> 'In diminished responsibility cases there are various courses open to a judge. His choice of the right course will depend on the state of the evidence and the material before him. If the psychiatric reports recommend and justify it, and there are no contrary indications, he will make a hospital order. Where a hospital order is not recommended, or is not appropriate, and the defendant constitutes a danger to the public for an unpredictable period of time, the right sentence will, in all probabilities, be one of life imprisonment.
>
> In cases where the evidence indicates that the accused's responsibility for his acts was so grossly impaired that his degree of responsibility for them was minimal, then a lenient course will be open to the judge. Provided there is no danger of repetition of violence, it will usually be possible to make such an order as will give the accused his freedom, possibly with some supervision.
>
> There will however be cases in which there is no proper basis for a hospital order; but in which the accused's degree of responsibility is not minimal. In such cases the judge should pass a determinate sentence of imprisonment, the length of which will depend on two factors: his assessment of the degree of the accused's responsibility and his view as to the period of time, if any, for which the accused will continue to be a danger to the public.'

Of 130 offenders (111 being males) convicted on this basis in the five years 1995-99, 63 received hospital orders (40 with s41 restriction), 50 (44 males) received immediate custody and 12 (six females) were placed on probation, three receiving suspended sentences.

INFANTICIDE

The elements of this offence, exclusive to mothers, under the Infanticide Act 1938 s1 are as follows:

(i) a woman's wilful act or omission;

(ii) causing the death of her child aged under 12 months;

(iii) at a time when the balance of her mind was disturbed by reason of her not having fully recovered from the effect of giving birth to the child or by reason of the effects of lactation consequent upon the birth of the child.

This offence can be charged by the prosecution, unlike manslaughter on grounds of diminished responsibility, in which event the accused does not have to prove her mental disturbance.

Rationale

The infanticide provision is very controversial (Maier-Katkin and Ogle, 1993). In summary, criticism of the measure has argued that:

(i)   it is based on unsubstantiated psychiatric assumptions, generating myths about linkage between childbirth and psychiatric disturbance;

(ii) it contributes to bogus sexist assumptions in law that women are not fully responsible for their actions, further portraying them as victims in need of sympathy rather than punishment and over-exposing them to psychiatry, and discriminates against fathers;

(iii) it operates improperly to introduce covert socio-economic and environmental stress factors which have contributed to the death of children;

(iv) it has been rendered redundant by the subsequent introduction of diminished responsibility manslaughter.

Proponents of the measure have responded that:

(i)   recent epidemiological studies confirm strong evidence for the existence of a link between childbirth and mental illness and that the post-partum period involves special risks of psychosis and emotional distress;

(ii) whether women who kill their infant children are psychiatrically disturbed or not, the measure is a compassionate and humane gesture; a more punitive stance would not have any deterrent effect; and the fact that it has a restrictively narrow ambit is not a basis for abolition;

(iii) reliance on 'diminished responsibility' would increase the punitiveness of the legal response, as the treatment of diminished responsibility offenders is becoming increasingly severe.

Ultimately, the issue is a matter of values rather than evidence or logic. The homicide rate among children under age of one year is greater than that of any other age group – virtually four times higher than the rate among the general population. About half of women convicted of infanticide are not suffering from any identifiable mental disorder and the legislation is used more widely than Parliament initially intended (see Wilczynski and Morris, 1993 and Mackay, 1993). By no means all women who kill their infant children benefit from the infanticide provision (of 56 women convicted of this kind of killing 1982-1988, 36 were convicted of infanticide and 20 of manslaughter/murder). There is also scope in cases of this nature for prosecution to be discontinued in the public interest (see instances identified by Mackay's research (1993) involving very young mothers who conceal their pregnancies, cases where there is doubt about whether there had been a live birth, and instances of puerperal psychosis where psychiatric intervention has taken priority over prosecution).

Sentencing

Though the maximum sentence is life imprisonment, the infanticide legislation has certainly promoted leniency for women who kill their children and offenders clearly tend to be dealt with invariably by non-custodial measures. The Court of Appeal in *R v*

Sainsbury (1989) 11 Cr App R(S) 533 was informed that, in 59 cases dealt with 1979-88, no custodial sentences were imposed, offenders being dealt with by probation, supervision or hospital orders. The *Supplementary Criminal Statistics* 1995-2000 show that, of a total of 21 convicted offenders, only one was sentenced to immediate custody, 19 receiving probation or supervision orders and one a s37 hospital order.

Learning Resources
Centre

7
HOSPITAL ORDERS

Power of compulsory commitment to hospital in criminal proceedings is given by MHA 1983 ss37 and 38, s 37 providing a final disposal of the case while s38 authorises the making of an 'interim hospital order' as a shorter-term, intermediate step. It is not necessary to make an interim order as a preliminary to a s37 order. A 'restriction order' under MHA 1983 s41 is not a disposal in its own right but an order attaching to a hospital order in cases of presenting special risk to the public of serious harm, and is thus addressed in this chapter. Because s37 also gives power to make a guardianship order in criminal proceedings, the statutory basis for this disposal is found in this chapter, though the measure is detailed in Chapter 11.

SECTION 37 HOSPITAL ORDER
MHA 1983 s37

(1) Where a person is convicted before the Crown Court of an offence punishable with imprisonment other than an offence the sentence for which is fixed by law or falls to be imposed under PCC(S)A 2000 s109, or is convicted by a magistrates' court of an offence punishable on summary conviction with imprisonment, and the conditions mentioned in subsection (2) below are satisfied, the court may by order authorise his admission to and detention in such hospital as may be specified in the order or, as the case may be, place him under the guardianship of a local social services authority or of such other person approved by a local social services authority as may be so specified.

(2) The conditions referred to in subsection (1) above are that –

   (a) the court is satisfied, on the written or oral evidence of two registered medical practitioners, that the offender is suffering from mental illness, psychopathic disorder, severe mental impairment or mental impairment and that either –

      (i) the mental disorder from which the offender is suffering is of a nature or degree which makes it appropriate for him to be detained in a hospital for medical treatment and, in the case of psychopathic disorder or mental impairment, that such treatment is likely to alleviate or prevent a deterioration of his condition; or

      (ii) in the case of an offender who has attained the age of 16 years, the mental disorder is of a nature or degree which warrants his reception into guardianship under this Act; and

   (b) the court is of the opinion, having regard to all the circumstances including the nature of the offence and the character and antecedents of the offender, and to the other available methods of dealing with him, that the most suitable method of disposing of the case is by means of an order under this section.

(3) Where a person is charged before a magistrates' court with any act or omission as an offence and the court would have power, on convicting him of that offence, to make an order under subsection (1) above in his case as being a person suffering from mental illness or severe mental impairment, then, if the court is satisfied that the accused did the act or made the omission charged, the court may, if it thinks fit, make such an order without convicting him.

(4) An order for the admission of an offender to a hospital (in this Act referred to as "a hospital order") shall not be made under this section unless the court is satisfied on the written or oral evidence of the registered medical practitioner who would be in charge of his treatment or of some other person representing the managers of the hospital that arrangements have been made for his admission to that hospital in the event of such an order being made by the court, and for his admission to it within the period of 28 days beginning with the date of the making of such an order; and the court may, pending his admission within that period, give such directions as it thinks fit for his conveyance to and detention in a place of safety.

In summary form, the statute specifies this power is available to the Crown Court or a magistrates' court, including a youth court:

(i) on convicting of an imprisonable offence (except murder) or where PCC(S)A 2000 s109 applies;

(ii) upon receiving oral or written evidence of two medical practitioners, one of whom must be approved under MHA 1983 s12 (see page 233) (s54(1));

(iii) on being satisfied that the offender is suffering from a specified form of mental disorder (see below) justifying detention in hospital for treatment, which (in the case of psychopathic disorder or mental impairment) is likely to be effective by alleviating the condition or preventing deterioration;

(iv) where detention is the most suitable disposal, given all the circumstances and other available options; and

(v) where admission to the hospital can take place within 28 days.

These procedural requirements are almost invariably satisfied by the medical practitioners' completion of standard s37 forms, in addition to any medical report.

Note that it is not necessary for a causal link to be established between the offender's mental disorder and the offence for which the order is made. It is sufficient that the criteria of s37 are satisfied. If the offender is aged under 18, an adult magistrates' court cannot make a hospital order (CYPA 1969 s7(8)).

For an illustration of the 'profoundly frustrating' inability of a court to make a hospital order, despite this disposal (combined with a restriction order under s41) being considered the most appropriate course, because the attitude of the relevant health authority meant that s37(4) was not satisfied, see *R v Barker* (2002, outlined on page 160).

Information from the Health Authority

Where a court is minded to make a hospital order (or an interim hospital order), it may request the Regional Health Authority (RHA) for the region in which the defendant resides or last resided, or any other RHA that appears to be appropriate, to provide information about hospitals in the region or elsewhere which may be able to admit the patient (MHA 1983 s39). The RHA thus has a duty to supply whatever information is available or can reasonably be obtained but is not obliged to locate a bed. RHAs should appoint a named person to respond to such request (MHA(COP) 1993 para. 3.4).

It is the court's responsibility to organise transport from the court to the receiving hospital (MHA(COP) 1993 para. 7.3).

Eligible Forms of Mental Disorder

Three of the four forms of mental disorder specified in s37(2)(a) and in MHA 1983 s1 are defined in s1(2), the exception being 'mental illness':

Psychopathic disorder: 'a persistent disorder or disability of mind (whether or not including significant impairment of intelligence) which results in abnormally aggressive or seriously irresponsible conduct on the part of the person concerned'.

Severe mental impairment: 'a state of arrested or incomplete development of mind which includes severe impairment of intelligence and social functioning and is associated with abnormally aggressive or seriously irresponsible conduct on the part of the person concerned'.

Mental impairment: 'a state of arrested or incomplete development of mind (not amounting to severe mental impairment) which includes significant impairment of intelligence and social functioning and is associated with abnormally aggressive or seriously irresponsible conduct on the part of the person concerned'.

Note that in the case of psychopathic disorder or mental impairment, the offender must also satisfy the 'treatability' criterion in s37(2)(a)(i), *ie* treatment is likely to alleviate or prevent deterioration of the offender's condition (see below).

Mental illness: the nearest that the Court of Appeal has come to an authoritative pronouncement was provided in *W v L* [1974] QB 711, a case involving a 23 year-old man who had put a cat in a gas oven, made a cat inhale ammonia before cutting its throat, hanged a puppy and strangled a terrier, and threatened to push his wife downstairs to kill the baby she was expecting. Having noted that 'mental illness' are 'ordinary words of the English language' to be 'construed in the way that ordinary sensible people would construe them', Lawton LJ stated:

> 'I ask myself, what would the ordinary sensible person have said about the patient's condition in this case if he had been informed of his behaviour to the dogs, the cat and his wife? In my judgement such a person would have said "well, the fellow is obviously mentally ill".'

Hoggett has unsurprisingly criticised this as 'the-man-must-be-mad' test, telling us nothing 'about why some people who are cruel to animals should be regarded as responsible for their actions and some should be not' and paying 'scant regard to the

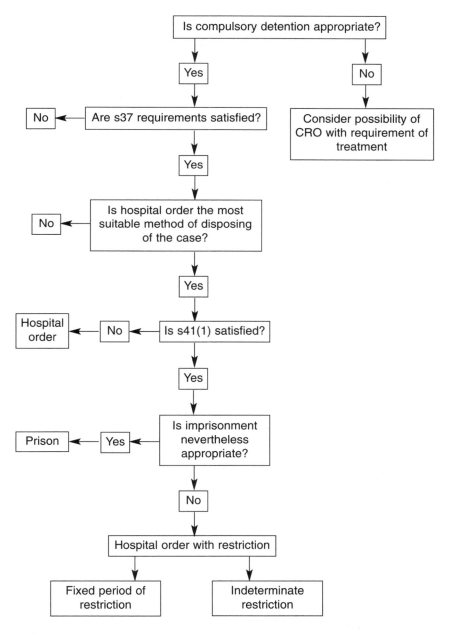

Sequence of Decision-Taking as outlined by Mustill LJ in R v Birch (1989)

painstaking efforts of psychiatrists to distinguish mental health from mental illness by means of carefully described deficiencies, not in behaviour but in mental functioning'. More assistance in defining mental illness is offered by the Northern Ireland Review Committee on Mental Health legislation:

'... a state of mind of a permanent or temporary (but not merely transient) nature in which the individual exhibits such disordered thinking, perceiving or emotion as impairs his judgement of his situation to the extent that he requires care, treatment or training in his own interests or in the interests of other persons.'

The court has to be precise in specifying from which form of disorder the offender is suffering. Additionally, the doctors must be in agreement as to the particular form of disorder from which the offender is suffering, though they may differ as to whether s/he is also suffering any other.

MHA 1983 s37

(7) A hospital order or guardianship order shall specify the form or forms of mental disorder referred to in subsection (2)(a) above from which, upon the evidence taken into account under that subsection, the offender is found by the court to be suffering; and no such order shall be made unless the offender is described by each of the practitioners whose evidence is taken into account under that subsection as suffering from the same one of those forms of mental disorder, whether or not he is also described by either of them as suffering from another of them.

Note also the caveat contained in s1(3) that a person cannot be detained under the Act as mentally disordered 'by reason only of promiscuity or other immoral conduct, sexual deviancy or dependence on drugs or alcohol'. In other words there must be other evidence to justify a finding of mental disorder, though Hoggett (1990) suggested that 'psychiatrists remain anxious to find evidence of other mental disorders in sexual deviants whom they wish to treat'. 'Psychopathy' is the obvious label that may be applied to those who have committed immoral or sexually deviant behaviour, yet Dell and Robertson (1988:128), writing about Broadmoor Special Hospital (as it was then known), identified that:

'In practice, the crime is regarded as proof of this disorder; had it not been committed, psychiatrists would not have considered the man to need hospital care. However, once the crime has occurred, the doctors – if they think a hospital disposal desirable – are forced into one of two procedures. Either they will cite little other than the offence as evidence of the disorder ... Alternatively, in an attempt to avoid this tautological approach, they will cite as proof of disorder a number of features (*eg* poor family or personal relationships) that existed before the offence but would never of themselves have caused the doctor to recommend hospitalisation ... The whole process can be regarded as a useful fiction'.

Treatability

An authoritative, six-point view of the meaning of 'treatment' in this context, albeit in regard to the judgement of a MHRT, was given by Roch LJ in *R v Cannons Park MHRT, ex p. A* [1995] QB 60:

'(i)   If a tribunal were to be satisfied that the patient's detention in hospital was simply an attempt to coerce the patient into participating in group therapy, then the tribunal would be under a duty to direct discharge.

(ii)   "Treatment in hospital" will satisfy the "treatability test" although it is unlikely to alleviate the patient's condition, provided that it is likely to prevent a deterioration.

(iii) "Treatment in hospital" will satisfy the "treatability test" although it will not immediately alleviate or prevent deterioration in the patient's condition, provided that alleviation or stabilisation is likely in due course.

(iv)   The "treatability test" can still be met although initially there may be some deterioration in the patient's condition, due for example to the patient's initial anger at being detained.

(v)   It must be remembered that medical treatment in hospital covers "nursing and also includes care, habilitation and rehabilitation under medical supervision" (see page 92).

(vi)   The "treatability test " is satisfied if nursing care etc are likely to lead to an alleviation of the patient's condition in that the patient is likely to gain an insight into his problem or cease to be unco-operative in his attitude towards treatment which would potentially have a lasting benefit.'

In the Scottish case of *Reid v Secretary of State for Scotland* [1999] 2 AC 512 it was considered that the test could be satisfied in circumstances where 'the anger management of (the patient) in the structured setting of the hospital in a supervised environment resulted in him being less aggressive'.

28 Day Rule

Because it may not be possible to admit the offender to hospital immediately, s37(4) provides a four-week period of flexibility and allows the court to order the offender's detention in a suitable 'place of safety' in the meantime. If unexpected circumstances arise after the order is made which make it impracticable for the offender to be admitted to the specified hospital, the Secretary of State has the discretion under s37(5) to direct admission to an appropriate alternative hospital.

MHA 1983 s37

(5)   If within the said period of 28 days it appears to the Secretary of State that by reason of an emergency or other special circumstances it is not practicable for the patient to be received into the hospital specified in the order, he may give directions for the admission of the patient to such other hospital as appears to be appropriate instead of the hospital so specified; and where such directions are given –

(a)   the Secretary of State shall cause the person having the custody of the patient to be informed, and

(b)   the hospital order shall have effect as if the hospital specified in the directions were substituted for the hospital specified in the order.

The Secretary of State may now make an order reducing the statutory length of time for which the offender may be held prior to hospital admission: CJA 1991 s27(2).

Permissible Concurrent Orders

When a hospital order is made, the court is prohibited by s37(8) from making any of the following sentences or orders in respect of the offence:

(i)   imprisonment;
(ii) detention;
(iii) community rehabilitation order;
(iv) supervision order;
(v)   fine;
(vi) bind over of parent of an offender aged under 18,

but 'may make any other order which the court has power to make apart from this section'. A community punishment order is not specifically excluded but is nevertheless an inappropriate tandem measure to combine with a hospital order. It may be appropriate, however, to make a compensation order or to disqualify the offender from driving.

Effect on Existing Hospital or Guardianship Orders

Where an offender is admitted to hospital in pursuance of a hospital order, any previous hospital or guardianship order ceases to have effect (s40(5)), unless a previous hospital order remains subject to a restriction order (s41(4)).

Sentencing Principles

In the leading Court of Appeal judgement on restriction orders, *R v Birch* (1989) 11 Cr App R(S) 202 (see page 99), Mustill LJ commented on the purpose of a hospital order without restriction:

> 'In general the offender is dealt with in a manner which appears, and is intended to be, humane by comparison with a custodial sentence. A hospital order is not a punishment. Questions of retribution and deterrence, whether personal or general, are immaterial. The offender who has become a patient is not kept on any kind of leash by the court, as he is when he consents to a probation order with a condition of in-patient treatment. The sole purpose of the order is to ensure that the offender receives the medical care and attention which he needs in the hope and expectation ... that the result will be to avoid the commission by the offender of further criminal acts.'

Sentencing in Practice

Robertson *et al* (1992) identified in their study of mentally disordered remand prisoners in 1989 (see Chapter 13) that 'almost without exception, magistrates and judges made hospital orders when they were given the option' in psychiatric reports to the court, 'but the procedures were slow and cumbersome'.

> 'The delays inherent in the hospital order system – delays in outside psychiatrists visiting, in courts making the orders, and in the admission of patients once orders were made – meant that the people who were made subject to orders (*ie* those in greatest need of hospital) spent longer in prison than any other group in our sample

... Everyone involved in the process – courts, prison doctors and outside psychiatrists – has come to take the attendant delays for granted'.

The great majority of the prisoners in the research sample who obtained a hospital order bed went to ordinary local hospitals. As it has been suggested that such people are 'ungrateful and unrewarding patients, intent on absconding at the earliest opportunity', the researchers sent out follow-up questionnaires after the patients had been in hospital for three months, receiving a 75% response. For over 90% of the cases, the doctors reported that the admissions had been appropriate and a similar proportion were said to have shown improvement.

'Few of the patients had caused major or unusual problems; well over half were still in hospital after three months ... the rest had been discharged as improved. Very few had left hospital prematurely by absconding. For those who obtained beds, hospitalisation had evidently been worthwhile.'

For a more detailed report of 101 men who had received hospital orders following a period of remand at Brixton prison, see Robertson *et al* (1994), reporting that 59% of the patients had shown 'marked improvement' as a consequence of hospital detention. Only 7% of patients showed 'no change'. Only five patients had left hospital within two weeks, three as a medical decision to transfer them to a less secure setting and only two by absconding.

Sentencing Statistics

Provisional figures (Johnson and Taylor, 2002) for persons given unrestricted hospital orders under s37(1) and (3) (see below) indicate a total of 614 in 2001, the lowest number in a decade, with 763 orders being made in 1994 though with a comparable 626 in 2000. As in preceding years, the largest offence category in 2001 was indictable (non-sexual) violence other than homicide (181 or 29.5%), the next most significant category being indictable criminal damage/arson with 99 (16%) orders. Some 82 orders were made in respect of summary offences. This evidence of static usage of s37 orders since HOC 66/1990 does not offer much encouragement for diversion of mentally disordered offenders into psychiatric care.

Hospital Orders Without Conviction

The power of a magistrates' court to make a hospital order without first convicting the offender, where the court is satisfied that s/he 'did the act or made the omission' (s37(3)):

'... is manifestly to deal compassionately, effectively and protectively with a mentally disordered person, who may not have had the necessary intention required in the offence, may not be able to conduct a defence in the normal way, ought not to be burdened in the future with a criminal conviction, and who needs the care and treatment provided under a hospital order. Furthermore the order will provide the necessary degree of protection for the public ...' (Samuels, 1995)

The power should be used very sparingly. *R v Lincoln (Kesteven) Justices, ex p. O'Connor* [1983] 1 WLR 335, where the offender had been charged with assault occasioning actual bodily harm of an occupational therapist at the hospital where he was a voluntary in-patient, illustrates an appropriate instance. It was very difficult for anyone to communicate with him and it was clear that he was not able to understand or make a decision when asked in court if he consented to summary trial. The Divisional Court considered this a proper case for an order to be made without proceeding to conviction, as requested by the defendant's solicitor and specifically recommended by one of the doctors submitting a report. This unusual power 'can save much cumbersome and time-consuming unnecessary procedure' but Lane CJ commented that the circumstances in which it will be appropriate 'are bound to be very rare and will usually require ... the consent of those acting for the accused'. In a subsequent case, *R v Ramsgate Justices, ex p. Kasmarek* (1985) 80 Cr App R 366, the Divisional Court ruled that magistrates could still exercise power under s37(3), even though the accused had earlier elected trial at Crown Court on charges of burglary and criminal damage, becoming mentally disordered prior to committal proceedings (now 'transfer for trial'). It is now clear that a magistrates' court has no jurisdiction to make an order under s37(3) in respect of a defendant charged with an offence triable only on indictment, as it has no power to convict him: *R v Chippenham Magistrates' Court, ex p. Thompson* (1996) 160 JP Reports 207 (a case of a man with a long history of schizophrenia who was facing allegations of robbery).

Samuels (1995) has identified the ambiguous meaning of 'did the act'. In the case of an alleged assault, for example, is it sufficient that the victim was injured at the hands of the defendant, irrespective of any question of intention, fault, self-defence or accident? Or is it necessary that an offence should be proved, *ie* that the defendant deliberately struck the injured party without justification? He argues that the latter is the more persuasive interpretation.

Legal Status of the Hospital Order Patient

A patient admitted to hospital on a hospital order is essentially in the same legal position as a civil patient compulsorily admitted to hospital for treatment under MHA 1983 s3 (s40(4)), modified in certain respects by sch 1 part 1 of the Act. As such, the duration of their detention is regulated by s20 which specifies detention for a period not exceeding six months from the date of the order, subject to renewal in the first instance for a further period of six months and thereafter at yearly intervals. Note that detention does not have to last for six months in the first instance as the patient may be discharged by the hospital at any time, on the authority of the doctor in charge of the patient's treatment (the 'responsible medical officer' or RMO) or of the hospital managers.

Renewal of the Order

Renewal is the responsibility of the RMO, who must examine the patient within two months of the current expiry date, consulting those professionally concerned with the patient's treatment. To justify renewal, the RMO must believe that the patient continues to suffer from one or more of the four statutorily specified forms of mental disorder and that it is necessary for the patient's own health or safety or for the protection of other persons that s/he should receive medical treatment in a hospital and that it cannot be provided unless s/he continues to be detained (s20(4)). If the RMO so reports to the hospital managers, authority for detention is renewed automatically for the appropriate period, unless the managers decide to discharge the patient against the RMO's advice.

Application to Tribunal

Mental Health Review Tribunals, comprising of legal, medical and lay members, operate regionally to conduct independent reviews of the exercise of compulsory powers upon psychiatric patients. Reviews are conducted upon the application of patients or their 'nearest relative' on obligatory referral by the hospital managers in specified instances (*eg* where detention is renewed and the patient has not been considered by a tribunal within the preceding three years) and on the discretionary referral of the Secretary of State for Health at any time.

Unlike a civil patient under s3, a hospital order patient cannot apply to a Tribunal within the first six months of their detention, nor can their 'nearest relative'. The first opportunity for application thus arises during the second six-month period of detention and in the course of each yearly detention thereafter (s69(1)(a)).

Tribunals are regulated by the Mental Health Review Tribunal Rules 1983 (SI 1983 No. 942). The Tribunal's task is to decide whether the patient should be detained any longer and must discharge the patient if grounds for detention do not exist, *ie* if s/he is not suffering from one of the four specified disorders, or the disorder is not of a nature or degree to make detention for treatment appropriate. The Tribunal needs to be satisfied 'on the balance of probabilities'. Technically speaking, it is for the patient to prove that the grounds for detention do not exist, not for the hospital to prove that they do, though Tribunals may well place an evidential burden upon the authorities. The patient may be legally represented and 'legal aid' is available.

'Nearest Relative'

This status is regulated by s26 which provides the following rank order of relationship: spouse (including co-habitant of at least six months), daughter/son, mother/father, sister/ brother, grandparent, grandchild, aunt/uncle, niece/nephew. However, any relative with whom the patient ordinarily resides or who cared for the patient prior to their detention takes precedence over any other relative, irrespective of their 'ranking' (s26(4)). Note that the nearest relative does not have the power to discharge a hospital order patient which would be available under s23(2) in respect of a civil patient.

Leave of Absence

As a detained patient, a s37 patient may be granted leave of absence by the RMO, either for a special purpose or for a fixed period or on an indefinite basis, under s17(1). Leave can be extended without the patient's return to hospital (s17(2)) or can be revoked at any time if the RMO considers this necessary in the interests of the patient's own health or safety or for the protection of other people. A patient on leave cannot be tied to s37 requirements indefinitely and cannot be recalled once the power to detain them has lapsed (s17(5)); *ie* once the patient has been on continuous leave for 12 months (extended from six months by MH(PC)A 1995). Though *R v Hallstrom* [1986] QB 1090 had determined that 'long leash' arrangements were not lawful and that authority to detain a patient could not be renewed while the patient was on leave of absence, nor could a patient be recalled from leave as a technical exercise simply to block the lapsing of detention power or to renew their detention, this decision was overruled by the Court of Appeal in *B v Barking, Havering and Brentwood Community Healthcare NHS Trust* [1999] 1 FLR 106. The Court decided that so long as the patient's treatment, viewed as a whole, involves treatment as an in-patient, the requirements of the provision can be met.

Absconding

If the patient goes absent from the hospital without leave or fails to return after leave of absence, s/he may be taken into custody and returned to the hospital by any police officer, approved social worker, officer on the staff of the hospital or any other person authorised in writing by the hospital managers (s18(1)). However, this is qualified by s18(4) (as amended by MH(PC)A 1995 s2(1) which increased the relevant period from 28 days):

> A patient shall not be taken into custody under this section after the later of –
>
> (a) the end of the period of six months beginning with the first day of his absence without leave; and
>
> (b) the end of the period for which he is liable to be detained ...

In other words, the absconder who is able to sustain their unlawful absence for six months normally achieves the unilateral termination of their order. Detention cannot be renewed while a patient is absent without leave and any renewal approved but not in effect at time of absconding does not come into effect. However, if he is absent on the date when his liability to detention expires or within a week of that date and he is then recaptured or voluntarily returns prior to expiry, authority to detain him is extended by up to a week, beginning with the date of his return, to allow the RMO to consider and apply for renewal (s21, as substituted by MH(CP)A 1995). If the abscondee returns or is returned within 28 days, renewal formalities may be completed under the usual renewal provisions of s20 (s21A); otherwise detention continues as before. However, if the patient has been at large for more than 28 days, the medical officer must examine the patient and review the case within a week, in consultation with an ASW and one or more professionals involved in his treatment, decide whether the renewal criteria are satisfied and report on the patient. If the RMO does not so report within a week of return, the patient is no longer liable to be detained, even if he would otherwise still have been detained under the earlier detention power.

As Hoggett (1996) notes, the old '28 day' law reflected an era in which the patient's ability to survive in the community for that length of time was considered proof that they were not ill, but this assumption or benefit of the doubt makes no sense in contemporary society, given concern about the number of s37 patients who had been achieving their discharge by that means.

Consent to Treatment

Under s63, 'the consent of a patient shall not be required for any medical treatment given to him for the mental disorder from which he is suffering', subject to certain safeguards provided by ss57 and 58. The general authority to impose treatment without consent is subject to these caveats:

(i) the treatment must be 'medical', though this is generously defined by s145(1) to include nursing and care, habilitation and rehabilitation under medical supervision;

(ii) the treatment must be for the patient's mental disorder and so there is no power to impose treatment for disorders unrelated to any mental disorder within the Act.

The specific safeguards are as follows:

(i) ECT and the administration of medicine beyond three months after it was first administered can only be given without the patient's consent if an independent medical opinion confirms that it should be;

(ii) a surgical operation destroying brain tissue or the surgical implantation of hormones for the purpose of reducing male sexual drive cannot be conducted unless the patient consents (as certified by an independent doctor and two non-doctors) and the independent doctor agrees that the treatment should be given.

After-Care

Patients leaving hospital at the end of their detention period, whether under s37 alone or in tandem with s41, have the benefit of s117(2):

> It shall be the duty of the District Health Authority and of the local social services authority to provide, in co-operation with relevant voluntary agencies, after-care services for any person to whom this section applies until such time as the District Health Authority and the local social services authority are satisfied that the person concerned is no longer in need of such services.

The 'local social services authority' means the authority for the area in which the ex-patient resides or to which s/he is sent on discharge (s117(3)). 'Services' are not defined but clearly can include social work support, access to day centre or residential facilities and the provision of domiciliary services. Whether this amounts to an individual entitlement to service is far from clear. Under s124, the Secretary of State for Health can make a default order declaring that a social services authority has failed to carry out its functions and directing the authority to discharge its duty.

CPA and Section 117 Registration

After-care under s117 is now part of the Care Programme Approach (CPA), introduced in 1991, to provide systematic assessment of health and social care needs, an agreed care plan, allocation of a key worker, now known as the Care Co-ordinator, and regular review for all mentally ill patients who are considered for discharge or accepted by specialist mental health services. This is outlined more fully in Chapter 15. A CPA Register is maintained as an information system for CPA patients. Patients subject to s117 (*ie* those discharged under MHA 1983 ss3, 37, 41, 47 and 48) will also be subject to CPA provisions, though health authorities are required to identify separately patients who are receiving s117 care so that they can demonstrate that they are fulfilling their statutory obligations. The DoH (2001, para. 71) has recommended that s117 registers become 'a discrete and identifiable subset of the CPA register'.

The Christopher Clunis Inquiry team (Ritchie *et al*, 1994) noted that 'the patient very often considers that the s117 aftercare plan is made at his expense rather than for his benefit' and that 'it is vital that the patient should participate in the formation of the plan', assisted by a befriender/advocate who should attend all s117 meetings to 'champion the patient's cause, ensure that action which is supposed to happen under the plan does in fact happen and ... be assertive in keeping in touch with the patient and in picking up any signs or symptoms of relapse'.

After-Care under Supervision

Concerns that there should be greater statutory control of discharged patients in the community prompted the passage of MH(PC)A 1995, amending MHA 1983 by introducing a new power of supervised discharge for detained patients aged 16 or over (including s37 patients) where (s25A(4)):

(a) the patient is suffering from mental disorder;

(b) 'there would be a substantial risk of serious harm to the health and safety of the patient or the safety of other persons, or of the patient being seriously exploited if he were not to receive after-care services under s117 after he leaves hospital'; and

(c) his being subject to after-care under supervision is likely to help to secure that he receives the after-care services to be so provided.'

Supervision Application

Supervised discharge arises upon the application of the RMO to the health authority which will be responsible for after-care services to the patient, after consultation with the patient, the nearest relative (if practicable), any informal carers and those professionally concerned with the patient's care. The RMO has to consider the services to be provided and the requirements to be imposed (s25B(1)(b) and (4)), though these are a matter for the after-care authority. The application must be accompanied by:

(i) a second medical opinion, normally by a doctor who will be professionally concerned with the patient's medical treatment after he leaves hospital(s25B(6)(a)). This doctor must certify (a) to (c) above and must agree with the RMO on at least one of the four forms of mental disorder;

(ii) a recommendation by an ASW (s25B(6)(b) who has to certify (b) and (c) above;

(iii) statements by the patient's community RMO and also his 'supervisor', (s25B(9)(a) and (b));

(iv) details of the after-care services to be provided under s117;

(v) details of any requirements to be imposed under s25D (see below).

On making an application, the RMO shall inform the patient both orally and in writing, the nearest relative in writing, and others who have been consulted (s25B(10) and (11)). Before accepting the application, the Health Authority must consult the local Social Services authority (s25A(7)). On accepting the application, the Health Authority must notify the patient and his or her professional and informal carers. In particular, the patient's right to apply to a MHRT must be explained.

Supervision

A nominated supervisor – normally the patient's key worker – will be responsible for supervising and monitoring the patient's after-care. 'Supervisor' is defined by s34 to mean the person acting in that capacity under s117(2A)(b), being professionally concerned with any of the after-care services so provided, who is supervising the patient with a view to securing that he receives those services. Supervision operates rather like guardianship but undertaken by health services and with power to 'take and convey'. Section 25D specifies that, where a patient is subject to after-care supervision or is to be so subject on leaving hospital, the 'responsible after-care bodies' (*ie* health and social services under s117) have power to impose any of the requirements specified in s25D(3):

(a) to reside at a specified place;

(b) to attend for medical treatment, occupation, education or training;

(c) to permit access at any place where the patient is residing to the supervisor, any registered medical practitioner, any ASW, or to any person authorised by the supervisor.

The supervisor, or a person authorised by the supervisor has power to 'take and convey' the patient to any place where they are required by s25D(3) to reside or attend under the specified after-care arrangements (s25D(4)). There is no power to administer medication or other medical treatment against the patient's will.

Duration
Supervision lasts for an initial period of six months, which may be extended in the first instance for a further six months if the grounds are still satisfied, and thereafter for renewable periods of one year. The patient may be discharged from supervision at any time, following the usual consultation.

Appeal
The patient, and the nearest relative, will have the right to appeal to a MHRT when supervised discharge is initially imposed and thereafter when supervision is renewed.

Sanction
Where the patient 'neglects or refuses' to comply with the after-care arrangements, there will be an immediate review and an ASW can be requested to consider applying for the patient's compulsory admission to hospital (s25E). There is no automatic power of recall to hospital. Though 'take and convey' power (above) has bite, there is no power to detain the person once they have arrived at the place to which they have been brought. Para. 49 of the Department of Health's *Guidance on Supervised Discharge* (see below) indicates that this power should only be used if:

(i) a patient has got into a situation which is putting him, or other people, at risk and needs to be taken home urgently; or

(ii) a patient is not attending for treatment but taking him is likely to lead him to co-operate with such services.

Jones (1999) has suggested that 'if the power ... is to escape contravening ECHR (by virtue of the decision in *X v United Kingdom* 4 EHRR 181) it would need to be shown that a failure by a patient to take his medication constitutes an emergency'.

Admission to Hospital or Prison
After-care under supervision ends if the patient is admitted to hospital under s3 or s37 powers. If admitted informally or under s2, after-care is suspended, though the period of supervision continues to run. Supervision resumes on re-discharge unless it has

expired meanwhile. Section 25I specifies that if the patient is detained in custody in pursuance of any sentence or order passed by a court in the United Kingdom, including a remand into custody, their supervision is suspended. If their custodial detention is for a period amounting in the aggregate to six months or less and supervision would otherwise have ceased during that period or would cease within 28 days of their release, their supervision shall be deemed not to have ceased until the expiry of 28 days from release. This permits time for consideration to be given to renewal of supervision.

Code of Guidance

The Department of Health issued a supplement to MHA(COP) as detailed guidance on supervised discharge, published under HSG(96)11/LA(96)8 and WHC(96)11.

At the time of its introduction this measure was subjected to substantial criticism as an erosion of basic rights, likely to operate in a discriminatory way and to destroy the basis of trust and patient involvement which is essential for successful community care, creating a new administrative burden, while at the same time achieving no improvements to inadequate community care resources. See Prins (1996).

INTERIM HOSPITAL ORDER

Before making a hospital order or dealing with the offender in some other way, the Crown Court or a magistrates' court (a youth court if the offender is aged under 18) may make an interim hospital order under MHA 1983 s38, the applicable conditions or criteria being almost the same as for a s37 order. Three differences should be noted:

(i) the court should be satisfied 'that there is reason to suppose that the mental disorder ... is such that it may be appropriate for a hospital order to be made' (s38(1)(b));

(ii) 'at least one of the registered medical practitioners whose evidence is taken into account ... shall be employed at the hospital which is to be specified in the order' (s38(3));

(iii) a magistrates' court cannot make an interim order without proceeding to conviction.

In *Birch* (1989, see page 99) Mustill LJ referred to s38 as a valuable provision, not used as often as it might be, giving the court and doctors further time to decide between hospital, with or without restrictions, and some other disposal. As the Court of Appeal has noted on various occasions, most recently in *R v Scarth* [2002] EWCA Crim 2737 (unreported), that Court is not able to make a s38 order unless it first quashes the sentence imposed in the Crown Court, the case then having to be remitted back to the Crown Court for the question of sentence to be considered afresh at the conclusion of the s38 period. As regards credit for time spent on remand, see page 49.

Duration

MHA 1983 s38

(5) An interim hospital order –

(a) shall be in force for such period, not exceeding 12 weeks, as the court may specify when making the order; but

(b) may be renewed for further periods of not more than 28 days at a time if it appears to the court, on the written or oral evidence of the responsible medical officer, that the continuation of the order is warranted;

but no such order shall continue in force for more than 12 months in all and the court shall terminate the order if it makes a hospital order in respect of the offender or decides after considering the written or oral evidence of the responsible medical officer to deal with the offender in some other way.

The mximum duration was extended from six to 12 months by C(S)A 1997 s49(1). Note that no minimum period is specified.

Proceedings without the Offender's Presence

Because it may be helpful for the court to proceed without requiring personal attendance of the offender, an interim order may be renewed (s38(6)) or a s37 order may be made (s38(2)) in the offender's absence, provided s/he is legally represented and the advocate is given an opportunity of being heard.

Absconding

The sanction in this instance is to bring the offender before the court making the order, not to return the offender to the hospital.

MHA 1983 s38

(7) If an offender absconds from a hospital in which he is detained in pursuance of an interim hospital order, or while being conveyed to or from such a hospital, he may be arrested without warrant by a constable and shall, after being arrested, be brought as soon as practicable before the court that made the order; and the court may thereupon terminate the order and deal with him in any way in which it could have dealt with him if no such order had been made.

Use of Section 38 Orders

Given relatively infrequent use of s38 orders in Special Hospitals and general psychiatric facilities, Kaul (1994) examined the somewhat greater use of interim orders at the Trent RSU during 1988. Of 32 patients admitted in that year, 11 were received under s38, of whom nine were diagnosed as suffering personality disorder with histories characterised by being processed by the criminal justice system rather than the mental health system. Noting that six were subsequently recommended for hospital orders and three for probation orders, Kaul suggested that s38 offers a valuable opportunity to evaluate psychopathic offenders' response in hospital without any irrevocable commitment being made.

RESTRICTION ORDER

Power to add a restriction order to a s37 hospital order is available only to the Crown Court but a magistrates' court may commit the offender to the Crown Court with a view to a restriction order being made (s43).

Power to Restrict Discharge

MHA 1983 s41

(1) Where a hospital order is made in respect of an offender by the Crown Court, and it appears to the court, having regard to the nature of the offence, the

antecedents of the offender and the risk of his committing further offences if set at large, that it is necessary for the protection of the public from serious harm so to do, the court may, subject to the provisions of this section, further order that the offender shall be subject to the special restrictions set out in this section, either without limit of time or during such period as may be specified in the order; and an order under this section shall be known as "a restriction order".

(2) A restriction order shall not be made in the case of any person unless at least one of the registered medical practitioners whose evidence is taken into account by the court under section 37(2)(a) above has given evidence orally before the court.

Note that one of the doctors involved must attend court and give oral evidence. If the court takes the unusual step (see below) of specifying a fixed period for the restriction order, then at the end of that period the hospital order continues to have effect as a s37 order without restriction (s41(5)).

Power to Specify Hospital Unit

Under provisions introduced by C(S)A 1997 s47, a court making a s41 restriction order may specify not only the hospital at which the defendant will be detained but a 'unit' of the hospital (defined by s47(3) to mean 'any part of a hospital which is treated as a separate unit'). This refinement is designed to enable the court to 'specify a level of security in which the patient needs to be detained' (MHA(COP) 1999 para. 3.15). In consequence, the Secretary of State's permission will be required for any transfer from the named unit, even to another part of the same hospital. The question of whether a unit should be designated is a factor for the doctors reporting to the court to consider (para. 3.14).

Power of Committal to Crown Court

This power if exercisable provided that:

(i) the offender is aged 14 or over and has been convicted of an offence punishable with imprisonment on summary conviction;

(ii) the criteria for making a hospital order under s37 are satisfied;

(iii) 'it appears to the court, having regard to the nature of the offence, the antecedents of the offender and the risk of his committing further offences if set at large, that if a hospital order is made a restriction order should also be made' (s43(1)(b)).

If committed, the offender must either be held in custody in the meantime, or committed to hospital under MHA 1983 s44:

(1) Where an offender is committed under section 43(1) above and the magistrates' court by which he is committed is satisfied on written or oral evidence that arrangements have been made for the admission of the offender to a hospital in the event of an order being made under this section, the court may, instead of committing him in custody, by order direct him to be admitted to that hospital, specifying it, and to be detained there until the case is disposed of by the

Crown Court, and may give such directions as it thinks fit for his production from the hospital to attend the Crown Court by which his case is to be dealt with.

(2)   The evidence required by subsection (1) above shall be given by the registered medical practitioner who would be in charge of the offender's treatment or by some other person representing the managers of the hospital in question.

The powers of the Crown Court on committal are:

(i)   to make an interim hospital order (s38), to remand to hospital for reports (s35) or for treatment (s36);

(ii)   to make a hospital order with or without a restriction order; or

(iii) to deal with the offender in any other manner available to the magistrates' court (*ie* the Crown Court's powers are limited to those of the lower court).

However, a magistrates' court may also commit the offender to the Crown Court for sentence under MCA 1980 s38, on grounds that greater punishment should be inflicted on the offender than can be exercised by magistrates, unless a hospital order with restriction is made. In this instance, the restriction in (iii) (above) will not apply.

Sentencing Principles

In the leading Court of Appeal guideline judgement on making a restriction order, *R v Birch* (1989) 11 Cr App R(S) 202, the following principles were outlined or confirmed:

- A restriction order fundamentally alters the nature of the patient's detention in hospital; the offender's interests are no longer paramount and the interests of public safety take priority.

- There need be no connection between the offender's mental state and the offence. It is sufficient that the defendant is a convicted offender and that the conditions of s41 are satisfied. Thus in *R v Hatt* [1962] Crim LR 647, the offender convicted of taking (a vehicle) without consent (TWOC) was said to suffer a psychopathic disorder and to have an uncontrollable impulse to take lorries, but the main basis for making a hospital order was his affliction with Munchausen's Syndrome (constantly seeking admission to hospital for unnecessary operations), not related to his urge to take vehicles.

- Though the court must hear the oral evidence of at least one of the doctors, the assessment of risk is a matter for the court and so an order may be properly made even though the doctors are unanimous that the offender is not dangerous, if the judge is satisfied that the offender is dangerous enough to warrant an inhibition on his or her release.

- Nevertheless, a restriction order cannot be made unless there is a basis for the court to conclude that such an order is necessary and the doctors' opinion will be a very important consideration. Thus in *R v Courtney* (1987) 9 Cr App R(S) 404, where the offender had strangled his wife as a result of a brief loss of control in the course of a quarrel, three medical witnesses agreed that he was suffering from depression of a nature warranting his detention in hospital. None considered that he was a danger to the public, though one doctor referred to the possibility that he might harm himself. The restriction order imposed by the trial judge was quashed, leaving a simple s37 order.

In *Birch*, the offender had pleaded guilty to manslaughter of her husband by reason of diminished responsibility. She had a depressive illness, aggravated by excessive alcohol consumption, and was considered a substantial suicide risk. The medical consensus was that she did not constitute a danger to the general public and that a s37 order without restriction was appropriate, but the trial judge considered that a restriction order was necessary as this was a serious offence of violence, with some degree of premeditation, and the possibility of further violence could not be ruled out. On her appeal that a s41 order was inappropriate, the Court of Appeal concluded that the court had nothing to go on in making its decision except the evidence of the doctors, which appeared responsible and sound, and that there was thus no basis for a restriction order.

- The court is required to assess not the seriousness of the risk that the defendant will re-offend but the risk that if s/he does so the public will suffer serious harm. Mustill LJ commented:

  'The harm in question need not, in our view, be limited to personal injury. Nor need it relate to the public in general, for it would in our judgement suffice if a category of persons, or even a single person, were adjudged to be at risk: although the category of person so protected would no doubt exclude the offender himself. Nevertheless the potential harm must be serious, and a high possibility of a recurrence of minor offences will no longer be sufficient.'

  Even a low risk of very serious harm may justify a restriction order.

- A restriction order should not be imposed simply to mark the gravity of the case and it is wrong to equate the seriousness of the offence with the likelihood of a restriction order being made, as this is only one of the factors to be taken into account. As Mustill LJ put it:

  'A minor offence by a man who proves to be mentally disordered and dangerous may properly leave him subject to a restriction. In theory the converse is also true. *Courtney* shows that a serious offence committed by someone who is adjudged to have a very low risk of re-offending may lead to an unrestricted hospital order.'

  Nevertheless, in the latter kind of case the court would have to be very sure of its ground and the Court of Appeal cited with approval the following statement of principle by Lord Parker CJ in *R v Gardiner* (1967) 51 Cr App R 187:

  'In the case of crimes of violence, and of the more serious sexual offences, particularly if the prisoner has a record of such offences, or if there is a history of mental disorder involving violent behaviour, it is suggested that there must be compelling reasons to explain why a restriction order should not be made.'

- Restriction for a fixed period (recommended for abolition by the Butler Committee) should be imposed only in 'the most exceptional kind of case'. In *Gardiner* (above) the Court of Appeal stated that unlimited orders should be made unless the doctors could confidently predict recovery within a limited period but the Review of the Mental Health Act 1959 (DHSS *et al*, 1978) commented that this view confused recovery from mental disorder with the duration of dangerousness. Though there may be instances where the court can make a reasonable prediction of when an offender may cease to be dangerous, an offender may continue to suffer some degree of mental disorder. It is, however, wrong for a court to determine the length of a restriction order by reference to the length of imprisonment that would otherwise be appropriate for the offence (*R v Haynes* (1981) 3 Cr App R(S) 330. See, however, the Case Illustration of Adam Self (page 110)). The *Gardiner* principle was subsequently reiterated by the Court of Appeal in *R v Nwohia* [1996] 1 Cr App R(S) 170: 'unless there is some foundation in the medical evidence for saying that the patient can be cured within a partcular period, it would be unwise to place a limit on the restriction order'.

- Where the pre-conditions for a s37/s41 order are satisfied and a bed is available in a secure hospital, a hospital order supplemented by a s41 order is the appropriate disposal rather than a life sentence. A judge should not pass a life sentence with a view to excluding the jurisdiction of the Mental Health Review Tribunal. Thus, in *R v Mbatha* (1985) 7 Cr App R(S) 373 the offender had been convicted of rape and buggery arising out of a number of attacks upon women. He had a history of sexual offences and was said to suffer manic depressive psychosis, which could be controlled by medication, but he could not be relied upon to take prescribed drugs without supervision. A bed was available for him in a Special Hospital. Sentence of life imprisonment was varied on appeal to a s37 order with s41 restriction. The subsequent case of *R v Fleming* (1993) 14 Cr App R(S) 151 (where the sentencer had been concerned that the medical authorities had previously determined erroneously that it was safe for the offender to go free when he had been subject to a hospital order with restriction, imposed for violent crime, and wished to ensure that in future this discretion should be exercised by the Home Secretary) had suggested that in very exceptional circumstances a sentence of life imprisonment could still be appropriate. However, in *R v Mitchell* [1997] 1 Cr App R(S) 90, followed in *R v Hutchinson* [1997] 2 Cr App R(S) 60, the Court of Appeal concluded that *Fleming* should be given little weight and 'is better disregarded'. The Court noted that that for offenders sentenced to 'discretionary' life imprisonment from 1 October 1992, the decision to release, once s/he has served the period specified as the tariff term under C(S)A 1997 s28, will be taken by the Parole Board, not the Home Secretary, using a procedure very similar to that exercised by an MHRT. [Following the recent decision in *Stafford v UK* (2002) 35 EHRR 32, determining that 'minimum term (tariff) expired mandatory lifers are entitled to have their continuing detention on the basis of risk considered by an independent tribunal conducted in a judical manner, all lifers will have the opportunity to be reviewed by the Board through an oral hearing.] A court may opt to impose a life sentence only if the offender is dangerous and no suitable secure hospital accommodation is available. Prisoners sentenced on that basis are known as 'technical lifers' (see Stone, 1997 and forthcoming).

The choice of prison as an alternative to hospital has sometimes arisen in the past where the sentencer has considered that, notwithstanding the offender's mental disorder, there was an element of culpability in the offence which merited punishment. This might happen where there was no connection between the mental disorder and the offence, or where the defendant's responsibility for the offence was 'diminished' but not wholly extinguished. However, even where there is culpability, the right way to deal with a dangerous and disordered person where the medical opinions are unanimous and a suitable bed is available seems always to make a hospital order with restriction (*R v Howell* (1985) 7 Cr App R(S) 360).

Recent Illustrations of the Restriction Order Threshold

Restriction Not Justified

Both the following cases involve instances of the summary offence of common assault (maximum term six months).

In *R v Martin* (1998, unreported) an offender with a long history of mental illness, on probation for common assault and threatening behaviour, was abusive to a woman probation officer who had sought to calm him when he was attending an office appointment, following her to the car park where he punched her three or four times to the back of the head. On his conviction for common assault, he was committed to Crown Court where a s41 order was added to a hospital order. Psychiatrists had recommended restriction so that his mental health could be more closely monitored, his discharge more controlled and his return to hospital if he deteriorated more readily achieved. Allowing his appeal against restriction, the Appeal Court noted that the sort of misconduct evidenced in his current offence 'is about the worst which can be foreseen'. The risk he presented did not justify s41. As Judge LJ put it:

> 'There should normally be some proportionate relationship between the instant offence and the history of offending, together with an assessment of risk on the basis of medical examinations before a s41 restriction is made.'

In *R v Kearney* [2002] EWCA Crim 2772 (unreported) the offender had been living in sheltered accommodation. Staff were concerned that his mental health was deteriorating but he resisted their efforts to persuade him to receive in-patient treatment. He produced a knife, threatening a community nurse who sustained a cut when she tried to restrain him. He pleaded guilty to common assault. He had two prior convictions for attempting to rob shops using a knife, though these had been committed several years previously. He was suffering paranoid schizophrenia and the psychiatrists treating him were recommending a hospital order, though they were not agreed whether restriction was justified. Two other consultants who had been asked to report considered that, given the offender's good level of insight into his illness and usual willingness to receive treatment, the appropriate course might be a community rehabilitation order. Upholding his appeal against s41, the Appeal Court considered that the overall history and the balance of the professional evidence did not justify a restriction order.

Restriction Justified

The following illustrations primarily concern offences of arson or violence which will almost inevitably pose substantial concern for public safety.

In *R v Beaumont* (1998, unreported) the offender, who had previously been diagnosed with severe borderline personality disorder, had set fire to her flat, then called the fire brigade. On further assessment, she was found to have been misdiagnosed as her true disorder was schizophrenia. Appropriate treatment was considered likely to reduce the risk of serious harm considerably. Dismissing her appeal against a s41 order, the Appeal Court noted that the making of a restriction order did not demonstrate any lack of faith in the hospital treating her. As Moses J put it:

> 'Setting fire to premises, even if it is difficult for them to ignite successfully, is likely to cause serious harm to others who may be affected by fire. ... There was a risk of serious harm despite the correct diagnosis of her symptoms.'

In *R v Goode* [2002] EWCA Crim 1698 (unreported) the offender aged 49, a long-term sufferer from paranoid schizophrenia but without previous convictions or episodes of violence, had stabbed his sleeping son unexpectedly but repeatedly with a knife in the delusional belief that he was in league with evil forces. His mental health had deteriorated after he had opted to pursue alternative therapy rather than conventional medication. Neither psychiatrist reporting to the Crown Court considered a s41 order necessary as the offender's condition was very manageable under medication combined with professional and family vigilance, and he was considered unlikely to commit further violence. The judge had taken a different view, given the very dangerous nature of the attack. Dismissing the appeal, the Appeal Court concluded that the judge had been right to conclude that a risk of further relapse did exist, that the level of vigilance required would need to be very high, and that the harm that might result in the event of relapse, given this present instance of extreme violence, could be very serious.

In *R v Griffith* [2002] EWCA Crim 1838 (unreported) the offender had attacked with a knife police officers who had attended his mother's home in light of a reported disturbance. He had been suffering paranoid schizophrenia which was responding well to treatment since his arrest for affray (an attempted murder charge was not proceeded with). Psychiatric advice was that a s41 order was not required as this incident had arisen at an early stage in his psychiatric history and he had not shown a sustained pattern of dangerous behaviour, though he had stabbed himself in the stomach in the year prior to the affray. The judge concluded that he had shown enough of a pattern of potentially dangerous behaviour to justify a restriction order and that it would not be right to wait until 'something else happened which might next time be someone's death'. Dismissing his appeal, the Appeal Court said that his improvement under treatment was a matter for the MHRT that would review his detention.

In *R v Chalk* [2002] EWCA Crim 2435 (unreported) the offender with a history of less serious but persistent acts of aggression, associated with his severe delusional and grandiose state leading to two s37 orders, had attempted to rob a post office, trying to use his hand in his pocket to give the impression of a gun. When he was refused money, he said he would not leave unless he was given £100 and he remained on the premises until the police arrived. In light of psychiatric advice that a s41 order was required, the judge said that he was fortified by this in his view that really serious harm might well be caused in the future. Dismissing his appeal against the order as unjustified, the Appeal Court noted that in the recent past he had demanded money from a bank armed with a potato and had previously placed a lighted newspaper through a shop letter box. Although the doctors had expressed their conclusions in terms of the risk of re-offending rather than the risk of serious harm, as they should have done, it was evident from his previous arson initiative that 'any repetition of such action would be likely to cause serious harm to the public'.

Sentencing in Practice

As a reflection of the recent use made of ss37/41, the *Statistics of Mentally Disordered Offenders 2001* (Johnson and Taylor, 2002) show that 239 restricted patients were admitted to hospital by this route in that year, an increase from 212 in 2000. In the decade 1991 (156 s41 admissions) to 2001, the average annual admission under this provision was 222 patients. Of the 239 s41 patients admitted in 2001, the overwhelming majority (203, 85%) were considered to be suffering mental illness, a further 10 being categorised as having mental illness in tandem with another disorder, leaving only 26 in another category of disorder (nine having psychopathic disorder and 12 mental impairment). *Criminal Statistics 2000* (Supplementary Vol. 2, Home Office, 2001) record only 35 men and one woman receiving s41 disposals (including for an offence of abstracting electricity in one instance) in that year (in contrast to 212 admissions recorded in the *MDO* Statistics) which appears to reflect a substantial shortfall in police recording procedures.

Street (1998) studied a sample of 372 offenders who received s41 orders in 1992 and 1993, all but 23 (6%) receiving orders without limit of time. Of those 23, the time limit ranged from one to seven years, with an average of five years. Those given time-limited orders were significantly less likely to have caused death and were also less likely to have been convicted of serious violence or arson. In other respects they did not differ from those given indefinite orders. The sample were aged from 16 to 84 with an average of 31 years, three-quarters being between 21 and 40. Though the majority of the sample were white (70%), some 21% were of black African/Caribbean ethnicity, higher than would be expected from their proportion in the population.

Offences

Just under a half of the total sample (49%) had been convicted of GBH (30%), manslaughter (16%) or attempted murder (11%); 13% of arson and 11% of sexual offences.

Diagnosis

The clear majority of the sample (77%) were diagnosed as mentally ill, with a further 13% as psychopathically disordered, 6% as mentally impaired and the remaining 4% as both mentally ill and having psychopathic disorder. Some 69% had been psychiatric in-patients before and, of these, 65% had been subject to compulsory detention under the Mental Health Act.

Criminal History

Nearly three in four had a prior criminal record, two-thirds for a sexual or violent offence. Four in ten of the sample had served at least one custodial sentence.

Psychiatric Recommendation

Though 70% of the sample were assessed as presenting a risk to others, s41 orders were expressly recommended in 41% of cases, although doctors often mentioned restriction orders as a possibility for the court to decide upon or recommended a s37 order involving detention in conditions of high security. Only 1% of reports expressly opposed a restriction order.

Judicial and Psychiatric Perspectives
The predominant opinion among seven judges interviewed perceived s41 orders as a means of protecting the public by removal from circulation, secure detention and restriction of discharge, some feeling that restriction status would guarantee patients treatment resources. Some judges considered that if a case was serious enough to come before the Crown Court and the defendant was sufficiently disordered to warrant a hospital order, then it would be rare not to add a restriction order. Psychiatrists (sample of six) also stressed the importance of public safety but placed more emphasis on s41 as a framework for ensuring long-term treatment, including ensuring compliance with medication, and supervision in the community. The real value of restriction for psychiatrists lay in the conditional discharge system and as a route to good quality community care. Section 41 status was felt to make little difference to a patient's management or care while in hospital.

Further evidence of the attitudes and practice of forensic psychiatrists regarding restriction orders can be gained from a survey conducted by Humphries *et al* (1998), yielding returns from 74 practitioners across the UK.

Recommendations in Reports to Court
Asked their approach when they considered a restriction order to be appropriate, 33 (45%) said that they would specifically state a view that such an order was necessary, 27 (36%) that they would make no mention of it and 14 (19%) that their practice would vary according to the circumstances of the individual case.

Time-Limited Restriction
Fifty-four (73%) of the respondents had never recommended a time-limited order but 20 had done so at least once. Forty (54%) stated that they would never regard such provision as appropriate.

Recommendations and Type of Offence
Twenty respondents said they would not automatically recommend a restriction order for a particular type of offence but 18 said that they would so recommend in any case of homicide, 12 in any instance of rape, and 10 in respect of sexual offending against children.

Basis of Recommendation
Sixty-eight (91%) indicated that retribution played minimal or no part in their thinking when making such recommendations, while a similar number stated that a high risk to the public in the event of relapse was a most important consideration. Other factors cited included ensuring adequate long-term follow-up, with extra supervision and scrutiny. The researchers suggest that recommendations for restriction orders may increase as practitioners come to regard this tool as a desirable alternative to unwieldy and possibly ineffective measures introduced by MH(PC)A 1995 (see page 94).

Court Concordance
Eight (10%) had experience of a court declining to make a restriction order despite such a recommendation. Seventeen (23%) has been involved in cases where a restriction

order had been made when their written recommendation and oral evidence had been to the contrary. Only eight were aware of conflicting evidence being heard in cases where their own recommendations were not accepted.

Limited Duration Restriction Orders

To gain a clearer understanding of the making and value of s41 orders of fixed duration Romilly *et al* (1997) reviewed their use in the ten years following the introduction of MHA 1983, identifying that 73 such orders were imposed, from three to 11 per year, accounting for 5% of all s41 orders. The typical duration was three years, though the range was from nine months to seven years. In only 11 instances had a psychiatrist specifically recommended a time-limited order but in only three instances had a link been drawn between prognosis and recommendation. Among justifications offered by psychiatrists when their views were sought by the researchers were:

(i)   an assumption that three or four years' compliance under statutory restriction would serve to ensure longer-term co-operation after the restriction had lapsed;

(ii)   that the fixed term proposed would provide ample time to assess treatability;

(iii) that limited duration provided a compromise between staff views opposed to restriction and the judge's preference for an unlimited order;

(iv)   that the fixed period reflected the time that the defendant could otherwise have expected to spend in prison.

Evidence for a tariff-based, punitive approach to imposing time-limited restriction was found in judges' sentencing comments, suggesting that courts have sought to reflect the seriousness of the offence. Longer determinate orders tended to be associated with more serious offences.

DELAY IN MAKING HOSPITAL ORDER

Scarcity of available bedspace may require a sentencer to delay the making of a hospital order, despite the clear justification for this disposal. The implications in law have recently been considered in *R v Galfetti* [2002] EWCA Crim 1916 where the offender, suffering a schizo-affective disorder and known to psychiatric services for 35 years, had been convicted of possession of an offensive weapon and indecent assault. The Crown Court judge was satisfied that the appropriate disposal was a s37 order with a s41 restriction but was unable to make these orders until over nine months following conviction because a suitable place could not be provided for him. Some ten interim hearings occurred in the interim in a bid to achieve progress. The defendant had been transferred from prison to hospital under MHA 1983 s48 while remanded prior to conviction but he was subsequently transferred back to prison because of an erroneous decision by a MHRT. On his appeal he contended that the s37/s41 order had been wrong in principle because of excessive delay and because his rights under ECHR had been infringed, in particular his right under Article 6(1) to receive determination of the criminal charge against him within a reasonable time.

The Court of Appeal recognised that the problem is 'endemic' and had no hesitation in deeming the delay both excessive and highly regrettable, keeping the defendant in suspense and in detention for far too long and affecting his right to apply to a MHRT for his discharge. It noted that in such circumstances a court is 'disabled from affording justice in the way which Parliament has provided'. In such circumstances the judge should first 'make every effort to persuade the hospital authorities to find a suitable place', as had been done here. Second, 'there may come a time when, by reason of delay, a sentence other than a hospital order should be considered ... but it could scarcely ever be satisfactory if a court is constrained to pass a different sentence simply because an appropriate hospital place is not available'. Third, 'the court will take delay into account in deciding the eventual disposal'. In this instance the appropriateness of a s37/s41 order remained clear when eventually passed, despite the unfortunate delay. The judge's duty had been to hold the balance between the defendant's rights and the rights of the public to be protected. No other order could realistically have been made. Taking the delay and its consequences into consideration, it could not realistically be maintained that the judge had been wrong in principle to make that order. The appeal was thus dismissed.

CASE ILLUSTRATION I: SECTION 37 HOSPITAL ORDER
Jon Binns (19)
Offences:
1. Arson by setting fire to rubbish in a stairwell at a block of flats when frustrated that a friend kept him waiting, subsequently calling the fire brigade for the excitement of watching them in action; little damage was caused and he admitted the offence to fire officers. Though subject to a supervision order supervised by Social Services, a pre-sentence report was prepared by the Probation Service, which noted that Jon Binns was in the process of being assessed for adult day or residential psychiatric services and was also being transferred from Social Services' Youth Justice team to an Adult Disability team, and proposed deferment of sentence. Sentence was deferred for six months with the expectation that Jon Binns should comply with assessment procedures and with the Consultant in Developmental Psychiatry, and should not re-offend.

2. During the deferment period, he was arrested for burglary having been found at night in disused commercial premises with the intention of committing criminal damage. He had reported a break-in at the premises and as the police had not responded, entered with the intention of starting a fire. He was granted bail subject to a condition of 24 hours' home curfew unless accompanied by his mother or other brother. Despite his subsequent arrest and return to court for breach of his bail condition (without re-offending), he was re-bailed as before.

Previous Convictions
Five sets of juvenile convictions, including two for arson; the remainder for burglary or theft, dealt with by absolute discharge.

Personal and Psychiatric History
Placed at a special day school at age seven because of developmental difficulties and learning disability, he was first referred to Social Services at age 14 because of concern about his behaviour in reaction to his step-father's violence towards his mother. Jon Binns was often required to call the police to deal with such incidents and this appeared

to trigger his fascination with the emergency services. It was also learnt that he had been sexually abused by males outside the family. Having been excluded from school for theft, he was placed in a special residential school where he was sexually abused by older boys. Behaviour problems increased, ranging from self-harm to wandering at night and frequent 999 calls.

Having returned home at age 16, he committed a number of theft offences while spending time in the town centre with youths who ridiculed him and incited him to steal, following which he would report himself to the police. His first arson offence was setting fire to a small rubbish heap in the town centre. Having next set fire to disused commercial premises when frustrated that his football team had been defeated, he was assessed by a child psychiatrist and a multi-disciplinary assessment team and sentenced to a supervision order, being placed in a new residential school for 12 months, returning to his mother's home at age 18. He remained vulnerable to ridicule and exploitation by his own age group and sought out the company of police officers on public order duties.

Psychiatric Assessment for Magistrates' Courts
Jon Binns readily volunteered information about his habit of starting small fires and generally seeking out other instances when he could call the police, *eg* waiting outside nightclubs so that he could report fights, believing that the police would praise him. He experienced intense frustration and distress if he felt ignored by other people and sought compensation by wanting to participate in the drama and activity of emergency services procedures, subsequently enjoying the satisfaction of being questioned and processed by the police. He had limited insight, little sense of risks and consequences of his behaviour, and recalled his court appearances with a sense of accomplishment. The risk of repeated fire setting was high.

'He is suffering mild mental impairment making it appropriate for him to receive further treatment in a hospital, and also a personality disorder of a psychiatric type ... His seriously irresponsible conduct requires further management within a secure environment.'

As a bed was not available in the consultant's own secure unit, offer of a bed had been obtained from a private sector secure unit.

Sentence
After a further adjournment because the evidence about arrangements at the private unit, required by s37(4), was not produced, a s37 order was imposed.

Comment
This disposal was not challenged by the defence (nor by the defendant, who was elated to be receiving a police escort to hospital) and the court was clearly relieved that a professional 'solution' had emerged, as hoped at the time of the original deferment of sentence. The possibility of a psychiatric probation order with a requirement of in-patient and community treatment was not canvassed, though this was clearly worth consideration. The Probation Service had had minimal links with the case and would have found it difficult to resist the combined weight of health and Social Services expertise unless the defence had been prepared to challenge and cross-examine the medical opinion. The private unit might be able to deliver what is claimed (Lee-Evans,

1993) to be the strength of the private sector: thorough assessment and planning of local community arrangements, followed by early discharge and after-care.

CASE ILLUSTRATION II: HOSPITAL ORDER WITH UNLIMITED RESTRICTION

William Power (46)

Offences

GBH with intent (in the course of an encounter in a park with two men whom he believed were speaking about him, he squirted one in the eyes with lemon juice or similar irritant and, when they followed him back to his flat, he threw a nut and bolt from his window striking one on the head and also fired an air pistol at them); wounding (he called at the victim's address and squirted ammonia in his eyes).

Personal History

Following a university degree in science, he had been unable to sustain employment or training opportunities and his social functioning had gradually deteriorated, with a number of instances of bizarre, irrational and aggressive behaviour, coupled with self-neglect and social withdrawal.

Psychiatric History

First referred for psychiatric assessment leading to compulsory admission under MHA 1959 s29 at age 31, he was diagnosed as suffering paranoid schizophrenia, though his state of mind was considered to have suffered as a result of using hallucinogenic drugs during the previous ten years. At age 33 he was made subject of a hospital order for offences of threats to kill and common assault. Following discharge and frequent further referrals, brief hospital admissions and various criminal convictions, he appeared to function better during a brief period of marriage from age 41 to 43 to another psychiatric patient, but he was re-admitted to hospital at age 44 following an incident when he caused concern for 'wandering' with an axe in his hand.

Psychiatric Probation Order

Later that year, following discharge, he contacted the police alleging that teachers at a school near his home were assaulting pupils and indicated that he would take steps to kill or assault the teachers if the police took no action. On the following day he visited the school and assaulted a member of staff with a piece of wood with protruding nails. Convicted at Crown Court of ABH, he was placed on probation for three years with a requirement to receive treatment as directed by the reporting psychiatrist who diagnosed manic depression and was 'prepared to supervise his management', adding that Mr Power's 'compliance and co-operation might be better guaranteed if coupled with a probation order'. No pre-sentence report was sought and the Crown Court liaison probation officer informed the judge that the Probation Service could do nothing to help Mr Power's problems. The judge concluded that a probation order was simply a device, the only way of ensuring that if Mr Power did not co-operate with his treatment, he would be brought back before the Court.

The subsequent history of the order illustrates some of the problems which can arise. As Mr Power did not respond to any appointment letters, the supervising officer approached the psychiatrist a month after sentence and was told that this was the doctor's first knowledge of the existence of the order. As appointment letters were subsequently returned, indicating that Mr Power no longer resided at that address, breach proceedings were initiated on grounds of failure to notify change of address, leading to Mr Power's arrest. It then came to light that he had informed the Crown Court of his new address at time of sentence but this had been overlooked in subsequent notification of sentence. This left Mr Power with a continuing sense of grievance, despite the withdrawal of breach proceedings and an apology, inhibiting work with him. Though he kept all subsequent appointments, the supervising officer concluded that supervision was not viable and should be reduced gradually to monthly, three-monthly and ultimately six-monthly contact. This was agreed with the officer's SPO, as a legitimate exception to normal National Standards expectations of frequency of contact, and was approved by the psychiatrist who was continuing to see Mr Power for out-patient appointments.

Around 13 months after the making of the probation order Mr Power committed the wounding and GBH offences. When the police investigating the park incident found him hiding in his loft, they conveyed him to a psychiatric unit where he was admitted under MHA 1983 s3 and transferred immediately to the regional secure unit. A number of home-made rockets, explosives and incendiary devices were found at his home (he had previously been placed on probation at age 32 for possessing explosives). It was now apparent that he had not been taking his medication and that his mental state had been deteriorating, so that his psychiatrist now considered that he was very dangerous and should be prosecuted to gain his admission to a Special Hospital.

Making of Hospital Order
Noting Mr Power's response to medication and the regime of the Secure Unit, the Consultant Forensic Psychiatrist identified that he had been suffering 'a severe mental illness' (not specified) over the past 15 years and that attempts to maintain him in the community under a psychiatric probation order had been unsuccessful in preventing the deterioration of his mental condition. A hospital order was therefore proposed, with the addition of a restriction order so that Mr Power's discharge could be subject to the condition that he continued to take his medication, in the light of his past relapses and subsequent offending, and in the interests of public protection. The judge thus imposed a s37/s41 order without limit.

Eight months later while still an in-patient at the RSU, Mr Power appeared again before the Crown Court and pleaded guilty to possessing explosive substances and a further s37/s41 order was made.

CASE ILLUSTRATION III: HOSPITAL ORDER WITH FIXED RESTRICTION PERIOD
Adam Self (21)
Principal Offences
Robbery (entering a bank and handing over a note stating that he was carrying an explosive device that he would detonate unless money was handed over; the note had been written by another patient at the hospital where he was receiving voluntary treatment and stated Adam Self's name); burglary and criminal damage (forcing entry through the roof into a girlfriend's flat).

Previous Convictions
None.

Personal History
Child of a black mother and white father, he was adopted at age two but subsequently found great difficulty in developing a secure identity and positive self-image as the only black person in an exclusively white family, school and community. Dyslexia severely inhibited his educational development. In adolescence he felt considerable doubts about his adoptive parents' motives and sincerity.

Psychiatric History
Referred to a Child and Family Psychiatry Unit at age 12 following overdose and other indications of emotional disturbance and conflict with his adoptive parents. Substance abuse and other illicit drug use from age 14. A number of episodes of psychotic illness from age 17 leading to hospital admission (including MHA 1983 s5(2) and s3), characterised by 'elevated mood, irritability, paranoid thinking and auditory hallucinations'. Having committed the burglary/criminal damage offences, he was placed at a probation hostel but, in the light of concern about his mental health, was admitted to hospital as a voluntary patient and committed the robbery during that stay. After an initial remand to prison he was admitted to the regional secure unit under MHA 1983 s35.

Consultant's Opinion
Though the acute symptoms of psychosis had resolved and the precise nature of his recurrent mental disorder remained unclear, it certainly amounted to a mental illness within the meaning of MHA 1983. 'There is still some fragility of mood swing with suicidal ruminations' (he had attempted to hang himself using a sheet and had hidden various sharp objects in his room).

Medical Recommendation
After proposing a s37 hospital order, the consultant stated that in view of Adam Self's long history of mental illness and his poor response to supervision in the past, 'it could be argued that if he was subject to the conditions of a discharge under s41 then this may be beneficial with regard to future supervision. However, the Court may take the view that, given that Adam Self has no previous convictions, in conjunction with the nature of the robbery, leads to the conclusion that a restriction order is not necessary to protect the public from serious harm'.

Court's Decision
Following an adjournment to allow the consultant to attend to give oral evidence, the judge stated that he was 'satisfied that there is a risk of further offences if you are at large' but felt that the restriction order should be limited to seven years.

MENTAL HEALTH BILL

Part Three, Chapter Two of the draft Bill sets out proposed new powers of criminal courts to make mental health disposals and the effects of these disposals on the person concerned. In brief, hospital orders (including interim hospital orders under MHA 1983 s38) and guardianship orders under MHA 1983 s37 are replaced by mental health orders

(MHOs) under clause 78, supplemented by clauses 79-83. MHOs are of wider ambit than the hospital order as the treatment may be provided to 'non-resident' patients. The Crown Court's power to add a restriction order under MHA 1983 s41 is now provided in clause 84 in respect of 'resident patients' (see below).

Jurisdiction to Make a Mental Health Order

Clause 77 specifies that power to impose the proposed new order will lie with the Crown Court and magistrates' courts essentially on the same basis as the current power to make a hospital order, including scope for a magistrates' court to make an order without convicting the accused as under s37(3). However, a court may not consider making a s78 order unless a care plan has been submitted to it by an approved clinician describing the treatment which would be provided to the subject. (The court may appoint a member of the Expert Panel to assist it in determining whether to approve the care plan, with or without modifications.) In addition, the clinician must recommend, in relation to the Crown Court, whether or not a restriction order should be made and, if not, whether the person should be provided with treatment on a 'resident' or 'non-resident' basis.

Conditions to be Met for a MHO

Clause 78(2) to (5) specifies the following conditions of which the court must be satisfied, on appropriate evidence (*ie*, in respect of (i)-(iii) below, that of two registered medical practitioners and an 'approved mental health professional', as specified in regulations, and, in respect of (iv) below, the evidence of a representative of the managers of the hospital in question), are met in respect of the defendant:

(i) the person is suffering from mental disorder (defined by clause 2(6) to mean 'any disability or disorder of mind or brain which results in an impairment or disturbance of mental functioning';

(ii) that mental disorder is of such a nature or degree as to warrant the provision of medical treatment to the person;

(iii) appropriate medical treatment is available;

(iv) if the court is minded to order that treatment should be provided to the person as a resident patient, arrangements have been made for his admission within 28 days of the making of the order to the hospital to be specified in the order. If treatment is intended to be ordered on a non-resident basis, the court must be satisfied that arrangements have been made for the provision of that treatment.

The court must also be of the opinion, having regard to all the circumstances (including the nature of the offence, the person's character and antecedents) and the other available methods of dealing with him, that a MHO is the most suitable method of dealing with him.

Nature and Effect of MHO

The order must state that the care plan is approved, either as submitted or as modified in agreement with the clinician and as specified by the court (clause 79(2)). Further, an unrestricted order must state whether the person is to receive treatment as a resident or non-resident patient. If the latter, the order must specify requirements (see below).

Unless it includes a restriction order, the MHO must specify the period for which it is to be in force, which may not exceed six months.

Non-Resident Patient Requirements

The requirements shall be imposed to secure that the treatment may be provided to him or to protect his health or safety or other persons. These may include:

(a) a requirement that the person –

    (i) attends at a specified place at specified times;

    (ii) resides at a specified place;

    (iii) makes himself available for treatment during specified periods;

(b) a requirement that the person does not engage in specified conduct.

Further, the order must make a recommendation to the clinical supervisor as to the action which might be taken if the person fails to comply with the requirements or there is a material change in the person's circumstances. In either of these arise, clause 81(3) empowers the clinical supervisor to determine whether medical treatment should be provided to him as a resident patient, but regard must be had to any recommendation specified by the court. Such a determination authorises the taking and conveyance of the patient to hospital, within a period of 24 hours beginning with the making of the determination. Alternatively, the clinical supervisor may determine that different treatment may be provided on a non-resident basis and may thus accordingly amend the requirements specified in the order.

Incompatible Disposals

If a court makes a MHO it may not impose a custodial sentence, a community order, a referral order or a fine for the offence, nor grant a discharge, absolute or conditional, or make a parenting order or a parental binding over order. However, it may make any other order which it has power to make (for example a disqualification from driving).

Restriction Orders

Clause 84, supplemented by clauses 85-88, empowers the Crown Court to augment a mental health order in respect of resident patients by the making of a restriction order. This power essentially replicates the provisions of MHA 1983 s41, save that the new provision makes no provision for a fixed restriction period. All such orders will thus be indeterminate in effect. The new provisions are further summarised at the conclusion of Chapter 14.

FALLON REPORT

In specific regard to psychopathic disorder, it is worth noting the view of the Fallon Report (1999) that patients with personality disorder (the term it preferred) should receive an appropriate custodial sentence and then be transferred from prison to appropriate therapeutic facilities, assuming they are considered to be suitable for treatment. It thus recommended that personality disordered offenders should no longer be eligible to be made the subject of hospital orders. Some psychiatrists are already adopting this view in their reports to courts.

8
PSYCHIATRIC COMMUNITY REHABILITATION ORDERS

First introduced into statute in 1948, the power to make treatment for mental condition an additional requirement of a probation order (now renamed community rehabilitation order by CJCSA 2000) is provided by PCC(S)A 2000 sch 2 para. 5. The term 'psychiatric community rehabilitation order' is not statutory language but is convenient shorthand for this form of community supervision. A thematic inspection by HM Inspectorate of Probation (1993, referred to in this chapter as HMIP) threw light on relatively recent practice in making and supervising this sentence, albeit that the samples studied were all imposed before the implementation of CJA 1991. In the absence of a more up-to-date comprehensive study, reference will be made to HMIP, albeit that the work of supervising offenders in the community has been transformed in the last decade. Power to make a new form of community order, a drug treatment and testing order, was introduced by CDA 1998 but this disposal is not likely to be made where an offender has substantial mental health problems and so is not addressed in this volume (see Stone, 2001).

POWER TO MAKE THE ORDER

A community rehabilitation order of any kind may be imposed for an offence, whether imprisonable or not, where the following pre-requirements are met (PCC(S)A 2000 s41):

(i) the offender is aged 16 or more when convicted;

(ii) the court is satisfied that supervision is desirable in the interests of –

    – securing the offender's rehabilitation, or

    – protecting the public from harm from the offender or preventing the offender's commission of further offences;

(iii) the court has explained the effect and consequences of the order in ordinary language.

As a community rehabilitation order is a 'community sentence', the court is also required by PCC(S)A 2000 s35(1) to reach the opinion that:

(i) the offence, either alone or in combination with other offences being dealt with, is 'serious enough' to warrant such a sentence which restricts the offender's liberty; and

(ii) the order is the most suitable form of community order for the offender; and

(iii) the restrictions on liberty imposed by the order are commensurate with the seriousness of the offences(s).

Special Prerequisites

In the case of a psychiatric community rehabilitation order, the following additional prerequisites apply (PCC(S)A 2000 sch 2 para. 5(1) and (4):

(i)   the court has received evidence (whether orally or in writing) from a registered medical practitioner approved under MHA 1983 s12;

(ii) the court is satisfied on that evidence that the offender's mental condition 'requires and may be susceptible to treatment' but does not warrant the making of a hospital order or guardianship order under MHA 1983 s37;

(iii) the court is satisfied that 'arrangements have been or can be made for the treatment intended to be specified in the order (including arrangements for the reception of the offender where he is to be required to submit to treatment as a resident patient)';

(iv) the offender has expressed willingness to comply with such a requirement. (The extent to which a defendant has proper opportunity to give genuinely informed consent to the order being proposed by the court will depend in practice on the initiative of the defence solicitor, the PSR reporter and the sentencer.)

Supervision will be exercised by a probation officer assigned to the petty sessions area specified in the order or, in the case of an offender aged under 18 at time of sentence, either by a probation officer or by a YOT member (in practice, the latter): s41(5)

Suitability: Pre-Sentence Report

As a psychiatric treatment requirement is a Schedule 2 requirement, a court is required to obtain and consider a PSR before forming an opinion about the offender's suitability for this form of order (PCC(S)A 2000 s36(4), subject to the rider in s36(5) that this provision does not apply if, in the circumstances of the case, the court is of the opinion that it is unnecessary to do so, though in this context that is an unlikely conclusion. In the case of offenders aged under 18, where the offence is triable only on indictment, a court may not reach that conclusion unless it has access and regard to a PSR prepared in previous proceedings (even if the old report concerned unrelated offences): s36(6). If more than one previous report has been prepared, the most recent should be considered. The court may feel that it has enough information from the medical practitioner to proceed to sentence, though it would seem strongly desirable and self-evident good practice to seek an assessment by the prospective supervising agency as well.

R v Thompson [2003] EWCA Crim 49 provides an instance where the PSR argued against the psychiatrist's proposal for a psychiatric community rehabilitation order (CRO) and indicates not only the weight that courts can give to the Probation Service's opinion but also the importance for courts to avoid giving an implied promise when adjourning for further information when considering making such an order. The Crown Court judge had been faced with a defendant whom the reporting psychiatrist assessed to be 'undoubtedly suffering from psychotic illness characterised by various bizarre delusional beliefs', aggravated by his illicit drug misuse, with a history of behavioural and emotional problems suggesting anti-social personality disorder. He had committed various offences during the 'at risk' period of a 30-month term of imprisonment for robbery, including racially aggravated threatening behaviour, witness intimidation, burglary and dangerous driving. The psychiatrist felt that a hospital order was not necessary as 'he can be managed in the community if he is compliant'. Though the longer-term prognosis was not encouraging, a sch 2 para. 5 requirement in a community rehabilitation order would enable mental health services to maintain regular contact with him. In light of this advice the case was adjourned, to ascertain if the psychiatrist was willing to act as nominated medical practitioner if a CRO was made and to enable the Probation Service to comment on such a proposal (a previous PSR had been unable to make any sentencing recommendation without the benefit of a psychiatric opinion). The doctor duly confirmed his willingness to act. However, the probation officer expressed concerns about the defendant's ability and motivation to comply, 'having regard to his inconsistent contact with the psychiatric services in the past'. The judge then imposed prison terms totalling four years, consecutive to 52 days for which he was returned to prison in respect of his earlier robbery sentence.

On appeal, the offender argued that in adjourning the case on the basis described without warning him that a custodial sentence remained an option, the judge had given the impression that a CRO would result if the doctor was willing to be identified. However, the Appeal Court rejected this submission, pointing out that the adjournment had also been designed to secure the Probation Service's view. It was clear that the service considered that a CRO would be inappropriate because of the offender's past inability to comply with medication and doctors' appointments. The judge's decision to heed that view was entirely proper, though the Appeal Court observed that the correct practice on adjournment would have been to have stated that custody might result, notwithstanding any information elicited from either source.

Range and Length of Treatment Requirements
PCC(S)A 2000 sch 2 para. 5

(2) ... the community rehabilitation order may include a requirement that the offender shall submit, during the whole of the community rehabilitation period or during such part or parts of that period as may be specified in the order, to treatment by or under the direction of a registered medical practitioner or a chartered psychologist (or both, for different parts) with a view to the improvement of the offender's mental condition.

(3) The treatment required by any such order shall be such one of the following kinds of treatment as may be specified in the order, that is to say –

    (a) treatment as a resident patient in a hospital or mental nursing home within the meaning of MHA 1983, but not hospital premises at which high security psychiatric services within the meaning of that Act are provided;

    (b) treatment as a non-resident patient at such institution or place as may be specified in the order; and

    (c) treatment by or under the direction of such duly qualified medical practitioner or chartered psychologist (or both) as may be so specified;

but the nature of the treatment shall not be specified in the order except as mentioned in paragraph (a), (b) or (c) above.

Community Punishment and Rehabilitation Orders
A community sentence imposed under PCC(S)A 2000 s51 combines the two elements of community punishment and community rehabilitation within a single order (formerly

known as a combination order). The community rehabilitation element (which must be made for a minimum period of 12 months) may include additional requirements, including a requirement as regards mental treatment, though the court would need to be satisfied that this could be imposed compatibly with the demands of community punishment work. Community punishment would clearly not be readily compatible with a requirement of in-patient treatment. A community punishment and rehabilitation order may be imposed only for an offence punishable by imprisonment.

AN ANALYSIS OF THE ORDER

Psychiatric community rehabilitation orders can thus be imposed more flexibly and with greater procedural ease than hospital orders (MHA 1983 s37), as follows:

- Evidence from only one medical practitioner is sufficient.

- It is not necessary for the offender to be suffering one of the four forms of mental disorder specified in s37 (see page 84). It is sufficient that the patient's mental condition requires and is susceptible to treatment. 'Mental condition' is not defined. The scope for discretion is clearly open to misuse, so that psychiatric orders are frequently made where the offender has no clearly identifiable illness or mental disorder. The HMIP Inspection (para. 3.14) found that:

  'A significant number of psychiatric reports ended with opinions that the subject was not mentally ill or even obviously disordered, was unlikely to respond to treatment (in at least one case explicitly not suitable for it) but that the psychiatrist was willing to see the person if the court wished to make a probation order with a requirement for treatment. In a number of cases where reports indicated the offender was in hospital and by inference likely to stay, discharge in fact took place almost immediately after the order was made.'

  This observation is echoed by a recent study of mental health problems in probation caseloads (Hudson *et al*, 1993) which found that, in a third of cases subject to treatment requirements, the supervising probation officer was unable to state a diagnosis.

- Treatment can consist of either in-patient or out-patient services or simply the more open-ended formula: 'by or under the direction of' a specified doctor. The spectrum of treatment thus ranges widely from admission to the quasi-custodial confinement of a regional secure unit to out-patient monitoring on a monthly or less frequent basis. CJPOA 1994 extended the range by introducing treatment by a 'chartered psychologist', *ie* a person so listed in the British Psychological Society Register. Thus, in the light of the parallel change allowing treatment to be specified during more than one period or 'part' of the order, an order might specify treatment by a doctor for a part of the order and by a psychologist for another part, though it does not appear possible for treatment by each professional to run in tandem, and this would certainly cause problems where the two professionals are in conflict about the needs of the patient.

- There is no requirement for admission to in-patient treatment to occur within 28 days of the date of the order.

- Following discharge from in-patient treatment, the offender-patient remains subject to statutory supervision (and usually continuing psychiatric oversight), whereas the discharged hospital order patient is free of liability but also may not receive any after-care follow-up.

HMIP (1993) noted the 'widespread ignorance among probation officers and managers of the law about requirements and the safeguards to the individual', so that 'the nature of the requirements for treatment as finally inserted by the court varied widely ... many not following the wording of the Act' (para. 3.20). This laxness had implications later if breach proceedings were contemplated (see page 130).

It is possible to combine both a treatment requirement and another sch 2 condition, provided that these are compatible. Thus a requirement of residence made under sch 2 para. 1, *eg* at an approved probation hostel, may be appropriate though not if the offender is 'suffering from severe subnormality or psychopathic disorder within the meaning of MHA 1983' (APBHR 1995 para. 12). HMIP noted (para. 6.3) that a number of wardens of approved probation hostels had taken probationers receiving psychiatric treatment and considered that this could be satisfactory provided the conditions and supports were right.

SENTENCING: PRINCIPLES AND PRACTICE
Court of Appeal Guidance
Limited guidance has been given by the Court of Appeal about the appropriate use of psychiatric probation/community rehabilitation orders since CJA 1991. In a few instances prior to implementation of the 1991 Act, the Court had indicated that such an order could be properly imposed in cases where a custodial sentence would otherwise be expected. In *R v Hoof* (1980) 2 Cr App R(S) 299, sentence of three years' imprisonment, neither 'wrong in principle or excessive', imposed on a 19 year-old offender for arson with intent to endanger life (setting fire to two dwellings in which the occupants were asleep and a car), was set aside in favour of a probation order with a requirement of psychiatric treatment 'as directed' but also a requirement of residence at a probation hostel. The Court of Appeal placed emphasis on a report from the custodial establishment where the offender had been serving sentence that his response was 'very good without being obsequious' and that he was demonstrating 'regretful resignation' to his sentence.

In *R v Taylor* (1983) 5 Cr App R(S) 241, a 21 year-old man with marked mental retardation was convicted of rape of a young woman with Down's Syndrome who attended the same special school. Given that he had desisted without full penetration and that his understanding of sexuality was severely limited, the Court of Appeal felt that this was a 'wholly exceptional case'. His behaviour was considered to be 'sexual exploration with no understanding of the possible consequences'.

> 'He did not appreciate at the time that what he was doing was not just something that he ought not to be doing but that it was something that was very wicked indeed.' (*per* Peter Pain J)

Noting that he had been subject to Rule 43 segregation (now Rule 45) in prison – 'just the wrong sort of thing for someone who has to be helped to live in the community' – and was not a serious danger to the public, the Court of Appeal overturned three years' imprisonment in favour of a probation order with requirement of both residence and treatment (as demonstration that the Court of Appeal can get things wrong, the Court ordered 'that he accept the probation officer's advice regarding medical treatment as agreed by his doctors, be this as an in-patient or out-patient' – clearly an irregular specification).

In *R v McDonald* (1983) 5 Cr App R(S) 419, the offender aged 24 had indecently assaulted a girl aged 11 on her way home from school. The Court of Appeal considered that the offence required either a 'substantial term of imprisonment or an individualised sentence which would assist the defendant and in the end assist and protect the public'. Two years' imprisonment was replaced by a probation order with a requirement of out-patient treatment coupled with a requirement to reside in accommodation close to the treatment centre arranged by the Probation Service.

In *R v Jones* (1992) 13 Cr App R(S) 275, sentence of four years' imprisonment for seven counts of robbery of building society branches was varied on appeal to probation with a requirement of out-patient treatment in the light of reports indicating that at the time of the offences the appellant 'was virtually out of her mind with desperation at her financial position'.

Such decisions may need to be viewed with caution in the light of the more distinct boundary between custodial and community sentences introduced by CJA 1991, as demonstrated by *Attorney-General's Reference No.20 of 1994* [1995] Crim LR 182. The offender aged 40 had unlawful sexual intercourse with a girl aged 12, a member of the majorette group which he trained. The Court of Appeal overturned a probation order with a requirement of psychiatric treatment and indicated that four years' imprisonment was the appropriate sentence, given his abuse of a position of trust, the element of corruption and his normal level of intelligence.

> 'The element of psychiatric or therapeutic need was not such as to bring the offender into the rare category of those who could be regarded as having a lesser criminal responsibility and therefore capable of being disposed of by means of a probation order with a condition of treatment'. (*per* Lord Taylor CJ)

This kind of dilemma had been presented in the pre-1991 Act case of *R v Cartwright* (1989) *The Times*, 18 April where the offender, who suffered a manic-depressive condition, had driven recklessly under the influence of alcohol during a hyper-manic episode, endangering life. The Court of Appeal overturned a custodial sentence in favour of a psychiatric probation order, indicating that the paramount consideration was to ensure that the offender received regular medical treatment and advice under supervision. As the Court had no power to require the offender to undergo medical treatment on release from a custodial sentence, and it would not be right to leave him to his own devices, the Court considered that it was in the public interest to set aside what was otherwise an appropriate custodial sentence in favour of a more constructive and rehabilitative disposal. This course is certainly open to the court under the provisions of PCC(S)A 2000 s158(3), outlined on page 154. The potential merits of therapeutic treatment may allow the court to take an exceptional course, even in cases of some seriousness.

In *R v Bunjo* [2001] EWCA Crim 1453 (unreported), an instance of robbery of a petrol station using an imitation firearm, use of a psychiatric community rehabilitation order seemed justified on a combination of reduced culpability on account of pre-offence mental disorder, combined with a strong professional view that although detention in hospital was no longer necessary, the offender still had psychiatric needs which would be better met via such a community disposal. The offender, aged 38 and regarded as of previous good character, had been transferred to hospital under MHA 1983 s48 during a remand period totalling 12 months. Doctors were unable to agree the nature of his mental disorder, though schizophrenia or a depressive illness with psychotic features were considered the most likely problem. By time of sentence he had responded well to treatment and a s37 order was not considered necessary. In light of this advice the judge concluded that a probation order would not be appropriate and that custody was the only viable alternative. This prompted a reporting psychiatrist to submit an unsolicited addendum stating that the defendant continued to suffer a depressive illness that required 'further intensive treatment if his mental health is not to deteriorate'. Though acknowledging that an immediate prison sentence might well cause such deterioration, the judge considered that this would be a matter for the Prison Service to deal with and said that this could not serve to 'reduce the normal tariff of sentence for this sort of offence'.

On his appeal against a three-year term of imprisonment, it was argued on his behalf that the judge had failed to have regard to PCC(S)A 2000 s82(3) (see page 154) and that insufficient regard had been given to his reduced culpability on account of his mental state at time of the robbery. The Court heeded the most up-to-date assessment from a psychiatrist and a probation officer favouring a CRO and determined to impose a psychiatric order, indicating that it had particularly in mind the evidence of 'an existing illness before the offence was committed'. It seems also worth noting that the psychiatric community order promised to help in maintaining the offender's improved mental health, whereas imprisonment could cause this to deteriorate.

Compare *R v Thatcher* [2002] EWCA Crim 1310, an instance of robbery at knifepoint of a taxi office committed by a 20 year-old homeless woman of previous good character in the company of an older man with criminal experience whom she had just met in a homeless persons' shelter. A psychiatric report diagnosed 'emotionally unstable borderline personality disorder' and recommended a community rehabilitation order with a treatment requirement. Dismissing her appeal against a term of 54 months' YOI, the Appeal Court noted her 'sad history' of physical and sexual abuse but concluded that a substantial custodial sentence was inevitable.

Attorney-General's Reference No. 83 of 2001 (Fidler) [2002] 1 Cr App R(S) 588 provides a contrasting instance where the Appeal Court has favoured the benefits of a psychiatric order instead of a tariff-based disposal, albeit in circumstances involving substantial mitigation. The offender had robbed an off-licence armed with a metal bar but he was not suspected of the crime. A few days later he was admitted to hospital as a voluntary patient where he disclosed his offence to his psychiatrist and a nurse, agreeing that they should break confidence and inform the police. Medical reports to the Crown Court had identified that he suffered schizophrenia, 'complicated by substance misuse and criminal behaviour' and had been experiencing auditory delusions prior to the robbery. His condition was now considered stable and compliant with treatment during the preceding seven months as an in-patient and he was assessed as likely to respond to careful management. One psychiatrist proposed a guardianship order but the offender's own consultant considered that this 'lacked sufficient teeth' for the purposes of his medical oversight and thus proposed a community rehabilitation order, affording clear breach powers.

Dismissing the Attorney-General's Reference on grounds that the resulting order was unduly lenient, the Court of Appeal considered this an instance where 'the individual circumstances of the offender and the mitigation available to him have led to a justified departure from the guidance' of reported decisions on robbery. In particular, the offender had sought treatment, made an unsolicited confession when he was not under any suspicion and was continuing to make good progress. It was thus justified for the judge to opt for a constructive course that was 'likely to provide both the offender and the community with the best long-term solution' to his problems through his full rehabilitation. Though the sentence was lenient, the balancing exercise had been properly conducted.

R v Arthur [2001] EWCA Crim 405 (unreported) also emphasised the importance of the mental disorder as a factor in assessing culpability. This case featured arson being reckless whether life would be endangered. Feeling depressed and sorry for himself on Christmas Day, and in a fit of frustration and temper aggravated by alcohol, the offender had started a fire in his own home. He had a history of chronic mood disorder, complicated by his drinking pattern and indications of brain (temporal lobe) dysfunction. The judge imposed a three-year prison term. On his appeal, the Appeal Court recognised:

'the balance to be struck between the need to punish and deter on the one hand and the possibility of rehabilitation and cure, if this is best to be achieved by a non-custodial means. It is always a matter of degree whether an offender's medical condition is such that his responsibility for his actions is reduced to a point where punishment as such may not be appropriate'.

As the Court considered that there was a strong possibility that the offender was suffering from a mental condition, or a combination of conditions, that had a considerable bearing on his mental state at the time', it felt able to substitute a CRO with a sch 2 para. 5 requirement combined with anger management course attendance (it is noteworthy that in making this order the Court omitted to establish the offender's willingness to comply).

R v Burns [2001] EWCA Crim 756 (unreported) featured two instances of public disorder directed against a shopkeeper well known to the offender. His record included previous occasions of violence, disorder and offensive weapons. A psychiatric report referred to the impact of loss of family members coupled with seeing a neighbour shot, causing post-traumatic disorder which was untreated and led to depression and self-medicating reliance on alcohol. He had attempted suicide. He now recognised his need for treatment, a view endorsed by the PSR which also pointed out the potentially counter-productive consequences of imprisonment. In sentencing him to a total of six months' imprisonment, the judge had observed that 'simply because he was depressed did not excuse the type of behaviour that he had exhibited' and that it was right that the court protected vulnerable small shopkeepers, adding that he could 'get on with seeing a psychologist' after his release.

On appeal, the Appeal Court appeared to agree that, though a custodial sentence had been 'essential' so that 'a local message should go out ... that attacks on corner shopkeepers will not be tolerated', at time of appeal when he was approaching release and the general deterrent purpose of imprisonment had been achieved, it was appropriate to substitute a psychiatric community rehabilitation order to provide a structured community programme, only possible through that means. With respect, this stance which can be characterised as 'having your cake and eating it', marking the seriousness and unacceptability of the misbehaviour while enabling a package of supervision that would not otherwise be attainable, does not offer much assistance to sentencers at first instance. Perhaps this is the kind of case that may attract a 'custody plus' sentence (page 168) following passage of the current Criminal Justice Bill.

R v Dowie [2002] EWCA Crim 27 (unreported) provides a further instance in which a switch to a psychiatric CRO was felt justified at appeal stage, after the initial punitive impact of the original sentence had served its purpose and had seemingly served to sharpen the offender's motivation to participate in treatment. It was also of significance that community-based treatment was considered likely to be more productive, given the offender's past adverse experience of institutional life.

The offender aged 19 had broken into a family home in the early morning, acting in a very violent and uncontrolled manner when confronted. He had numerous previous convictions, including offences of violence and disorder. A psychiatric report detailed his history of ill-treatment from early childhood and the failure of institutional care to provide him with emotional security or control over his disruptive and anti-social behaviour. His extreme vulnerability required 'therapeutic intervention focusing on the abuse he suffered in childhood'. Treatment was considered unlikely to be successful in an institutional setting where he would be at increased risk of suicide. However, the judge concluded that the nature and frequency of his offending meant that 'the need for (him) to be contained outweighs the substantial arguments' for a therapeutic disposal. The judge was not convinced that he would be able to respond to therapy at that stage.

On his appeal against a four-year custodial term, the Appeal Court had a further psychiatric assessment indicating that the personal deterrent impact of custody had already been achieved and the offender had shown his willingness to work with the psychiatric services to overcome his depression and tackle his personality problems. It concluded that though no criticism could be made of the judge's decision to impose a custodial sentence, the offender's age, background and need to address his problems sooner rather than later meant that four years was rather too long. Further, it was desirable now in the public interest, 'following ... the short, sharp shock of a prison sentence ... to capitalise on (his) substantially improved attitude'.

R v Gibson [2001] EWCA Crim 656 (unreported) presents an instance where the Court of Appeal opted not to use the opportunity of appeal to substitute a psychiatric CRO for a custodial sentence despite agreeing that this would have been the proper disposal at Crown Court. The offender aged 21 had joined with others in burglary of an old cemetery and disinterring a body from a coffin in a crypt. He was diagnosed as suffering from Asperger's Syndrome, having an obsession with death and insects, and said by the probation officer to present a high risk of self-harm. Since arrest he had co-operated well with treatment, drawing some comfort from the diagnosis which had helped to explain his difference from other people. He was likely to need help for some years to come. As he had by now served the equivalent of a six-month term, the Appeal Court simply reduced sentence of 18 months' imprisonment to six months, so as to allow his immediate release. This meant that he would not be subject to statutory supervision but the Court appears to have judged that his excellent co-operation with his clinical psychologist, CPN and key worker indicated that he did not require the structure of a CRO to facilitate further treatment.

R v Hayward [2001] EWCA Crim 3070 (unreported) can be contrasted with *R v Higgins* [1996] 1 Cr App R(S) 271, both featuring wives killing their husbands and facing sentence for manslaughter on grounds of diminished responsibility. In *Higgins* the wife had suffered domestic violence from her husband. When he handed her a knife during one such episode, challenging her to stab him, she did so. Given her clinical depression, the violence and provocation offered, her remorse and the feelings of the deceased's family in her support, the Appeal Court was persuaded that a custodial sentence would not serve any further useful purpose and substituted a probation order with a treatment requirement. In *Hayward* the wife had stabbed her husband with a carving knife having picked it up to frighten him in the course of a quarrel. In this case too the offender was suffering a depressive illness and had been under increasing stress. She felt considerable remorse and the family wanted her release. However, on her appeal against two years' imprisonment, arguing that she should have been dealt with by a psychiatric CRO (or a suspended sentence), the Appeal Court concluded that the case fell on the other side of the line to *Higgins*. In particular, she had not been subject to direct violence from the victim, rather intimidated by his bullying personality. An immediate custodial sentence was necessary but, in light of the family's feelings, the Court reduced the term to permit her immediate release, as an act of substantial mercy.

R v Crittenden [2002] EWCA Crim 2859 (unreported) presented a further instance of family violence, the offender, of previous good character, attacking his brother repeatedly with a knife in response to a mild slight. Psychiatrists advising the judge found this a complex case without a clear diagnosis. The most recent opinion had been that he was of relatively low intelligence with schizophrenic traits and in consequence 'solitary, introspective and emotionally blunted'. The psychiatrist conclude that he required a long period of community treatment in which he could develop a good relationship with his professional helpers. On his appeal against eight years' imprisonment for s18 wounding, the Appeal Court found the proposal of a community disposal quite unrealistic, given this savage and frenzied attack, but substituted an extended sentence comprising a five-year custodial term with a three-year extension as a means of facilitating the psychiatrist's view.

Practice Dilemmas and Possibilities

Community rehabilitation orders, with their emphasis on rehabilitation and help, do not fit easily within the framework of sentencing introduced by the 1991 Act and this form of probation has been particularly difficult to locate in a discourse centred on punishment, commensurability and restriction of liberty. As Lewis (1980) pointed out in his study of psychiatric probation orders in Nottinghamshire in the late 1970s, such orders constitute an uneasy meeting point of very different disciplines: the law, medicine and social work. Now the tensions are more acute as the Health Service's concern for treatment, offered essentially on the basis of the patient's need, free consent and active co-operation (outside of the enforced detention and treatment authorised by MHA 1983), has to be reconciled with a sentencing approach which in this context locates psychiatric treatment, like any other additional probation requirement, primarily as an additional element of penalty and restriction of liberty, backed by sanctions in the event of non-co-operation. Addressing the 'central dilemma' of punishment *v* treatment posed by psychiatric probation orders, HMIP (para. 4.6) commented:

> 'Many of the problems and frustrations observed in the supervision of these orders appear to have some root in a failure by those concerned to address and come to an accommodation and agreement about these fundamental issues ... Pretending they do not exist is a recipe for frustration, waste of resources and ineffectiveness.'

Despite the encouragement offered to chief probation officers by HOC 66/1990 (para. 26(iii)) to 'facilitate a wider use of treatment and non-custodial disposals, including ... psychiatric probation orders', and the recommendation in the Reed Report that 'the possible use of probation orders with a condition of psychiatric treatment should be considered more frequently' (para. 11.17), HMIP were wary of promoting greater use of this sentence, preferring instead to advocate resources and schemes for diverting mentally disordered offenders away from prosecution into the health, rather than the criminal justice, system and improving the quality of advice to courts (para. 2.14).

HMIP recognised the superficial or expedient attractiveness of psychiatric probation orders for sentencers and practitioners when faced with difficult, complex decisions about potentially dangerous or high risk offenders. Many of the offenders in their study sample:

> 'presented the courts with agonising decisions balancing culpability, sympathy for the offender, danger to the public, fears of violence and madness, bizarre behaviour and strong defence pleading. It seemed likely that quite often probation orders with requirements for treatment were seen as a way out of the court's dilemma rather than a more objective decision based on soundly prepared and weighed expert evidence from doctor and probation officer alike.' (para. 3.16)

> 'With hindsight about what happened almost immediately after the court hearing and in view of the complexities surrounding the preparation of reports, it was difficult to escape the conclusion that courts often did not fully understand the proposals that were put before them and, in a small proportion of cases were being, wittingly or unwittingly, misled.' (para. 3.17)

Probation officers can feel that a formal treatment requirement can act as a useful lever to gain priority access to community mental health resources. However, HMIP (para. 7.16) suggested that increasing Health and Social Services experience of offenders' needs should ensure that services are provided on the basis of need rather than compulsion.

In so far as it is possible to offer some rudimentary guidelines to bear in mind when considering the possibility of a psychiatric community rehabilitation order as a sentence, the HMIP report prompts the following considerations:

- Start by considering the seriousness of the offences to be dealt with; do not propose the inclusion of an additional requirement under sch 2 para. 5 if this would be disproportionately restrictive for offences of a less serious nature merely because it appears to reflect either the defendant's needs or the offer of psychiatric treatment.

- Propose a psychiatric order only if there is a clear consensus and agreed treatment plan negotiated by the psychiatrist (or psychologist) and the probation officer. As HMIP (para. 7.11) noted:

  'If there is uncertainty in the medical recommendation, it is likely that a straight probation order would be a more realistic option. This would enable treatment to proceed on a truly voluntary basis and avoid the ethical difficulty of breach proceedings if the patient does not wish to continue with treatment that does not appear to be helpful.'

- 'For most patients in the community whose illness (usually schizophrenia) has to be kept in control by long-acting drugs ('depot' drugs) the community medical services, out-patient facilities and CPNs can cater satisfactorily without a coercive requirement. However, for schizophrenic patients who lack insight, the additional level of a treatment requirement may be essential'. (HMIP, para. 7.14)

- 'For some personality disordered offenders or those with learning disabilities, a requirement for treatment can provide a framework of structured, disciplined living, possibly with other services such as financial management, provision of accommodation which will lead to a better prospect of rehabilitation than any agency is likely to be able to offer alone.' (HMIP, para. 7.13)

There is little empirical evidence to support the belief that a requirement of treatment enhances the prospects of completion of treatment. One seemingly encouraging research study of out-patients seen by the Regional Forensic Service at Prestwich Hospital, Manchester (Mendelson, 1992) gave this impression but the numbers were small (11 out of 18 probationers completed their treatment compared with seven out of 29 voluntary patients). This was not a properly matched trial and the researcher accepted that the probationers may have been selected on the basis of a more promising initial prognosis. The study does not allow the conclusion that probationer patients responded better because of their requirement of treatment. More recently, Clark *et al* (2002) have reported a retrospective study, based on case notes, of 29 male probationers resident as a requirement of their order at Elliott House approved probation hostel, a specialist resource for mentally disordered offenders and bailees (Geelan *et al*, 1998/9, 2000). Of the 29 who had completed a period of residence since the hostel opened in late 1993, 17 had also been subject to a treatment requirement. A greater proportion of those with a treatment requirement (14 out of 17) had a diagnosis of a psychotic illness compared with those without (five out of 12). Having a treatment requirement had little effect on the offenders' management at Elliott House. Though the hostel enjoyed a high degree of inter-agency collaboration, 'more than one in three probationers had no contact with local psychiatric teams during their period of residence', though 'nearly two out of three residents were in contact with local psychiatric services' at time of leaving the hostel. 'There was no difference in the proportion who received follow-up between those with and those without' a treatment requirement – only three of the 17 received regular continuous follow-up despite the specific focus and structure of their orders.

'This seems to suggest a lack of understanding of psychiatric probation orders on the part of psychiatrists and perhaps the courts. The lack of subsequent treatment suggests that adequate arrangements for treatment could not have been in place when the order was made.'

Recent Use of Mental Treatment Requirements

The use of psychiatric orders has shrunk somewhat from 1,012 (2.2% of all probation order commencements) in 1990 to 671 (1.2%) in 2001, of which 421 (63%) specified non-residential treatment while 215 (32%) specified treatment as directed by a medical practitioner (*Probation Statistics 2001*, Home Office, 2002). The most significant shrinkage has concerned orders requiring residential mental treatment, declining from 122 (14% of treatment orders) in 1991 to 35 (5%) in 2001. A survey by Pritchard *et al* (1992) of probation caseloads in two Probation Areas (Hampshire and Dorset), found that 21% of probationers aged 18-25 had psychiatric disorders. Only a very small number of community punishment and rehabilitation (combination) orders contained mental treatment requirements – 0.2% (28) of orders in 2001.

The use of orders will almost certainly have been affected by the implementation of the 1991 Act. First, the 'serious enough' threshold introduced for community sentences may have reduced the number of eligible defendants. HMIP (para. 3.5) estimated that one half to three-quarters of the offences in their sample would have been 'serious enough', suggesting that at least 25% of the orders surveyed would now fall into the fine/discharge sentencing zone (though many commentators have considered that this threshold has become so flexible, especially in the light of the weight that can now be given to previous convictions, as to be almost meaningless). Secondly, a number of previously eligible offenders have doubtless been considered more suitable for a requirement of treatment for drug or alcohol dependency (introduced by CJA 1991 and now regulated by sch 2 para. 6).

Inappropriate Deferment of Sentence

Power to defer sentence with the defendant's consent for a period of up to six months under PCC(S)A 2000 s1, usually with clear expectations being specified of what should be achieved by the defendant during the deferment period, may prompt a court to consider deferment linked to the expectation that the defendant will seek or receive psychiatric treatment. This was criticised by the Court of Appeal in *R v Skelton* [1983] Crim LR 686 where the judge had deferred sentence on the basis of the defendant's undertaking to reside at a mental hospital as a voluntary patient during the deferment period, but the *Skelton* decision left the appropriate use of deferment very unclear. Clarification was given in *R v George* [1984] 1 WLR 1082 where Lord Lane CJ indicated:

'... deferment of sentence will be more appropriate where the conduct required of the defendant is not sufficiently specific to be made the subject of a condition imposed as part of a probation order without creating uncertainty in the mind of the probation officer and to the defendant as to whether there has been a breach of the order. Deferment may be the appropriate course where the steps to be taken by the defendant could not of their nature be the subject of a condition ...'

In *Skelton*, what amounted via deferment to a substantial restriction on the defendant's freedom should have been imposed by a specific order of the court, either a hospital order or a psychiatric probation order. Deferment should not be adopted as an 'easy option', in effect hedging the court's bets, when the intentions of the court could be achieved by a specific immediate sentence.

Inserting a Treatment Requirement by Amendment: Time Limit

Whilst it is in force, a probation order may be amended by inserting any requirement which could have been included at the time that the order was made, either in addition to or in substitution for any existing requirement, upon the application either of the offender or, more usually, the supervising officer (PCC(S)A 2000 sch 3 para. 19(1)), though no such application may be made while an appeal against the order is pending (para. 23). Where the applicant is the supervising officer, the offender must attend, upon summons, and, following the basic requirement of consent to a treatment requirement (page 115), must express willingness to comply with the requirement of the amended order (para. 19(2)(b)(i)). If the offender does not appear in answer to summons, the court may issue a warrant for their arrest (para. 24(1)).

By a special provision in para. 19(2)(b)(ii), the supervising court may not insert a requirement of treatment for mental condition unless the amending order is made within three months after the date of the original order. This limitation appears to affect the scope to vary the kind of treatment given within an already existing psychiatric order, as detailed at page 129, though this awaits judicial clarification.

Note that the enforcement provisions of the 2000 Act allow the insertion of additional demands without requiring any consideration of the provisions of s35(3)(b) requiring restrictions to be commensurate with seriousness of offence(s). If the original order was deemed to impose restrictions on liberty appropriate for seriousness, on what basis can additional restrictions be inserted? Logic suggests that only if the restrictions contained in the original order fell below the 'commensurability' ceiling, in the light of the offender's 'suitability', would it be appropriate to add requirements which do not exceed that ceiling, in the light of changes in the offender's personal circumstances. In practice, an amendment of this nature will only be sought rarely, where the offender is clearly willing to accept the new requirement. In such instances it might seem unnecessary to place the proposed treatment on a formal statutory basis.

THE ADMINISTRATION OF A PSYCHIATRIC COMMUNITY REHABILITATION ORDER

The nature of the order, with dual responsibility held by psychiatrist/psychologist and probation officer, requires professional liaison and co-operation and also a proper degree of flexibility in the treatment arrangements in the light of the probationer-patient's response and progress. The long-term difficulties in securing reliable, close collaboration and also the rewards of effective inter-disciplinary and inter-agency communication are well recognised. HMIP (1993) noted that often 'neither side knew what the other was doing, unless the patient himself acted as go-between and messenger' (para. 3.28). 'Instances were seen of work being duplicated between probation officers, approved social workers of the local authority and CPNs' (para. 3.30).

'Probation officers often expressed anger and cynicism over what they saw as inactivity and failure to co-operate on the part of some psychiatrists, confusion over the roles being played out within the health service or promises of treatment that turned out to be a "non event". Whether or not these attitudes reflect reality it is important that they are addressed and that measures are devised to enhance understanding between the services at all levels.' (para. 3.31)

On the brighter side, however:

'There were some excellent examples of collaboration, particularly where probation officers exhibited confidence in their own roles and were able to take initiatives in contacting health service personnel and suggest discussions, conferences and role clarification. Many psychiatrists (especially forensic psychiatrists) valued this approach and recognised the special skills with offenders, that probation officers brought to their shared cases. Clarity of role and purpose leads to confidence and confidence leads to authority when dealing with the chaotic.' (para. 3.32)

As some indication of the extent of progress since the 1993 report, see Richardson *et al's* (2003) study of the records of probation orders with treatment requirements supervised by Leicestershire Probation area in 1999, a total of 33 cases. They note the considerable heterogeneity in types of offences and clinical diagnoses (psychotic disorders accounted for 55% of cases and substance misuse featured in 84% of the sample). The files revealed limited record keeping in the psychiatric notes, poor communication between probation and medical staff and some doctors were clearly not aware of the existence of the order. Most noteworthy was the rarity of CPA documentation.

In-Patient Treatment

To mark the professional primacy of the medical authority in dealing with probationer in-patients, whether subject to a specific requirement of in-patient treatment under para. 5(3)(a) or within the flexibility of an 'under the direction' order (para. 5(3)(c)), and the residual role thus played by the supervising probation officer, sch 1A para. 5(5) provides:

'While the offender is under treatment as a resident patient in pursuance of a requirement of the probation order, the probation officer responsible for this supervision shall carry out the supervision to such extent only as may be necessary for the purpose of the revocation or amendment of the order.'

This curtailment of responsibility was considered unhelpful by the Butler Committee on Mentally Abnormal Offenders (1975) who suggested that it should not inhibit the principles of good practice, maintaining regular contact, linking to the patient's family back at home and planning for discharge. This message was echoed by HMIP (paras. 3.23-3.24) who noted that it was quite common for patients who were in hospital at the time that the probation order was imposed to be discharged very quickly thereafter, sometimes leaving the probation officer handling 'a normal, but very difficult, probation case with the doctor keeping a watching brief through monthly or longer check-ups'.

Changing the Place of Treatment

The legal framework allows the responsible medical practitioner a degree of flexibility in the arrangements for treatment, to the extent of changing the location of treatment to an alternative institution or place without requiring a formal referral back to the supervising court seeking an amendment of the order, though the supervising probation officer must be notified. This can be achieved even though the new place of treatment is not one which could have been specified in the requirements (para. 5(7)), *eg* because the 'place' at which it is now intended to offer residential treatment is not a 'mental hospital' for the purposes of para. 5(3)(a) and (10).

PCC(S)A 2000 sch 2 para. 5

(6) Where the medical practitioner or chartered psychologist by whom or under whose direction an offender is being treated for his mental condition in pursuance of a community rehabilitation order is of the opinion that part of the treatment can be better or more conveniently given in or at an institution or place which –

  (a) is not specified in the order; and

  (b) is one in or at which the treatment of the offender will be given by or under the direction of a duly qualified medical practitioner,

  he may, with the consent of the offender, make arrangements for him to be treated accordingly.

(7) Such arrangements as are mentioned in sub-paragraph (6) above may provide for the offender to receive part of his treatment as a resident patient in an institution or place notwithstanding that the institution or place is not one which could have been specified for that purpose in the community rehabilitation order.

(8) Where any such arrangements as are mentioned in sub-paragraph (6) above are made for the treatment of an offender –

  (a) the medical practitioner or chartered psychologist by whom the arrangements are made shall give notice in writing to the probation officer responsible for the supervision of the offender, specifying the institution or place in or at which the treatment is to be carried out; and

  (b) the treatment provided for by the arrangements shall be deemed to be treatment to which he is required to submit in pursuance of the community rehabilitation order.

Amendment of Treatment Requirements

For more substantial changes in psychiatric orders, beyond that of location, amendments of the order must be sought under the provisions of PCC(S)A 2000 sch 3 paras. 18-25, detailed more fully in Stone (1999). However, specific provision is made for the amendment of treatment requirements, whether in respect of mental condition or alcohol dependency (sch 2 para. 6).

PCC(S)A 2000 sch 3 para. 20

(1) Where the medical practitioner or other person by whom or under whose direction an offender is, in pursuance of any requirement of a community rehabilitation or CPR order, being treated for his mental condition, or his

dependency on or propensity to misuse drugs or alcohol –

(a) is of the opinion mentioned in sub-paragraph (2) below; or

(b) is for any reason unwilling to continue to treat or direct the treatment of the offender, he shall make a report in writing to that effect to the responsible officer and that officer shall apply under paragraph 19 above to a magistrates' court for the petty sessions area concerned for the variation or cancellation of the requirement.

(2) The opinion referred to in sub-paragraph (1) above is –

(a) that the treatment of the offender should be continued beyond the period specified in that behalf in the order;

(b) that the offender needs different treatment, being treatment of a kind to which he could be required to submit in pursuance of a probation order;

(c) that the offender is not susceptible to treatment; or

(d) that the offender does not require further treatment.

The scope of this provision is wide, covering instances where the additional requirement appears to be no longer necessary or viable because the offender has completed treatment or has proved to be non-responsive (where a 'cancellation' amendment could be sought) or the wording of the order should be varied to embrace a different or an additional form of treatment (a 'substitution' amendment). Note that the supervising probation officer is placed under a duty to make the appropriate application. The usual requirements under sch 3 para. 19, regarding the offender's attendance and consent, apply; these procedures are necessary unless the proposed amendment simply cancels or reduces the period of any requirement. It would appear to follow from the wording of para. 19(1)(b) that an amending order must be made within three months after the date of the original order (see page 127), even in instances where the original order contained a treatment requirement, since a substitution of a requirement nevertheless counts as an insertion of a requirement.

Termination of Treatment
HMIP noted that in some instances in their study sample 'the doctor appeared to be making arbitrary decisions to end treatment, sometimes only a few days after recommending it to the court, which the probation officer was obliged to accept' (para. 3.36). This could thus mean a referral back to the supervising court which would almost certainly feel concern that the intentions of the sentencing court were being overridden so quickly and throwing into doubt the basis of the original proposal to the court. Such rapid and unexpected terminations should be reduced if the quality of co-ordinated advice to sentencers is improved. HMIP also noted unanticipated terminations arising not from the needs of the patient but 'owing to changes in staff in either the NHS or the probation service' (para. 3.35).

Breach of the Order
Given the problems likely to be experienced by probationers with treatment requirements, it is not surprising that, among the HMIP sample, 'failure to keep

appointments and difficulty about treatment were almost universal, stemming from the nature of the mental disorder' (para. 3.37), though a very few cases ran through 'almost obsessionally'. The Inspectorate thus conclude that the psychiatric complexities in such cases made 'a full application of *National Standards* for probation supervision unrealistic, particularly over enforcement', suggesting that a specific *National Standard* is needed for these cases. Subsequent versions of *National Standards* (1995 and 2000) have not pursued this proposal and it would appear that generic scope for variation and discretion in application is considered adequate in dealing with mentally disordered offenders.

Breach action, where appropriate, can prove difficult because the wording of the requirements is insufficiently precise, though HMIP note that this may not prevent a professional consensus that breach proceedings are the appropriate way of dealing with awkward probationer-patients. Given the lax drafting of treatment requirements and the consequent lack of clarity in the terms of psychiatric orders (see page 118) HMIP suggested:

> 'It would often have been difficult to prove a breach of requirement of the order if the law were to be strictly observed. Often it was not and there appeared a covert acceptance by all concerned that the probationer had proved difficult and it was therefore right that there should be a conviction for failing to comply with what was a very unclear requirement.' (para. 3.20)

Even more worryingly, it appeared that, on occasion, probationers in the HMIP study sample were being convicted of breach of requirement,

> 'because they were reacting exactly in accordance with the mental condition diagnosed in the first place to a poorly managed situation.' (para. 3.21)

Reasonable Refusal to Comply with Treatment

Procedures to be adopted in breach proceedings under PCC(S)A 2000 sch 3 paras. 2A-9 are outlined more fully in Stone (1999) but note the specific defence to an allegation of failure to comply with a treatment requirement, offered by sch 3 para. 6(2):

(2) An offender who

   (a) is required by a community rehabilitation order or CPR order to submit to treatment for his mental condition, or his dependency on or propensity to misuse drugs or alcohol, or

   (b) (*not relevant*)

   shall not be treated for the purposes of paragraph 4 or 5 above as having failed to comply with that requirement on the ground only that he has refused to undergo any surgical, electrical or other treatment if, in the opinion of the court, his refusal was reasonable having regard to all the circumstances.

This clearly applies in the case of an offender who declines to submit to a lobotomy or electro-convulsive therapy but it is less clear whether refusal to participate in less drastic intervention, such as prescribed medication, would be considered 'reasonable'.

FACTORS IDENTIFIED AS CONTRIBUTING TOWARDS THE EFFECTIVENESS OF PSYCHIATRIC ORDERS (*HMIP*, para. 3.43)

i   understanding by the doctor of criminal justice and court procedures and their implications;

ii   a well argued and well presented joint plan agreed by doctor and probation officer, in a good quality pre-sentence report (PSR);

iii   adequate pre-trial information available to the probation officer;

iv   procedures, recognised by each agency, within which main grade practitioners could work with confidence;

v   good basic probation practice by probation officers, including efficient recording so that information is immediately accessible in emergency or when officers change;

vi   skilled counselling by the probation officer;

vii   accessibility of a resource providing long-term treatment mainly available to the probation service;

viii   effective case conference and liaison procedures and clear understanding of what information should be shared both ways and how often;

ix   risk management procedures clearly documented and operated;

x   good multi-agency and multi-disciplinary input;

xi   objectives and roles of all concerned with the case clearly defined;

xii   effective resettlement plan (housing repair/decoration, home help, finance);

xiii   vigorous, pro-active work by the probation officer;

xiv   removal from chaotic lifestyle to therapeutic but firm situation;

xv   good motivation and co-operation from the probationer and informed, genuine concern to the requirement;

xvi   careful targeting of resources;

xvii   social and medical management arrangements well co-ordinated;

xviii   effective action when there was failure to comply;

xix   proper consultation between probation and medical services about termination of orders.

FACTORS MILITATING AGAINST EFFECTIVENESS (*HMIP*, para. 3.44)

i   inappropriate order or requirement not in accordance with the Act;

ii   conflicting recommendations to court by probation officer and psychiatrist;

iii   lack of interest in the doctor's therapy by the probation officer;

iv   frequent re-offending disrupting appointments;

v   lack of support by the psychiatrist;

vi   very complex personality problem resulting in disruptive behaviour;

vii   home visits and influences which prove unsettling where the family has strong feelings about the criminal justice system;

viii   shortfall in resources, especially appropriate medium/low care accommodation for resettlement programme;

ix   duplication of each others' work by agencies lacking shared knowledge;

x   lack of understanding and agreement about criteria for breach action.

CASE ILLUSTRATION I
Adrienne Head (35)

Offences

Assault (ABH) x 5. Following chance encounters with her ex-husband who lives in the same town, Ms Head felt certain that he must be stalking her. Accompanied by her new partner, she called at her ex-husband's home in a very intoxicated and agitated state and aggressively confronted his present wife who telephoned both her husband's place of work and the police for help. On the arrival of her ex-husband, some of his work colleagues and a police officer, Ms Head lashed out and committed these assaults.

Previous Convictions

None.

Personal and Psychiatric History

Having married at age 22, Ms Head first suffered psychiatric illness in the following year when she experienced 'symptoms of a depressive illness with features of obsessionalism' (a pre-occupation with hygiene rituals) coupled with moodiness and temper outbursts. Her illness led to increased marital stress and her husband had an affair and finally left her when she was aged 26. She received sustained out-patient supervision and day patient care, interspersed with short periods of in-patient treatment, though she was admitted for nine months at age 29, when she suffered more psychotic symptoms including auditory hallucinations. More recently, she formed a new relationship with another psychiatric patient, a man 15 years younger than her who also suffered depression and was very dependent upon her. Ms Head had two short in-patient admissions in the four months prior to her offences. She complained after the assaults that she felt strangers were looking at her, could read her mind and were ridiculing her.

Court Reports

Her consultant psychiatrist reported that, following a further brief in-patient admission, Ms Head was now more self-controlled under medication and that a non-custodial sentence would permit her current programme of psychiatric treatment to continue, backed by CPN nursing and counselling to address the sexual abuse she suffered as a child and her subsequent relationship difficulties. The probation officer's report noted Ms Head's unresolved feelings towards her ex-husband and her related problems of low self-esteem, isolation and anger. A short community rehabilitation order was proposed to help her to come to terms with her past life experiences and to address the risk of further offending, especially against her ex-husband. The probation officer felt that it would only be possible to supervise Ms Head constructively and safely if she continued to receive medication. It was considered that a requirement of treatment as directed by the consultant psychiatrist would go some way to ensuring this, giving the supervising officer the scope to refer the matter back to the court in breach proceedings should Ms Head fail to take her prescribed medication, even if she had not defaulted on her other probation requirements.

Sentence

Community rehabilitation order for 12 months with requirement to receive psychiatric treatment at the direction of the consultant psychiatrist.

Progress of the Order

Regular contact was maintained throughout the order in accordance with National Standards, backed by the involvement of a probation volunteer. Ms Head's volatile mood swings made supervision sessions difficult. Though she was able to discuss issues and feelings with her probation officer that she felt unable to share with anyone else, she also directed her anger and frustration onto that supervisor, particularly when her partner's dependence and passivity got on top of her. Innocuous incidents could cause Ms Head to direct great hostility towards her probation officer who, at times, felt it too risky to undertake visits to their home. It was possible to address the violence and paranoia in that relationship in joint sessions with the couple, though it was important to give Ms Head individual time, even though this caused her partner to feel jealous of the attention she was receiving.

Liaison with the consultant psychiatrist was almost entirely one-way, through numerous letters from the probation officer updating the doctor on progress. It proved impossible to contact the doctor by telephone for a discussion except on one occasion during the entire course of the order. Efforts by the probation officer to secure the involvement of a CPN in readiness for the termination of the probation order proved fruitless. Nevertheless, Ms Head and her partner were reviewed by the consultant periodically and they both sustained their medication.

Termination of the Order

By the halfway stage of the order it was clear that Ms Head was no longer pre-occupied with her past marriage and the risk to her ex-husband had thus abated. Though still angry, frustrated and unfulfilled in many respects, Ms Head had made a commitment to her present partner and had learnt to manage that relationship with less violent swings of emotion and reduced peaks of crisis. Despite the difficulties in fulfilling all the aims of this probation order, it was possible to apply successfully to the court for revocation of the order after ten months, in recognition of Ms Head's progress and the reduced risk of re-offending.

CASE ILLUSTRATION II
David Mellors (32)

Offence

Arson by setting light to a maintenance shed at the block of flats where he lived, denied throughout by Mr Mellors who unsuccessfully claimed an alibi.

Personal and Psychiatric History

First came to psychiatric attention following a road traffic accident when aged 22, causing serious head injuries, brain damage and an apparent change of personality, leading to instability of mood, irritability, aggressive outbursts, impaired concentration and memory, difficulty in planning ahead. He was first admitted to hospital following violence towards his wife and criminal damage to his home, causing the end of the marriage. He subsequently led an unsettled life, acquiring a number of convictions for assault, criminal damage, affray and possession of an offensive weapon, in addition to some offences of dishonesty, and he received three consecutive probation orders. Supervision had been marked by concern about his misuse of alcohol and both prescribed and illicit drugs, incidents of self-harm and threats to kill himself at times of stress. He had been attending a psychiatric out-patient clinic irregularly prior to the offence but with insufficient commitment to allow any stabilisation.

Court Reports

Assessing Mr Mellors on prison remand, a psychiatrist who had not previously dealt with him was somewhat sceptical of the suggestion that his mental state was attributable to brain damage, found no evidence of mental illness and gave the opinion that Mr Mellors suffered from an abnormal personality characterised by irritability, impulsiveness and disorganisation, causing severe social difficulties and exacerbated by his improper use of prescribed and illicit drugs. The doctor noted that Mr Mellors was adamant that he did not wish to enter hospital and that compulsory hospital admission was unlikely to be successful as in-patient treatment would depend largely on his co-operation. Out-patient treatment was proposed, 'possibly as part of a community rehabilitation order', to deal firstly with Mr Mellors' drug dependency; when this had been tackled, his personality problems and possible brain damage would be properly assessed. Eventually, voluntary hospital admission or placement in a therapeutic community would be helpful, but the doctor predicted that Mr Mellors would have difficulty in complying with the proposed order. The pre-sentence report considered that it was 'essential that Mr Mellors receives the appropriate medical treatment for his problems', whether or not he was given a custodial sentence, but added that 'he could remain in the community to serve his sentence only if he is required to attend psychiatric treatment as a condition of the order'.

Sentence

Community rehabilitation order for 12 months with a requirement that he attend treatment as a non-resident patient at the local forensic psychiatry unit.

Progress of the Order

Though Mr Mellors kept his probation appointments throughout, his involvement with the psychiatric unit was of far more crucial importance. Initially, he attended out-patient appointments regularly and, though extremely angry and in dispute about his conviction, he was generally co-operative, if argumentative, especially when accompanied by his girlfriend who had a stabilising influence. After five months he had successfully stopped use of illicit drugs and prescribed tranquillisers.

Shortly afterwards the structure of the order went badly awry. He committed a serious assault upon his girlfriend, attempting to throttle her and causing her to fear for her life, and subsequently cut his own wrist deeply. She opted not to press charges despite advice to the contrary. He was admitted to psychiatric hospital as a voluntary patient but, in view of the serious risk he presented both to himself and his girlfriend, he was detained under MHA 1983 s3 with the aim of securing his admission to a Regional Secure Unit (RSU). As no beds were available and his threatening behaviour made detention and treatment in an open ward unsafe, the s3 order was rescinded after three days and he was discharged. Thereafter, he started to use illicit drugs again and was increasingly aggressive and irregular in his out-patient attendance, raging, making threats and being abusive to staff and turning up without an appointment demanding medication, so that it was necessary for security staff to be present whenever he was on hospital premises. He was also abusive and intimidating to his probation officer and she transferred responsibility to a colleague who initiated a minimal reporting schedule of three-weekly or monthly appointments, seeing Mr Mellors only when accompanied by another officer.

After his further brief (two-day) and unproductive admission to psychiatric hospital at Mr Mellors' own request and a further overdose, the psychiatrist concluded that his violent mood swings and dangerous behaviour towards himself and others had made it impossible to carry out the order and requested that the supervising officer should refer the order back to the supervising court with a view to revocation, remand in custody and re-sentence to a s37 hospital order, so that he could be admitted to a secure unit.

Breach Proceedings

The supervising officer obtained a summons alleging that Mr Mellors had failed to attend out-patient appointments on four dates. A psychiatric report to the court was prepared by the consultant who had dealt most extensively with him prior to the order, in anticipation that breach would be established, stating that Mr Mellors was suffering serious mental disorder, requiring hospital treatment, *ie* a personality disorder arising from severe brain damage, and recommending the exceptional course of a remand in custody to obtain the necessary reports and await a RSU vacancy, as he could not be held safely in open hospital conditions.

Though his non-attendance was not disputed, the defence was able to argue successfully that as the doctors had sent Mr Mellors prescriptions for medication through the post (as they had on two occasions around the time of his most recent overdose) they were, in effect, encouraging him to take very large doses and that he could not be blamed for his consequent erratic behaviour. Persuaded by this argument of 'reasonable excuse', the breach allegations were dismissed.

Feeling considerable frustration that this route to achieving secure hospital detention had been blocked, the psychiatrists informed the supervising officer that they were no longer able to see Mr Mellors as an out-patient or to carry out the treatment requirement any further. The probation officer considered various alternative courses such as seeking amendment of the order to delete the treatment requirement or seeking revocation of the order and replacement with a conditional discharge.

Latter Phase of Order

Before a decision was reached and with less than two months of the order remaining, Mr Mellors was admitted to a general hospital having attacked his former girlfriend's new partner, who retaliated, causing him a fractured skull. The psychiatrist again asked the supervising probation officer to refer the order back to court to seek revocation and re-sentencing by a hospital order. The supervising officer replied that this did not seem a promising course, in the light of the previous unsuccessful prosecution of breach. The psychiatrist then admitted Mr Mellors to psychiatric hospital, where a new more secure facility had been opened, under MHA 1983 s3, with the hope of stabilising him and transferring him to a head injury rehabilitation clinic. However, his aggressive behaviour continued to cause serious concern, no bed was available at the area's RSU and it was learnt that the lengthy waiting list for a head injuries unit made early transfer out of the question. As a consequence, Mr Mellors was discharged two days after his community rehabilitation order expired. It had already been resolved that he should be entered on the local Supervision Register.

Comment

This case clearly caused real concern, in the light of Mr Mellors' potential for violence, particularly against women, and self-harm. As in the previous case illustration, it was hoped that the structure and enforcement powers of the order would ensure that the probationer sustained a consistent relationship with the psychiatric unit and followed their medication regime. The psychiatric prediction that Mr Mellors would prove problematic was entirely correct but how might the enforcement powers of the order be mobilised in search of a more constructive solution?

Powers of amendment of the order under PCC(S)A 2000 sch 3 para. 19 by establishing in-patient treatment for the existing requirement would not be sufficient as the psychiatrist's objective was to secure Mr Mellors' detention in hospital and to mobilise the scarce resource of a RSU bed. In any case, it would be doubtful whether Mr Mellors would consent to such a substitution. The doctors thus wanted a different form of sentence and felt that a remand in custody pending re-sentence was the only realistic way of gaining a RSU bed, perhaps under MHA 1983 s48 transfer in the first instance, which was clearly not forthcoming under MHA 1983 s3 civil procedures.

Breach proceedings presented the most promising course but this plan came unstuck, thus illustrating HMIP's observation (page 131) that breach allegations often arise unfairly because patients behave exactly in accordance with their diagnosed mental condition in reaction to poorly managed situations. Mr Mellors' failure to keep appointments was clearly part of his pattern of erratic, unpredictable behaviour and his difficulty in planning ahead, exacerbated by his misuse of drugs and medication. Though many offenders will admit breach despite this possible defence, in this instance the defence challenged the prosecution and persuaded the court that to send prescriptions by post to Mr Mellors was asking for trouble and that the offender should not be held legally at fault for the consequences. As Mr Mellors was adhering to the standard requirements of his probation order, the only scope for breach action lay in his response to the medical requirement and it would have been necessary for the doctors and the supervising officer to plan a very specific, carefully structured out-patient medication regime for Mr Mellors with a view either to his adherence or to establishing a watertight, provable default.

Once the breach prosecution had foundered, either it meant going back to the drawing board, albeit that relations with the patient would have suffered meantime and that the order had only 12 weeks to run, or giving up on enforcement powers as a solution. To refer the case back to court in revocation proceedings on the grounds that it would be in the interests of justice for the offender to be dealt with in some other manner (PCC(S)A 2000 sch 3 para. 10(1)) would probably not have been effective because the defence would surely argue that it would be unjust and wrong to expose Mr Mellors to remand in custody and re-sentencing to a more substantial sentence, especially at such a late stage in the order, when there would be no suggestion of fault on his part.

An additional consideration that the defence would probably raise in any re-sentencing exercise is that the probation order was arguably made on the basis that the offender's mental condition was 'not such as to warrant the making of a hospital order'. It could be submitted that Mr Mellors' condition remained essentially as before and that the psychiatric evidence would have to demonstrate the basis on which his condition did now warrant a s37 order.

There was thus no happy ending to this worrying and frustrating illustration of the difficulties of bringing legal, medical and resource considerations into harmony through a psychiatric community rehabilitation order.

CRIMINAL JUSTICE BILL

Clause 187 of the Bill currently before Parliament provides power for a court to attach a mental health treatment requirement to a 'relevant order', a term that includes a 'community order' under the proposals for a single generic community sentence for offenders aged 16 or older. This power essentially re-enacts the provisions of PCC(S)A 2000 sch. 2 para. 5 and continues the procedural requirement that the offender must express willingness to comply with the proposed treatment requirement. Allied clause 188 reproduces the provisions of para. 5(6) to (8) (above at page 129).

9
PSYCHIATRIC SUPERVISION ORDERS

Though not a statutory term, a 'psychiatric supervision order' is a convenient shorthand term for a supervision order imposed upon a young person aged under 18 at point of conviction in criminal proceedings that includes a requirement to receive treatment for their mental condition, made under PCC(S)A 2000 sch 6 para. 6 (succeeding CYPA 1969 s12B). The provisions are essentially a shortened version of the legislation governing psychiatric community rehabilitation orders under PCC(S)A 2000 sch 2 para. 5, and reference should thus also be made to Chapter 8, particularly in regard to practice considerations which apply to both forms of supervisory order. This chapter seeks to outline the provisions specific to supervision orders and address the differences between the two forms of order. For general coverage of the enforcement of supervision orders under PCC(S)A 2000 sch 7, see Stone (1999). For more information about psychiatric morbidity among young offenders, see Lader *et al* (2000).

As some indication of the very small numbers of supervision orders containing such a requirement, it is worth noting that a total of only 25 supervision orders made in the five years 1996-2000, out of a total of 10,873 where the probation service was the nominated supervising agency, included a psychiatric requirement, 18 being for non-residential mental treatment. In the period 1990-2000 only eight instances of residential mental treatment requirement are recorded as being linked to probation service supervision (*Probation Statistics, 2000*). The Youth Justice Board has not been able to identify the number of psychiatric supervision orders imposed since youth offending teams took responsibility for youth justice since their statistical returns do not require that specific information. It may be worth noting that the Board has set youth offending teams a performance task of referring all young people with acute mental health problems to the appropriate child and adolescent mental health service for formal assessment which should commence within five working days of receipt.

POWER TO MAKE THE ORDER
PCC(S)A 2000 sch 6 para. 6

(1) This paragraph applies where a court which proposes to make a supervision order is satisfied, on the evidence of a registered medical practitioner approved for the purposes of section 12 of the Mental Health Act 1983, that the mental condition of the offender–

   (a) is such as requires and may be susceptible to treatment; but

   (b) is not such as to warrant the making of a hospital order or guardianship order within the meaning of that Act.

(2) Where this paragraph applies, the court may include in the supervision order a requirement that the offender shall, for a period specified in the order, submit to treatment of one of the following descriptions so specified, that is to say–

(a) treatment as a resident patient in a hospital or mental nursing home within the meaning of the Mental Health Act 1983, but not a hospital at which high security psychiatric services within the meaning of that Act are provided;

(b) treatment as a non-resident patient at an institution or place specified in the order;

(c) treatment by or under the direction of a registered medical practitioner specified in the order; or

(d) treatment by or under the direction of a chartered psychologist specified in the order.

Evidential Prerequisites

Evidence under para. 6(1) need not be but will usually be given through a written report. The court must be satisfied that arrangements either have been or can be made for treatment and, in the case of residential treatment, for the patient's reception (para. 6(3)(a)) (though there is no specified time limit within which reception must occur – compare MHA 1983 s37(4)).

Requirements

Whereas there was no provision for treatment under a s12B order to be undertaken or directed by a chartered psychologist, this is now an option under para. 6(2)(d), such a professional being defined by para. 6(5) as 'a person for the time being listed in the British Psychological Society's Register of Chartered Psychologists'. However, evidence satisfying para. 6(1) must be from an appropriate medical practitioner and a report from a chartered psychologist does not satisfy that evidential prerequisite. The rider to sch 2 para. 5(3), that the nature of the treatment shall not be specified in a community rehabilitation order except as mentioned in the explicitly stated options, does not appear in para. 6 but it is submitted that this does not give a court making a psychiatric supervision order wider scope or discretion. Also, the scope under sch 2 para. 5(2) to specify treatment of different kinds during different parts of a psychiatric community rehabilitation order does not apply to para. 6 orders. In other words, the sentencing court must opt for one form of treatment from options (a) to (d) above.

Consent

Though the consent of the offender is not required before a 'standard' supervision order is imposed, an additional requirement under para. 6 cannot be included in respect of a young person aged 14 or older (at point of sentence) without their consent (para. 6(3)(b)). Any such requirement ceases to have effect after the consenting young person's 18th birthday even if their order remains in force (para. 6(3)).

Duration

A treatment requirement remains in force for the period specified in the order, either for the duration of the order or for the period of treatment within the overall term of the order as specified by the court. However, this is subject to the 'guillotine' mentioned above where the supervised person attains the age of 18, even if the supervision order continues.

AMENDMENT TO INSERT, VARY OR CANCEL A TREATMENT REQUIREMENT

Adding a para. 6 requirement

An existing supervision order cannot be amended to include a para. 6 requirement unless the court dealing with the amendment application is satisfied in accordance with sch 6 para. 6(1): sch 7 para. 8(1)(c). Such amendment of an existing order cannot be made unless ordered by the court before the expiration of three months from the date when the order was originally made, unless it is in substitution for such a requirement already included in the order: PCC(S)A 2000 sch 7 para. 5(3)(a).

Amendment on Report of Medical Practitioner

If a medical practitioner by whom or under whose direction an offender is being treated for his mental condition under sch 6 para. 6 is either:

(a) unwilling to continue to treat or direct the treatment of him, or

(b) is of the opinion that the one of the following applies –

– treatment should be continued beyond the period specified for it in the order;

– the offender needs different treatment;

– the offender is not susceptible to treatment;

– the offender does not require further treatment,

that medical practitioner shall make a report to that effect to the supervisor of the order: sch 7 para. 6(1) and (2). On receiving such a report, the supervisor is required to refer it to the appropriate court: para. 6(3). The court then has discretion whether to order the variation or cancellation sought. Where the para. 6 requirement specifies treatment by or under the direction of a chartered psychologist (para. 6(2)(d)) there is no scope for that professional person to trigger an application by reporting to the supervisor but this does not prevent the supervisor exercising discretion to seek amendment, following consultation with the psychologist.

The 'Care or Control' Test

A youth court dealing with a supervised person aged under 18 shall not exercise its power to insert, vary or even cancel a Schedule 6 requirement unless:

the court is satisfied that the supervised person is unlikely to receive the care or control he needs unless the court makes the order or is likely to receive it notwithstanding the order.

'Care' for this purpose includes 'protection and guidance' and 'control' includes 'discipline': sch 7 para. 8(2). This 'care or control' test, specified by sch 7 para. 8(1), applies even where the supervisor is required by sch 7 para. 6(3) (see above) to refer the order back to the court after receiving a report from the medical practitioner: sch 7 para. 8(1)(b).

Offender's Consent

Where the supervised person has attained the age 14, even if he was aged under 14 when the order was originally made, then an amendment order inserting or amending a para. 6 requirement shall not be made without their consent, unless the variation is simply a reduction of the treatment period's duration or removal of the requirement: sch 7 para. 9.

SUPERVISION OR COMMUNITY REHABILITATION ORDER?

An overlap of powers means that a court may select either disposal when dealing with a young offender aged 16 or 17. No statutory criterion is provided to guide sentencers but earlier guidance provided by HOC 30/1992: *Young People and the Youth Court* suggested that the most suitable measure should be identified in the light of 'the offender's circumstances and of the stage of his/her emotional, intellectual, social and physical development in the transition from childhood to adulthood' (para. 9). Among factors suggested as relevant which may be particularly pertinent in the context of a young person with mental health problems are:

(i)   the offender's continuing dependence on or independence from his or her parents;

(ii) whether s/he is leading a stable independent life and has family responsibilities of his/her own;

(iii) whether s/he accepts personal responsibility for his/her actions;

(iv) whether s/he is intellectually impaired.

A further consideration is that the period that must elapse before a conviction resulting in a supervision order is 'spent' under the provisions of ROA 1974 is currently shorter than that specified for a community rehabilitation order (see Stone, 2001). A persuasive argument can be made that all persons aged under 18 are in the stage of transition into adulthood and need help in achieving that development and are thus more appropriately dealt with under supervision order powers, but courts may be more influenced by the seriousness of the offence and assumptions that community rehabilitation orders are administered more rigorously, albeit by the same practitioners. However, members of Youth Offending Teams may take a more expedient view, favouring community rehabilitation orders, because the contact rate demanded by the *National Standards* governing community rehabilitation orders (Home Office, 2000) is less exacting than that specified by the equivalent *Standards* for supervision orders (Youth Justice Board, 2000).

10
SUPERVISION AND TREATMENT ORDERS

Introduced by CP(IUP)A 1991 and detailed in sch 2 to that Act, a supervision and treatment order may be made by the Crown Court in cases other than murder where:

(i)   a special verdict is returned that the accused is not guilty by reason of insanity (Chapter 6); or

(ii) a finding that a defendant who is unfit to plead did the act or made the omission charged (Chapter 5).

The order is modelled substantially upon the psychiatric community rehabilitation order, outlined in Chapter 8, the main differences being:

(i)   the order may be made only on the oral or written evidence of two doctors (at least one of whom must be approved under MHA 1983 s12) rather than one;

(ii)   the court must consider the order to be 'the most suitable means of dealing with the accused', 'having regard to all the circumstances of the case';

(iii) supervision may be exercised by a local social services authority social worker or by a probation officer;

(iv)   the proposed supervisor must indicate prior willingness to undertake supervision;

(v)   the supervised person's consent to the order is not required;

(vi)   the maximum period of the order is two years.

RATIONALE OF THE ORDER
In the words of HOC 93/1991 para. 17(c)(v):

> 'The order is not a punitive measure: its purpose is to benefit the accused. In the generality of cases, it is envisaged that it will be used where the court is satisfied that release into the community will not pose an unacceptable risk to the safety of the public – for example, in the case of a mentally disordered person who will be able to live independently with the help and support of health and social services, and who has been charged with a relatively minor offence. The aim will be to ensure that such persons receive medical treatment either as in-patients for a short period or as out-patients, and receive social support to help them to lead settled lives.'

REQUIREMENTS OF THE ORDER
As its name implies, the order combines social supervision with medical care.

Supervision
'The supervised person shall keep in touch with the supervising officer in accordance with such instructions as he may from time to time be given by that officer and shall

notify him of any change of address' (sch 2 para. 3(5)). This is qualified by the usual caveat that, in respect of an in-patient, 'the supervising officer shall carry out the supervision to such extent as may be necessary for the purpose of the revocation or amendment of the order' (para. 4(3)).

An order 'may include requirements as to the residence of the supervised person' (para. 5(1)) but, before including such a requirement, the court 'shall consider the home surroundings of the supervised person' (para. 5(2)). If a residence requirement specifies residence in 'an approved hostel or any other institution', the period of residence must be specified in the order (para. 5(3)).

Treatment

The order 'shall include a requirement that the supervised person shall submit, during the whole of the period specified in the order or during such part of that period as may be so specified, to treatment by or under the direction of a registered medical practitioner with a view to the improvement of his mental condition' (para. 4(1)). The required treatment shall be one of the following (para. 4(2)):

(i)   treatment as a resident patient in a hospital or mental nursing home, not being a special hospital within the meaning of the NHSA 1977;

(ii) treatment as a non-resident patient at such institution or place as may be specified in the order; and

(iii) treatment by or under the direction of such registered medical practitioner as may be so specified;

but the nature of the treatment shall not be specified except in these terms. There is no provision for treatment by a registered psychologist.

Before making the order, the court is required by para. 3(2) to explain to the supervised person in ordinary language:

(i)   the effect of the order, including any requirement as to residence, and

(ii) that a magistrates' court has power to review the order on the application either of the supervised person or of the supervising officer.

Once the order is in force the doctor responsible for treatment has legal discretion to vary the location of treatment, including in-patient treatment, from that institution or place specified in the order where this would be a better or more convenient arrangement and the supervising person consents (para. 4(4) and (5)), though written notice of the change must be given to the supervising officer (para. 4(6)).

SUPERVISOR'S CONSENT AND TREATMENT ARRANGEMENTS

CP(IUP)A 1991 sch 2 para. 2

(2)   The court shall not make a supervision order and treatment order unless it is also satisfied –

(a)   that the supervising officer intended to be specified in the order is willing to undertake the supervision; and

(b) that arrangements have been made for the treatment intended to be specified in the order (including arrangements for the reception of the accused or appellant where he is to be required to submit to treatment as a resident patient).

Choice of Supervising Agency

HOC 93/1991 para. 17(c)(v) suggests that in the majority of cases Social Services will be the appropriate supervising agency but indicates that this is ultimately for the court to decide after consultation and advice. In the light of that choice, sch 2 para. 3(1) states that the order shall either:

(a) specify the local social services authority area in which the supervised person resides or will reside, and require him to be under the supervision of a social worker of the local social services authority for that area; or

(b) specify the petty sessions area in which that person resides or will reside, and require him to be under the supervision of a probation officer appointed for or assigned to that area.

ENFORCEMENT OF THE ORDER

Jurisdiction

Jurisdiction to deal with the amendment and revocation of an order lies with a magistrates' court acting for the 'petty sessions area concerned', *ie* the PSA in which the supervised person resides, either as explicitly specified in the order (in the case of supervision by a probation officer) or by implication (where a local social services area is specified) (para. 3(4)).

Amendment of the Order

Upon Change of Residence

Where the supervised person changes residence from the social services or petty sessions area specified in the order to another area, 'the court may, and on the application of the supervising officer shall, amend the order by substituting the other area for the area specified' (para. 7(1) and (2)). This is subject to the caveat of para. 7(3):

The court shall not amend under this paragraph a supervision and treatment order which contains requirements which in the opinion of the court, cannot be complied with unless the supervised person continues to reside in the area specified in the order unless, in accordance with paragraph 8 below, it either –

(a) cancels those requirements; or

(b) substitutes for those requirements other requirements which can be complied with if the supervised person ceases to reside in that area.

Amending a Requirement of the Order

Upon the application of either the supervising officer or the supervised person, the court may amend the order (para. 8(i)):

(i) by cancelling any of the requirements of the order; or

(ii) by inserting in the order (either in addition to or in substitution for any such requirement) any requirement which the court could include if it were the court by which the order was made and were then making it.

This power cannot be used to extend the period of the order beyond the end of two years from the date of the original order (para. 8(2)). *R v Maidstone Crown Court, ex p. London Borough of Harrow* (1999) *The Times*, 14 May (see page 76) illustrated inappropriate and invalid exercise of amendment powers. An order specifying supervision by a probation officer was made without consulting the probation service which promptly took steps to transfer supervision to Social Services. This purported 'amendment' was achieved not by application to the court but by requesting the office of the relevant Crown Court centre to re-issue the order 'administratively', specifying Harrow Social Services who were not consulted at any stage as to their willingness to supervise the order. Social Services then referred the order back to the court to complain that the order had not been made lawfully.

Amendments in Pursuance of a Medical Report
The supervising officer is required to seek variation or cancellation of any requirement relating to treatment following a written report from the responsible doctor, in the same way as specified by PCC(S)A 2000 sch 3 para. 20 in the case of a psychiatric community rehabilitation order (see page 129).

Revocation of the Order in the Interests of Health or Welfare
Revocation of the order may be sought by either the supervising officer or the supervised person, under sch 2 para. 6:

> Where a supervision and treatment order is in force in respect of any person and, on the application of the supervised person or the supervising officer, it appears to a magistrates' court acting for the petty sessions are concerned that, having regard to circumstances which have arisen since the order was made, it would be in the interests of the health or welfare of the supervised person that the order should be revoked, the court may revoke the order.

No Scope for Breach
Unusually for statutory supervision, there is no provision for breach proceedings to be initiated in the event of failure to comply with requirements. HOC 93/1991 (para. 17(c)(vi)) comments:

> 'Should the accused refuse to co-operate with his supervision or treatment, penal sanctions will not apply. The court will have no power to enforce the order or otherwise intervene in cases of non-compliance. It will be for the accused's medical and social supervisors to decide on the appropriate action: if they believe that compulsory medical treatment is necessary it will have to be under the relevant provisions of MHA 1983 Part II. In cases where supervisors believe the accused poses a risk to others, but does not meet the requirements for detention under the civil powers, they should act in the same way as they would in respect of any other person in this position. This will involve liaising closely with the police to ensure they are aware of any concern about possible danger to others.'

CASE ILLUSTRATION

Dolan and Campbell (1994) offered an example of the use of this relatively new and unfamiliar order. Only four orders were imposed in 1992 (Mackay and Kearns, 1994). The Home Office was unable to supply the author with figures for more recent years.

Offence

Attempted murder of spouse. A polydrug user until the year prior to the attack, the defendant aged 42 had subsequently developed a florid illness characterised by persecutory ideas and auditory hallucinations but had not received psychiatric attention. He had attempted to throttle his wife and gouge her eyes out, believing he was ridding her of demonic possession.

Process

His psychosis was identified soon after his remand into custody and he was transferred to a regional secure unit under MHA 1983 s35. He improved within two weeks and was transferred back to prison after six weeks. He remained symptom-free until his trial, where he was found not guilty by reason of his temporary insanity.

Order

Two years' supervision and treatment order with a requirement to reside in a hostel and to attend for psychiatric out-patient treatment. He remained well and free of problems throughout, the only minor hiccup arising when the Social Services department refused to allow the social worker attached to the RSU clinical team to undertake the statutory supervision, requiring a reference back to court to amend the order.

11
GUARDIANSHIP ORDERS

Though guardianship powers are usually conferred upon application in civil procedure under MHA 1983 s7, a guardianship order may also be made in criminal proceedings under MHA 1983 s37, including cases where the accused is found unfit to plead (see Chapter 5) or not guilty by reason of insanity (see Chapter 6). As this section primarily provides the legislative basis for a hospital order, the statutory provisions are cited in Chapter 7.

POWER TO MAKE THE ORDER
In summary form, the power is available:

(i) to the Crown Court or a magistrates' court, including a youth court;

(ii) on convicting an offender aged 16 or older of an imprisonable offence (except murder), though an adult magistrates' court cannot make an order in respect of an offender aged under 18;

(iii) upon receiving oral or written evidence of two medical practitioners, one of whom must be approved under MHA 1983 s12;

(iv) where the court is satisfied that the offender is suffering from mental illness, psychopathic disorder, severe mental impairment or mental impairment (see page 84), and that the mental disorder is of a nature or degree which warrants the offender's reception into guardianship;

(v) where guardianship, in the court's opinion, is the most suitable disposal, given all the circumstances and other available options.

Mental Disorder
- It is not necessary for a causal link to be established between the offender's mental disorder and the offence for which the order is made; it is sufficient for the criteria of s37 to be satisfied.

- The court has to be precise in specifying from which form of disorder the offender is suffering and the doctors must be in agreement as to the particular form of disorder (s37(7), see page 86).

- For offenders suffering either psychopathic disorder or mental impairment, it is not necessary to satisfy the 'treatability' test, as required in the case of a hospital order, *ie* that treatment is likely to alleviate or prevent a deterioration of the condition.

- Mere mental disability will not be a sufficient ground for guardianship; the impairment must be 'associated with abnormally aggressive or seriously irresponsible conduct' (MHA 1983 s1(2)).

- The caveat of MHA 1983 s1(3) applies that a person should not be made subject to guardianship 'by reason only of promiscuity or other immoral conduct, sexual deviancy or dependence on drugs or alcohol'.

Consent of the Guardian

The court must be satisfied that the local social services authority (which will almost certainly be the appropriate guardian), or 'such other person' approved by the authority for the task, 'is willing to receive the offender into guardianship' (s37(6)). Note that the consent of the offender is not a pre-requisite. CJA 1991 s27(1) inserted a further provision to allow a court which is considering a guardianship order to seek the views and proposals of the local social services authority:

MHA 1983 s39A

Where a court is minded to make a guardianship order in respect of any offender, it may request the local social services authority for the area in which the offender resides or last resided, or any other local social services authority that appears to the court to be appropriate–

(a)   to inform the court whether it or any other person approved by it is willing to receive the offender into guardianship; and

(b)   if so, to give such information as it reasonably can about how it or the other person could be expected to exercise in relation to the offender the powers conferred by section 40(2) below;

and that authority shall comply with any such request.

The Reed Committee (1992, para. 5.14) suggested that this new provision might increase the use of s37 guardianship. Responsibility for decisions regarding potential guardianship is likely to rest at a senior level within the authority's Social Services directorate.

Making the Order without Conviction

Power of a magistrates' court to make a s37 order without first convicting the offender, where the court is satisfied that s/he 'did the act or made the omission' (s37(3)) is available equally in respect of guardianship but is likely to be exercised only on very rare occasions (see pages 83 and 89).

Permissible Concurrent Orders

The provisions of s37(8) (see page 88) apply equally to guardianship orders.

EFFECT OF THE ORDER

A guardianship order confers on the authority or person named in the order the same powers as a guardianship application made and accepted under MHA 1983 s7(s40(2)), subject to minor modifications detailed in sch 1 part I. It is not possible to address the precise, detailed legal provisions for administering guardianship in this book, so the following simply summarises the main features.

Powers and Duties of the Guardian

Powers are specified by MHA 1983 s8(1) as follows:

(i)   to require the patient to reside at a specified place ('this may be used to discourage the offender from sleeping rough or living with people who may exploit or mistreat him, or ensure that he resides at a particular hostel': HOC 66/1990 para. 8(iv)(c));

(ii) to require the patient to attend at specified places or times for medical treatment, occupation, education or training;

(iii) to require access to the patient to be given, at any place where the patient is residing, to any doctor, approved social worker or other person (*eg* a nurse) specified by the guardian ('this power could be used to ensure that the offender did not neglect himself': HOC 66/1990 para. 8(iv)(c)).

The guardian must fulfil the duties specified by the *Mental Health (Hospital, Guardianship and Consent to Treatment) Regulations 1983*, reg.13 specifying that the local authority:

> 'shall arrange for every patient ... to be visited at such intervals as the authority may decide, but in any case at intervals of not more than three months, and at least one such visit in any year shall be made by a medical practitioner approved under MHA 1983 s12.'

Ill-treatment or wilful neglect of a guardianship patient by any private guardian or by any individual responsible for the custody or care of the patient is a criminal offence punishable with imprisonment (s127(2)).

Absence of Sanctions

Guardianship rests on the assumption that patients will co-operate with those given authority to oversee their lives and the 1983 Act provides neither power to oblige the patient to receive medical treatment (as a person subject to guardianship is not 'liable to be detained' within s56 and Part IV of the Act), nor sanction in the event of refusal to co-operate with the guardian's requirements. The only enforcement power arises if a patient 'absents himself without leave of the guardian from the place at which he is required by the guardian to reside'. Such unauthorised absence renders the patient liable to 'be taken into custody and returned to that place by any officer on the staff of a local social services authority, by any constable, or by any person authorised in writing by the guardian or a local social services authority' (s18(3)). However, a patient will cease to be subject to guardianship if s/he remains absent without leave after a period of six months (or the end of the period for which he is subject to guardianship, if that is sooner) (s18(4) as amended by MH(PC)A 1995 s2(1), extending the period from 28 days).

Medical Oversight

The 1983 Act assigns certain medical responsibilities in guardianship to 'the responsible medical officer' (RMO), the 'appropriate medical officer' (AMO) or the 'nominated medical attendant' (NMA). The RMO (who has power to discharge the order) is a medical officer authorised by the local authority so to act, either generally or in any particular case or for any particular purpose. The AMO, who examines the patient to determine if there are grounds to renew the order, is either the RMO (in the case of a local authority guardianship) or the NMA (in the case of private guardianship), who is the doctor appointed by the guardian to act in this capacity.

Duration of the Order

Guardianship provisions mirror those pertaining to hospital orders without restriction, lasting initially for six months but renewable for a further six months and subsequently for a year at a time (s20(1)). The appropriate medical officer must examine the patient within the last two months of the period of the order and report to the guardian (and the local social services authority in the case of private guardianship) if the criteria for guardianship still exist. Unless the local authority opts nevertheless to discharge the order, the guardianship will be automatically renewed. The criteria justifying continuance are that (s20(7)):

(i) the patient continues to suffer from one of the four statutorily specified forms of mental disorder;

(ii) the disorder is of a nature or degree which warrants the exercise of guardianship;

(iii) it is necessary in the interests of the welfare of the patient or for the protection of other persons that the patient should remain under guardianship.

Discharge of the Order

Power to discharge the guardianship can be exercised at any time during the life of the order, either by the responsible local social services authority or by the responsible medical officer (s23(2)(b)). Though the 'nearest relative' has power of discharge in respect of s7 guardianship, they cannot discharge a s37 patient.

USE OF THE ORDER

The Butler Committee (1975, para. 15.8) considered that guardianship orders:

'offer a useful form of control of some mentally disordered offenders who do not require hospital treatment ... particularly suited to the needs of subnormal offenders including those inadequate offenders who require help in managing their affairs',

and in some circumstances would be more effective than a probation order. HOC 66/1990 para. 8(c) suggested that as the purpose of guardianship is primarily to ensure that the offender receives care and protection rather than medical treatment, the power could be used 'to ensure the offender did not neglect himself'. MHA(COP) 1999 para. 13(1) identifies the purpose of guardianship generally thus:

'To enable patients to receive care in the community where it cannot be provided without the use of compulsory powers. It provides an authoritative framework for working with a patient, with a minimum of constraint, to achieve as independent a life as possible within the community. Where it is used it must be part of the patient's overall care and treatment plan.'

The 1993 Code of Guidance suggested that guardianship orders may be particularly suitable in helping to meet the needs of mentally impaired offenders who could benefit from occupation, training and education in the community.

In fact the use of this measure by the courts has been extremely limited. In the year ending 31 March 1993 only four new s37 orders were imposed in England and the total number of s37 orders in force on that date in England was 22, the lowest figure since the 1983 Act was implemented. However, the 1994 figures showed a modest but encouraging increase, with 18 orders being imposed, the highest number for any year since implementation. Since then, the annual number of new s37 orders has remained low, with an average of 11 per year in the period 1995-2001. However, in the 12 months ending 31 March 2002 only three orders were made in criminal proceedings. The number of current s37 guardianship orders at that date was 22, the lowest number in the period since 1995 (Department of Health, 2002).

It may be that local authorities are reluctant to take on additional responsibilities in an unfamiliar area of work which may be considered beyond their proper remit. It is also possible that there is simply a widespread ignorance about the availability of this little-known measure.

THE FUTURE OF GUARDIANSHIP

The Department of Health, considering the potential future use of guardianship, issued a Discussion Paper in October 1994 which acknowledged that there does not seem any clear consensus about the kind of patients for whom guardianship (civil or criminal) might be suitable. The Paper noted that a common belief prevails that guardianship cannot work without the subject's co-operation but is redundant if the subject co-operates. Ways of strengthening guardianship by including a 'power to convey' the subject or to require them to accept medication were under consideration but the Government then decided to test the effectiveness of the new power of supervised discharge (see page 94) before amending the present powers of guardianship. However, under the draft Mental Health Bill (2002), the provisions of guardianship would be abolished in favour of new provisions enabling compulsory treatment to be provided in the community and in hospital.

12
CUSTODIAL SENTENCING

This chapter should be considered in the context of advice in HOC 66/1990 para. 26(ii) that courts should 'ensure that alternatives to custody are considered for all mentally disordered persons ... and that persons who are in need of medical treatment are not sent to prison'. *Mentally Disordered Offenders: Inter-Agency Working* (Home Office/DoH, 1995) reiterated that:

> 'the Government attaches importance to ensuring that those suffering from mental disorder are not imprisoned unnecessarily ... In the case of defendants whose mental disorder is not amenable to, or does not require, medical treatment, the courts will wish to consider their suitability for other non-custodial measures.'

Though life sentences are noted briefly below, the law and issues pertaining to this form of custodial sentence are dealt with more fully in Stone (1997 and forthcoming).

MENTAL DISORDER AND PCC(S)A 2000

Within the broad framework of proportionality originally introduced by the 1991 Act and now reproduced largely unchanged in PCC(S)A 2000, recognition of the special demands of mentally disordered offenders is given in three particular instances or safeguards when the court would otherwise be considering a custodial sentence. 'Mentally disordered' in this context means 'suffering from a mental disorder within the meaning of MHA 1983' (s82(5)), *ie* suffering from one or more of the four kinds of disorder outlined in MHA 1983 s1(2) (see page 84).

Duty to Obtain a Medical Report

Before forming an opinion that a custodial sentence is justified and, if so, what the length of that sentence should be, a court, faced with a defendant who is either known to be 'mentally disordered' or appears to be so in the lay opinion of the court, should obtain a medical report (see Chapter 4), subject to the familiar caveat that this can be dispensed with if the court reaches a specific opinion that such a report is not necessary. A medical report is defined by s82(6) as: 'a report as to an offender's mental condition made or submitted orally or in writing by a doctor who is approved' under MHA 1983 s12 (see page 233). If the court fails to obtain a report without first reaching an opinion that a report is unnecessary, any custodial sentence passed is nevertheless valid but will clearly provide grounds for appeal and, in the event of an appeal, the higher court will be required to obtain and consider a report. The requirement does not apply where a custodial sentence is 'fixed by law'.

PCC(S)A 2000 s82

(1) Subject to subsection (2) below, in any case where section 3(1) above applies and the offender is or appears to be mentally disordered, the court shall obtain and consider a medical report before passing a custodial sentence other than one fixed by law.

(2) Subsection (1) above does not apply if, in the circumstances of the case, the court is of the opinion that it is unnecessary to obtain a medical report.

...

(4) No custodial sentence which is passed in a case to which subsection (1) above applies shall be invalidated by the failure of a court to comply with that subsection, but any court on an appeal against such a sentence –

(a) shall obtain a medical report if none was obtained by the court below; and

(b) shall consider any such report obtained by it or by that court.

Duty to Consider the Effects of Custody

Except in cases where a mandatory life sentence will apply, the court should not impose a custodial sentence on a defendant known or suspected to be mentally disordered without first considering any available information from whatever source about the defendant's mental condition and the impact of a custodial sentence upon that condition and the implications of such a sentence for any treatment that the defendant is receiving or could receive.

PCC(S)A 2000 s82(3)

Before passing a custodial sentence other than one fixed by law on an offender who is or appears to be mentally disordered, a court shall consider –

(a) any information before it which relates to his mental condition (whether given in a medical report, a pre-sentence report or otherwise); and

(b) the likely effect of such a sentence on that condition and on any treatment which may be available for it.

Discretion to Sentence as Appropriate

Offenders who would otherwise attract a custodial sentence but who are mentally disordered may be dealt with flexibly to allow the sentence most appropriate to their circumstances.

PCC(S)A 2000 s158(3)

Nothing in this Part shall be taken –

(a) as requiring a court to pass a custodial sentence, or any particular custodial sentence, on a mentally disordered offender; or

(b) as restricting any power (whether under the 1983 Act or otherwise) which enables a court to deal with such an offender in the manner it considers to be most appropriate in all the circumstances.

Though he was probably not intending to give definitive guidance in a case which was primarily addressing the right of courts to make hospital orders without obstruction from 'nurses, porters and union officials' who may seek to resist the admission of difficult offender-patients to insecure conditions, it is worth noting the comments of Lawton LJ in *R v Harding* (1983) *The Times*, 15 June:

'Putting people who are severely mentally ill into prison is a form of cruelty. Not only that but it imposes a great strain on the prison staff. They are there to deal with inmates of ordinary mental stability. If they have among the inmates some who are mentally disordered ... the prison routine could be seriously upset.'

R v Cartwright (1989, outlined on page 119) offers a pre-1991 Act illustration of a sentencer's discretion to avoid a custodial sentence in favour of a psychiatric probation order. More recently, in *R v Fell* [2000] 2 Cr App R(S) 464, a young woman, then aged 20, had been in a relationship from age 14 with a man five years older than herself who had been persistently domineering and violent to her. In the course of an argument in which she told him to leave he received a fatal knife wound. Psychiatric opinion considered that she exhibited features of 'battered woman's syndrome', including chronic depressive illness and a feeling of hopelessness and despair. Since her arrest she had made remarkable progress in changing her mode of life, flourishing in her new circumstances while on bail. The Court of Appeal was able to conclude that the circumstances justified the 'wholly exceptional course' of imposing a community sentence. Sentence of detention for four years was quashed in favour of (what was then) a probation order.

Effect of Imprisonment on a Mentally Disordered Offender

Information may be available about the impact of custody on a mentally disordered offender, while on remand or following sentence (and thus brought to the attention of the Appeal Court). In *R v Dainty* [2002] EWCA Crim 2993 (unreported), the offender suffered physical and mental disabilities. Following special schooling, he had spent numerous periods in psychiatric hospital followed by out-patient support, being prescribed anti-depressants, anti-convulsants and depixol. After his last discharge from hospital, he had not received his medication for some reason and this seemed to have contributed to his episode of offending following an acrimonious separation from his girlfriend. Having committed deception by issuing a worthless cheque, he had stolen a handbag from a parked car, ramming another vehicle in escaping the scene and driving dangerously while uninsured in a bid to evade police in pursuit. When interviewed, he said voices had told him to take the bag. Bailed, he had been able to secure specialist accommodation as part of a community care programme. A psychiatric report considered at sentence identified his poor impulse control and judgement but doubted whether the claimed auditory delusions were genuine. The psychiatrist concluded that though he was certainly vulnerable, with considerable and pervasive psychological difficulties, he might well cope within the prison system if given adequate support.

On his appeal against 18 months' imprisonment, he claimed that insufficient account had been taken (a) of the fact that he had been without medication through no fault of his own, thus causing him to behave out of character (he had previous convictions but none in the preceding 13 years, being then aged 42), and (b) of the negative effect of imprisonment. A prison-based probation officer's report indicated that he had been located in three different prisons within six weeks, having been attacked by other prisoners in the mistaken belief that he was a sex offender against children and having had an epileptic fit. The reporter could not 'recall having met a more vulnerable prisoner'. The specialist accommodation remained available as part of the care plan but only up to the date of the appeal hearing. Though concluding that the sentence was fully justified in normal circumstances, the Appeal Court, taking a view that seems to echo the sentiments of Lawton LJ in *Harding* (see above), felt satisfied that his time in prison 'will have been a far greater punishment and, therefore, a far greater deterrent for him than for a conventional prisoner'. It was clearly in the public interest to quash the sentence and substitute a community rehabilitation order.

Compare *R v Waterfield* [2002] EWCA Crim 2680 (unreported), where a psychiatric report before the Appeal Court stated that the offender was suffering an obsessive compulsive disorder and that her condition had deteriorated since she was sentenced. Dismissing this ground of her appeal against a term of five years for conspiracy to supply cannabis, the Court concluded that 'the mere fact that an applicant suffers from a serious medical condition of this type, which is not readily treatable in the prison in which she is detained, is no ground for a reduction of sentence'. It may have been significant that her condition appeared not to have been a factor in her crime.

Mental Disorder and Mitigation

It may be legitimate for a sentencing court to maintain its belief that a custodial term is required but to mitigate sentence by taking into account the offender's mental disorder, either as information which it is required to consider about the circumstances of the offence or by exercising its general discretion under PCC(S)A 2000 s158(1) to take account of 'any such matters as are relevant'. This can be illustrated by recent cases involving domestic violence:

R v Wornock (1998, unreported) where the breakdown of the offender's marriage caused his severe depressive illness. Having told his GP about his violent outbursts and threats of violence towards his wife, he had been referred to a psychiatrist to whom he explained his fear that he could not control himself. After becoming angry he left the consulting room and refused to attend again, though he later appeared calmer and no longer making threats. Thereafter, however, he stabbed his former best friend with whom his wife was now in a sexual relationship. Though his premeditation was clear, having taken a knife with him to the victim's flat, his illness, together with his previous good character save for one unrelated conviction, was considered a mitigating factor and his sentence was reduced on appeal from seven years to 54 months.

R v Parsons (1999, unreported) where the offender had wounded his wife with intent (s18), by stabbing her in the back as she slept. He had persisted in face of her screams and resistance and he had to be restrained by intervening neighbours. A medical report indicated that he had been suffering a moderately severe depressive illness, had experienced a range of stressful circumstances which robust individuals would have found difficult and thought that 'people had it in for him'. It was unlikely that the attack, though sustained, had been premeditated. He was considered vulnerable in prison and at high risk of fatal self-harm. Given his previous essentially good character, and evidence that his crime was wholly out of character, the Court of Appeal considered that in the light of the medical evidence 'the criminality was significantly lower than that of somebody who was not similarly afflicted', reducing sentence from seven years to 54 months.

R v Korkmen [2001] EWCA Crim 777 (unreported), where the offender had caused GBH with intent to his estranged wife out of pathological jealousy and anger that she would not reconcile. He had been under psychiatric out-patient care in the nine months prior to this attack. The Court of Appeal concluded that the sentencer had given insufficient recognition to his severe depressive state and thus reduced a term of nine years to one of six years.

In a case not concerned with domestic violence but with arson, *R v Manuel* [2002] 1 Cr App R(S) 526, the offender's mental disorder appears not to have prompted any mitigation, given no clear indication of the nature of her condition. A woman aged 48 of previous good character had been under intermittent psychiatric care from the 1980s, receiving treatment for 'a depressive disorder associated with personality difficulties'. She was convicted of arson with intent to endanger life and arson being reckless as to whether life was endangered, having placed lighted rags through the letter boxes of two homes some two weeks after discharge from hospital where she had been admitted because of her 'very bizarre behaviour', including attempting to suffocate her boyfriend with a pillow. In one instance she had been motivated by the belief that the occupant had reported her for shoplifting. The psychiatric evidence disclosed no basis for a disposal under MHA 1983 and she was described as 'emotionally detached', indicating that she found prison no hardship. Though her sentence of 12 years was reduced to ten years on appeal, this was on the basis of her lack of previous convictions, not her mental condition.

PUBLIC PROTECTION

PCC(S)A 2000 s79(2)(b) and s80(2)(b) (formerly CJA 1991 s1(2)(b) and s2(2)(b)) permit a court dealing with a violent or sexual offence to consider that only a custodial sentence would be adequate to protect the public from serious harm from the defendant and to pass a longer-than-commensurate sentence in the interests of such public protection. Though not statutorily restricted to the Crown Court, this issue will almost always arise only in the superior court, and the provision will only be invoked when there is a substantial risk of further violence or sexual offending causing serious harm. See Stone (2001) for a fuller account.

'Violent Offence'

This is defined descriptively by PCC(S)A 2000 s161(3) as:

> an offence which leads, or is intended or likely to lead, to a person's death or to physical injury to a person, and includes an offence which is required to be charged as arson (whether or not it would otherwise fall within this definition).

This definition has proved ambiguous in contexts where the victim has been threatened with a weapon but no actual injury was inflicted, *eg* where a robbery is committed using an unloaded firearm (*R v Touriq Khan* (1995) 16 Cr App R(S) 180). In the absence of a specific finding that the offence was likely to lead to injury or that the offender intended to use the weapon, the court is not able to invoke public protection powers to impose a longer sentence. The mere risk of injury is insufficient for an offence to qualify as 'violent' but it does not have to be shown that injury was a necessary and probable consequence. In *R v Szczerba* [2002] Crim LR 429, where a man assessed to be suffering from dissocial personality disorder had broken into his older victim's home and detained her, spraying her face with hairspray, knocking her spectacles from her face and placing his hands round her throat and applying pressure, the Court of Appeal considered that this offence of false imprisonment was violent as it involved conduct that 'could very well lead to injury', such as cardiac arrest or vagal inhibition.

Sexual Offence

This is defined by PCC(S)A 2000 s161(2) not by description but by reference to a list of statutory offences:

(i)   an offence under the Sexual Offences Act 1956, other than an offence under ss30, 31 or 33 to 36 of that Act;

(ii)   an offence under the Mental Health Act 1959 s128;

(iii) an offence under the Indecency with Children Act 1960;

(iv)   an offence under the Theft Act 1968 s9 of burglary with intent to commit rape;

(v)   an offence under the Criminal Law Act 1977 s54;

(vi)   an offence under the Protection of Children Act 1978;

(vii) an offence under the Criminal Law Act 1977 s1 of conspiracy to commit any of the offences in paras. (i) to (vi) above;

(viii)an offence under the Criminal Attempts Act 1981 s1 of attempting to commit any of those offences;

(ix)   an offence of inciting another to commit any of those offences.

'Protection from Serious Harm'

This is defined by PCC(S)A 2000 s161(4) as meaning:

> protecting members of the public from death or serious personal injury, whether physical or psychological, occasioned by further such offences committed by him.

Range of Danger

Though reference to protection of 'the public' might be interpreted to mean risk or threat of harm only of a broad or general nature, the Court of Appeal has held that s80(2)(b) is not limited to cases where the threat extends beyond one individual or a very small number of people. In *R v Hashi* (1995) 16 Cr App R(S) 121 the offender stabbed a man whom he saw drinking in the company of a woman with whom the offender had previously lived, having already been convicted of a jealous knife attack on another male who had formed a relationship with her. The Court was satisfied that s2(2)(b) applied even though the offender presented a serious risk only to his former partner and any man associating with her.

Psychiatric Factors

Use of longer than proportionate, protective sentencing is by no means confined to offenders presenting psychiatric ill-health and allied instability. It is thus not necessary to obtain a psychiatric report before passing such a sentence (*Hashi*), though PCC(S)A 2000 s82(1) may make this a prerequisite in many such cases. In *R v Fawcett* [1994] Crim LR 704, where the defendant had attacked another woman aged 86, the Court of

Appeal stated that the court should call for a medical report before concluding that a s80(2)(b) sentence is required, if the danger appeared to arise from a mental health or personality problem, to allow the court to consider whether a medical disposal is appropriate.

R v Bavaghens [2003] EWCA Crim 31 (unreported) illustrates the application of s80(2)(b) in a psychiatric context. The offender, who had been made subject to a s37 hospital order on grounds of mental illness for possession of cocaine, had afterwards attacked his barrister, a woman, through the opening of his cell door in the custody area at court, punching her to the face. On subsequent conviction for ABH he was given a three-year term, expressed as a longer-than-commensurate term, instead of two years which the judge considered would otherwise have been justified. He appealed, arguing that a s80(2)(b) sentence was not indicated, given that he had inflicted a single punch and had not caused lasting physical injury. Noting his record of aggression, particularly directed against women, the Court of Appeal determined that he posed a significant risk of serious harm, justifying a longer term. However, the commensurate term should have been 12 months. The Court noted that in many cases where s80(2)(b) is applied some 50% has been added, which in this instance would indicate a total term of 18 months. Given the medical evidence and the concerns expressed in the PSR, the Court concluded that this was 'a wholly exceptional case' requiring a longer extension and substituted a term of two years (*ie* 100% increase). See also *R v Barker* (see page 160).

Extended Sentence

Separate provisions in respect of offenders convicted of violent or sexual offences under PCC(S)A 2000 s85 empower a court to order the extention of the period for which the offender would otherwise be subject to licence on release, where the period that would otherwise apply would not be adequate for the purpose of preventing the commission of further offences and securing his or her rehabilitation. This power can be used in tandem with a longer-than-commensurate sentence under s80(2)(b) (above) or in respect of a commensurate custodial term. The Court of Appeal has given guidance on the appropriate use of different combinations of these powers in *R v Nelson* [2002] 1 Cr App R(S) 134. Extended sentence provisions are detailed in Stone (2001) but for an example of use in the context of a mentally disordered offender and in addition to use of s80(2)(b) powers, see *Barker* (outlined at page 160).

DISCRETIONARY LIFE SENTENCE

Leading judgments in the Court of Appeal prior to CJA 1991 (especially *R v Hodgson* (1968) 52 Cr App R 113 and *R v Wilkinson* (1983) 5 Cr App R(S) 105) established that life imprisonment will be justified for offences carrying that statutory maximum sentence where three conditions are satisfied:

(i)   the offence(s) are in themselves grave enough to require a very long sentence;

(ii) it appears from the nature of the offence(s), or from the defendant's history, that s/he is a person of mental instability who, if at liberty, would probably re-offend and present a grave danger to the public;

(iii) the defendant will remain unstable and a potential danger for a long and/or an uncertain period of time.

In *Attorney-General's Reference No. 34 of 1992* [1993] Crim LR 801 the Court of Appeal confirmed that these criteria continue to be applicable following implementation of the 1991 Act. However, as an indeterminate custodial sentence must be regarded as a longer-than-commensurate sentence (PCC(S)A 2000 s80(4)), a discretionary life sentence may be imposed only in the case of a 'violent' or 'sexual' offence.

In *Attorney-General's Reference No. 32 of 1996 (Whittaker)* [1997] 1 Cr App R(S) 261 the qualifying conditions were posed thus:

(i)   the offender has been convicted of a very serious offence;

(ii) there are good grounds for believing that the offender may remain a serious danger to the public for a period that cannot reliably be estimated at the date of sentence.

R v Trowbridge [2002] 2 Cr App R(S) 154 provides a recent illustration of the application of the *Hodgson* criteria in respect of a mentally disordered offender, a man aged 50 and of previous good character at the time of committing arson being reckless as to whether life was endangered. He had started a fire in his own flat when police had been summonsed to investigate an emergency water leak emanating from that address causing flooding in properties below. No one was injured. Following his bail to hospital to assess his suitability for a probation order with requirement of treatment, a psychiatrist had reported that he had 'limited capacity to cope and is of borderline intellectual ability' with social and intellectual deficit. His marked antipathy to hospital treatment made that proposed form of disposal unfeasible. The PSR identified his vulnerability, social isolation, mistrust of others and considerable difficulties in coping with day-to-day demands, combined with refusal to co-operate with help on offer. The probation officer concluded that, should factors such as his social isolation and prolonged grieving not be addressed, the risk of re-offending would appear high. A clinical psychologist reported that he needed assistance in the community as regards accommodation, occupation and development of self-care skills. Apparently prompted by the psychiatrist's reference to the defendant's marked antipathy to the County of Devon (where he had been living) and its inhabitants, the judge concluded that he posed 'a significant threat to the inhabitants of Devon' and that a life sentence was justified.

On appeal, the Court of Appeal agreed with defence counsel that the psychiatrist could not have held the view that the offender posed a significant threat to Devon residents because he had been willing to support the proposal of a probation order provided that the offender was willing to accept treatment. Such an order would not have been appropriate for someone posing a grave danger to the public. Further, the judge had failed to appreciate that the factors at stake resided not in the offender's mental instability or personality disorder but in his social circumstances, which were open to remedy, through Social Services for example. Accordingly, the life term was quashed and a period of four years was substituted.

See also *R v Barker* [2003] 1 Cr App R(S) 212, an instance of attempted robbery, where the Court of Appeal considered that a hospital order with s41 restriction would have been the best disposal but was unable to take that course (see page 83). While sympathising with the dilemma faced by the sentencing judge in trying to deal most effectively with a defendant who posed a serious risk to the public, the Court concluded that his offence did not call for a sentence of sufficient severity to justify the imposition of a discretionary life sentence. However, in light of the psychiatric evidence, a longer than commensurate term of ten years (four years as the commensurate period plus an additional six years) was imposed, combined with extension of licence to constitute an extended sentence.

Mental Instability

A medical report should normally be available to the court (*R v De Havilland* (1983) 5 Cr App R(S) 109), though in very exceptional cases it has been held that evidence of this nature justifying the imposition of a life sentence was sufficiently apparent to the court from the facts of the case and the defendant's record, *eg De Havilland*, where the defendant was judged very unlikely to co-operate and the judge had the benefit of observing a six-day trial, and *R v Allen* (1987) 9 Cr App R(S) 169. For discussion of the possible use of life imprisonment in circumstances where the offender is eligible for a hospital order with restriction, see page 101.

AUTOMATIC LIFE SENTENCE

Under the provisions of PCC(S)A 2000 s109 (formerly C(S)A 1997 s2), the Crown Court is required to impose a life sentence on a defendant convicted of a second 'serious offence' (committed after 30 September 1997 when the offender was aged 18 or older and had already incurred a conviction for such an offence) unless there are 'exceptional circumstances' justifying the avoidance of this course. This measure is detailed in Stone (2001). Suffice it to clarify here that the test for exceptionality is that the offender does not represent an unacceptable risk or danger to the public (*R v Offen* [2001] 2 Cr App R(S) 10). Accordingly, the defendant's mental disorder does not constitute an exceptional circumstance. This was confirmed in *R v Newman* [2000] 2 Cr App R(S) 227, where the offender had killed his grandmother, prompting his guilty plea to manslaughter on grounds of diminished responsibility. He clearly fell within the scope of s2/s109 as he had a previous conviction for s18 GBH. However, psychiatrists were agreed that he was suffering a paranoid psychotic illness considered treatable under the provisions of a hospital order and a bed was available for him at a special hospital. Though expressing concern that a defendant 'so obviously and acutely suffering from mental illness should be ordered to prison, not hospital', the Appeal Court concluded that in the absence of any other exceptional circumstance, this was a case to which the automatic life sentence plainly applied, given the parallel amendment to MHA 1983 s37(1) to exclude the making of a hospital order where a case falls to be sentenced under s109 (see page 82). The possibility of avoiding this course had been explicitly blocked by MHA 1983 s45A(1). It was thus a case in which the offender would be eligible instead to receive hospital treatment as a life sentence prisoner by means of a s47 transfer from prison (see Chapter 13). In a commentary on *Newman*, Thomas suggested that this kind of case would be suitable for a 'hospital direction' (see below) and that the conditions of eligibility should be extended accordingly. Laing (1997) has speculated that this measure will prompt more resort to defence claims of unfitness to plead and insanity.

The approach in *Newman* has since been challenged unsuccessfully on human rights grounds. In *R v Drew* [2002] 2 Cr App R(S) 189 a defendant pleading guilty to s18 wounding, a frenzied attack with a kitchen knife on a man who sought to intervene in an altercation he was having with a pub landlord, had a previous conviction for s18 GBH, incurred less than five years previously, thus rendering him liable to an automatic life sentence. However, examining psychiatrists were unanimous that he was suffering from a mental illness within MHA 1983 and that the appropriate course was a s37/s41 hospital order with restriction. The trial judge had expressed regret that he had to pass a life sentence, but concluded that he had no other option, in light of *Newman*. The offender appealed, arguing that the life sentence was in breach of the ECHR Article 3 (prohibition of inhuman treatment) and Article 5 (right to liberty). His representatives argued that it was wrong to treat someone who was mentally ill as a deliberate wrongdoer deserving of punishment and subject to a tariff set by the court. Since his sentence he had been transferred from prison to hospital under MHA 1983 s47 (see Chapter 13).

Dismissing the appeal, the Court of Appeal agreed that a sentence of imprisonment carries a certain stigma but noted that the offender had been found fit to plead and had been properly convicted. The Court took into account that there are instances where an offender presents such a serious and continuing danger to public safety that a s37/s41 order affords inadequate protection, a life sentence affording greater protection. There was no evidence that a life sentence prisoner will not receive appropriate medical treatment, the offender being in the same institution as he would have been under s37/s41. Accordingly, it could not be said that his Convention rights had been infringed. In a commentary on *Drew*, Thomas [2002] Crim LR 222 has suggested that if a mentally defendant is facing an automatic life sentence, the defence should consider running an insanity defence (see Chapter 6) since this, if successful, avoids conviction and thus the mandatory consequences of s109(1). He also suggests that it could be helpful for the Home Secretary to extend scope for use of hospital and limitation directions under MHA 1983 s45A (see page 163) to any form of mental disorder, thus enabling a court obliged to impose a life sentence in such instances as *Drew* to direct that the offender be detained in hospital.

In *R v Harkin* [2002] EWCA Crim 2700 (unreported) the offender had attacked first a man he had met in a public house and accompanied to his home and then a woman police officer who attended the scene. At the time he had been a ss37/41 restricted patient following conviction for s18 wounding of a police officer but on day release in the community approved by the Home Office. He suffered paranoid schizophrenia but had 'deceived the doctors into believing that his illness had improved'. On conviction for attempted murder and s18 wounding, an automatic life term was inevitable but, on appeal, the specified period was reduced from 12 years to 8+ years.

Mental Health Bill

Clause 77(1) of the draft Bill indicates that power to impose a mental health order under clause 78 applies to an offence punishable by imprisonment 'other than an offence for which the sentence ... falls to be imposed under s109(2)', clause 111(9) interpreting that a sentence so falls to be imposed 'if it is required by that provision and the court is not of the opinion there mentioned'. The *Explanatory Notes* (para. 105) indicate that the effect is 'that where the court is of the opinion that there are such exceptional circumstances which justify not imposing a life sentence, a mental health order may be made'. This appears to replicate the current law.

MANDATORY CUSTODIAL SENTENCES FOR DRUG TRAFFICKING AND DOMESTIC BURGLARY

Though the Crown Court is required to impose a custodial sentence of a minimum length of seven years (in respect of a drug trafficking offence) or three years in respect of a domestic burglary offence) where the offender incurs a third conviction for an offence of that nature, under PCC(S)A 2000 s110 (drug offence; formerly C(S)A 1997 s3) or s111 (burglary offence; formerly C(S)A 1997 s4), the scope for variation from this statutory expectation is more flexible than applies in respect of an automatic life sentence under s109 (see above). The 1997 Act amended MHA 1983 s37 to include s37(1A) which states that nothing in s3 (s110) or s4 (s111) 'shall prevent a court from making an order under s37(1) for the admission of the offender to hospital'. For further details of s110 and s111, see Stone (2001). The present law is replicated in respect of mental health orders under clause 78 in clause 77(9) of the draft Mental Health Bill.

PROPORTIONALITY AND MENTAL DISORDER

In cases other than those involving violent or sexual offences where public protection justifies a longer than proportionate sentence, it is clear that a disproportionate sentence is not legitimate on grounds either (i) to keep the offender out of harm's way (*ie* with the aim of extended containment or incapacitation) or (ii) to seek to ensure that s/he receives treatment for their mental condition.

In *R v Fisher* (1981) 3 Cr App R(S) 112, sentence of three years' imprisonment imposed on an offender convicted of burglary, theft and criminal damage who was described as 'an inadequate psychopathic personality' with very low intelligence, not eligible for a hospital order but likely to remain unmanageable in the community, was reduced on appeal to 18 months. Though a 'social nuisance', the original term was clearly excessive for the offences in question. *R v Roote* (1980) 2 Cr App R(S) 318 illustrates the inappropriateness of lengthening sentence to protect offenders from themselves. The defendant was addicted to morphine and had self-harmed by overdose. A medical report indicated that she had a 'tenuous hold on life' and that a longer sentence would probably save her life. The Court of Appeal confirmed that this was not a proper basis for a disproportionate sentence.

Possibility of Grendon

Sentencers may hold a belief that the defendant would benefit from spending part of their prison sentence at HMP Grendon, designated to operate a therapeutic prison regime and that their prospects of having that opportunity will be better if either the sentence is longer or the sentencer indicates such a preference. However, as made clear in *R v Hook* (1980) 2 Cr App R(S) 353, where sentence of three years was reduced on appeal to 18 months for an offender who had broken windows at the hospital where he had previously been an in-patient, it is improper to extend sentence artificially in the hope that the offender will be allocated to Grendon and undesirable to refer to Grendon when passing sentence as this raises expectations which are frequently disappointed.

HOSPITAL DIRECTION

C(S)A 1997 s46 amended MHA 1983 by including a new provision, s45A, empowering the Crown Court, when imposing a custodial sentence upon a mentally disordered offender suffering from psychopathic disorder, to direct the offender's immediate admission to hospital. As explained in HOC 52/1997, power to make a hospital direction is intended:

'to give the courts greater flexibility in dealing with cases where they conclude that a prison sentence is the appropriate disposal in spite of evidence that the offender is mentally disordered .... either because the offender falls to (receive an automatic life sentence under C(S)A 1997 s2 – *now PCC(S)A 2000 s109*) or because the court is satisfied that a prison sentence with a hospital direction will be the most effective way to protect the public from harm.'

Whereas the sentencer previously had to opt between making a hospital order without any penal element or a prison sentence without any guarantee that the offender would receive any specialist treatment for his or her disorder, the new measure is intended to resolve the apparent dilemma, combining what Baroness Blatch, as Minister of State at the Home Office sponsoring the Bill through the Lords, described as 'the security of a custodial sentence with the immediacy of medical treatment.' The measure gives legislative effect to a proposal for a 'hybrid order' first suggested by the Reed Committee in 1994 as a way of encouraging psychiatrists to 'have a therapeutic go' in working with psychopaths of uncertain treatability, so that if the offender proves untreatable, doctor and patient would not be locked into a non-therapeutic relationship. The additional notion included in a subsequent Home Office/Department of Health discussion paper (1996), that courts could use the hybrid order in circumstances where the offender was considered to be 'partially responsible' for their crime, has not been pursued in the statutory criteria justifying the present measure.

It remains questionable what merits this provision has in terms of public protection over a hospital order with a s41 restriction order attached. For a fuller exploration of the conceptual and practical problems of this provision, see Eastman (1996); Eastman and Peay (1998). As currently designed, the number of offenders anticipated to be affected by this measure is very small. A hospital direction is available in respect of offences committed on or after the commencement date: 1 October 1997. *Statistics for Mentally Disordered Offenders: England & Wales, 2001* (Johnson and Taylor, 2002) indicate that three restricted patients were admitted to hospital in 2001 under hospital and limitation direction, with eight such admissions in 1999 and three in 2000.

Unsurprisingly, this power has received little attention in the Court of Appeal. However, in *R v Martin* [2001] EWCA Crim 2132 (unreported), the Court, in replacing a 30-month term of imprisonment imposed for a single instance of indecent assault (a street attack on a woman unknown to the offender by grabbing her genital area) on a man without previous convictions with a s37 hospital order, indicated that hospital and limitation directions were not necessary. Two months into his sentence the offender had been transferred to hospital, where he had been diagnosed to be suffering 'mild mental impairment associated with abnormally aggressive behaviour and seriously irresponsible conduct'. Both doctors advocated a hospital order and the Court agreed, having regard to the nature of the offence and the character and antecedents of the appellant.

Criteria to be Fulfilled

The conditions to be fulfilled are specified by s45A(2). The court must be satisfied on the evidence of two medical practitioners that:

(a)   the offender is suffering from psychopathic disorder;

(b)   the mental disorder from which the offender is suffering is of a nature or degree which makes it appropriate for him to be detained in a hospital for medical treatment; and

(c)   such treatment is likely to alleviate or prevent a deterioration of his condition.

At least one of the medical practitioners must give oral evidence to the court: s45A(4).

Cases Attracting an Automatic Life Sentence

Offenders for whom PCC(S)A 2000 s109 applies, requiring an obligatory life sentence (see page 161) in the absence of exceptional circumstances, are not eligible to receive a hospital order instead (see page 82). However, if the above conditions are satisfied the court may consider a s45A hospital direction as an adjunct to the life sentence.

Other Eligible Cases

In other instances where the offender satisfying the above conditions is convicted of an offence for which the sentence is not fixed by law, the court must first consider making a s37 hospital order before deciding to impose a sentence of imprisonment instead: s45A(1)(b). Note that the section does not include any indication of the circumstances in which a judge might properly prefer a hospital direction to a fully fledged hospital order. In determining length of sentence, the court has the scope in dealing with a sexual or violent offence (as most cases liable to be dealt with under this power are likely to be) to impose a longer than commensurate sentence under s80(2)(b) (see page 157), if the criteria for that protective measure are satisfied. If s80(2)(b) is not applicable, the sentence will need to be commensurate with seriousness, so that the issue of the offender's culpability and responsibility will still be a pertinent consideration. This is thus one of the sentencing challenges of a s45A order: the assessment of custodial punishment for an offender who is mentally disordered and the extent to which that disorder affords mitigation.

Procedural Prerequisite

The court must be satisfied on the oral or written evidence of the medical practitioner who would be in charge of treatment (or of a representative of the hospital managers) that arrangements have been made for the admission of the offender to the hospital to be specified in the order within 28 days of the direction: s45A(5). Pending admission to hospital, the offender may be detained in a 'place of safety' as defined by MHA 1983 s55. If, within 28 days, it appears to the Home Secretary that it is not practicable for the patient to be received into the specified hospital, by reason of an emergency or other special circumstance, he may give instructions for admission to another hospital: s45A(6). In this instance, the hospital direction shall have effect as if the substitute hospital were the specified hospital: s45A(7). Under s45A(8), discretionary power to make a s38 interim hospital order is extended to instances where the Crown Court is satisfied that it may be appropriate to make a hospital direction.

Directions Available to the Court

Section 45A(3) specifies that 'the court may give both of the following directions:

(a) *hospital direction:* 'a direction that the offender shall be moved to and detained in such hospital as may be specified in the direction';

(b) *limitation direction:* 'a direction that the offender be subject to the special restrictions of MHA 1983 s41.'

Though the drafting of s45A is not completely clear in this respect, the Government's intention, as reflected in HOC 52/1997 para. 7 is that the two directions must be imposed together, *ie* that the sentencer cannot make a hospital direction without a limitation direction. The effect is amplified by s45B(2) which states that a hospital direction shall have effect as a transfer direction (*ie* as if the patient has been transferred to hospital from prison under MHA 1983 s47) and a limitation direction shall have effect as a restriction direction under MHA 1983 s49. For the status of ss47/49 transferees, see Chapter 13. Where s45A directions are made, they apply to any other sentence of imprisonment imposed on the offender on the same or any previous occasion: s45A(9).

Power to Specify Hospital Unit
Under provisions introduced by C(S)A 1997 s47(1)(b), a court making a s45A order may specify not only the hospital at which the defendant will be detained but a 'unit' of the hospital (defined by s47(3) to mean 'any part of a hospital which is treated as a separate unit'). This is designed to enable the court to 'specify a level of security in which the patient needs to be detained' (MHA(COP) 1999 para. 3.15). In consequence, the Secretary of State's permission will be required for any transfer from the named unit, even to another part of the same hospital. The question of whether a unit should be designated is a factor for the doctors reporting to the court to consider (para. 3.14).

Extension to Other Mental Disorders
The Home Secretary may by order extend the provisions of s45A to offenders suffering other kinds of mental disorder under MHA 1983 in addition to psychopathic disorder.

Mental Health Bill
Clause 89 of the draft Bill, supplemented by clauses 90-91, incorporates this Crown Court power in the new statutory framework, though the power is extended beyond psychopathic disorder to 'persons suffering from mental disorder'. The procedure for making a hospital direction is designed to be very similar to that for making a mental health order, the first three conditions being the same as clause 78(2)-(4) and a fourth condition specifying that arrangements have been made for the admission of the person to the hospital specified by the Court within 28 days of the date of the directions (clause 89(6)).

SUSPENDED SENTENCE OF IMPRISONMENT
A suspended term of imprisonment under PCC(S)A 2000 s118 may only be imposed where the court is of the opinion (s118(4)):

(i) a sentence of imprisonment would have been appropriate even without the power to suspend sentence; and

(ii) suspension can be justified by the 'exceptional circumstances of the case'.

The Court of Appeal has not sought to define 'exceptional circumstances', preferring to retain wide discretion, but has made clear that exceptionality should not be found in relatively commonplace features such as previous good character or the adverse consequences of conviction. However, psychiatric considerations may amount to exceptional circumstances, as illustrated by *R v French* (1994) 15 Cr App R(S) 194 where the offender had pleaded guilty to conspiracy to obtain property by deception, falsely claiming that her car had been stolen to obtain an insurance payout. She had been under considerable financial and emotional strain at the time of the offence and had a 'significant' psychiatric history of depression. The psychiatrist's report indicated that she had been receiving treatment while awaiting trial and, though the prognosis was good, there would be concern about her stability if she were sent to prison. 'It would be highly likely that she would become significantly depressed and perhaps in need of hospital treatment. It would also substantially undermine her ability to succeed on release. As so much progress has been made since her arrest, imprisonment would be counter-productive'. The Court of Appeal concluded that suspension of sentence was justified.

See also *R v Ullah Khan* (1994) 15 Cr App R(S) 320 where a 69 year-old solicitor, following conviction for a £150,000 conspiracy to defraud, who was suspected to be suffering either depression or Alzheimer's Disease, was found on psychiatric examination to be suffering treatable paranoid psychosis which would have significantly jeopardised his concentration and judgement. The Court of Appeal considered that 'the serious health problems that face this ageing man are capable of being exceptional circumstances'.

Note, however, that the courts' preparedness to find exceptionality is not readily predictable. In *R v Bradley* (1994) 15 Cr App R(S) 597 a college lecturer with departmental budget responsibilities, who had misappropriated £7,000, had a history of mental health problems since childhood, including post-traumatic stress which had affected her at the time of her dishonesty. The psychiatric report indicated that since her arrest she had received in-patient treatment for severe reactive depression and remained highly suicidal. In both this case and *R v Lowery* (1993) 14 Cr App R(S) 559 (a very similar case involving a police officer) the Court of Appeal, placing emphasis on the breach of trust, was unable to find exceptional circumstances but was able to reduce the custodial term so as to facilitate the offender's almost immediate release.

More recently, in *R v Smith* [2002] 1 Cr App R(S) 250 suspension of sentence was rejected in circumstances where the offender aged 34 had set fire to his canal boat home because he believed that his relationship with his partner was over. The fire damaged other boats moored nearby. Though he had contemplated suicide in the fire, he escaped as the fire took hold. A psychiatric report had identified that he had been under a great deal of personal stress and anguish at the time, associated with his experience of childhood abuse and his subsequent propensity to depression, agoraphobia, angry and impulsive thinking, self-harm and emotional distress. There was no evidence, however, that he presented a continuing danger. The Court of Appeal agreed that sentence of three years was excessive, in light of his impulsive recklessness rather than any intent to harm others or their property, his full co-operation with police and his remorse, and substituted a term of two years but determined that there were no exceptional circumstances that could begin to justify suspension. As the Appeal Court has subsequently stated in *R v Stevens* [2002] EWCA Crim 2706 (unreported), serious health problems have to be 'truly exceptional' to justify suspension.

CRIMINAL JUSTICE BILL

Clause 187 of the Bill currently before Parliament provides power for a court to attach a mental health treatment requirement to a 'relevant order', a term that includes a 'custody plus order', a 'suspended sentence order' and an 'intermittent custody order', under the Bill's new scheme for shorter prison terms for offenders aged 18 or older.

Variations in Shorter Custodial Sentences

Suspended Sentence (Clauses 170-174)

A court will be able to suspend a short custodial sentence of under 12 months for between six months and two years on condition that the offender undertakes activities in the community, including mental health treatment.

Custody Plus (Clauses 163-164)

This proposed new sentence will replace all short sentences of under 12 months (with the exception of intermittent custody), combining a short period in custody of up to three months with a subsequent period of supervision in the community of a minimum period of six months. The court will be able to attach specific requirements to that supervision on licence, including mental health treatment.

Intermittent Custody (Clauses 165-168)

Under this proposed new sentence, where the offender consents, the custodial period may be served in blocks, while the licence period will run between those blocks and may continue after the final custodial period. Mental health treatment may be specified as a requirement of licence supervision.

This power essentially re-enacts but extends the provisions of PCC(S)A 2000 sch. 2 para. 5 governing community rehabilitation orders (Chapter 8) and continues the procedural requirement that the offender must express willingness to comply with the proposed treatment requirement. Allied clause 188 reproduces the provisions of para. 5(6) to (8) (above at page 129).

Dangerous Offenders

The Bill introduces a new scheme of sentences for offenders who are convicted of a specified sexual and/or violent offence and are assessed as dangerous (*ie* the court considers that 'there is a significant risk to the public of serious harm occasioned by the commission by the offender of further specified offences'. If the offence carries a maximum sentence of less than ten years, an offender who satisfies the criterion will be given an extended sentence with a minimum term in custody of half of total sentence length. Release during the remaining portion of sentence will be on the recommendation of the Parole Board. In addition, the court must attach extended supervision periods to the sentence of up to five years for violent offenders and nine years for sexual offenders.

If an offender has been assessed as dangerous and their offence carries a maximum term of ten years or longer, he will receive either a sentence of 'imprisonment for public protection' (clause 205) or a discretionary life sentence. For both forms of sentence, the court will specify a minimum term that the offender will be required to serve in custody. Beyond that point the offender will remain in prison until the Parole Board is satisfied that their risk has diminished sufficiently for them to be released and supervised in the community.

Clause 209 deals with the assessment of dangerousness at point of sentence, depending on whether at the time the current offence was committed the offender had been previously convicted in any part of the United Kingdom of any relevant offence. If not so convicted, the court, in making its assessment of dangerousness:

(a) must take into account all such information as is available to it about the nature and circumstances of the offence,

(b) may take into account any information which is before it about any pattern of behaviour of which the offence forms part, and

(c) may take into account any information about the offender which is before it.

If so convicted, the court must assume that the offender is dangerous unless, after taking into account:

(a) all such information as is available to it about the nature and circumstances of each of the offences,

(b) where appropriate, any information which is before it about any pattern of behaviour of which any of the offences forms part, and

(c) any information about the offender which is before it,

the court considers that it would be unreasonable to conclude that there is such a risk.

The Bill also repeals the 'automatic' life sentence provisions of PCC(S)A 2000 s109 (see page 161).

13
MENTALLY DISORDERED PRISONERS

This chapter primarily addresses the scope afforded the Home Secretary to direct the transfer of mentally disordered prisoners to hospital, while casting a wider glance at the evidence of prevalence of mental disorder among prisoners and the current face of in-house mental health care provision for mentally disordered prisoners.

HOC 66/1990 asked prison medical officers:

> 'to ensure that action is taken to arrange transfer to hospital under the provisions of MHA 1983 s48 in respect of any mentally ill or severely mentally impaired person remanded in custody who appears to require urgent treatment in hospital, and to consider advising the courts of the suitability of any other mentally disordered person on remand for treatment as part of a non-custodial disposal, such as a psychiatric probation order or guardianship order, after conviction. Prison medical officers are asked to ensure that action is taken to arrange the transfer to hospital under the provisions of MHA 1983 s47 of any sentenced prisoner who appears to require treatment in hospital for mental disorder.'

On a more general note, the Reed Committee (1992, para. 11.74) recommended:

> 'There should be a clear statement of policy, complementary to the existing policy on diversion, in relation to the care and treatment of prisoners with mental heath care needs. This statement should cover the role of the mental health care services in the identification and assessment of mental disorder, crisis intervention, and continuing treatment on the basis of individual care plans for those for whom transfer from prison is either not possible or delayed.'

Reference may also be made to Section 6 of *Mentally Disordered Offenders: Working Together* (Home Office/DoH, 1995, though that has been largely overtaken by subesequent developments in joint initiatives between the two Departments, as outlined at the end of this chapter. Though some issues pertaining to life sentence prisoners are noted below, the specific law and related provisions for indeterminate sentences are dealt with in Stone (1997 and forthcoming).

THE MENTAL HEALTH PROBLEMS AND TREATMENT NEEDS OF PRISONERS
Sentenced Male Prisoners
Gunn and colleagues (1991) assessed the psychiatric needs of a 5% sample of the sentenced male prison population, interviewing 404 young offenders and 1,365 adults in 25 prisons in 1988-89 about past and present medical and psychiatric problems, substance misuse and self-harm. They found that 37% had a psychiatric disorder, including 2% (34) with psychosis (comparable with the prevalence of psychosis in the community) and 10% (177) with personality disorder. Fifty-two prisoners (3%) were

judged to require transfer to hospital for psychiatric treatment, 17 in Special Hospitals, 21 in Regional Secure Units and 14 in district psychiatric service facilities. Reasons for recommending hospital transfer included: unpredictable violence, life threatening self-harm, victimisation by other prisoners, refusal to take prescribed drugs. Of the 30 psychotic prisoners recommended for hospital treatment, 21 had schizophrenia, six had affective disorder and three had paranoid psychosis. Twelve of the 37 prisoners recommended for hospital treatment for mental illness or organic disorder had developed their illness during their imprisonment. In addition to those for whom hospital care was proposed, 10% of the sample were assessed to need psychiatric help from the Prison Medical Service and over 5% were considered to require treatment in a therapeutic community setting within the prison system (currently available at HMP Grendon and HMP Wormwood Scrubs Annex, and at HMYOI Glen Parva for young offenders).

Studying the records of 834 remanded and convicted prisoners resident in Leeds prison on 16 September 1991, Mitchison et al (1994) found that 23% had a recorded history of having seen a psychiatrist and 16% a history of depression or self-harm, a probable under-estimate given that 18 of an interviewed sample of 43 prisoners admitted failing to declare such matters on reception. Only ten prisoners (1.2% of the prison's population) were awaiting transfer to psychiatric hospital.

Women Prisoners
Seeking to apply the same methods as used in Gunn's (1991) study to a sample of sentenced women to see if, as often claimed, women in prison have higher levels of psychiatric disorder, Maden et al (1994) surveyed a total of 262 women, over 20% of the sentenced population at that time. While the prevalence of psychosis was the same as in Gunn's male sample, women had a higher prevalence of intellectual impairment (6% compared to 2%), personality disorder (18% compared to 10%), neurotic disorder (18% compared to 10%) and substance misuse (26% compared to 12%). In consequence, women were noted to make greater demands on prison health services.

Some 45% of women reported psychiatric contact prior to their current imprisonment (compared to 36% of men). Prevalence of deliberate self-harm (DSH) during current period in custody was the same for both sexes at around 5% and lifetime prevalence of self-harm by cutting at 10% was comparable with male prisoners but women had a higher lifetime prevalence of DSH, mainly because of over-dosing outside prison. Sixty-eight women (26%) reported receiving treatment with psychotropic medication during the current imprisonment (compared to 8% of men), though none reported being treated against their will (women, like men, complained most frequently of doctors' reluctance to prescribe sedatives on request). No evidence was found of 'drugging up' reluctant or difficult prisoners. The four women with a psychosis were rated to require transfer to hospital and had been so recommended, as had eight others, four on the basis of mental handicap, three with severe personality disorder and one with severe neurotic depression. The main unmet need for treatment of women in prison was considered to be for substance misuse and personality problems. The authors concluded that the presence of women with mental disorder in prison reflected failings in multi-agency services elsewhere.

171

Remand Prisoners

A national prevalence study in the 1990s, interviewing a 9.4% sample of the male unconvicted prison population (Maden *et al*, 1996; Brooke *et al*, 1996) reported that about one-third of unsentenced prisoners met the criteria for a psychiatric diagnosis, with about 5% being acutely psychotic. Some 55% of remanded male prisoners were deemed to require immediate treatment, with 9% requiring transfer to the NHS for urgent psychiatric attention.

Older prisoners may be particularly likely to experience mental health problems. Taylor and Parrott (1988), studying remand prisoners in one local prison, found that over half of 23 prisoners aged 65 or over had active symptoms of psychiatric illness.

To assess the prevalence of disorder and the psychiatric needs among new remand prisoners, Birmingham *et al* (1996) approached all unconvicted men on their reception into HMP Durham, October 1995 to March 1996, gaining a sample of 569 willing to be screened. Mental disorder (excluding substance misuse) was present in 148 (26%), though a further 22 men had a history of mental disorder but no current symptoms. Among these, 24 had psychotic disorders, 38 had personality disorder and 34 had anxiety disorders. Some 50 men were assessed to require urgent attention, 16 requiring immediate transfer to an outside psychiatric hospital, while 29 needed prison healthcare placement.

In comparison, screening by prison medical and nursing staff was rated insensitive and inaccurate, identifying current mental disorder in 52 men. Of these, 34 were among the 148 identified by the researchers, but only six of the 24 with acute psychosis were identified. Mental disorder was said to be present in a further 18 men in whom the researchers had found no evidence. Of the 50 thought to require urgent intervention, 17 were identified, the others being allocated to normal cell location.

Women Remands

To gain a more accurate understanding of levels of mental disorder among women remand prisoners, Parsons *et al* (2001) assessed all new remands (aged 18 and over) to two prisons (Holloway and New Hall) over 14 weeks, April to September 1998, gaining a sample of 382 women. The lifetime prevalence of mental disorder for the sample was 68% (psychotic disorders 19%; mood disorders 43%; anxiety disorders 42%). Current mental disorder (excluding substance dependence) was identified in 227 (59%), with psychotic symptoms in 42 women (11%). The CPNs who undertook the screening considered that a further 21 women needed to be placed in the prison healthcare centre (HCC) and that another 18 should be referred for psychiatric assessment. All 21 non-psychotic women were exhibiting substance-withdrawal symptoms in addition to other psychiatric symptoms. A significantly higher proportion of women diagnosed as suffering from a mental disorder were charged with an offence of violence compared with those who were not found to have a mental disorder.

Of the 227 identified as mentally disordered, 73 (32%) were also identified by the normal prison screening process which also found disorder in eight women where the research found no evidence. Only 10 of the 42 women identified with psychotic symptoms were detected as psychotic by the prison screen. Of the 81 women who the researchers judged should be located in the HCC or referred to psychiatric hospital, 64 were placed in the HCC, 35 on the basis of mental disorder and 29 for detoxification. Twelve of the women assessed as psychotic were placed on ordinary wings. The researchers note the Prison Service is changing radically the way in which new receptions are screened, with the prospect of more accurate detection of psychiatric morbidity (see below).

ONS Survey of Psychiatric Morbidity

In 1997 the Office of National Statistics was commissioned to survey the extent of psychiatric morbidity among prisoners in England and Wales to inform policy decisions about services. Some 3,142 prisoners of both sexes, male and female, remanded and sentenced, were interviewed, with one in five being approached for a follow-up clinical interview. The findings (Singleton *et al*, 1998), reinforcing what is already known about the high levels of early social disadvantage experienced by offender populations and indicating level levels of psychiatric morbidity than had previously been suggested, are summarised by Coid *et al* (2002).

Psychoses

In comparison with an estimated prevalence of psychotic disorder among 0.4% of the general population, 7% of sentenced men, 10% of remanded men and 14% of women in both categories were assessed as having a psychotic illness in the last year.

Neurosis

Neurotic symptoms were particularly widespread, especially among women and remanded prisoners. Even sentenced males had over three times the prevalence of their counterparts in the general population. These results were considered to highlight the high level of stress in prisoners' lives prior to their imprisonment and the highly stressful nature of prison conditions.

Personality Disorder

Confirming provisional assessments in previous surveys of the extent of PD among prisoners, now using standardised diagnostic instruments, it was found that 78% of remanded men, 64% of sentenced men and 50% of women received one or more diagnoses of PD. Anti-social personality disorder was estimated as the most prevalent condition, followed by paranoid PD for men and borderline PD for women. Prisoners with PD were most likely to present management problems and indicate risk factors.

Substance Misuse

Some 58% of remanded men, 63% of sentenced men and 39% of sentenced women had engaged in hazardous drinking, though this was most associated with young, white, single males with previous convictions and detained in respect of a violent offence. Some form of drug dependence in the year prior to imprisonment varied from 41% (sentenced women) to 54% (remanded women).

Medication

Around 20% of men and 50% of women were taking some form of psychotropic medication. Between 25% and 59% of those thought to suffer from psychosis had received treatment from a psychiatric professional while in prison. However, between 13 and 21% of respondents reported asking for help with psychiatric/emotional problems since coming into prison but had been refused, particularly among those thought to have been suffering from psychosis.

Previous Use of Psychiatric Services

Some 21% of male and 40% of female remand prisoners had received psychiatric help in the year prior to entering prison. Some 65% of male and 79% of female remand prisoners had received such help at some previous point.

In a commentary on the ONS survey, Fryers *et al* (1998) highlight the considerable resource implications for the NHS if an adequate response is to be made to the estimate, based on this sample, that there may be about 4,500 men and 400 women in prison with recent or current psychotic illness.

Elderly Prisoners

To study the prevalence of psychiatric morbidity among prisoners aged 60 and over, Fazel *et al* (2001) interviewed 203 sentenced men (mean age 65.5) in 15 prisons in 1999-2000. Psychiatric illness was diagnosed in 64 men (31.5%), the most common diagnosis being depressive disorder, found in 60 individuals, of whom seven were being treated with anti-depressant medication at time of interview. Twenty-four had a past or present history of depression noted in their medical records. Two men had dementia, with onset during their imprisonment. Personality disorder was diagnosed in 61 men, combined with psychiatric illness in 19 instances. In total, 53% of the sample had a psychiatric diagnosis. The rate of depression was higher than the rates found in studies of younger adult prisoners and of elderly men in the community (6%).

The researchers suggest that if these results were to be extrapolated to the total elderly prison population at any one time, 52 elderly men would be psychotic, most with a depressive psychosis, while 312 men would be found to be depressed. As only 12% of the depressed prisoners in the sample were being treated with anti-depressants, this would suggest large unmet treatment needs.

Care of Mentally Disordered Persons in Prison

Expectations for prison health care, based on *Prison Service Health Care Standing Order 13*, with nine health care standards (one covering mental health services), were approved by the Prisons Board for implementation by mid-1997. The standard of health care for mentally ill persons in prison has caused concern for many years. To gauge standards in individual prisons, Reed and Lyne of the Prisons Inspectorate (1997 & 2000) have reported their findings regarding healthcare centres (described as 'more like sickbays with primary health cover) during the course of semi-structured inspections of establishments during a year's Inspectorate programme, 19 in 1995-96 and 13 in 1997-98. In the latter year, covering 20% of all prison-based beds, they found that no doctor in charge of in-patients had completed specialist psychiatric training, while 24% of nursing staff had mental health training. Two prison healthcare centres had input from a clinical psychologist. Only one prison had a full multi-disciplinary team. No prison met the Standards expectations in respect of therapeutic activity. Patients had restricted days with little constructive to do. While most staff were assessed to be caring professionals who were trying to do their best under difficult circumstances, the management, staffing and clinical facilities was rated 'much worse than in the NHS'.

For a small-scale survey of the accuracy of identification of mentally disordered prisoners, the extent to which their needs were being met and the level of communication and information exchange between prison-based professionals and outside agencies, indicating shortfall in effective practice, see Vaughan *et al* (1999).

The current *Standard for Health Services for Prisoners* was issued in July 2002 (HM Prison Service). In the context of mental health, the Standard specifies:

(i) 'an initial assessment of all newly received prisoners is conducted by a suitably trained healthcare worker to identify immediate ... mental health needs, indicators of recent substance abuse and the potential for self-harm so they can be properly managed';

(ii) 'a doctor is available for consultation throughout the normal reception period. If not in the establishment, the doctor is contactable by telephone and able to attend the establishment if necessary for clinical reasons';

(iii) 'a ... mental health assessment is undertaken by a doctor within 24 hours of reception';

(iv) establishments must provide services for the observation, assessment, treatment and care of prisoners with mental healthcare needs. Prisoners must be treated by a multi-disciplinary team in line with good practice laid out in the Code of Practice on the operation of MHA 1983 and standards set out in the National Service Framework for Mental Health.

TRANSFER TO HOSPITAL OF SERVING PRISONERS: MHA 1983 SECTION 47

In circumstances where a court could order admission to hospital under s37, the Home Secretary may direct that a person serving a custodial sentence shall be 'removed to and detained in such hospital ... as may be specified in the direction' (s47(1)). This is known as a 'transfer direction'. The prohibition of transfer to 'a private nursing home', as specified in the original wording of s47, was removed by C(S)A 1997 s49(3), thus empowering transfer under s47 and s48 (below) to private psychiatric hospitals.

In summary, the criteria to be satisfied are:

(i) the prisoner is suffering from mental illness, psychopathic disorder, severe mental impairment or mental impairment (see page 84);

(ii) the mental disorder is of such a nature or degree that makes it appropriate for the prisoner to be detained in a hospital for medical treatment (and, in the case of psychopathic disorder or mental impairment, treatment is likely to alleviate the condition or prevent deterioration) (see page 86);

(iii) the Home Secretary has received reports from at least two medical practitioners (one of whom is approved under s12) which concur on the form of mental disorder suffered and is of the opinion that detention in hospital is expedient, having regard to the public interest and all the circumstances.

Note that although there is no statutory requirement upon the Home Secretary to obtain the consent of the receiving hospital before making the necessary direction, this is normally secured in practice. Under provisions introduced by C(S)A 1997 s47, the Secretary of State, in making a s47 direction, may specify not only the hospital at which the defendant will be detained but a 'unit' of the hospital (defined by s47(3) to mean 'any part of a hospital which is treated as a separate unit'). This refinement is designed to enable the Home Office to specify a level of security in which the patient needs to be detained. In consequence, the Secretary of State's permission will be required for any transfer from the named unit, even to another part of the same hospital. The question of whether a unit should be designated is a factor for the doctors reporting to Home Office to consider.

Note also that there is no provision enabling prisoners to be transferred to hospital for assessment, only treatment, though the Reed Committee (1992, para. 9.6) felt that this would be helpful to allow thorough assessment, especially where diagnosis is problematic. See now the draft Mental Health Bill proposals (page 194).

Prisoners eligible for transfer include those subject to any form of detention in criminal proceedings, even those committed to custody for non-payment of financial penalties or for failure to comply with an order to enter into recognisances to keep the peace or be of good behaviour.

Treatability

In *W (R on the application of) v South West London and St George's Mental Health NHS Trust* [2002] EWCA Admin 1770, a prisoner aged 20 with a personality disorder, who was approaching his date of release from a term of 42 months' YOI detention for an unprovoked instance of s18 GBH, was made subject of a s47 transfer direction. The Administrative Court was required to determine if the transfer order was lawful, the prisoner claiming that the treatability provision of s47(1)(b) had not been met. The Court adopted the schema offered by the consultant psychiatrist giving evidence that treatment can take three forms or 'limbs':

(i)   treatment of the patient's core disorder;

(ii) seeking to give the patient the skills necessary to cope with situations that they had previously found difficult or stressful but without attempting to change the core disorder;

(iii) management focused on managing the patient's environment so that conflict in situations is minimised, this including management in the hospital, when the patient is on leave from hospital and in the community, but neither altering the core disorder or giving skills to the patient.

The clinical aim in this instance was to achieve 'a staged or phased discharge' which would be likely to reduce the very negative effect on the patient's mental well-being that would otherwise occur following sudden release from prison, principally aggressive behaviour, self-harm and drug abuse. Admission to hospital would lead in due course to increasing periods of leave linked to occupational therapy. Efforts would be made to locate a hostel placement providing mental health staff. An alternative assessment by another psychiatrist argued that the prisoner would be too angry and resistant to having his freedom postponed to be responsive to these efforts. However, noting that the prisoner was someone who would cope badly with change, in particular the sudden loss of structure on leaving prison, Crane J decided that s47 transfer in these circumstances (under limb (iii) above) amounted to 'treatment' likely to alleviate or prevent a deterioration of condition. Since his transfer, the prisoner had proved difficult to manage and had even absconded for three days but there was some basis now for thinking that he might be responsive at the level of limb (ii).

Transfer Direction

A transfer direction under s47 has broadly the same effect as a hospital order under s37 (s47(3)) but must take effect within 14 days (s47(2)). There is thus no automatic application of restrictions but the Home Secretary may (and, in the clear majority of cases, will) add a 'restriction direction' under s49, the effect of which is detailed below.

Provision of Reports

Where a prisoner is transferred to hospital from a prison or remand centre, any relevant pre-sentence reports should be sent promptly to the hospital along with an up-to-date medical report including details of medication and a report from prison health care staff covering the patient's day-to-day care and management (MHA(COP) 1999 para. 7.1).

Effect of Transfer without Restriction

A s47 patient without a restriction direction is liable to be detained in hospital beyond the point of sentence when s/he would have been released from prison if the medical basis for compulsory detention continues and s/he is not considered fit for discharge from hospital. However, unlike a s37 patient, an unrestricted s47 patient may apply to a MHRT within the first six months of their detention in hospital (s69(2)(b)). The patient can, of course, be discharged at any time by the hospital. If discharged by either the hospital or a MHRT prior to the point of sentence when s/he would be released from prison, the s47 transferee is at liberty and is not liable to be returned to prison to complete their sentence. For this reason, transfer directions without restrictions have customarily been made only where the prisoner is reaching their point of early release. However, MHA(COP) 1999 para. 3.21 states that transfer of a prisoner to hospital under the Act should not be delayed until close to release date. 'A transfer in such circumstances may be seen by the prisoner as being primarily intended to extend their detention and result in an unco-operative attitude towards treatment'. But note the case of *W* (page 176).

Transfers to High Security Hospitals

In a study of 351 (309 men) prisoners admitted to the three Special Hospitals (as they were then known) under s47 transfer in the period 1984-91, Huws *et al* (1997) found that s47 accounted for 23% of the total number (1,502) of admissions, being 39% of the total number of s47 transfers to hospital during that time. Of the 351, 172 went to Ashworth (26% of Ashworth admissions), 94 to Rampton (22% of Rampton admissions) and 85 to Broadmoor (21% of Broadmoor admissions). Almost all (336 or 96%) were also subject to s49 restriction. Fifteen were transferred within a week of their EDR (date of release). The clear majority (281, 80%) were transferred on the basis of mental disorder, though 31 (9%) were transferred because of dangerous or violent behaviour and 21 (6%) because of 'worry about their release'. In eight cases the basis for transfer was unclear. Of transfers, 118 (60%) were returned to prison and 77 (39%) were discharged to a local hospital or to the community. Of the 64 transferees serving determinate terms, seven were discharged on EDR or before.

The researchers wanted to test the continuimg validity of previously expressed concerns (Grounds, 1991, addressing the period 1960-83): that transfers were frequently delayed, often until late in sentence, with prisoners being detained in hospital for prolonged periods, Special Hospitals being used to detain prisoners (especially sex offenders) preventively. They concluded that this study does not support many of those concerns. In most cases the average time from request for opinion to transfer was less than two months. There was also little evidence that transfer was used to lengthen a sentence and no evidence that the time spent in hospital reflected the gravity of the offence. Though there was basis for concern regarding the 21 transferred in light of worry about their release, the average length of sentence for these prisoners was 3.7 years, considerably less than the average length for the group overall (6.5 years). Of the 21, only five suffered from a mental illness and it is speculated that those with personality disorder may have come to attention less quickly than those with more noticeable problems. Although transfer resulted in increased length of detention, there was little evidence that their treatment in hospital differed from that of other patients.

THERAPEUTIC COMMUNITY TREATMENT IN PRISON

The scope to harness custodial community life within the Prison Service for England and Wales to therapeutic advantage was first given serious attention when HMP Grendon was opened in 1962 as a specialist prison establishment run on 'democratic' principles, open to prisoner volunteers housed in five 'therapeutic community' wings and selected primarily on the basis of their personality disorder coupled with a high risk of reconviction. Selection criteria have included: motivation to change, willingness to participate in group work and having sufficient time left to serve to be able to commit to an extended stay. For a full account of Grendon, see Genders and Player (1995). A recent study (Taylor, 2000) of the reconviction rate within seven years of a sample of prisoners who went to Grendon in the years 1984 to 1989 (the admitted group), compared with a sample who had been selected for Grendon but did not go (the waiting list group), provides some measure of the prison's effectiveness.

In summary, lower rates of reconviction were found for admitted prisoners than for waiting list prisoners. However, the length of time spent at Grendon was a critical factor, varying from 71% for those staying for under six months to 62% for those staying over 18 months. There was also a significant reduction in levels of re-imprisonment and violent offending for those staying over 18 months. For shorter periods, such as those under 12 months, the reduction in reconviction rates compared with the control group was only slight. Older (over 30) repeat (two or more convictions) violent offenders demonstrated some treatment effect, though this lacked statistical significance. Repeat sexual offenders in the waiting list group proved much more likely to be reconvicted of a sexual/violent offence than admitted prisoners with a similar history. For those with a single sexual conviction there was no treatment effect. In fact, there was some indication that once-only admitted offenders were more likely to be reconvicted than their waiting list counterparts.

A task force established in 1993 to determine strategy for managing prisoners with personality disorders and to consider the need for further Grendon-style regimes estimated that by 2001 there would be at least 2,392 prisoners in the system falling outside the scope of MHA 1983 but likely to benefit from a therapeutic regime. Further therapeutic community units have been initiated in HMPs Gartree and Wormwood Scrubs, HMYOIs Aylesbury and Ashworth. In addition, 'hierarchical' therapeutic communities for drug users have been developed in Channings Wood, Holme House and Portland. For a review of the literature, see Rawlings (1999 and 2000). Further, a 'second Grendon' was established in HMP Dovegate, a new prison in the West Midlands that opened its therapeutic community in November 2001.

DANGEROUS AND SEVERE PERSONALITY DISORDER PROGRAMME

As part of the overall plan to reform mental health law, the Department of Health, Home Office and the Prison Service are currently pursuing a joint initiative to develop and pilot new mental health services for people who are assessed as dangerous as a result of a severe personality disorder and who have generally not had previous access to mental health services. The relevant factsheet (Home Office, 2002) clarifies that 'DSPD' is not a diagnosis but a 'working title' for a programme to develop better ways of working with the very small numbers who pose a significant risk of serious harm to others because of their disorder. It has been estimated that there are about 1,400 prisoners at any one time who can be considered as DSPD (Farrington and Jolliffe, 2002). The concept was first introduced in a Green Paper (Home Office/Department of Health, 1999) and pursued in the White Paper *Reforming the Mental Health Act* (Department of Health/Home Office, 2000).

The DSPD programme will straddle penal and hospital provision, thus offering 'criminal' and 'civil' routes. A wing has opened at HMP Whitemoor (a dispersal prison) for assessment and intervention units with a further unit at another dispersal prison (HMP Frankland) expected to be ready by the end of 2003. Within the high security hospital system, the opening of a small pilot unit at Broadmoor is anticipated in the first half of 2003, with another unit at Rampton Hospital expected to become available in late 2003. One further unit at Broadmoor Hospital is scheduled for completion in late 2004. A total of 320 places are planned to be operational by April 2004.

The Home Office anticipates that most candidates will be identified at point of sentence or during a prison sentence and will thus access prison facilities. However:

'people who are already in prison but at the end of a determinate sentence may also be eligible for assessment (by the civil route). With time, assuming the criminal route works well, the use of the civil route will diminish. It will be possible to use the civil route for particularly dangerous people with a severe personality disorder who are no longer in prison but living in the community.'

Currently, potential DSPD prisoners are identified in the eight prisons within the high security estate, are screened, and asked if they are willing to participate in the Whitemoor unit. Though admission is voluntary, many prisoners are keen to demonstrate that they are willing to address and reduce their perceived risk, with the hope of increasing their probability of release on licence. The 90 bed unit (36 for assessment and 54 for treatment) had assessed 63 prisoners up to March 2002, of whom about half were considered suitable for treatment (using Dialectical Behaviour Therapy which aims to improve personal and social functioning and emotional regulation, to reduce the risk of harm to self and others, to reduce the subject's distress and to improve their amenability to other treatment for sexual and/or violent offending). Only four of those who completed the assessment were not assessed as DSPD. Treatment in DSPD units is likely to continue for two to three years. For more details, including consideration of the feasibility of a randomised control trial, see Farrington and Jolliffe (2002).

PAROLE REVIEW AND LICENCE
Prisoners serving determinate terms of four years or longer are long-term prisoners who are subject on their application to discretionary conditional early release on parole licence at or after the half-way point of their sentence, with automatic conditional release on non-parole licence at the two-thirds point of sentence. Their applications for parole are considered by the Parole Board on the basis of documentation gathered in a dossier which is considered by a panel of three Board members. Certain applicants are referred to a 'psychiatric panel', *ie* where one of the members is a psychiatrist, to enable the Board to make a properly informed judgement. The criteria for this facility currently are:

(i)   nature of sentence offence (manslaughter on grounds of diminished responsibility; a serious sexual or violent offence with exceptionally savage or bizarre elements; arson other than for financial gain or to destroy evidence); or

(ii) psychiatric history (current or previous diagnosis of mental disorder within MHA 1983; admission to psychiatric hospital and/or serious attempt at suicide or pattern of repeated self-harm and/or pattern of bizarre behaviour during sentence; parole dossier includes a psychiatrist's or psychologist's report indicating a mental health problem with proposals for addressing it and/or current or recent treatment from a psychiatrist or psychologist other than participation in an offending behaviour or thinking skills programme); or

(iii) sexual offending featuring additional elements of special concern, such as excessive/gratuitous violence/humiliation/degradation or sadistic behaviour, or multiple non-familial victims, or a sustained pattern of jealous or obsessive behaviour, or admission to deviant fantasies persisting over time.

Licence, whether on parole or non-parole, lasts until the three-quarter point of sentence, unless in respect of a sexual or, more rarely, a violent offence the sentencing court has ordered extension of licence, now regulated by PCC(S)A 2000 s58 and known as an extended sentence (see page 159). In appropriate cases a licence may include an additional condition that the licensee attends upon a duly qualified psychiatrist or psychologist or medical practitioner for such care, supervision or treatment as that practitioner recommends. That practitioner should be named and be willing to fulfil the role anticipated.

RECALL FROM LICENCE: OFFENDER DETAINED UNDER MHA 1983
The situation may arise where a prisoner, short or long-term, subject to licence causes concern that may prompt consideration of their recall to prison but where the offender is also subject to MHA intervention. This arose in *R (on the application of S) v Secretary*

of State for the Home Department and the Parole Board [2002] EWHC 2424 Admin, where S was on licence following release in respect of an 18-month term for breach of a restraining order imposed for harassment. Admitted as a voluntary patient to hospital, he had refused to remain and was detained under s3 civil powers on grounds of mental illness (bipolar affective disorder). Prior to his admission he had not complied with his medication regime, thus leading to bizarre behaviour, including indecent exposure and threatening/abusive behaviour at his brother's workplace. The day after the s3 order was made, his supervising probation officer had requested revocation of his licence, apparently unaware of medical developments. The Home Office then learned of the s3 order but nevertheless revoked S's licence, not with the intent of removing him from hospital to prison but to have that power in readiness when he was discharged or if he absconded. He was recalled by the Home Secretary under CJA 1991 s39(2) powers (where immediate recall is expedient in the public interest), without any reference in the revocation notice to his s3 status. While still unaware that his licence had been revoked, S absconded from hospital and was quickly arrested and taken to prison. He made written representations against his recall which were rejected by the Parole Board. S sought judicial review, arguing that revocation of his licence had been unlawful while he was subject to s3 detention.

The Administrative Court upheld his claim and quashed both decisions, determining that though the separate provisions of MHA 1983 and CJA 1991 are separate and without any attempt to cross-reference them, s3 normally takes precedence over recall, being based on certified expert opinion that detention is necessary for the health and safety of the patient or for the protection of others so that he should receive treatment. Maurice Kay J ruled that the Home Secretary should not have proceeded without any reference to or consultation with the hospital doctors, such as an inquiry whether there was any likelihood of an imminent release. Further, once he had been received back in prison, the Home Secretary should have considered transferring him back to hospital under MHA 1983 s47, yet there had been no consultation with the doctors at that stage and S had been kept in the prison's healthcare centre. Similarly, the Parole Board should have taken into account the views of the treating clinicians.

> 'Without doing so they were unable properly to consider why the usual procedure that s3 takes precedence should be overridden in the circumstances of this case. Instead of addressing current material considerations, emphasis was misplaced on the hypothesis or contingency that the hospital might discharge S before his prison release date.'

TRANSFER TO HOSPITAL OF UNSENTENCED PRISONERS: MHA 1983 SECTION 48

The following categories of prisoners may be transferred to hospital by order of the Home Secretary in circumstances akin to s47 transfer:

(i)   remand prisoners awaiting trial or sentence (either by a magistrates' court or in the Crown Court);

(ii) civil prisoners;

(iii) detainees under the Immigration Act 1971.

Powers under s48 differ from s47 provisions in the following ways:

- The unsentenced prisoner must be suffering either mental illness or severe mental impairment. The Reed Committee (1992, para. 9.6(iv)(a)) proposed that the ambit should be extended to include persons suffering from mental impairment or psychopathic disorder to ensure that all kinds of mental disorder within the 1983 Act receive treatment as soon as practicable.

- The Home Secretary must be satisfied that the unsentenced prisoner 'is in urgent need of treatment'. The Reed Committee (1992, para. 9.6(iv)(b)) noted that this requirement is often interpreted unnecessarily narrowly and recommended that it should be applied where a doctor would recommend in-patient treatment if a person were seen as an out-patient in the community.

- Where the prisoner is remanded in custody unsentenced in criminal proceedings, the Home Secretary does not have a discretion whether to impose a restriction direction under s49 but is required to do so (s49(1)).

In other respects, *eg* the requirement regarding doctors' reports and the need for the direction to take effect within 14 days, s48 transfers follow the same procedure as s47 and have the same effect as a hospital order, subject to the special provisions of:

(i)   s51: persons detained in prison or remand centre other than remanded in custody by a magistrates' court;

(ii) s52: persons remanded by magistrates' courts;

(iii) s53: civil prisoners and Immigration Act detainees.

As regards credit for time spent on remand, see page 49.

Provision of Pre-Sentence Reports
See above (page 177) under MHA s47 transfer.

Magistrates' Court Remands
The transfer direction ceases to have effect on the expiry of the remand period unless the court further remands the accused or the accused is committed/transferred in custody to the Crown Court. Further remands may be ordered in the absence of the accused provided that s/he has appeared before the court within the previous six months (s52(4)).

The magistrates have power to direct that a transfer direction shall cease to have effect, even though the remand has not expired or committal/transfer to Crown Court has taken place, if satisfied on the written or oral evidence of the responsible medical officer that the patient no longer needs treatment in hospital for mental disorder or that no effective treatment for the disorder can be given in the specified hospital (s52(5)).

Persons Awaiting Trial or Sentence in the Crown Court
For transferred patients waiting to appear in the Crown Court, the transfer continues until the court disposes of the case (s51(2)), unless:

(i)   the Home Secretary, upon notification by the responsible medical officer, any other doctor or a MHRT that

(a) the patient no longer requires treatment in hospital for mental disorder, or

(b) that no effective treatment can be given, orders that s/he should be transferred back to prison custody (s51(3)); or

(ii) the Court is notified by the RMO that either (a) or (b) above applies and orders that s/he be either transferred back to prison custody or released on bail (s51(4)).

Power to make a Hospital Order in Defendant's Absence

If the patient remains in hospital at the point when required to appear for trial or sentence, the Court has the power to make a hospital order in the absence of the defendant and, in the case of a person awaiting trial, without convicting the defendant, provided that the following conditions are fulfilled:

(i) it is 'impracticable or inappropriate to bring the defendant before the court';

(ii) the court is satisfied on the oral or written evidence of at least two doctors, one approved under MHA 1983 s12, that the defendant is suffering from mental illness or severe mental impairment of a nature or degree which makes detention in a hospital for treatment appropriate; and

(iii) the court is of the opinion that such an order is 'proper', having considered the depositions and any other documents supplied to the court.

In *R (on the application of Kenneally) v Snaresbrook Crown Court* (2001, unreported) the meaning of 'impracticable and inappropriate' (in s51(5)(a)) was considered in the case of a man charged with indecent assault to which he had pleaded not guilty. Having considered medical evidence that detention under a hospital order was appropriate, the court was invited to make the order without the defendant being present, even though he was in the court building, in the light of the doctors' opinion that this might cause his mental state to deteriorate and thus result in disruption to proceedings. He was brought into court at the conclusion of the hearing so that the judge could explain what had been decided. When he subsequently challenged the lawfulness of the s51 hospital order, the Divisional Court noted that his presence was clearly not 'impracticable' and concluded that the word 'inappropriate' should be construed restrictively. The power 'must not be used as a routine and easy way of avoiding a potentially troublesome trial'. Pill LJ stated:

'I would not necessarily restrict the word so as to mean "physically impossible" but a high degree of disablement or relevant disorder must be present. The section does not apply where all that is involved is possible inconvenience for the Court and inevitable distress for the defendant and others likely to be concerned in a trial, if a trial is held. ... To pass sentence, even a sentence one of the objects of which is to assist the defendant, without first convicting him is a drastic step, one that should be taken only in exceptional circumstances.'

The procedure followed was thus ruled to be defective and the s51 order was quashed.

The Crown Court's power to make a hospital order under s51(5) (which can include a restriction order) without convicting the accused compares with the power of a magistrates' court under s37(3) (see page 89) but the Crown Court is not required by statute to be satisfied that 'he did the act or made the omission charged'.

In *R v Kingston Crown Court, ex p. Mason* (1998, unreported), the making of a s51(5) order combined with a s41 order was challenged through judicial review, the applicant arguing that the judge had not had sufficient basis for concluding that the public would suffer serious harm (see page 100). The applicant, with no previous convictions but a history of severe schizo-affective disorder, had been prosecuted for attempted child abduction, the prosecution alleging that had sought to persuade two girls aged 10/11 to accompany him in a car to his home for sex. He had not attempted to use physical force against them. He had earlier opted to stop taking his medication. He had denied mentioning the prospect of sex or having a sexual motive, though he agreed that he had wanted to find out if they were engaging in sex as he wished to 'sort this country out' and thus needed to know what was going on. He had been transferred to hospital from prison under s48. He had been found unfit to stand trial because he would not allow himself to be prosecuted by a woman or tried by a woman juror. The Divisional Court determined that the judge was entitled to rely on the complainants' and other witness statements and reach the conclusion that serious harm could result if a restriction order was not made, without having to 'embark on an elaborate fact-finding exercise' to resolve the factual dispute – in all the circumstances, 'the outcome was inevitable.'

Civil Prisoners and Immigration Act Deportees

A transfer direction in this context ceases to have effect on the expiration of the period of detention, had the transfer to hospital not occurred. If a restriction direction was also made, and the Home Secretary, prior to the expiry of detention, is notified by the RMO, any other doctor or a MHRT that the patient no longer requires detention in hospital for treatment or that no effective treatment can be given, the person may be returned to prison custody on the Home Secretary's warrant.

Scope for Greater Use

In the light of their survey of mentally disordered remand prisoners in three prisons (see page 51), Dell *et al* (1992) proposed that far greater use should be made of s48 transfer, avoiding the delays attendant on court proceedings and enabling mentally ill people to be moved rapidly.

'Our study showed that it was rarely employed because prison doctors believe it covers only those people whose physical health is at risk from their mental illness. There seems to be no justification for this interpretation and we would recommend that transfers rather than court orders should become the way in which mentally ill prisoners are initially hospitalised. This would inject an appropriate degree of urgency into the process. Hospital orders can be made subsequently.'

In fact, this appeal coincided with a substantial increase in use of s48, from only 77 instances in 1987 rising to 536 in 1994 and subsequently averaging 479 per year in the five years 1995-99 (Home Office, 2000). The numbers of transfers appears to have reached a plateau of late (Department of Health, 2000).

In their recent study of 370 (321 men and 49 women) cases transferred under s48 in 1992, Mackay and Machin (2000) report as follows:

Offence charged: Two-thirds of transfers concerned prisoners whose most serious charge concerned allegations of physical/sexual harm to others. Murder, attempted murder/

GBH and other (non-sexual) violence accounted for 59% of this sample. Over half (53%) were subject to magistrates' court remand and 44% to the jurisdiction of the Crown Court. Mackay and Machin suggest that the use of s48 for cases involving less serious offences 'could indicate that the word "urgent" is being interpreted more broadly and thus that the Reed Committee's recommendation (see page 182) of removal of this requirement is unnecessary'.

Diagnosis at time of transfer: A diagnosis of schizophrenia accounted for half of the sample, the next largest diagnostic group being 'other psychosis' (11%) and non-psychotic depression (11%). Some 9% suffered 'manias/other affective disorders' and 4% alcohol or drug-induced psychosis. In 13% of instances there was 'no definite diagnosis'. Some 15% were also diagnosed as having a personality disorder.

Psychiatric history: Some 72% had a psychiatric history, 36% having previously been subject to a section of MHA 1983. Of those 97 prisoners, 46 had been subject to a s37 hospital order, seven with a s41 restriction.

Nature of hospital: Over half (54%) were transferred to a regional secure unit or a medium security unit, a further 25% transferring to a locked hospital ward, and only 9% moving to open ward conditions.

Transfer process: For over half the sample (56%) transfer was requested within 25 days of the defendant being first remanded in custody, the average being 35 days. The Home Office warrant authorising transfer was issued, on average, in seven days. Transfer took longest in respect of patients charged with the most serious violent offences awaiting a Special Hospital placement. Of 45 patients remitted back to prison, 28 were assessed not to require further treatment and in 24 instances no effective treatment was considered possible. The average time interval between transfer and final court decision was 138 days. The degree of co-operation between the Home Office Mental Health Unit, consultants and other agencies was assessed as very high.

Court outcomes: Some 76% of the sample were found guilty (8% with diminished responsibility) and only 3% were found not guilty but 65 persons (18%) had their case discontinued or their charge withdrawn, often because the prosecution was no longer considered to be in the public interest. Over half of those sentenced (57%) received a hospital order (27% with s41 restriction). Some 11% received a psychiatric probation order, usually with a requirement of in-patient treatment. Only 15% received a custodial sentence.

RESTRICTION DIRECTIONS
MHA 1983 s49

(1) Where a transfer direction is given in respect of any person, the Secretary of State, if he thinks fit, may by warrant further direct that that person shall be subject to the special restrictions set out in s41 above, and where the Secretary of State gives a transfer direction in respect of any such person as is described in paragraph (a) or (b) of s48(2) above, he shall also give a direction under this section applying those restrictions to him.

(2) A direction under this section shall have the same effect as a restriction order under s41 above and shall be known as 'a restriction direction'.

A restriction direction under s49 is thus to be interpreted as a s41 restriction order but subject to the provisions of ss50-51 and s74 which regulate the special status of prisoner-patients. The responsible medical officer must examine each patient in this category and report to the Home Secretary at least yearly, and at more frequent intervals if the Home Secretary so requires, and reports shall contain such particulars as the Home Secretary may require (s49(3)).

Serving Prisoners
As noted earlier, most s47 patients will be subject to s49 restriction.

End of Sentence
The restriction direction ceases to have effect upon 'the expiration of sentence' (s50(2)). 'Expiration' refers to the point of sentence at which the prisoner would cease to be liable to be detained in prison custody (s50(3)) and so the patient is able to benefit from the normal early release provisions of CJA 1991, time in hospital counting towards the calculation of time served. The only exception to this is that any period during which the patient is unlawfully absent from the institution will not count towards the calculation (s50(4)). Upon the restriction direction ceasing, the patient has the status of someone subject to a hospital order without restriction as if such an order was made on the date of cessation (s41(5)), and so remains subject to detention in hospital (see page 90).

No Longer Requiring Treatment
If the Home Secretary is notified by the RMO, any other doctor or a MHRT that the patient no longer requires treatment in hospital for mental disorder (or that no effective treatment for that disorder can be given), three possibilities arise under s50(1):

(i)   the Home Secretary can direct the patient's return to prison custody to continue serving sentence, in which case the transfer direction terminates (s51(3)); or

(ii)   the patient can be released on licence or supervision if eligible for 'early release' under the usual provisions; or

(iii) in any other case, it appears that the Home Secretary always retains the residual discretion to leave the patient in hospital for the time being, with the restriction direction remaining in force.

Role of Mental Health Review Tribunal
The prisoner-patient is entitled to apply to a MHRT in the usual way and can do so within the first six months of their hospital detention (s69(2)(b)). Referrals to the Tribunal are also made as if the patient were subject to a s41 restriction order (see Chapter 7). After the hearing, the Tribunal must notify the Home Secretary whether the patient would, if subject to s41, be entitled to an absolute or conditional discharge, according to the usual criteria (see page 199). In the case of conditional discharge, the Tribunal may recommend that the patient should remain in hospital rather than be returned to prison (s74(1)(b)). The Home Secretary then has the following options and should normally notify the Tribunal of the decision within 90 days:

(i)   to allow the patient's discharge, according to the Tribunal's recommendation; or

(ii) to order the patient's return to prison custody to continue sentence, unless the

Tribunal has recommended that, if not discharged, the patient should remain in hospital. If such a recommendation was made, the patient will remain in hospital detention.

If the Home Secretary does not respond to the Tribunal within 90 days, the patient must be returned to prison custody, unless the Tribunal had added a recommendation that the patient should remain in hospital, in which case s/he remains in hospital detention and the restriction direction continues (s74(3)).

Even if the Tribunal does not consider that the patient qualifies for discharge, either absolute or conditional, it may nevertheless notify the Home Secretary that s/he no longer requires treatment or that no effective treatment can be given (s50(1)) in which case the Secretary of State has the discretion outlined above (page 186).

These provisions and the interpretation of s50(1) has recently been considered by the Court of Appeal in *Morley v Nottinghamshire Heathcare Trust and Another* [2002] EWCA Civ 1728. A prisoner sentenced to life imprisonment for sexual violence had been transferred to Rampton Hospital for treatment for his psychopathic disorder, in a bid to move him on from becoming 'stuck' within the prison system. Just over two years later, the RMO concluded that he was not benefiting from treatment, was a security risk and should be returned to prison, notifying the Home Secretary accordingly. The Home Office ordered that he should be remitted to prison. He had not been notified of the hospital's decision to issue a s50(1) notification, nor was he consulted by the Secretary of State. He challenged both exercises of decision-making through judicial review, arguing first that the RMO should have done more than present his opinion and should have drawn the Home Secretary's attention to the view of psychologists at the hospital that he was capable of benefiting from treatment and the opinion of an external consultant whom the hospital had asked to advise. He also submitted that the Home Secretary was exercising a quasi-judicial function and had a duty of fairness that involved giving the patient-prisoner an opportunity to make representations. He sought to assert that his ECHR rights under Article 8 (right to respect for private life and physical and psychological integrity) were at stake.

The Appeal Court ruled, in respect of the first claim, that while the RMO must make proper inquiries within the hospital as to whether the treatability test is satisfied and to consider views expressed before giving a s50(1) notification, he was entitled to make a clinical judgement. He had done enough to discharge his duty and was not required to disclose reports on individual components of the patient's medical regime or to present contrary views in addition to his own judgement. On the second claim, the Court concluded that a right to make representations did not arise. While there will be cases where the Home Secretary has a duty to make further inquiries, that situation did not apply here and the Secretary of State was able to make a decision based on the RMO's judgement. As for Article 8, interference with private life was an inevitable consequence of his lawful sentence and the decisions made had been within the proper ambit of discretion.

Unsentenced Prisoners
The somewhat complex provisions relating to s48 prisoners subject to restriction directions have been addressed earlier in this chapter, save in respect of the role of a

MHRT under s74. A s48 patient is entitled to apply to a Tribunal for review within six months of the date of the direction (s69(2)(b)). The position of s48 patients and the powers of a Tribunal are very similar to the provisions with regard to s47 patients, except that if the Tribunal notifies the Home Secretary that the patient would be entitled to absolute or conditional discharge, if a s41 patient, the Home Secretary is required by s74(4) to order the patient's transfer back to prison custody unless the Tribunal also added a recommendation that, if only conditional discharge would be appropriate, the patient should remain in hospital rather than be returned to custody, in which case the patient will be allowed to remain in hospital. In other words the Home Secretary does not have the discretion in any instance to allow the patient's discharge.

Even if the Tribunal does not consider that a patient (other than a patient remanded in custody by a magistrates' court) qualifies for discharge, either absolute or conditional, it may nevertheless notify the Home Secretary that s/he no longer requires treatment or that no effective treatment can be given (s51(3) or s53(3)), in which case the Home Secretary may order the patient's transfer back to prison custody or may opt to allow the patient to remain in hospital for the time being.

RECENT USE OF SECTIONS 47 AND 48

As an indication of recent use of ss47 and 48 and the contribution of transfers from prison to the population of restricted patients, *Statistics of Mentally Disordered Offenders, England and Wales 2001* (Johnson and Taylor, 2002) shows that, in 2001, 214 sentenced prisoners (compared with 270 in 2000 and 251 in 1997) and 410 unsentenced prisoners (compared with 392 in 2000 and 495 in 1997) were transferred to hospital on restriction directions, constituting 28% and 47% respectively of the total number of restricted patients admitted to hospital that year. No s47 prisoners were transferred on an unrestricted basis. As regards the numbers of transferred prisoners within the population of restricted patients, 414 sentenced and 181 unsentenced prisoners were detained in hospital on 31 December 2001, together constituting 20% of the total number. This proportion has remained relatively stable between 18% and 24% in the period since 1995.

MHA statistics (DoH Bulletin 2002/26) give a slightly different numerical picture, reporting that, in the 12 months ending 31 March 2002, 226 prisoners were transferred under s47, 41 without s49 restriction, 209 of the 226 being admitted to NHS facilities. Of those 209, 188 were classified as mentally ill and 18 as psychopathically disordered. As for s48 transfers, 362 are recorded, though 13 are stated to have been without s49 restriction, which is not a lawful option. Of 326 admitted to NHS facilities, 323 were classified as mentally ill.

The Chief Inspector of Prisons (Annual Report, 1992-93) has in the past addressed the difficulties which can inhibit the effective use of transfer to hospital, noting that the prospects of transfer in eligible cases varies between prisons. Though 'better co-operation from the NHS' had made the use of s48 more possible in a number of establishments (*eg* Norwich, Bristol and Lincoln),

> 'these improvements were only relative and all those prisons still had to look after gravely psychotic inmates for several weeks when they should have been in a

psychiatric hospital ... We have felt in the past that the law should be reviewed on this point and we still do. It remains important that when there are difficulties in transferring the gravely ill to hospital, the local health authority should be informed and asked to find a solution.' (para. 6.04)

Taking stock of the mental health care of remand prisoners in 2000, the Chief Inspector (HM Inspectorate of Prisons, para. 6.30 *et seq.*) observed that though the numbers of prisoners transferred to outside hospitals had increased dramatically after the Reed Report, the figures had since stabilised and, given high bed occupancy rate and the dearth of secure psychiatric beds, transfer from prison of those for whom the need for NHS treatment is agreed can be 'painfully slow'. He estimated that prisoners for whom the optimal placement on clinical grounds would be NHS psychiatric care account for some third of all prison-based healthcare in-patients, suggesting a need for a minimum of 500 additional secure beds in the NHS. Reed and Lyne (2000) noted that four patients in one prison for whom transfer had been agreed had been waiting between four and 20 months, with an average of just under 11 months.

As part of the solution to these delays and uncertainties, the Chief Inspector (2000) commended the provision of dedicated NHS facilities for the treatment of mentally disordered prisoners, as described for male remand prisoners in North-West London by Weaver *et al* (1997). The 14-bed Bentham unit was established in 1994 to provide rapid assessment and (where appropriate) transfer, offering regular outreach assessment sessions at HMP Wormwood Scrubs and more timely treatment, combined with expedited contact with local service providers. However, as the Chief Inspector noted, the scope for such provision is made complicated by disputes about which Health Authority is responsible for the cost of treatment and the level of security required.

Noting the six-fold increase in use of s48 between 1987 and 1996, reflecting a particularly marked increase as a proportion of the average annual population of unsentenced prisoners, Churchill *et al* (1999) suggest that this may be due to the following factors: more psychiatrists visiting prisons than they did 15 years ago; while court-based schemes may not divert, they do prompt more identification of psychiatric disorder, so that on reception prison staff are more likely to have a description of the offence and a psychiatric history as an impetus to seeking onward referral; ss35, 36 and 38 of MHA 1983 are failing to achieve diversion of MDOs from prison so that the burden is increasingly carried by s48.

AFTER-CARE SERVICES
Prisoners discharged into the community from hospital detention under ss47 or 48 are included within the requirement upon health and local authorities under MHA 1983 s117 to provide after-care services (see page 93). Many prisoners assessed as being mentally disturbed are released without any formal referral to any other agency, particularly those serving terms of less than 12 months who are subject to unconditional early release provisions. NACRO (1993) has recommended that:

'Any prisoner assessed as being mentally disturbed but who will not be subject to statutory supervision by the probation service on his or her release should be referred to the relevant local authority social services department. That department should have a duty to assess his or her need for community care services and support at least one month before the earliest possible release date to ensure that the necessary arrangements and services will be in place on release.'

The Wessex Project (Barker and Swyer, 1994) demonstrated the scope to link prison and community services, assessing all newly sentenced or remanded prisoners at Winchester Prison for mental disorder. About 13% are considered to need follow up, the majority because of mental illness. 'Prisoners with identifiable mental health problems are being offered services through care management and the care programme approach exactly as they would if they were being discharged from hospital or any other institution'.

As an illustration of the project's work, Barker and Swyer described a prisoner ('Robert Rhodes') serving a 21-month sentence for unlawful sexual intercourse and assault, both against his step-daughter. He was diagnosed as suffering paranoid schizophrenia.

'After consultation with Mr Rhodes, the prison medical officer and others involved in his care, the project team organised a care programme meeting. The priorities at this stage were to secure an address to which he could be released, to arrange support and medical services for his release and to ascertain from social services the likelihood of him being allowed to return home. Present at this first meeting were the consultant psychiatrist, the probation through-care officer, the children's social worker, a member of the Wessex Project team and the client. The meeting agreed to arrange Mr Rhodes' medication and accommodation for the period immediately after his release. It was made clear to him that there was no immediate prospect of him returning home.

Just after Robert Rhodes' release on licence, a second care programme meeting was held. The same services were represented as at the first meeting though some personnel had changed. His full programme of support and care was formalised at this meeting. His probation officer was nominated as key worker, giving him overall responsibility for ensuring that the care programme was delivered as agreed, and providing Mr Rhodes with a named person to go to in times of crisis. The consultant psychiatrist and his team committed themselves to providing Mr Rhodes' medication and monitoring his mental illness. Local child protection services agreed to conduct a risk assessment in relation to his eventual return home.'

To ascertain the views of mentally disordered prisoners on the responsiveness of mental health and criminal justice agencies to their needs while in the community, Vaughan and Stevenson (2002) undertook a survey for the Wessex Project at HMP Winchester of a sample of 50 prisoners with mental health problems. The findings suggested that their disorder and offending had not been considered serious enough to warrant the intervention of forensic psychiatric services but their needs had been too complex for them to access mainstream community care. The sampled prisoners had felt 'vilified and marginalised by many professional workers' and were unlikely to seek help themselves. Psychiatric intervention was usually determined by a psychotic breakdown or suicide attempt. After they had been stabilised in hospital or prison, after-care and follow-up was not adequately pursued, often resulting in deterioration in mental health and further offending.

The researchers conclude that community agencies should broaden their referral criteria to avoid excluding mentally disordered offenders. Key workers should maintain contact with service users during periods of imprisonment and hospitalisation in order to sustain family and community links and facilitate re-engagement with services on release or discharge. More care is required in placing MDOs in suitable accommodation and helping them access their benefits. Frontline housing and Benefit Agency staff should be trained in dealing with such persons to reduce the risk of alienation and exclusion. Workers with criminal justice roles should seek to temper their authority role with 'practical and therapeutic help'.

Detention under Civil Section on Release

It is sometimes considered appropriate to assess a prisoner for admission to hospital as a detained patient under MHA 1983 ss2 or 3 close to the point of release from custody. MHA(COP) 1993 para. 3.12 states that if an ASW has to be called for this purpose, as much advance warning as possible should be given and the ASW must be given ample interview time and facilities, access to the pre-sentence report 'as it is difficult within the confines of a prison to assess how a prisoner might be able to benefit from alternative treatment in the community'.

THE FUTURE OF PRISON HEALTH CARE

In the light of severe criticism of Prison Service health care, firstly by the Chief Inspector of Prisons who has argued (1996) that responsibility for health care provision should move to the NHS and subsequently by the standing Health Advisory Committee to the Prison Service (1997) which highlighted the uncoordinated way in which mental health care to prisoners has been formulated and delivered, with inadequate continuity on release, a Prison Service and NHS Executive Working Group reported in 1999 on the future organisation of Prison Health Care, in a spirit of frank recognition of deficiency in provision. Instead of embracing the solution of integration, the Group's report advocated an approach based on formal partnership between Prison Service and NHS, designed to ensure that health care standards in prison are the same as those in the NHS, thus serving to influence custodial regimes in positive directions and lift low morale so that isolation of clinical staff is minimised and that continuity of care is maintained on reception to and release from prison.

In particular, the report highlighted the following aims:

- The care of mentally ill prisoners should develop in line with NHS mental health policy and national service frameworks, including new arrangements for referral and admission to high and medium secure psychiatric services.

- Special attention should be paid to better identification of mental health needs at reception screening.

- Mechanisms should be in place to ensure the satisfactory functioning of a Care Programme Approach within prisons and to developing mental health outreach work on prison wings.

- Prisoners should receive the same level of community care within prison as they would receive in the wider community and policies should be put in place to ensure adequate and effective communication and joint working between NHS mental health services and prisons. Health Authorities should ensure that service agreements with NHS Trusts include appropriate mental health services for their local prison population.

To oversee and manage these new arrangements the report proposed that the Prison Health Care Directorate should be replaced by (a) a new Prison Health Policy Unit, responsible for strategic direction and the application of Department of Health policies and objectives, and (b) a task force responsible for ensuring that health needs assessments and other changes are delivered in practice. For an analysis of the report's implications and the challenge facing the new structures in delivering 'the principle of equivalence', see Grounds (2000).

In pursuing its commitment to improving mental health services for prisoners, the Government issued *Changing the Outlook: A Strategy for Developing and Modernising Mental Health Services in Prisons* (Department of Health, December 2001), acknowledging that 'the way services are currently organised, in terms of volume, range and quality, does not meet prisoners' needs' and offering 'a vision of where services should be in 3-5 years' time'. By September 2002, all prisons and their local NHS partners would be 'expected to have completed a detailed review of mental health needs, based on their existing needs assessment work, to identify gaps in provision between what is currently available and that set out in the strategy document, and to have developed action plans to implement the changes needed to fill those gaps'. The key five-year aims include:

(i)   a reduction in the number of prisoners located in prison healthcare centres, with resources redeployed to provide increased day care (HMP Brixton is cited as a positive illustration of this kind of facility) and improved wing-based support (report notes the 'crisis card scheme' developed by the Mental Health Liaison Team at HMP/YOI Moorland, whereby prisoners assessed as likely to benefit from immediate access to a mental health professional are issued cards that they can show to wing staff if they feel in crisis. The team aims to respond within 30 minutes, day or night);

(ii) a reduction in the average length of time mentally ill prisoners spend in remaining healthcare beds;

(iii) more appropriate skill mix among those providing mental health care, so that prisoners have access to the right range of services to NHS standards (note is taken of HMP Leeds' pilot Custody Plan, profiling needs on reception and bringing together those agencies and services that can best meet mental health and allied social welfare needs on release);

(iv) quicker and more effective arrangements for transferring the most seriously ill prisoners to appropriate NHS facilities and receiving them back (the report notes Broadmoor's dedicated 'waiting list support CPN' whose role is to manage the hospital's waiting list and provide active support/advice to those presently managing those awaiting admission);

(v)   increased collaboration by NHS in the management of those who are seriously mentally ill, including those vulnerable to suicide and self-harm while they are in prison.

The mental health 'in-reach' project in prisons commenced with a first wave of 12 English prisons and all four Welsh prisons from July 2001. Funded from the NHS budget, in-reach involves the establishment of multi-disciplinary teams, similar to Community Mental Health Teams, aiming to provide a range of services to prisoners. A further six prisons commenced funding from November 2001, being those establishments linked directly or indirectly to the DSPD programme (see page 179). Another 25 prisons are expected to join the project during 2002-03 and it is anticipated that 'in-reach' will cover around half of all prisons by March 2004. In September 2002, the Home Secretary and the DoH agreed that funding responsibility will transfer to the latter Department with effect from April 2003. Prisoners come within the ambit of the revised Care Plan Approach, as outlined in Chapter 15.

CASE ILLUSTRATION: SECTION 47 TRANSFER TO HOSPITAL
Eve Tyde (24)
Offence
Robbery (robbing the cashier of a petrol station of £40 at knifepoint, having consumed a quantity of alcohol).

Personal and Psychiatric History
Following the end of her marriage, Ms Tyde's dependence on alcohol increased, despite in-patient detoxification, and care of her children was transferred to their father by court order. After a second admission to hospital for detoxification, she was able to reduce her alcohol consumption substantially but difficulties in a further relationship caused depression, leading to her voluntary admission to psychiatric hospital six months prior to the offence, where she overdosed with paracetamol. Unable to return to work after discharging herself, she experienced a range of financial demands and debts, and the offence appeared to be committed out of desperation.

Prior to Sentence
The pre-sentence report commented that Ms Tyde was still depressed, anxious and periodically self-harming by scratching her wrists. She was assessed as at risk of suicide if she received a lengthy prison sentence. The probation officer had suggested to the defence that a psychiatric report would be helpful but legal aid funding for such a report was refused and the court did not order a medical assessment.

Sentence
Thirty months' imprisonment.

Transfer Decision
At an early stage in her sentence, Ms Tyde attempted to throttle another prisoner with a belt and subsequently claimed no memory of the incident. An EEG test revealed an abnormality and she was referred to a consultant forensic psychiatrist based at the RSU in her home area who recommended transfer under s47 (with restriction) for an assessment. After her admission to the unit she became more floridly ill and was

diagnosed to be suffering from paranoid schizophrenia with an abnormality of brain functioning akin to temporal lobe epilepsy. With hindsight it seemed clear that she should have been psychiatrically assessed prior to sentence and would have been better dealt with by a s37 hospital order, probably with s41 restriction.

She remained in the RSU beyond the point when she would otherwise have been released from prison on ACR licence, *ie* at the half-way point of sentence, and was subsequently granted indefinite 'leave of absence' under MHA 1983 s17(1), to reside at a specialist rehabilitation hostel, 19 months after her date of sentence. It was anticipated that she would continue to require long-term forensic psychiatric oversight.

Legal Status

As a s47 patient, Ms Tyde's restriction direction automatically ceased at the point when she would otherwise have ceased to be liable to be detained in prison, taking account of her early release entitlement (s50(2) and (3)). This meant that she then held the same status as if subject to a s37 hospital order (s47(2)). If she were then discharged from hospital in the period prior to date when her ACR would have terminated (*ie* the three-quarters point of sentence), would she be liable to ACR licence requirements for the remainder of that period? Or would she simply have the status of a s37 patient entitled to receive aftercare or discharge under MHA 1983 s117? The answer appears to be that her residual liability to licence under CJA 1991 would assume belated active life and that she should be statutorily supervised by a probation officer. In practice this requires both the doctor to notify the Probation Service and the prison from which she was transferred to hospital to raise a licence for the purpose.

In this instance, however, Ms Tyde was not discharged but granted leave of absence which could be revoked at any time if the RMO thought this necessary in the interests of the patient's own health or safety or for the protection of other people, notice being in writing. Leave can be subject to whatever conditions the RMO thinks necessary in the patient's own interests or to protect others (s17(1)). The patient is thus still liable to detention and can be obliged to accept medical treatment. While she was subject to such legal status, it is submitted that MHA 1983 takes precedence over CJA 1991 and that she would not be subject to ACR licence requirements.

A final question concerns Ms Tyde's liability to be returned to prison under PCC(S)A 2000 s116 (formerly CJA 1991 s40) upon conviction for any offence during the currency of the original sentence, *ie* prior to the expiry of the full 30 months. It is submitted that Ms Tyde retained the status of short-term prisoner and thus in principle fell to be dealt with under s116 powers, including return to prison. However, in practice the court would wish to take account of the likely effect of a return to prison on her mental condition and on the treatment which she was receiving. Returning to prison someone who had been transferred out of prison for reasons of their mental health, where those medical factors remain pertinent, would seem wrong in principle, if not in law.

MENTAL HEALTH BILL

Chapter Three of Part Three of the draft Bill is designed to replace the provisions of MHA 1983 ss47-48 and their associated provisions, replicating current provisions but adding a new power in clause 92 to direct transfer of a sentenced prisoner to hospital for a mental health report, thus enabling the assessment of individuals who cannot be adequately examined in prison.

Transfer for Report

Clause 92 empowers the Secretary of State to transfer a sentenced prisoner (including one detained for non-payment of fine) to hospital for a mental health report where satisfied that there is reason to believe that the person is suffering from mental disorder. The person must be admitted to the specified hospital within 14 days of the making of the direction; otherwise the direction will cease to have effect. Transfer will last for 16 weeks from date of admission to hospital or until the person's release date, whichever is sooner. Transfer can be terminated sooner if the clinical supervisor notifies the Secretary of State that he is not satisfied that there is reason to suspect mental disorder. The prisoner does not have to be returned to the same prison in which he was detained prior to transfer.

14
RESTRICTED PATIENTS

Patients fall into the category of 'restricted patient' if they are subject to any of the following (s79(1)):

(i)   a s37 hospital order with a s41 restriction order attached (see Chapter 7);

(ii)   a 'restriction direction' under s49 relating to a prisoner subject to a 'transfer direction' on removal from prison to hospital under ss47-48 (see Chapter 13);

(iii) an order under CP(I)A 1964 s5(1) or CAA 1968 s6 (following a finding of insanity or unfitness to plead) (see Chapters 5 and 6);

(iv)   removal to a hospital in England or Wales from Northern Ireland, Scotland, the Channel Islands or the Isle of Man under ss82 or 85 or MH(S)A 1984 s73, while subject to a restriction order under legislation in that jurisdiction;

(v)   a restriction direction under s46(3) relating to a member of an armed service ordered to be detained under military law during Her Majesty's pleasure.

Patients in sub-categories (iii), (iv) or (v) are treated in law as subject to a s37 order with s41 restriction and reference hereafter to the latter applies also to them.

EFFECT OF RESTRICTION
While the restriction order continues, the effect is as follows:

(i)   the patient cannot be discharged, transferred to another hospital or given leave of absence without the consent of the Home Secretary (s41(3)(c));

(ii)   if leave of absence is granted, the patient may be recalled by the RMO (see page 91) or the Home Secretary, in the latter instance at any time (s43(3)(d));

(iii) there is no requirement that the patient's detention should be renewed periodically under s20 (s41(3)(a));

(iv)   though there is no statutory requirement for any authority to consider whether the criteria for detaining the patient continue to apply, the RMO must examine the patient and report to the Home Secretary at such intervals (not exceeding a year) and containing such particulars as the Minister may require (s42(6)). This is intended to prevent restricted patients being detained for unjustifiably long periods;

(v)   if the patient absconds, s/he may be taken into custody at any time and the 'six month rule' under s18(4) (see page 92) does not apply (s43(3)(d)).

EUROPEAN CONVENTION
It is worth noting at the outset that the key questions relating to detained patients have to be viewed in the context of ECHR, now incorporated into domestic law by HRA

1998. Article 5 of the Convention provides:

(1) Everyone has the right to liberty and security of person. No one shall be deprived of his liberty save in the following cases and in accordance with a procedure prescribed by law...

   (e) the lawful detention of ... persons of unsound mind...

(4) Everyone who is deprived of his liberty by arrest or detention shall be entitled to take proceedings by which the lawfulness of his detention shall be decided speedily by a court and his release ordered if his detention is not lawful.

The leading relevant decision of the Strasbourg Court is *Winterwerp v The Netherlands* [1979] 2 EHRR 387 which established the following principles:

(i) a mental patient cannot lawfully be detained unless he has been reliably shown to be of unsound mind;

(ii) the nature of the mental disorder must be of a kind or degree to warrant compulsory confinement;

(iii) continued detention will only be justified if the disorder persists;

(iv) a person detained must have periodic access to an authority with the characteristics of a court in order to obtain a review of the lawfulness of his detention.

POWERS OF THE HOME SECRETARY

The main powers of the Secretary of State in respect of hospital orders are as follows:

(i) to direct that the patient shall cease to be subject to restriction;

(ii) to discharge the patient from hospital 'absolutely' under s42(2), so that the hospital order thereby terminates;

(iii) to discharge the patient from hospital 'conditionally' under s42(2) so that the patient remains subject both to compulsory supervision in the community and to recall to hospital;

(iv) to give consent under s41(3)(c) to the RMO or the hospital managers to discharge (under s23), transfer (under s19) or grant leave of absence to (under s17) the patient;

(v) to refer the patient to a MHRT;

(vi) to recall the conditionally discharged patient to hospital;

(vii) to recall the patient from leave of absence.

These powers are detailed more fully in the remainder of this chapter, while the special provisions relating to restricted prisoner-patient are addressed primarily in Chapter 13. It may be noted here in respect of (iv) above that C(S)A 1997 s49(2) amended MHA 1983 s41(3) to provide that any transfer of a restricted patient between hospitals under s19 is subject to the Secretary of State's agreement, even where the hospitals are managed by the same NHS Trust or authority.

Advisory Board on Restricted Patients

In dealing with patients considered to need 'special care in assessment' (*ie* the risk is high or the prognosis particularly difficult), where either their discharge or transfer from secure to open conditions are under consideration, the Home Secretary has scope to refer a case to an independent Advisory Board, sometimes known as the 'Aarvold Board' after the Committee chaired by Sir Carl Aarvold which reported in 1973 (Cmnd 5191) recommending its creation. Comprising two lawyers, two psychiatrists, a Chief Probation Officer and a Director of Social Services, the Board has no statutory basis, is purely advisory and is not subject to judicial review. In recent years very little use has been made of this facility which can cause protracted delay in decision-making.

Role of Home Office

The Home Secretary's responsibilities under MHA 1983 and related legislation is undertaken by the Mental Health Unit (formerly C3 Division) of the Home Office, holding responsibility for:

(i) arranging the admission to hospital of patients transferred from prison or under CP(I)A 1964;

(ii) considering recommendations from RMOs for the leave, transfer or discharge of restricted patients;

(iii) seeking the personal authority of a Minister in certain instances of discretion;

(iv) preparing documentation for MHRTs;

(v) monitoring the progress of conditionally discharged patients and considering questions of variation of conditions, recall to hospital or absolute discharge.

The Unit is organised in teams, each holding responsibility for a proportion of the restricted patient population according to the patient's surname initial.

LIFTING SECTION 41 RESTRICTIONS

The Home Secretary is able to direct at any time that the restriction order shall cease, if 'satisfied that a restriction order is no longer required for the protection of the public from serious harm' (s42(1)). If the patient is still in hospital when the direction is given, the patient's status is now as if s/he had been admitted to the hospital under a normal s37 hospital order without restriction made on the date that the restriction order ceased (s41(5), with the exception that the patient can apply to an MHRT during the first six months of their new status (s69(2)(a)).

If the patient had already been conditionally discharged from hospital before the Home Secretary's direction, s/he is deemed to be absolutely discharged on the date when the order ceases to have effect (s42(5)).

APPLICATIONS AND REFERENCES TO A MENTAL HEALTH REVIEW TRIBUNAL

Patient's Application

Restricted patients, including prisoner-patients subject to a restriction direction, have the same right to apply to a MHRT as an ordinary s37 patient and under s70 may apply:

(i)   in the period between the expiration of six months and the expiration of 12 months beginning with the date of the relevant hospital order or transfer direction; and

(ii)   in any subsequent period of 12 months.

HOME SECRETARY'S REFERENCE

The Home Secretary has both a discretionary power of reference at any time under s71(1) and a duty to refer under s71(2) in respect of restricted patients who have not been considered by a tribunal within the last three years.

MHA 1983 s71

(1)   The Secretary of State may at any time refer the case of a restricted patient to a Mental Health Review Tribunal.

(2)   The Secretary of State should refer to a Mental Health Review Tribunal the case of any restricted patient detained in a hospital whose case has not been considered by such a tribunal, whether on his own application or otherwise, within the last three years.

The discretionary power extends also to conditionally discharged patients. The Home Secretary also has an obligation under s75(1)(a) to refer the case of a conditionally discharged patient who has been recalled to hospital, within one month of their return.

A Tribunal considering the case of a restricted patient should be chaired by 'a lawyer with substantial judicial experience in the criminal courts'. The proceedings of MHRTs are governed by the *Mental Health Review Tribunal Rules 1983* (SI 1983 No. 942). Thus r6 requires the Home Secretary to send a statement and detailed reports on the patient to the Tribunal within three weeks of being notified that an application has been made. The Tribunal must give at least 14 days notice of the hearing to the Home Secretary and supply copies of all the documents (r20) so that the public interest can be represented. Failure to comply with the latter has been held to invalidate the Tribunal's proceedings.

Tribunal's Power to Discharge

When dealing with a restricted patient other than a prisoner-patient subject to a restriction direction, a MHRT does not have general discretion to order the patient's discharge but it has a duty under s73(1) and (2) (as amended by the MHA 1983 (Remedial) Order 2001 – SI 2001 No. 3712) to direct the patient's discharge as follows.

● It shall direct the *absolute discharge* of the patient under s73(1) if:

(a)   it is not satisfied –

(i)   that he is then suffering from mental illness, psychopathic disorder, severe mental impairment or mental impairment or from any of those forms of disorder of a nature or degree which makes it appropriate for him to be liable to be detained in a hospital for medical treatment; or

(ii)   that it is necessary for the health or safety of the patient or for the protection of other persons that he should receive such treatment;

and

(b) the tribunal is satisfied that it is not appropriate for the patient to remain liable to be recalled to hospital for further treatment.

• It shall direct the *conditional discharge* of the patient under s73(2) if:

(a) paragraph (a) above applies; but

(b) paragraph (b) above does not apply.

Under the original wording of s73 the Tribunal had to be satisfied that one of the following criteria applied:

(i) that the patient is not suffering from mental illness, psychopathic disorder, severe mental impairment or mental impairment; or

(ii) that the patient is suffering from one of the four specified forms of disorder but not of a nature or degree which makes it appropriate for detention in hospital for medical treatment; or

(iii) that it is not necessary for the health or safety of the patient or for the protection of other persons that s/he should receive such treatment.

However, in *R (on the application of H) v London North and East Region MHRT* [2001] 2 WLR 512 the Court of Appeal ruled that in so far as this provision imposed the burden on the patient to establish that at least one of the criteria for his continued detention is no longer satisfied, and thus to disprove the lawfulness of his own detention, it infringed his right to liberty under ECHR Article 5(1) and (4) and that to comply with that right the Tribunal should be required to discharge a patient if it cannot be shown that he is currently suffering from a mental disorder that warrants detention. This judgment prompted the remedial order by statutory instrument noted above.

Risk and Prevention
A patient cannot be detained on purely preventive grounds. However, a wide definition of 'medical treatment' (see page 87) means that it is not essential in justifying further detention that further treatment in hospital has the prospect of alleviating or improving the patient's condition. *In R v Merseyside MHRT, ex p. D* (1987) *The Times*, 13 April, a patient suffering psychopathic disorder who had been detained in secure hospitals since 1939 sought judicial review to challenge the Tribunal's decision to continue his detention, arguing that further treatment stood no chance of achieving any positive change. Dismissing his application, the Divisional Court considered that he could benefit from nursing and care, even if there was no prospect of preventing the deterioration of his condition. Note also that the Tribunal does not have to consider whether it is necessary to protect the public from serious harm.

It is still valid for a Tribunal to consider that a patient should appropriately remain liable to recall, even though s/he has been found not to be suffering any mental disorder. In *R v Merseyside MHRT, ex p. K* [1990] 1 All ER 694, a patient placed on a hospital order with restriction in 1971 because of psychopathic disorder satisfied the Tribunal in 1986 that he was not suffering any mental disorder but the Tribunal nevertheless considered that he should remain liable to recall because, having regard to the period he had been detained in hospital, it was necessary to test his behaviour in the community and it was clear that he needed strict supervision. His claim that, as he was not suffering mental disorder, he was no longer a 'patient' within the meaning of the Act and thus was entitled to unconditional discharge was dismissed.

Conditions

The conditions to which the conditionally released patient will be subject are not specified by statute and will be determined by the Tribunal; the usual requirements relate to residence, supervision, medical treatment and conduct. A requirement of medical treatment is subject to the proviso of s56(1)(c) that a conditionally discharged patient may not be subjected to enforced treatment against their consent. Other requirements may specify, for example, that the patient does not enter on-licence premises. The Home Secretary may subsequently add to or vary the Tribunal's conditions at any time (s73(4) and (5), and will normally require social and psychiatric supervision if these have not been specified.

Though, as indicated below, it is not open to a MHRT to direct a patient's transfer from one detaining institution to another, the question arises whether conditions of a patient's discharge are so restrictive as to amount to ordering such a course. This problem was posed in *Secretary of State for the Home Department (R on the application of) v Mental Health Review Tribunal and PH* [2002] EWCA Civ 1868 (unreported) where the Tribunal considering a 77 year-old patient with chronic paranoid schizophrenia as well as significant physical health problems, who had been detained in a high security hospital for 44 years following a finding of unfitness to plead to allegations of s18 wounding, directed his conditional discharge subject (among other conditions) to the following:

(i) that he should reside at suitable specialist accommodation which provides 24-hour trained nursing care and daytime trained psychiatric nursing care and appropriate security;

(ii) that he should not leave the accommodation without an escort.

The Home Office which had considered that the patient still required detention in hospital sought judicial review, arguing that the Tribunal had acted outside its powers because those conditions were so restrictive as to deprive him of his liberty, so that he would continue to be detained, albeit in conditions of lower security. The Court of Appeal rejected this argument, being unable to accept that the conditions:

'inevitably mean that this man would be in a regime so restrictive that he would be deprived of his liberty. (The first) is sufficiently broadly phrased as to allow for measures which would fall short of such deprivation and both it and (the second) have as their purpose the protection of (the patient) and would be in his interests.'

The fact that any registered care home or similar establishment would be likely to qualify as a 'hospital' (within the meaning of MHA 1983 s79(6)) did not affect the issue. 'If he is discharged from detention, that is still an effective discharge, even though he may be required to reside in another institution that qualifies as a hospital.'

Communicating Decisions

The Tribunal's decision, with reasons, must be communicated to the patient and to the Home Secretary within seven days of the hearing, though the decision may be announced immediately after the hearing, at the Tribunal's discretion (MHRTR 1983 r24(1)).

Power to Defer Discharge

Under s73(7), a Tribunal may defer conditional discharge 'until such arrangements as appear ... to be necessary for that purpose have been made to their satisfaction'. Where such a provisional decision has been made, 'any further decision in the proceedings may be made without a further hearing' (MHRTR 1983 r25(1)). If, however, the deferment causes such delay that a second application or reference is made in the meantime, the second consideration will supersede the first (s73(7)).

In *Johnson v United Kingdom* (1997) 27 EHRR 296 the European Court stated that while the imposition of conditions could justify a deferred conditional discharge, it is of paramount importance that discharge is not unreasonably delayed and that safeguards had to be in place to ensure deferral was consonant with Article 5(1).

In *R v MHRT and others, ex p. Hall* [2000] 1 WLR 1323, a Tribunal considering the detention of a patient found not guilty of manslaughter by reason of insanity had been concerned by the risk of recurrence of his mental illness and the need to protect the community. It had imposed stringent conditions as to residence, medical and social supervision. Neither the local authority nor the health authority provided the required care plan to meet those conditions, with the result that he remained in detention. On his application for judicial review, the Court of Appeal held that, as the Tribunal had considered that he should be subject to recall, it had been required to order conditional discharge. Those conditions, although likely to be difficult to satisfy, were neither unusual nor unreasonable. Once the Tribunal had stipulated its conditions and deferred discharge for the necessary arrangements to be made, the burden passed to the local authority and health authority to make the arrangements within a reasonable time. The Tribunal had no authority to require those authorities to produce a care plan, or to set a time limit for its preparation, nor was it required to have such a plan available setting out workable arrangements before imposing those conditions. While it is desirable for a Tribunal to encourage agencies to fulfil their statutory duties, and a more interventionist approach might have been possible here, the Tribunal was not subject to judicial review on that account. The position was not affected by Article 5.

In *K (R on the application of) v Camden and Islington Health Authority* [2002] QB 198, the Tribunal ordered a s41 patient's conditional discharge on condition that she should live at her parents' home and co-operate with supervision provided by a consultant forensic psychiatrist, deferring her discharge until satisfactory arrangements had been made to meet those conditions. Her RMO did not agree with the residential condition and considered that she should transfer to a residential care facility. The health authority was unable to find a psychiatrist willing to supervise her on the basis of the conditions set by the Tribunal. She sought judicial review of the health authority's actions, arguing that it was under a duty to provide the psychiatric services necessary to enable compliance with the Tribunal's condition. The Court of Appeal dismissed her application, holding that the authority owed no such absolute duty under MHA 1983 s117. Its duty in exercising its discretion, having regard to other demands on its budget, was to use reasonable endeavours to provide the services in question. In this instance it had fulfilled that duty. It was in no position to order a psychiatrist to supervise the patient if the psychiatrist had declined to do so on grounds of professional judgement.

The problems posed by this kind of impasse were further considered in *IH (R on the application of) v Secretary of State for the Home Department and others* [2002] EWCA Civ 646. The patient, who had suffered paranoid psychosis, had cut off his three year-old son's genitals, resulting in him being found not guilty of s18 GBH by reason of insanity and detained in Rampton Hospital. On being informed that his illness was in remission, the Tribunal had indicated that it considered his conditional discharge to be appropriate and adjourned to enable a care plan to be drawn up, stating the conditions that it anticipated. Despite extensive efforts, the Health Authority was unable to locate appropriate forensic psychiatric supervision, primarily because the consultant who serviced its area considered supervised discharge to be clinically inappropriate and unsafe. The Tribunal nevertheless ordered his conditional discharge on the conditions proposed, deferred until arrangements had been made. The patient remained in limbo in hospital for a further 21 months until the Home Secretary, at the suggestion of the High Court, referred him to a further Tribunal which determined that he should remain detained in hospital for continuing treatment of his illness. He then contended that his detention violated Article 5 and that the statutory provisions were incompatible with the Convention.

The Court of Appeal noted that to comply with *Winterwerp* (page 197) and *Johnson* (above), a conditional discharge must not be deferred under s73(7) beyond a reasonable period. After that, the MHRT must discharge the patient, whether or not it has proved possible to put in place arrangements to accommodate the conditions the Tribunal wished to impose. If such arrangements have not proved possible, the MHRT must make appropriate modifications to the conditions and direct discharge. As for the risk of impasse, the Court observed:

'The critical impasse arises where a Tribunal considers that it is necessary for the health or safety of the patient or the safety of others that the patient continues to receive psychiatric treatment, and that it is reasonable for such treatment to be provided in the community, but the psychiatrists who would have to provide such treatment refuse to do so because they disagree with the Tribunal's view that the patient can safely be treated in the community. We think that it is unlikely that this impasse will arise in circumstances where the Tribunal has concluded that it is not satisfied that the patient is any longer suffering from a mental illness, although the present may be such a rare case. The impasse in question will classically arise in the case of a patient who, while of unsound mind, can be expected to remain free of symptoms provided that he continues to receive treatment. In such a situation there is more scope for disagreement between a Tribunal and the psychiatrists called upon to provide such treatment as to whether it can be safely be provided in the community or only under detention in hospital.'

The Court considered that in a case such as the one under consideration the provisions of s73 operate as follows:

'Where a Tribunal decides (i) that a restricted patient is suffering from mental illness for which psychiatric treatment is necessary for the health or safety of the patient or the protection of other persons and (ii) that detention in hospital for that treatment is not necessary if, but only if, psychiatric treatment is provided in the community, the Tribunal can properly make a provisional decision to direct a conditional discharge, but defer giving that direction to enable arrangements to be made for providing psychiatric treatment in the community. The Health Authority subject to the s117 duty will then be bound to use its best endeavours to put in place the necessary aftercare. If it fails to use its best endeavours it will be subject to judicial review. If, despite its best endeavours, the Health Authority is unable to provide the necessary services, the Tribunal must think again. If, as is likely in those circumstances, it concludes that it is necessary for the patient to remain detained in hospital in order to receive the treatment, it should record that decision.'

If a patient considered that the psychiatrist was seeking to foil the intention of the Tribunal in this way, the Court expressed the view that the patient would have a remedy under judicial review, seeking to establish that the doctor was in breach of a public law duty. However, the ECHR does not require psychiatrists to administer treatment or supervision in the community when, as a result of professional judgement made in good faith, they refuse to undertake responsibility.

Helpfully summarising the position of a MHRT considering conditional release, the Court offered the following step-by-step process, considered compatible with Article 5(1):

- The Tribunal can, at the outset, adjourn the hearing to investigate the possibility of imposing conditions.

- The Tribunal can make a provisional decision to make a conditional discharge on specified conditions, including submitting to psychiatric supervision, but defer directing a conditional discharge while the authorities responsible for after-care under s.117 of the Act make the necessary arrangements to enable the patient to meet those conditions.

- The Tribunal should meet after an appropriate interval to monitor progress in making these arrangements if they have not by then been put in place.

- Once the arrangements have been made, the Tribunal can direct a conditional discharge without holding a further hearing.

- If problems arise with making arrangements to meet the conditions, the Tribunal has a number of options, depending upon the circumstances:

  (a) it can defer for a further period, perhaps with suggestions as to how any problems can be overcome;

  (b) it can amend or vary the proposed conditions to seek to overcome the difficulties that have been encountered;

  (c) it can order a conditional discharge without specific conditions, thereby making the patient subject to recall; or

  (d) it can decide that the patient must remain detained in hospital for treatment.

- It will not normally be appropriate for a Tribunal to direct a conditional discharge on conditions with which the patient will be unable to comply because it has not proved possible to make the necessary arrangements.

If a MHRT grants a deferred conditional discharge, the issue can arise that leave of absence is necessary to enable the patient to spend a trial period at a hostel. Such a proposal was put forward in *RA (R on the application of) v Secretary of State for the Home Department* [2002] EWHC 1618 Admin. in respect of a patient diagnosed as suffering paranoid schizophrenia who had been detained following plea of insanity in respect of offences of kidnapping and assault. Following deferral of his discharge by the MHRT until appropriate accommodation was available, the hospital sought Home Office approval and consent under s41(3)(c)(i) for him to spend six weeks' trial leave at a hostel. The Home Office declined to approve leave of absence under s17, arguing that this section, though appropriate for testing unrestricted patients, is not suitable for restricted patients since it places discretion in the hands of the RMO and does not provide for the Home Secretary to attach conditions to his consent. The Home Office nevertheless recognised the merits of the hostel initiative and proposed as the way forward the use of the Home Secretary's s42(2) powers of conditional discharge, suggesting that if the placement proved not to be a success the offender could either be recalled if his mental health justified resort to that power or be re-housed, perhaps by voluntary admission to hospital.

On his application for judicial review of the Home Office stance, Crane J upheld the patient's claim that the delay to his discharge thus caused had violated his Article 5(1) and (4) rights and that he had been unlawfully detained. The Court considered that the Home office view that conditions cannot be attached to s17 consent was incorrect.

'It is true that neither s17 nor s41(3) provides in terms for such conditions to the consent. However, s17 enables conditions to be imposed by the RMO on the patient. I can see no reason why the Secretary of State cannot in law decline to give consent unless suitable conditions are imposed. He can obviously refuse consent to leave for a particular period. And since the Secretary of State has a power of recall under s41(3)(c), there is every reason why he should be able to insist upon conditions that have the effect of providing the necessary information to him. The power to recall would then be no less effective than under s42(2). The suggestion of voluntary readmission or a civil section are not likely to be effective.'

Decisions Beyond a Tribunal's Power
A MHRT is not able to make the following decisions:

• To remove the patient's s41 restriction, leaving the s37 order intact.

• To release a patient who does not qualify for mandatory discharge.

• To impose a condition of continued residence in a hospital.

• To grant leave of absence or direct transfer to another hospital.

These limitations do not prevent a Tribunal from forming views and passing these to the Home Office.

Patients Subject to Restriction Directions
In dealing with patients transferred to hospital from prison under ss47-48 and subject to a s49 restriction direction, Tribunals cannot authorise their discharge. Instead, under s74(1), the Tribunal must notify the Home Secretary whether the patient, if s/he had

been subject to a restriction order, would have been entitled to absolute or conditional discharge under s73. Further, if notifying the Home Secretary that the patient would have been entitled to be conditionally discharged, the Tribunal may recommend that the patient should continue to be detained in hospital rather than returned to prison. This is further addressed in Chapter 13.

DISCHARGE OF THE PATIENT BY THE HOME SECRETARY

A restricted patient can be discharged by the RMO or the hospital managers under s23, where the Home Secretary's consent has been obtained, but discharge is much more likely to occur upon exercise of the Home Secretary's own powers of absolute or conditional release under s42(2):

> At any time while a restriction order is in force in respect of a patient, the Secretary of State may, if he thinks fit, by warrant discharge the patient from hospital, either absolutely or subject to conditions; and where a person is absolutely discharged under this subsection, he shall thereupon cease to be liable to be detained by virtue of the relevant hospital order, and the restriction order shall cease to have effect accordingly.

This power runs parallel to the provision for discharge by a MHRT and gives the Home Secretary much broader discretion than is available to a Tribunal, for example in regard to a patient who still has some mental disorder, for whom it is difficult to conclude whether hospital treatment is still appropriate.

Absolute Discharge

This has the effect of terminating both the s37 hospital order and the s41 restriction order.

Conditional Discharge

In summary, this requires the patient to be subject to compulsory supervision in the community while remaining liable to be recalled to hospital.

CONSULTATION WITH VICTIMS

CJCSA 2000 s69 placed on a statutory footing the duties of the Probation Service towards victims of sexual or violent offences (including 'an offence against a child' as designated by sch 4 para. 1 to the Act) when a 'relevant sentence' has been imposed on the offender. The local probation board is required to take all reasonable steps to ascertain whether 'any appropriate person' wishes to make representations about whether the offender should be subject to any conditions on release or to receive information about any conditions to which the offender is to be subject on release. If an appropriate person wishes to participate in either or both of those ways, the board must forward representations to the decision-makers and inform the person with appropriate information. The ambit of 'relevant sentences' does not include hospital orders, only custodial sentences of 12 months or longer, thus presenting an obvious anomaly. In its Consultation Document (para. 4.2) on the draft Mental Health Bill (2002), the Government has indicated that:

> 'there will be provision in the Bill to provide the same rights to victims of mentally disordered offenders. This will not involve breach of medical confidentiality. The

right to information will cover basic management issues such as the fact that an offender is no longer detained in hospital'.

CONDITIONAL DISCHARGE

The current *Notes for the Guidance of Social Supervisors* (NGSS), issued by the Home Office, Department of Health and Welsh Office (1997), indicate that discharge will usually be subject to conditions, the normal requirements being: residence at a stated address; supervision by a local authority social worker or a probation officer; and psychiatric supervision.

'The purpose of the formal supervision resulting from conditional discharge is to protect the public from further serious harm in two ways: first, by assisting the patient's successful reintegration into the community after what may have been a long period of detention in hospital under conditions of security; second, by close monitoring of the patient's progress so that, in the event of subsequent deterioration in the patient's mental health or of a perceived increase in the risk of danger to the public, steps can be taken to assist the patient and protect the public. Conditional discharge also allows a period of assessment of the patient in the community before a final decision is taken whether to remove the control imposed by the restriction order by means of an absolute discharge.' (para. 17)

Upon discharge, a 'warrant of discharge' is prepared, stating the terms and requirements of the patient's status in the community.

In a general review of the management of conditionally discharged patients (and others who present similar risks in the community) Snowden *et al* (1999) identify the lack of literature on the styles of service provision for the supervision of higher-risk mentally disordered offenders, especially s41 patients. They consider the confusing but prevalent use of the terms 'integrated' and 'parallel' as a description of care provision, *ie* the extent to which patients are returned to local psychiatric services for community care or remain subject to specialist forensic mental health teams. In the light of experience of the Manchester and Preston Forensic Mental Health services, they argue that these terms or categories have no value in present-day practice and propose that conditionally discharged patients fall into four service model groups, depending on level of risk, from local community mental health team care (low risk) to forensic community health team care (high risk), with shared care at intermediate risk levels.

Preparation for Supervision and After-Care
The following points distil the *Notes of Guidance* (NGSS, Section 5):

- The multi-disciplinary clinical team seek to understand what led to the dangerous behaviour which resulted in the patient's detention and to assess the extent to which treatment for the mental disorder is likely to reduce the risk of the patient behaving dangerously if returned to the community.

- Only when the patient's condition has so improved that the level of risk to the public is reduced to the extent that detention in hospital is no longer considered necessary, will the clinical team consider recommending conditional discharge. Preparation for conditional discharge will begin before authority for discharge is sought.

Choice of Social Supervisor

Both Social Services and the Probation Service have the experience and the statutory basis (either under MHA 1983 s117 or the *Probation Rules*) for exercising supervision. The choice will depend on a number of factors (NGSS, para. 24):

- The view of the RMO and clinical team, having regard to the patient's history, mental state and likely requirements in the community.

- The wishes of the patient, though this is not a determining factor.

- Supervision of the patient by an agency prior to admission to hospital.

- Any ongoing contact with an agency during the patient's stay in hospital.

In clear-cut cases, the hospital social work department will write to either the Director of Social Services or Chief Probation Officer for the area to which the patient is likely to be discharged, giving background information and seeking nomination of a social supervisor. In other cases, the discharging hospital is advised to write to the Directors of Social Services for the areas from which the patient came and to which the patient is likely to be discharged, and also to the appropriate Chief Probation Officer, informing them of the likely discharge, giving information about the patient's social history, criminal history, history of mental disorder and supervision needs, inviting both agencies to contribute to the decision and to meet with the hospital's social work department to discuss selection of a social supervisor.

Role of Social Supervisor

Pre-Discharge

The social supervisor should receive full information at the earliest opportunity covering the following aspects:

(i) pen-picture of the patient including diagnosis and current mental state;

(ii) admission social and medical history;

(iii) summary of progress in hospital;

(iv) present medication, reported effects and any side-effects;

(v) any warning signs indicative of a relapse of mental state or repetition of offending, together with the time lapse in which this could occur;

(vi) report on home circumstances;

(vii) supervision and after-care arrangements considered appropriate or inappropriate.

'Wherever possible, pre-discharge contact should include at least two visits to the hospital by the social supervisor to meet the patient and participation in at least one multi-disciplinary case conference at which the prospective social supervisor can discuss the case and the plans for discharge with the responsible medical officer, the hospital social worker, the nursing staff who know the patient well, any other hospital staff who have been involved and the prospective supervising psychiatrist. If a social supervisor is asked to take on the case of a restricted patient shortly to be conditionally discharged and is not invited by the hospital to participate in pre-discharge discussions in this way, he or she should request contact with the hospital clinical team through the responsible medical officer, the hospital social worker or the liaison probation officer where one exists. The Home Office Mental Health Unit may be able to help in cases of difficulty.' (NGSS, para. 21)

Frequency and Nature of Supervision

While it is impossible to offer a blueprint for successful, effective supervision, the NGSS (Section 8) makes the following recommendations:

- Meetings should take place at least once each week for at least the first month after discharge, reducing to once a fortnight and then once each month as the social supervisor judges appropriate. These are considered to be minimum periods and sometimes the Home Office will request more frequent meetings (para. 44). If, after some time, monthly contact is considered unduly frequent, the supervisor should consider recommending discharge from conditions (see below).

- 'Meetings should usually take place on the patient's home territory but some meetings away from the home, perhaps in the supervisor's office, may also prove valuable' (para. 44) (Note that this advice may need to be qualified by health and safety considerations to reduce or avoid possible risk to the supervisor).

- 'If the patient is in close contact with, or living with, friends or relatives, the social supervisor should see them regularly also' (para. 41).

- 'The patient should consult the supervisor when considering any significant change in circumstances, *eg* a new job or home, financial matters or a holiday' (para. 40). Any proposed change of circumstances has to be assessed for the degree of risk involved and some proposals should be reported to the Home Office (see below).

- Responsibility for difficult decisions concerning the patient should be shared with senior officers/line managers (para. 40).

- If a social supervisor is absent from post, even for a short period, responsibility should be transferred temporarily to a colleague and the supervising psychiatrist notified (para. 45). If the absence is for longer than two months, the Home Office should also be informed.

- An outgoing supervisor should brief their successor fully, passing full information, supplemented with an oral briefing. Care should be taken to ease the transition which may be unsettling for a patient (para. 46).

Disclosure of Information

Though there are no hard and fast rules, the social supervisor will need to consider whether certain information about the patient should be disclosed to people who may become involved with the patient in the community (para. 48). In general, information should be disclosed only with the full knowledge and agreement of the patient, unless there are strong overriding reasons for doing so against their wishes. 'Such reasons may include the patient's known propensity for offending which arise from the accommodation, workplace or some types of job' (para. 49). (Supervisors will, of course, be particularly alert to child protection issues and the precautionary procedures to be adopted in regard to 'Schedule One' offenders).

Liaison with Other Professionals

Close liaison with the supervising psychiatrist is essential. If the patient is taking medication, the supervising psychiatrist should inform the social supervisor (and the patient's GP) of the nature of the medication, its effects and possible side effects, and the arrangements made for the medication to be given (para. 54). The social supervisor may identify aspects of the patient's state of mind which might be helpful to the psychiatrist. The GP should be kept informed of any significant development in the case. Other links, *eg* with the CPN, hostels and day centres, will be maintained and the social supervisor will usually be the key worker in liaison between those involved in the patient's care and support, inviting others to contact the supervisor if there is any cause for concern about the patient's condition or behaviour. Prior to the patient's discharge all those practitioners involved with the future care and support of the patients should be invited to a multi-disciplinary meeting at which a comprehensive plan of care and strategy for intervention will be agreed. Subsequently, the social supervisor will need to arrange regular meetings to review the after-care arrangements (para. 58).

Reports to the Home Office

Reports on the patient's progress are usually sought by the Home Office from both the social and the psychiatric supervisor, as follows (para. 59):

(i)   one month after conditional release;

(ii) every three months thereafter, unless more frequent reports are requested.

If the social supervisor subsequently considers it appropriate to submit reports at longer intervals but nevertheless feels that some formal supervision remains necessary, a written recommendation should be sent to the Home Office proposing reports at six-monthly intervals (the minimum reporting rate to which the Home Office will agree) (para. 60).

The social supervisor should send a copy of reports to the supervising psychiatrist and discuss these with him/her as necessary (para. 62). For the first year following discharge, two copies of each report to the Home Office should also be sent for information to the RMO at the discharging hospital (in cases where that doctor is not also the supervising psychiatrist). The social supervisor can also seek further background information from the hospital social work department.

Reports to the Home Office Mental Health Unit (MSU) should wherever possible follow a standard format, (Annex A) supplying initial summary data:

(i)   patient's name, address and HO reference number;

(ii)   social supervisor's name;

(iii) length of time since conditional discharge;

(iv)   frequency of meetings with patient since last report;

(v)   whether the patient shows signs of becoming a danger to self or others;

(vi)   if so, the action recommended by the supervisor.

This should be followed by the main report, covering (para. 61):

(i) a detailed account of the patient's current circumstances including accommodation, employment, training, major relationships and other interests and spare time activities;

(ii) any changes since the previous report, the reasons for those changes and any notable improvements or achievements by the patient;

(iii) a detailed description of any signs of deterioration in the patient's mental health or behaviour, with any steps taken to improve the situation and any further proposals for doing so;

(iv) the social supervisor's plans for the patient's continued rehabilitation;

(v) any other information to enable the Home Office to consider whether the patient may remain in the community or that steps should be taken to return the patient to hospital.

The report should include at the end the line manager's comments.

Changes of Address or Supervisor

If the patient wishes to change address from that specified in the warrant or direction of discharge or to be away from that address for more than a short absence, and the social supervisor agrees that the proposed accommodation is suitable, the supervisor should write to MSU to seek agreement, giving details of the new accommodation and the reasons for the change (para. 63). In an emergency, where the social supervisor may have to agree to a change of address without prior reference to the Home Office, MSU should be contacted as soon as possible afterwards. In agreeing to a change, the Home Office will issue a formal amendment to the warrant of discharge. The supervising psychiatrist should also be informed.

A conditionally discharged patient is not precluded from taking holidays from home but should always discuss such plans with the social supervisor so that suitability of arrangements can be considered. During the first six months after discharge, absence from home of more than a few days is not usually advisable (para. 65). If absence will be for two weeks or longer, the social supervisor should notify the Social Services Department or Probation Area (as appropriate) in the holiday area and should inform the patient whom to contact there if any problems arise. Any proposal for holiday abroad or travel outside the United Kingdom should be referred to MSU for prior approval. The supervising psychiatrist should be informed of any holiday/travel absences and consideration of special medication arrangements to cover the period away may be necessary (para. 66).

Though the names of supervisors are not usually entered on the warrant of discharge, it is helpful if the Home Office is notified as soon as possible of any permanent change of social supervisor (para. 64).

Transfer across UK Jurisdictions

C(S)A 1997 s48 amended both MHA 1983 and MH(S)A 1984 to enable the responsibility for supervising conditionally discharged patients to be transferred between jurisdictions within the United Kingdom, without having to receive absolute discharge. The detailed provisions are contained in C(S)A 1997 sch 3, inserting ss80A, 81A, 82A, 83A and 85A, governing transfers to or from Scotland, Northern Ireland, the Channel Islands or the Isle of Man. As HOC 52/1997 summarised the changes:

'If the Secretary of State, or appropriate authority responsible for the supervision of a patient in one jurisdiction accepts that it would be in the patient's best interest to move to another, there can be a transfer of responsibility, enabling the receiving authority to set up equivalent arrangements. Where such a transfer is agreed, the patient will be treated as if conditionally discharged in the receiving jurisdiction on the date of the transfer.'

Action in the Event of Concern

Where concern arises about the patient's mental state or behaviour, this should be discussed first with other professionals involved, particularly the supervising psychiatrist who should be contacted immediately if the social supervisor has reason to fear for the safety of the patient or others. The consultant may decide to initiate local action to admit the patient to hospital without delay with the patient's consent. 'Whether or not such action is taken and even if the supervising psychiatrist does not share the social supervisor's concern, the social supervisor should report to the Home Office at once so that consideration should be given to the patient's formal recall to hospital' (para. 69). Social supervisors should inform their line managers of the situation as soon as possible. Recommendations by probation officer supervisors should be accompanied by the views of a senior probation officer and of the Chief Probation Officer, where this is possible without undue delay. Telephone discussion with the staff of MSU is welcomed and outside office hours the Home Office duty officer should be contacted. A telephone report should be followed up by a written report as soon as possible (which can, of course, be faxed to MSU).

A report to the Home Office should always be made in the following instances (para. 71):

(i)   there appears to be an actual or potential risk to the public;

(ii)   contact with the patient is lost or the patient is unwilling to co-operate with supervision;

(iii) the patient's behaviour or condition suggests a need for further in-patient treatment in hospital;

(iv)   the patient is charged with or convicted of an offence.

In all cases where it seems that admission is necessary to protect the public from possible harm, the recommendation must have the support of the supervising psychiatrist that the patient be formally recalled to a hospital. 'The Home Secretary would normally be prepared to act on such a recommendation.' (NGSS, para. 73)

RECALL TO HOSPITAL

MHA 1983 s42

(3)   The Secretary of State may at any time during the continuance in force of a restriction order in respect of a patient who has been conditionally discharged

under subsection (2) above by warrant recall the patient to such hospital as may be specified in the warrant.

(4) Where a patient is recalled as mentioned in subsection (3) above –

(a) if the hospital specified in the warrant is not the hospital from which the patient was conditionally discharged, the hospital order and the restriction order shall have effect as if the hospital specified in the warrant were substituted for the hospital specified in the hospital order;

(b) in any case, the patient shall be treated for the purposes of section 18 above as if he had absented himself without leave from the hospital specified in the warrant, and, if the restriction order was made for a specified period, that period shall not in any event expire until the patient returns to the hospital or is returned to the hospital under that section.

Reference to s18 in s42(4)(b) means that the patient is in the same position as if s/he had gone absent without leave on the warrant date and can thus be taken into custody in accordance with s18(1) (see page 92). If the patient is not prepared to return to hospital willingly, the police should be informed.

The Act does not specify any grounds for recall and the Home Secretary thus has unfettered discretion, without being required to obtain medical evidence beforehand. This has implications for cases where the Home Office holds a different view of a patient who has been conditionally discharged by a MHRT, as illustrated by *R v Secretary of State for the Home Department, ex p. K* [1991] QB 270. On pleading guilty to manslaughter, on grounds of diminished responsibility, of a girl aged 12, the offender had been made subject of a hospital order with restriction because he was found to be suffering a psychopathic disorder. The Home Secretary had opposed his discharge because the offender's motive for this violent, sexual assault leading to asphyxiation and other mutilations had not been satisfactorily established and there was continuing concern about his pattern of violence. His conditional discharge was ordered by the Tribunal in 1985 because they were satisfied that he was not then suffering a mental disorder, but later that year he committed two unprovoked attacks on young women and was sentenced to six years' imprisonment. He applied to a Tribunal for the conditions of his discharge to be lifted so that he would be absolutely discharged. The Tribunal made no order but remained satisfied that he was not suffering any mental disorder. As his release date approached in 1989, the Home Secretary, without seeking any further expert medical opinion, issued a warrant for his detention in Broadmoor Hospital immediately upon his release. His application that the Secretary of State had acted unlawfully was dismissed by the Court of Appeal, despite the unanimity of expert medical opinion at two hearings of the MHRT and both decisions of the Tribunal, and the Home Secretary's exercise of discretion, balancing the interests of the patient against those of public safety, was upheld. The Court noted that the Act safeguards the interests of the patient by requiring the Home Secretary to refer a recalled patient's case to a MHRT within a month of their return to hospital (see page 216).

This might suggest that the Home Secretary could recall a patient immediately after a Tribunal's unwelcome decision to discharge him or her, though the judge who dealt with *ex p. K* in the first instance ([1990] 1 WLR 168) expressed the view that this would be unlawful, being irrational or unreasonable, 'unless in the meantime something had happened which justified the belief that a different view might now be taken about one of the factors on which his release had depended'.

Recall Policy Perspective

The Notes of Guidance (para. 74) advise as follows:

'Whether the Home Secretary decides to recall a patient depends largely on the degree of danger which the particular patient might present. Where the patient has in the past shown himself capable of serious violence, comparatively minor irregularities in behaviour or failure of co-operation would be sufficient to raise the question of the possible need for recall. On the other hand, if the patient's history does not suggest that he is likely to present a serious risk, the Home Secretary may not wish to take the initiative unless there are indications of a probable physical danger to other persons. There are cases in which recall to hospital for a period of observation can be seen as a necessary step in continuing psychiatric treatment. There are other cases in which anti-social behaviour may be unconnected with mental disorder, so that recall to hospital is not an appropriate sanction and there may be no alternative to leaving the conditionally discharged patient to be dealt with as necessary by the normal processes under the criminal law. Each case is assessed on its merits in the Home Office and a decision is reached after consultation with the doctor(s) concerned and with the social supervisor.'

Absconding

The patient may leave their approved address without consent or notification and/or cease contact with both the social supervisor and the supervising psychiatrist. NGSS paras. 77-78 state:

'In such cases the social supervisor should report the fact to the Home Office immediately and then make every reasonable effort to locate the patient, contacting his colleagues in other areas if he has reason to believe that the patient may have gone to a particular place in a different locality. The Home Office may decide simply to wait until the patient's whereabouts are known. If necessary, however, the Home Secretary will issue a warrant for the recall of the patient, thus providing the police with the powers to bring the patient into custody.

If a conditionally discharged patient is suspected of having left his approved address to go abroad the Home Secretary may decide to issue a recall warrant and alert the immigration authorities who would detain the patient on re-entry to the country.'

Informal or Civil Admission to Hospital

The supervising psychiatrist may decide to initiate local action to admit the patient to hospital informally for a short period of observation or treatment. The Home Office and the social supervisor should be kept informed since the patient will remain subject to the formal conditions of their earlier discharge when leaving hospital. However, NGSS para. 72 states:

'it is generally inappropriate for a conditionally discharged patient to remain in hospital for more than a short time informally and the Home Secretary would usually wish to consider the issue of a warrant of recall if the period of in-patient treatment seemed likely to be protracted.'

Further Offending

If a patient is facing prosecution for an offence alleged to have been committed since conditional release, and is remanded in custody, 'the Home Secretary will usually consider it advisable, if the patient is in safe custody and presents no danger to others, to let the law take its course so that the court may reach a fresh decision on the need for medical treatment or other measures, rather than recall the patient to hospital' (para. 79). (The Notes of Guidance do not give explicit advice in regard to a remand on bail, though this could imply that the defendant's present circumstances do not rebut the normal presumption in favour of bail and that therefore s/he is not posing a danger to others.)

If the patient is convicted of and dealt with for an offence, the Home Office view will depend on the sentencing decision:

- The patient may be recalled if that is in agreement with the court's wishes and the doctor concerned agrees (for example if the court decides, on conviction, to take no action or to impose a nominal penalty in the knowledge that the patient will be returned at once to hospital)' (para. 79).

- If a non-custodial sentence is imposed, 'the terms of the previous conditional discharge will continue and the supervisors should resume their roles' (para. 80).

- If a custodial sentence is imposed:

  'the Home Secretary will usually decide to reserve judgement on the patient's status under the Mental Health Act 1983 until he nears the end of his prison sentence. At that stage, the Home Secretary will decide whether to authorise the patient's absolute discharge from liability under that Act, to allow his continued conditional discharge under conditions of residence, social supervision and psychiatric supervision or to direct his recall to hospital on release from prison. Which decision is taken will depend largely on the length of the prison sentence imposed, the nature of the offence, the patient's mental state, both at the time of the offence and during the sentence of imprisonment, and the risk of danger to the public' (para. 81).

AFTER RECALL

Duty to Give Reasons

Recalled patients should be informed of the reasons for their recall, following the two stage procedure introduced by DHSS Circular LASSL (80) 7 paras. 3-4:

'Stage 1 – the person taking the patient "into custody" should inform him in simple terms that he is being recalled to hospital by the Home Secretary under the Mental Health Act and that a further explanation will be given later.

Stage 2 – will take place as soon as possible after admission to hospital and in any event within 72 hours. The responsible medical officer or his deputy should explain to the patient the reasons for his recall. He should ensure that so far as the patient's mental condition allows, he understands those reasons. The responsible medical officer will also be responsible for informing the patient's supervising officer in the community and a responsible member of the patient's family (or his legal adviser) of the reasons for his recall.'

'Where a social supervisor is involved in returning the patient to hospital, this duty should be borne in mind' (NGSS, para. 75).

Status Following Recall

The patient is once again detained as a restricted patient in pursuance of the legal authority that applied immediately prior to their conditional discharge. 'In some cases, the patient may need to return to hospital for only a short while but, in others, the lessons learned in the community may point to the need for a longer stay in hospital' (NGSS, para. 76).

Referral to a MHRT

A conditionally discharged patient who is recalled to hospital must be referred to a MHRT by the Home Secretary within a month of their return to hospital (s75(1)). Additionally, the patient's right to apply to a MHRT under s70 (see page 198) applies so that application can be made in the period 6-12 months after their recall and in any subsequent period of 12 months.

On referral to a MHRT after recall, the Home Secretary's statement to the Tribunal will address the circumstances that led to the recall and give views on whether the patient is yet fit again to be discharged.

'In referring to the decision to recall, the Home Secretary is likely to draw on reports received from supervisors. In some cases the Tribunal may decide to ask the supervisors to appear at the Tribunal hearing.' (NGSS, para. 93)

LENGTH OF SUPERVISION AND SCOPE FOR ABSOLUTE DISCHARGE

Where a conditionally discharged patient is subject to a s41 restriction order of specified duration, their absolute discharge occurs automatically on the date of the order's expiry. In the much more likely case of indefinite duration, the Home Secretary 'normally requires active supervision and reporting' to be maintained, 'particularly where a patient requires continued medication in the community for the control of symptoms which might otherwise lead to violent behaviour' (NGSS, para. 83).

A patient can secure absolute discharge by one of two means: by order of the Home Secretary; on application to a MHRT.

Order of the Home Secretary

Before converting the patient's conditional discharge into an absolute one under s42(2), the Home Secretary 'will wish to see evidence of a prolonged period of stability in the community which has been tested by a variety of normal pressures or experiences' (NGSS, para. 84).

Social Supervisor's Recommendation

'If a social supervisor considers that the patient no longer requires active supervision and that the safety of the public will not be put at risk if the patient were not subject to supervision, the matter should be discussed with the supervising psychiatrist before an appropriate recommendation is put forward to the Home Office ... supported by detailed reports on the patient's activities and behaviour in the community.' (NGSS, para. 84)

Note that the 1987 advice that supervision be kept up for at least five years after discharge in serious cases, and for at least two years in less serious ones, has been superseded.

Discharge Warrant

Where the Home Secretary agrees to absolute discharge, a warrant will be issued and copied to the patient and to the supervisors. This action does not preclude continued contact between patient and supervisors on a non-statutory basis.

Application to a MHRT

MHA 1983 s75

(2) Where a restricted patient has been conditionally discharged (by the Home Secretary or by a MHRT) but has not been recalled to hospital he may apply to a Mental Health Review Tribunal –

(a) in the period between the expiration of 12 months and the expiration of two years beginning with the date on which he was conditionally discharged; and

(b) in any subsequent period of two years.

(3) ... on any such application the Tribunal may –

(a) vary any condition to which the patient is subject in connection with his discharge or impose any condition which might have been imposed in connection therewith; or

(b) direct that the restriction order or restriction direction to which he is subject shall cease to have effect;

and if the Tribunal give a direction under paragraph (b) above the patient shall cease to be liable to be detained by virtue of the relevant hospital order or transfer direction.

Thus the patient may seek either a variation of conditions or an absolute discharge.

When a conditionally discharged patient applies to a Tribunal, the Tribunal will require the Home Office to provide information as specified in MHRTR 1983 sch 1 parts C and D. This includes: an up-to-date medical report and a full report on the patient's mental condition; an up-to-date report prepared for the Tribunal by the social supervisor on the patient's progress in the community since discharge from hospital; and a report on the patient's home circumstances.

On receiving the Tribunal's request, the Home Office will write to the social supervisor asking for a report, including the supervisor's views on the value of continuing social supervision, to be completed within four weeks. The Home Office statement, including the supervisor's reports, will be disclosed to the patient in full unless the Home Secretary recommends, and the Tribunal agrees, that part of it, submitted separately, be withheld from the patient. If the social supervisor considers that part of their report should not be disclosed, that part should be prepared separately and the reasons for non-disclosure explained. 'Supervisors will be informed by the Tribunal of the date of the Tribunal hearing and invited to appear at the hearing (NGSS, para. 91).

The Tribunal's decision in the case of a conditionally discharged patient is notified to the patient and interested parties, including the supervisor, and to the Home Office, who will also inform both supervisors of the decision (NGSS, para. 86). Time periods in s75(2) are calculated from the date of actual release from hospital, not the date when a Tribunal decides that the patient should be discharged subject to satisfactory arrangements being made (*R v Cannons Park MHRT, ex p. Martins* (1995) 26 BMLR 134).

RESTRICTION IN PRACTICE

The following quantitative information has been drawn from *Statistics of Mentally Disordered Offenders: England and Wales 2001* (Johnson and Taylor, 2002).

Key Statistical Data

Legal Category on Admission

Of the 980 restricted patients entering hospital in 2001 (894 being male), 239 were subject to s41 orders, 214 on s47 transfer, 410 on s48 transfer, 62 on recall following conditional discharge, 44 as unfit to plead, with only three on hospital and limitation directions.

Type of Disorder on Admission

Of the 980 patients, the predominant diagnosis was 'mental illness' (870 or 88.8%), with 'psychopathic disorder' a poor second (37 or 3.8%). There were only 17 instances of 'mental impairment' and three of 'severe mental impairment'.

Type of Hospital on Admission

Only 9.9% of restricted patients were admitted to High Security Hospitals in 2001 (88 men and nine women).

The Detained Population

At the end of 2001, the restricted patients population stood as follows:

	Male	*Female*
High Security Hospitals	1,004	140
Other Hospitals	1,666	192
Total	2,670	332

Legal Category

Of the 3,002 patients, 1,929 (64%) were detained on s41 orders, 414 on s47 transfer, 181 on s48 transfer, 151 as unfit to plead and 268 on recall following conditional discharge. Only ten were subject to hospital and restriction direction.

218

Mental Disorder
Of the 3,002 patients, 2153 (72%) were classified as suffering 'mental illness' (153 in tandem with other disorders), 415 (14%) psychopathic disorder (29 in combination with mental impairment) and 201 (7%) mental impairment.

Length of Detention
The period of years spent by the 2,670 men in hospital (including all previous periods in hospital under the relevant order), as at the end of 2001, by their present location, was as follows:

	Unsent-enced	Under 2	2–5	5+–10	10+–20	20+–30	30+
High Security	6	66	118	240	316	176	82
Other Hospitals	160	472	455	354	156	48	21

Discharges
Of 213 patients who were conditionally discharged into the community in 2001, 187 were discharged by MHRT and 26 by the Home Secretary. Only 10 patients gained absolute discharge, while 79 s48 transfer patients were discharged from court.

Reconviction
Of 1,989 restricted patients first discharged between 1984 and 1999, 160 (9%) were convicted of a 'standard list' offence and 18 (1%) of a 'grave' offence within two years of discharge. Of 1,559 patients first discharged between 1984 and 1996, 239 (17%) were convicted of a 'standard list' offence and 46 (3%) were convicted of a 'grave' offence within five years of discharge. Those discharged by the Home Secretary have had a generally lower reconviction rate than those discharged by a MHRT but the five-year rate for conviction of a grave offence has proved similar for both types of discharge. Reconviction rates have been higher for those discharged from High Security Hospitals and also for those with a psychopathic disorder (Home Office, 2002). Between 1995 and 1999, 11 (2%) restricted patients were reconvicted of a violent or sexual offence within two years, compared with an expected (based on the rate that would be expected of released prisoners and those sentenced to community penalties) reconviction rate of 11%.

Recall
In 2001, 62 restricted patients were admitted to hospital on recall from conditional discharge. The yearly recall rate fluctuated in the preceding decade, from 38 in 1992 to 106 in 1997. Of the 62, 50 were categorised as mentally ill with seven as psychopathically disordered. Of 2,632 patients first discharged between 1972 and 1993, 282 (11%) were recalled within two years of discharge. Of 2,265 patients first discharged between 1972 and 1990, 350 (15%) were recalled within five years (Kershaw *et al*, 1997. More recent recall statistics have not been published).

Leave of Absence
The Home Office issued updated *Guidance to Responsible Medical Officers* in September 2001 on applications for leave of absence for restricted patients, introducing new

arrangements for rehabilitation leave and clarifying the circumstances in which the Home Secretary's consent may be treated as given (appearance at court or attendance for medical treatment) or is specifically required. Special provisions apply to High Security Hospitals. The guide and attachments are available at: www.homeoffice.gov.uk/cpg/mhu2.htm but in brief summary they are as follows:

Leave for Rehabilitation

All such leave should be for a definable purpose and should relate to the overall care and treatment programme to which the RMO and the care team are working, and set personal objectives for the patient. The request should explain what, specifically, each leave will seek to achieve and how they will be monitored, with an explanation of how the assessment of the result will be made.

Transferred Prisoners

Given that patients in this category continue to be liable to detention under a prison sentence, leave (other than court attendance or for medical treatment) will not normally be considered appropriate until the prisoner is approaching parole eligibility date or (if serving under four years) shortly before automatic release date. Section 48 prisoners will not be considered for leave unless there are exceptional grounds for granting this opportunity.

Lifers

In considering proposals for life sentence prisoners, distinction will be drawn between 'technical lifers' (see Stone, 1997 and forthcoming) for whom 'no regard will be paid to the fact that in law they remain subject to a sentence of imprisonment', and lifers whose mental health has deteriorated since sentence. The latter category will normally become eligible to be considered for leave during the period of three years prior to expiry of their minimum term (tariff date).

THE EXPERIENCE OF HIGH SECURITY HOSPITALS

Dell and Robertson's study of offenders in Broadmoor, *Sentenced to Hospital* (1988) provides a fascinating if somewhat dated insight into the experiences of male restricted patients, differentiated according to whether they are psychotic (*ie* admitted with mental illness) or non-psychotic (*ie* admitted with psychopathic disorder). It is possible to offer only a flavour of their findings here.

The consultants clearly felt on more assured clinical ground in treating their psychotic patients, whereas they frequently confessed ignorance or puzzlement about what treatment was appropriate for psychopathic patients. However, even in the case of psychotic patients, the impressive efforts to assess and diagnose patients on their arrival at the hospital were not matched by continuous systematic examination of their mental states. Though their illnesses were the focal point of their hospitalisation, psychotic restricted patients continued to be judged by their past behaviour, as well as by their present state, so that it became difficult, 'certainly for the patients', to separate penal from psychiatric custody.

As a result of being detained alongside active young men categorised as psychopaths, the chronically debilitated schizophrenic patients had to endure massive security, even though only 28% of the psychotics were considered to require conditions of maximum security. However, consultants argued for the continued detention at Broadmoor on grounds that patients needing long-term care would be difficult to place in less secure units and in some instances were better off in Broadmoor, enjoying a better standard of nursing, with higher staff-patient ratio and a more agreeable ward environment.

The researchers found that, while periodic access to psychotherapy or social skills training was usual, the majority of non-psychotic restricted patients were not currently receiving any treatment other than being at Broadmoor. Staff adhered more to the hope that, with the passing of time, young men would 'simmer down' and 'mature'. Tariff considerations coloured clinical judgements, albeit marked by a psychiatric vocabulary. As Grounds (1987) noted:

'I commonly hear from nursing colleagues the view that a particular individual who has committed a grave crime has a long time to do or that his problems will take a long time to resolve – the two notions are interchangeable.'

Thus in making their discharge judgements about men who were not mentally ill, the doctors were essentially making predictions about offending.

'They were guided by a variety of non-medical considerations, including both what they called their gut feelings and the basic criminological principles of re-conviction, one of which is that young men generally calm down as they get older.'

It should be noted that this research was undertaken prior to the implementation of the 1983 Act which requires patients to be referred automatically to a MHRT and gave tribunals power to discharge restricted patients in certain instances (see page 199). Only 57% of the sample of psychotic patients had ever applied for discharge to a tribunal and the consensus among these patients was that the MHRT system was, for them, a waste of time, as tribunals were very unlikely to make discharge recommendations against the advice of consultants. This was supported by the statistical evidence. In only 11% of cases where applications had been made did a MHRT recommend discharge against a consultant's advice.

Surveying Patients' Views

In a small-scale survey of 20 (19 male) patients (13 in high security and seven in medium secure units), NACRO (2002) sought to ascertain their views on daily life in longer-term secure settings. The sample expressed a wish for a more fulfilling and well-structured daily life through a variety of activities, including paid work, education linked to future goals, sport, the opportunity to cook and to arrange social events. Staff were seen as key in setting the tone of any unit and patients wanted an older staff group and the opportunity to choose the sex of their primary nurse. Greatest emphasis was placed on having some say about their daily lives, regimes and treatment, rather than just having to fit in with a regime dictated by staff.

National Standards

Following a turbulent decade for High Security Hospitals and in light of recommendations in the Lewis Report (1999) on social work provision in these establishments, the Department of Health has issued *National Standards for the Provision of Social Care*

Services in the High Security Hospitals (2001). Six free-standing but overlapping sections address the responsibilities of the different organisations with a stake in services for patients, including the hospital itself, the local council for the area in which it is located, the local council for the patient's home area and the Probation Service. Among the specifications of Standard Six on the responsibilities and requirements of the Service are the following points:

- When a patient is admitted to a high security hospital from prison, the Service should provide the social care service (SCS) based at the hospital with a risk assessment and should co-operate in providing information that will assist the hospital in proving appropriate care and treatment. In particular, the Service should provide details of Schedule One and Sex Offender Act status.

- The relevant Probation Area should be kept informed by the hospital-based SCS when a patient is transferred back to prison.

- When discharge planning is begun, the Service should agree jointly at the s117 planning meeting who is to be the social supervisor/community probation officer for the patient.

- Supervising probation officers should be invited to CPA reviews and provided with information about a patient's progress at least annually by the SCS.

- Particular regard must be paid to the exchange of information when planning for discharge or when a patient is granted leave of absence.

- In each Probation Area there should be a named senior manager for formal liaison purposes with each of the hospitals and for strategic and policy issues.

DISCHARGE IN PRACTICE

In attempting to assess the effectiveness of restricted hospital orders in the longer term, Street (1998) examined the progress of a sample of 391 (83% male) patients subject to a court-imposed restriction order who had been discharged from hospital between 1987 and 1990, focusing principally on any reconvictions and recalls to hospital up until the end of 1994. Some 64% had been detained under the category of mental illness and a further 24% had been classified as psychopathically disordered. In almost half the cases the offence had been manslaughter, attempted murder or GBH. He also interviewed members of MHRTs and the Home Office Mental Health Unit (MHU). As a general observation arising from the study, Street noted that information available to decision-makers on patients' index offence, offending history and any dangerous behaviour post-discharge was not always sufficiently detailed.

Specific Research Findings

Discharge

These patients had spent an average of nearly nine years detained in hospital before their discharge. MHU staff emphasised that no 'tariff' considerations dictated how long patients would spend in hospital before the Home Office would be prepared to consider release. Every case, in their view, should be dealt with on the merits, the central consideration being whether the patient can be safely managed in the community. Some

MHRT members, particularly 'legal' members, acknowledged giving consideration to 'proportionality'.

Mentally impaired patients spent longer in hospital on average than those detained under other categories of disorder. Some 95% (370) had been conditionally discharged. Nearly two-thirds had been discharged by a MHRT. The principal reason for Tribunal discharge (given in 86% of cases) was that the patient's disorder was not of a nature or degree warranting detention. The Home Office in its statement to the Tribunal had opposed discharge in 86% of the MHRT cases, though strong opposition had been expressed in only 6% of cases. Home Office discharge (38% of cases) usually followed the receipt of favourable reports from those caring for the patient. Patients in the category of mental illness were more likely to gain Home Office discharge.

Circumstances Following Discharge

Of the 370 conditionally discharged patients, over half were initially placed in a group home or hostel. About one-third formed a relationship with a partner. Some 70% were on psychiatric medication for at least some part of their conditional discharge. The mental state of 40% of the sample deteriorated to the stage where some psychiatric intervention was required – over one-third of the sample had a non-recall admission to hospital. While the period of supervision progressed well for the majority, nearly one-third caused supervisory anxiety, 43 patients (12%) causing 'significant' problems (other than refusing medication), ranging from persistently failing to co-operate with discharge conditions to absconding. Problems arising from drug and alcohol misuse were reportedly experienced by 88 patients (24%). Some 59 patients (16%) reported being victimised, most allegations concerning violent or sexual assault or threatening behaviour. Those presenting supervision problems or having difficulty in socialising appeared more at risk of violence. Four patients killed themselves and a further 43 deliberately self-harmed. By the end of the follow-up, 45% of conditionally discharged patients were no longer under restrictions, the majority of those having been absolutely discharged by a MHRT.

Reconviction

Overall, 12% of the total sample were reconvicted of any type of offence. Some 5% were reconvicted of serious offences in the follow-up period. There was no difference between MHRT and Home Office discharges in rate of reconviction for serious crime. Such reconvictions were more likely in cases where there were previous convictions for sexual or violent offences, particularly previous sexual offences. In addition to reconviction, 13% of conditionally discharged patients had been reportedly involved in incidents viewed as harmful or potentially harmful to others, not resulting in conviction. However, over one-third of such incidents had resulted in recall to hospital. Perhaps not surprisingly, patients who misused alcohol or drugs, or who suffered a deterioration in their mental state that required intervention, were also more likely to have been reconvicted of a serious offence or to have been involved in such incidents.

Recall

A quarter of conditionally discharged patients were recalled to hospital in the follow-up period, including 5% who were recalled on more than one occasion. Concern about mental state was the most common reason for recall, though concern about risk (often following reported incidents of dangerous behaviour) featured in over half of recalls. By the end of the follow-up just over three-quarters of those recalled had been re-discharged from hospital, having spent an average of 15 months back in hospital.

CASE ILLUSTRATION: CONDITIONAL AND ABSOLUTE DISCHARGE BY MHRT

Michael Higham

Offence

Unlawful wounding, when aged 28 (under the paranoid belief that he was being pursued by a number of men, he became agitated and sought the victim's attention, stabbing him when the victim tried to reassure him).

Previous Psychiatric History

Several admissions to hospital, with various diagnoses, including personality disorder and schizophrenia.

Verdict

Having been diagnosed as suffering from a schizophrenic illness whilst on remand, he was found not guilty by reason of insanity and an order was made admitting him to a Special Hospital under CP(I)A 1964 s5(1) (*ie* having the same effect as a s41 restriction order).

In Hospital

No positive symptoms of schizophrenia were observed during his 15 years as an in-patient.

First Conditional Discharge

At age 44, he was conditionally discharged by a MHRT. In addition to the usual requirement of psychiatric and social supervision (by the Probation Service), he was required to reside at a therapeutic hostel run by a specialist voluntary agency and to abstain from drinking alcohol. Two months later he returned to the hostel intoxicated and it was suspected that he had been drinking covertly on a regular basis. As the hostel was unwilling to continue his residence and no suitable alternative accommodation was available, his social supervisor recommended that he be recalled to the Special Hospital and this was ordered on the advice of the psychiatric supervisor.

Second Conditional Discharge

Following a further seven months as an in-patient, Mr Higham was further reviewed by a MHRT which was satisfied that he was not suffering from mental illness. He was considered an 'inadequate personality' who had 'sufficiently matured' to justify conditional release geared particularly to his avoidance of excessive drinking. He was discharged to reside at the same hostel as before, subject to the following conditions:

(i) to attend the psychiatric supervisor's out-patient clinic as the psychiatrist may require;

(ii) to reside at such hostel as the psychiatrist should specify and observe the rules of such hostel;

(iii) to accept the supervision of the probation officer and abide by his advice;

(iv) at no time to drink in excess of what the probation officer may advise.

Progress on Conditional Release

Mr Higham sustained his re-settlement, moving in due course from the hostel to bed and breakfast accommodation, obtaining a council tenancy after two years. His probation officer initially dealt with the issue of alcohol consumption by prescribing a limit of two pints of beer a day and requiring him to drink at one specified public house. This issue ceased to be an active concern as it became clear that he was able to drink in moderation without a close degree of oversight, with occasional lapses into drunkenness when faced with setbacks or stress. He formed a relationship with a woman with a lengthy, continuing history of schizophrenia who was considered to be both 'a drain on his energy and a reason to survive'. He reported satisfactorily for all appointments.

After five years' supervision, a possible application to a MHRT to seek an absolute discharge was discussed between the two supervisors and Mr Higham, but the psychiatrist indicated that he could not yet recommend this, given doubts about the stability of Mr Higham's relationship with his partner. After seven years' supervision and by now keen to move to a new area, Mr Higham obtained offer of a tenancy exchange. Fresh supervision arrangements were negotiated and the move was approved by the Mental Health Unit.

After nine years' supervision and after Mr Higham had ended his relationship with his partner, the social supervisor asked the supervising psychiatrist to consider a joint recommendation of absolute discharge to the Home Office. The psychiatrist replied:

'I think it likely that, given the difficulties, although minor, that Mr Higham has experienced recently, particularly becoming anxious and depressed in response to his ex-girlfriend's difficulties, and given that he has only been in (new area) for about a year, the Home Office would take the view that at the present time he should remain liable to be recalled to hospital. I would also lean towards a cautious approach as I feel that the conditions do not really restrict Mr Higham's life to any great extent.'

Mr Higham then applied for a MHRT review, obtaining legal representation by a solicitor specialising in mental health. The report for the Tribunal by the psychiatric supervisor concluded that the pre-trial diagnosis of schizophrenia was probably incorrect and that:

'his presentation is more consistent with a diagnosis of a severe personality disorder with mixed inadequate, dependent and histrionic features. I think it is also likely that he suffered with transient psychotic episodes which were derived from his abnormal personality and compounded by his alcohol and possibly drug abuse ...

His mental state has remained stable for many years and he has clearly matured greatly with passing time. However, he remains a vulnerable individual and has a tendency to become reactively anxious and mildly depressed. He continues to gain benefit from on-going supervision. On balance, I take the view that he should remain liable to be recalled to hospital.'

The Statement of the Home Secretary to the Tribunal noted the encouraging progress made but could 'not agree that an absolute discharge would be the most appropriate course of action' and thus recommended that conditions should remain unaltered.

Absolute Discharge

When the Tribunal sat, nine years after Mr Higham's second conditional release, it directed his absolute discharge, stating:

'The Tribunal convened (when the patient was 44) determined that he was not then suffering from schizophrenia. The Tribunal today can find no evidence to support a finding of mental illness nor psychopathic disorder. The patient has been in the community for the last ten years without medication and without disturbance to any other person. He has complied scrupulously with the conditions imposed. The evidence is that he does not constitute a significant danger to others. Moreover the Tribunal accepts that he has cared for another disadvantaged person for many years. The Tribunal is satisfied that the requirements of Section 117 of the Act adequately suffice to monitor the future of the patient.'

CASE ILLUSTRATION: REVIEW BY MHRT AND PAROLE BOARD OF MANDATORY LIFER ON SECTION 47 TRANSFER

Scott Barker

Offence

Murder at age 23 of a woman he had met at a public house, killing her in a drunken rage by multiple blows to the head, by his account because she had led him to expect sexual intercourse but had changed her mind at a late stage.

Previous Psychiatric History

None and no indication of mental disorder on examination while remanded in custody. Several admissions to hospital, with various diagnoses, including personality disorder and schizophrenia. He pleaded guilty. He was set a tariff (minimum term) of 10 years.

In Prison

During his first decade in prison Mr Barker was described as 'difficult to get through to', a poor communicator, unwilling to discuss his crime, negative in his outlook and 'stuck in a rut'. Periodically he would try to assault prison staff. By the 15-year point concern was raised about his mental state on account of his 'mechanical behaviour' and 'regression into his own world'. After an unsuccessful attempt to achieve improvement at HMP Grendon, he was transferred to a Regional Secure Unit for six months where he stabilised on medication.

Some three years later, Mr Barker was described once again as abnormally withdrawn and was diagnosed as suffering from paranoid schizophrenia and mental impairment. He was virtually mute and engaged in ritualised behaviour. When reviewed by the Parole Board he was seen as continuing to pose risk to others because of his propensity to react violently when he felt provoked or frustrated. His proposed transfer under ss47/49 was considered the proper course.

Time in RSU

Back in the same secure unit as before, some 21 years after sentence, Mr Barker stabilised on medication and made slow but steady progress. The MHU authorised first escorted and then unescorted community visits, followed by overnight stays at a residential care home, his proposed release address. Though he had 'limited insight' into his mental illness, he understood the need to comply with medication and also to abstain from alcohol.

MHRT Hearing

Four years after his second admission to RSU, 25 years following sentence, Mr Barker applied to a MHRT which concluded that he continued to suffer from schizophrenia but that there was no need for him to be detained in hospital. If he had been a s41 patient, the Tribunal would have conditionally discharged him to reside at the residential care home. As that was not within its power, it indicated that he should continue his detention in hospital rather than be returned to prison.

Parole Board Review

In light of the MHRT's opinion, based on the clear consensus of professional opinion that Mr Barker was suitable for conditional discharge, the Home Secretary referred his case to the Board for the first time since his second s47 transfer. Reviewing him 26 years after sentence, the Board considered him suitable for release on life licence.

Licence

Subject to life licence, the question might arise as to the appropriate avenues to be followed in the event that Mr Barker's mental health deteriorated. He could be made subject to civil powers under MHA 1983. If the Probation Service reported to the Home Office that he should be subject to recall, he would have to be recalled to prison rather than returned direct to hospital but it would be open to the Secretary of State to direct his further transfer to hospital under s47.

MENTAL HEALTH BILL

Clause 87 of the draft Bill provides for the Secretary of State to terminate a restriction order if satisfied that the order is no longer necessary to protect the public from serious harm. Such termination would not affect the mental health order itself (see page 112) but the patient's case must be referred to a MHRT under clause 103(1) for a fresh determination. The Secretary of State should receive reports about a restricted patient from the clinical supervisor at intervals of not more than a year (clause 87(6) and (7)).

Clause 88 empowers the Secretary of State to lift conditionally a requirement that a restricted patient shall be detained as a resident in hospital, thus providing a measure equivalent to the conditional discharge provisions of MHA 1983 s42. Such an order may be made on the recommendation of the clinical supervisor. This will not cause the restriction order to cease effect and the patient will remain subject to compulsory treatment in the community, unless the mental health order is lifted by a MHRT. The Secretary of State may impose conditions when lifting a residence requirement and may thereafter vary these as is seen fit. The restricted patient will remain subject to recall to hospital. Where a patient has been recalled, the Secretary of State must refer their case to a MHRT within seven days of their readmission to hospital (clause 106). Thereafter, a recalled patient whose recall has been confirmed by the Tribunal will be entitled to apply to the Tribunal once within the period between 6 to 12 months after such confirmation and thereafter once in every 12 month period.

Resident restricted patients may also apply under clause 102 to have their residence reviewed by a MHRT. The powers of the Tribunal are provided in clauses 104 (restriction orders) and 105 (other restricted persons).

15
THE CARE PROGRAMME APPROACH

The Care Programme Approach (CPA) was introduced in 1989-91 to provide a generic framework for the delivery of mental health care to all adults with mental health problems in contact with secondary mental health services, whether on discharge from hospital, in residential care, the community or in prison. It has four main elements:

1. Systematic assessment of the health and social needs of persons receiving specialist services.

2. A care plan identifying the care required from providers of services.

3. Appointment of a key worker to maintain close contact with the service user and to monitor/co-ordinate care.

4. Regular review and agreed changes to the care plan, as appropriate.

The DoH (2000) has recently sought to revitalise CPA, now integrated with Care Management, to achieve greater consistency while reducing its potential to be unhelpfully bureaucratic. For the information of readers who are less familiar with CPA developments, the following key changes can be summarised:

- *Lead Officer:* Each health and social services mental health provider must jointly identify a Lead Officer with authority to work across all agencies to deliver an integrated approach.

- *Beyond After-care:* CPA should no longer be considered simply as a framework for after-care but for care wherever service users are in the system, including residential as well as community settings.

- *Assertive Outreach and Inreach:* CPA must be utilised to seek to ensure that those with complex needs stay in contact with services and do not lose contact. This may also require 'the development of assertive inreach approaches into prisons'.

- *MHA Status:* An individual's status under MHA 1983 can be reviewed at their CPA review meeting which can serve to determine all care planning aspects, MHA issues and discharge planning, etc, without the need for separate occasions.

- *GPs and Primary Care:* All those subject to CPA should have a GP who will play a key role in maintaining continuity of care, alongside other members of the primary care team.

- *Shared Responsibility between MH and CJS:* Where those subject to CPA are the shared responsibility of mental health and criminal justice agencies, close liaison and effective communication is essential over care arrangements, including ongoing risk assessment and management.

- *Those Posing Risk to Others and Disclosure of Information:* Where a person does not have formal contact with the CJS but is assessed as a potential risk to others, careful liaison with the police is necessary. In the absence of a statutory requirement to share information provided in confidence, such information should only be shared with the informed consent of the individual.

'This duty is not absolute and can be overridden if the holder of the information can justify disclosure as being in the public interest (including a risk to public safety) (see HSG (96)18 *The Protection and Use of Patient Information*). Decisions to disclose information against the wishes of an individual should be fully documented and the public interest justification clearly stated.' (para. 46)

- *Shared Information:* Information shared between different agencies should be governed by strict protocols to ensure that all parties concerned, including the service user, are aware of how information will be used, who will have access to it and how it will be safeguarded. NHS organisations are required by HSC 1999/012 to have Guardians of Patient Information with the task of overseeing information-sharing protocols and it is recommended that other agencies adopt this model.

- *Multi-Agency Participation:* All agencies involved in complex care arrangements should use the CPA framework, including Probation, Police and Housing.

- *Prisoners:* If service users are located in prison and present longer-term and complex needs, the responsible psychiatric team should maintain contact with the individual and make plans for their care on release, in collaboration with prison and probation staff as appropriate.

- *Two Levels of Need:* CPA should be delivered on a Standard or Enhanced Level:

  (a) Standard Level: for persons characterised as –

    (i) either requiring support/intervention from one agency or only low key support from more than one agency/discipline;

    (ii) more able to self-manage their mental health problems;

    (iii) posing little danger to themselves;

    (iv) more likely to maintain appropriate contact with services.

  (b) Enhanced Level: for persons characterised as –

    (i) having multiple care needs, including housing, employment etc, requiring inter-agency co-ordination;

    (ii) only willing to co-operate with one professional agency yet have multiple care needs;

    (iii) likely to be in contact with a number of agencies (including the CJS);

    (iv) likely to require more frequent and intensive interventions, perhaps with medication management;

    (v) more likely to have mental health problems co-existing with other problems such as substance misuse;

(vi) more likely to be at risk of harming themselves;

(vii) more likely to disengage with services.

- *Abolition of Supervision Registers:* Development of an enhanced level of CPA to identify and provide for the most vulnerable users supersedes the need for Supervision Registers which were thus abolished from 1 April 2001. [Supervision registers as part of CPA had been introduced from 1 April 1994 with the aim of ensuring that services are focused effectively on patients who have the greatest need. They had been the cause of considerable criticism for creating a bureaucratic demand rather than offering a useful procedural tool and as a political response to public disquiet, which added little to achieving good clinical practice.]

- *Key Worker:* Formerly designated 'key worker', the professional with responsibility for co-ordinating care, keeping in touch with the service user and ensuring that the care plan will be delivered and reviewed is now known as the Care Co-ordinator. This person should have: competence in delivering mental health care (including an understanding of mental illness); knowledge of service user/family; knowledge of community services and agency roles; co-ordination skills; access to resources.

- *Streamlined Care Co-ordination:* To reduce over-bureaucratisation and duplication of effort, CPA will require integrated operational practice, including maintenance of shared records and a single system of referrals.

- *Review of Care Plans:* Past requirements for a review period of six months have ceased in favour of a flexible and responsive practice. At each review meeting the date of next meeting must be set. All requests for a review of the care plan must be considered by the care team. It is particularly important to review a service user's plan on their discharge from hospital and consequent transfer in location of delivery of care.

Appendix I
CIVIL POWERS UNDER MHA 1983

Though a detailed account of powers to admit and detain mentally disordered persons in hospital under Part II of the 1983 Act cannot be given here, a brief summary of the main provisions may be helpful.

DETENTION FOR ASSESSMENT: MHA 1983 SECTION 2

This provision authorises a person's compulsory admission to hospital and detention for up to 28 days. Application is made to the managers of the hospital by the person's 'nearest relative' (see page 91) or by an ASW. The applicant must have seen the patient personally within 14 days prior to making application; an ASW must also interview the person before applying and take into account the wishes of the nearest relative. The application must be based on the separate or joint written recommendations of two doctors.

The grounds for an application are that the person:

(i)   'is suffering from mental disorder of a nature or degree which warrants the detention of the patient in a hospital for assessment (or for assessment followed by medical treatment) for at least a limited period'; and

(ii) 'ought to be so detained in the interests of his own health or safety or with a view to the protection of others'.

A completed application allows the applicant (or any person authorised by the applicant) to convey the person to hospital, usually by ambulance. The police may be asked to help if the person is violent or dangerous. The person must be taken to hospital within 14 days of the second doctor's examination. Application may be made in respect of someone who is already in hospital as an informal patient.

The patient may be discharged prior to time expiry by the RMO, the hospital managers or the patient's nearest relative. There is no power to extend the patient's detention by renewal of the application.

DETENTION FOR TREATMENT: MHA 1983 SECTION 3

This provision authorises the person's compulsory admission to hospital and detention for treatment for an initial period of up to six months. It may be used for patients already in hospital as informal patients or detained under s2. Application to the managers of the hospital can be made by the nearest relative or an ASW but the ASW must consult the nearest relative (unless it appears that such consultation is not reasonably practical or would involve unreasonable delay) and cannot proceed if the nearest relative objects, unless a successful application is made to the County Court to displace the relative. The ASW must interview the person.

The application must be based on the separate or joint written recommendations of two doctors.

The grounds for an application are stricter than for s2 and are akin to the grounds for a s37 hospital order, specifying that the patient is:

(i)   'suffering from mental illness, severe mental impairment, psychopathic disorder or mental impairment and his mental disorder is of a nature or degree which makes it appropriate for him to receive medical treatment in a hospital'; and

(ii) 'in the case of psychopathic disorder or mental impairment. such treatment is likely to alleviate or prevent a deterioration of his condition'; and

(iii) 'it is necessary for the health or safety of the patient or the protection of other persons that he should receive such treatment and it cannot be provided unless he is detained under this section'.

Blom-Cooper *et al* (1995) considered the meaning of 'suffering from' and concluded that many psychiatrists have interpreted this too narrowly, being reluctant to invoke compulsion until the patient becomes demonstrably psychotic once more, for example after ceasing to take medication, even when relapse can be confidently expected on the basis of previous medical history. Their report argues that there is no need to 'wait for a psychosis to ripen' as the person is already 'suffering from' the disorder. Applications for admission may be renewed for a further six months and thereafter at yearly intervals, provided that the patient is medically assessed and the legal criteria for detention continue to be met.

Patients discharged from detention under s3 are subject to the requirement upon health and local authorities to provide after-care services under s117 and will be eligible for 'supervised discharge' (see page 94).

EMERGENCY DETENTION FOR ASSESSMENT: MHA 1983 SECTION 4

This provision authorises a person who would otherwise fall to be dealt with under s2 to be compulsorily admitted to hospital for a period of up to 72 hours, 'in a case of urgent necessity', where an application under s2 would involve 'undesirable delay'. Application is made by the nearest relative or an ASW. The applicant must have seen the patient within the 24-hour period prior to making application. The grounds are the same as in a s2 application but the application is based on a single (not necessarily 'approved') doctor's recommendation, if practicable given by a doctor who has 'previous acquaintance' with the person. Thus s4 is intended for use only for genuine emergencies where the need for admission is so urgent that a second or an approved doctor cannot be found in time. The application ceases to have effect after 72 hours unless the second medical opinion necessary for s2 detention for 28 days reaches the hospital managers within that initial period.

HOLDING POWERS TO DETAIN CURRENT IN-PATIENTS: MHA 1983 SECTION 5

A doctor in charge of an in-patient's treatment (including treatment for a physical disorder) may detain the patient for up to 72 hours on the grounds that an application ought to be made for the compulsory admission of the patient to hospital. The doctor simply has to provide the hospital managers with a written report to that effect.

In-patients receiving treatment for mental disorder may be detained for up to six hours if a registered mental nurse believes that 'the patient is suffering from mental disorder to such a degree that it is necessary for his health or safety or for the protection of others for him to be immediately restrained from leaving the hospital' and 'it is not practicable to secure the immediate attendance of a doctor' to exercise their holding power.

GUARDIANSHIP: MHA 1983 SECTION 7

This provides for a person aged 16 or over to be placed under the guardianship of a local Social Services Department (or someone who is acceptable to that authority), on the application of the nearest relative or an ASW, supported by two doctors' recommendations. The grounds on which a patient may be received into guardianship are that:

(i)   the patient is suffering from a mental disorder as defined by MHA 1983 s1(2);

(ii) the mental disorder is of a nature or degree which warrants reception into guardianship;

(iii) guardianship is necessary in the interests of the health or safety of the patient or for the protection of other people.

The initial period of guardianship is six months, renewable for a further six months and thereafter at yearly intervals.

The powers under s7 guardianship are the same as apply under a s37 guardianship order (see Chapter 11).

APPROVED MEDICAL PRACTITIONERS

Whenever MHA 1983 requires the recommendation of two doctors in the exercise of civil or criminal powers, one of them must be 'approved' under s12(2) 'as having special experience in the diagnosis or treatment of mental disorder'. Approval is also necessary for the purposes of making a psychiatric probation order. Approval is undertaken by district health authorities, on behalf of the Secretary of State, on the advice of an advisory panel. Approval is not limited to doctors holding consultant status, nor are all approved doctors qualified psychiatrists; some doctors within the Prison Health Care Service are listed.

In all applications, s12(2) requires that one of the doctors must, if practicable, have 'previous acquaintance' with the patient.

As a safeguard against collusion, s12(3) provides (in the case of a patient being admitted to an NHS hospital as a non-paying patient) that not more than one of the two doctors making recommendation may be a member of the hospital's staff. Exceptionally, both doctors may be hospital staff, provided that three criteria are satisfied (s12(4)): (i) securing an outside doctor would cause delay involving serious risk to the patient's health or safety; (ii) one of the doctors works at the hospital for less than half of their NHS contractual time; (iii) where one of the doctors is a consultant, the other does not work under that consultant's direction. A s4 emergency admission may be recommended by a hospital staff doctor.

PATIENTS IN CUSTODY

Where a patient subject to civil detention or s7 guardianship is sentenced, committed or remanded in custody for a period exceeding six months, their status ceases to have effect at the expiration of six months (MHA 1983 s22(1)). If their time in custody does not exceed six months but their status would otherwise have expired during that time, their liability to hospital detention or guardianship is extended and deemed to run until the end of the day of custodial discharge (s22(2)). Additionally, they are then treated as though absent without leave for the purposes of MHA 1983 s18 and remain liable for 28 days to be detained or returned. There follows a period of seven days during which the RMO should examine the patient and determine whether his liability to detention should be renewed. MH(PC)A 1995 s22(3) made explicit provision to retain the 28 day liability in this respect and the revised (six months) provisions of s18(4) (see page 92) do not apply.

MENTAL HEALTH ACT COMMISSION

Established as a special health authority under the National Health Service Act 1977, the functions of the Commission include a general protective responsibility for all detained patients to 'keep under review the exercise of the powers and the discharge of the duties conferred or imposed by (the 1983 Act) so far as relating to the detention of patients or to patients liable to be detained' (MHA 1983 s120(1)). The Commission visits and interviews detained patients and investigates patients' complaints.

Appendix II
DRUGS GLOSSARY

Space permits only a very brief description of some of the drugs prescribed in psychiatric practice, intended as a rough guide for non-medical practitioners. Names in brackets indicate the active drug in proprietary brands. Some of the proprietary brands may no longer be marketed but are included as they have been available in the recent past. For further reference, see MIMMS (the *Monthly Index of Medical Specialities*, Haymarket Publishing) or the BNF (*British National Formulary*, BMA).

Allegron (nortriptyline)	anti-depressant (TCAD)
Amitryptyline	generic anti-depressant sedative commonly used for agitated or violent patients
Amisulpride	'atypical' antipsychotic drug, for schizophrenia
Anafranil (clomipramine)	anti-depressant and for obsessional or phobic states
Androcur – see *Cyproterone acetate*	
Anquil (benperidol)	used in the control of anti-social behaviour
Asendis (amoxapine)	anti-depressant (TCAD)
Ativan (benzodiazine)	tranquilliser for anxiety
Benzodiazepines	minor tranquillisers and hypnotics (sleep promoters), *eg* Valium, Librium, Ativan
Bolvidon (mianserin)	anti-depressant
Camcolit (lithium)	for manic and manic-depressive illness and in the control of aggression or self-mutilation
Carbamazepine	for manic-depressive illness
Clopixol (zuclopenthixol)	for psychoses, especially schizophrenia, particularly for patients who are agitated or aggressive
Chlorpromazine	generic name for an antipsychotic drug, with a marked sedating effect
Citalopram	anti-depressant; also used for panic disorder
Clopixol – see *zuclopenthixol decanoate*	
Clozapine	'atypical' antipsychotic drug, for schizophrenia
Clozaril – see *Clozapine*	
Concordin (protriptyline)	anti-depressant, especially for apathetic, withdrawn patients
Cyproterone acetate	libido inhibitor used in treatment of male hypersexuality and sexual deviation
Depixol (flupenthixol)	for schizophrenia and other psychoses, particularly for patients who are withdrawn or apathetic, by depot injection

Dolmatil (sulpiride)	for schizophrenia, especially where characterised by lack of social contact
Dozic (haloperidol)	for schizophrenia, mania, organic psychoses and alcohol withdrawal
Droleptan – see *Droperidol*	
Droperidol	major tranquilliser for calming manic, agitated patients
Efexor (venlafaxine)	anti-depressant
Epanutin (hydenoin)	anti-convulsant
Faverin	anti-depressant with less sedative effect
Fentazin (perphenazine)	tranquilliser for treatment of anxiety, violent or dangerously impulsive behaviour, schizophrenia and other psychoses, especially paranoia
Fluanxol (flupenthixol)	anti-depressant
Fluoxetine	for depression and bulimia
Flupentixol Decanoate	anti-psychotic maintenance by intramuscular injection for schizophrenia and other psychoses
Gamanil (lofepramine)	anti-depressant (TCAD)
Haldol (haloperidol)	antipsychotic especially for manic behaviour
Haldol Decanoate (haloperidol)	long-term maintenance drug for schizophrenia and other psychoses
Haloperidol	generic name for an antipsychotic drug which may be used for rapid control of hyperactive psychotic states
Haloperidol Decanoate	anti-psychotic maintenance by intramuscular injection for schizophrenia and other psychoses
Heminevrin (chlormethiazole)	short acting hypnotic and sedative, used primarily for management of restlessness and agitation (especially in older people) and for alcohol withdrawal states
Largactil (chlorpromazine)	for schizophrenia, mania, affective disorders and other psychoses, especially paranoia, and in the control of violent or dangerously impulsive behaviour
Lentizol (amitriptyline)	sedatory anti-depressant
Limbitrol (amitriptyline and chlordiazepoxide)	for depression and depressive anxiety
Liskonum (lithium)	for acute mania and preventing recurrent manic depressive illness
Lithium	generic name of anti-psychotic drug for acute mania, manic-depression and to prevent recurrent affective disorders

Lofexidine	for management of opioid withdrawal
Ludiomil (maprotiline)	sedating anti-depressant
Lustral	anti-depressant
Marplan (isocarboxazide)	anti-depressant (MAOI)
Methadone	narcotic analgesic commonly used as prescribed substitute for heroin
Moclobemide	anti-depressant, for major depression (MAOI)
Modecate (fluphenazine)	for schizophrenia and paranoid psychoses, by injection, particularly for chronic patients who are unreliable in taking oral medication
Moditen (fluphenazine)	anti-psychotic, for management of anxiety, agitation and behavioural disorder
Mogadon (benzodiazine)	sedative for insomnia
Molipaxin (trazodone)	for depression and depressive anxiety
Motipress (phenothiazine)	tranquiliiser for anxiety/depression
Motival (fluphenazine and nortriptyline)	for depression and depressive anxiety
Naltrexone	to prevent relapse by previously opioid-dependent patients
Nardil (phenelzine)	for depression and phobic states (MAOI)
Nembutal	a barbituate sedative
Neulactil (pericyazine)	for schizophrenia and other psychoses, anxiety, violent or dangerously impulsive behaviour
Nitrazepam (benzodiazine)	mild sedative for anxiety/insomnia
Norval (mianserin)	anti-depressant
Nortiptyline	antidepressant (TCAD)
Nozinan (methotrimeprazine)	sedating drug, alternative to largactil
Olanzapine	'atypical' anti-psychotic; may maintain improvement in those who have responded to initial treatment
Orap (pimozide)	general tranquillising anti-psychotic and for agitated, excited states
Paroxetine	for depression, obsessive-compulsive disorder, panic attacks, social phobia (SSRI)
Pertofran (desipramine)	anti-depressant (TCAD)
Phenothiazines	a class of anti-psychotic drug
Physeptone	form of methadone
Piportil (pipotiazine)	anti-psychotic maintenance by intramuscular depot injection for schizophrenia and other psychoses
Priadel (lithium)	for mania, manic depression, affective disorders, control of aggression or self-mutilation

237

Procyclidine	to correct parkinsonian side-effects of anti-psychotic drugs
Promazine	anti-psychotic for severe anxiety
Prothiaden (dothiephin)	sedating anti-depressant and for acute anxiety (TCAD)
Prozac – see *fluoxetine*	
Quetiapine	'atypical' antipsychotic drug, for schizophrenia
Reboxetine	antidepressant
Risperidone	'atypical' antipsychotic drug, for acute and chronic psychoses
Serenace	see haloperidol
Seroxat (paroxetine)	anti-depressant and for depressive anxiety
Sertraline	anti-depressant; may also be used for obsessive compulsive disorder
Sinequam (doxepin)	sedating anti-depressant (TCAD)
Solian	see amisulpride
Soneryl	a barbituate sedative
Stelazine (trifluoperazine)	for anxiety states in low dosage; for schizophrenia, especially paranoia and dangerously impulsive behaviour, in high dosage
Stemetil (prochlorperazine)	tranquilliser for chronic schizophrenia, acute mania and anxiety states (or minor emotional disturbance in low doses)
Sulpitil – see *sulpiride*	
Sulpiride	for acute and chronic schizophrenia and related psychoses
Surmontil (trimipramine)	sedatory anti-depressant where anxiety, agitation or sleep disturbance (TCAD)
Tegretol	an anti-convulsant for epilepsy and for manic-depressive psychosis
Temazepam	a benzodiazepine hypnotic for sleeping difficulty
Thioridazine	for schizophrenia, mania and the management of anxiety, agitation, violent or dangerously impulsive behaviour (once marketed as Melleril)
Tofranil (imipramine)	anti-depressant, especially for withdrawn, apathetic patients (TCAD)
Triptafen (amitriptyline)	tranquilliser for depression linked to anxiety (TCAD)
Tryptizol (amitriptyline)	sedatory anti-depressant (also for eneuresis) (TCAD)
Valium (benzodiazepine)	tranquilliser for anxiety, with or without insomnia, and for alcohol withdrawal

Vivalan (viloxazine)   non-sedating anti-depressant

Zispin (mirtazapine)   anti-depressant

Zuclopenthixol Decaoate   anti-psychotic maintenance by intramuscular injection for schizophrenia and other psychoses, particularly with aggression and agitation

Zyprexa – see *olanzapine*

SIDE EFFECTS

The following adverse effects may be experienced:

Anti-Psychotic Drugs: (for schizophrenia, etc) spasms of the eye, face, back or neck muscles (dystonia); motor restlessness and inability to sit still (akanthisia); Parkinsonian syptoms of tremor; dry mouth; nasal stuffiness; weight gain; difficulty in passing urine; constipation; blurred vision; rapid heart beat; impotence. 'Atypical' anti-psychotics have no marked Parkinsonian side-effects.

TCAD (tricyclic anti-depressants): dry mouth; constipation; urine retention; blurred vision; palpitations; tremor; dizziness; sweating; weakness or fatigue; ataxia (lack of co-ordination, clumsiness in movement or speech); allergic skin reactions.

MAOI (monomine oxidase inhibitors): insomnia; postural hypotension; dry mouth; constipation; urine retention; tremor; dizziness, drowsiness, weakness or fatigue; gastro-intestinal difficulties.

SSRI (selective serotonin re-uptake inhibitors): gastro-intestinal effects; weight variation; dry mouth; nervousness; anxiety; insomnia; dizziness; sexual dysfunction; movement disorder.

Lithium-based Anti-Depressants: nausea; diarrhoea; tremor; muscle weakness; weight gain.

Other Anti-Depressants: nausea; sweating; tremor; dry mouth; drowsiness; diarrhoea.

Benzodiazepines: drowsiness; light-headedness; vertigo; visual disturbance; ataxia; hypotension; urine retention; libido change. More toxic when taken with alcohol.

Barbiturate-based Drugs: hangover with drowsiness; dizziness; ataxia; headache; paradoxical excitement; confusion.

REFERENCES

Association of Chief Officers of Probation (1994) *Probation actively working with Health and Social Services in the management of Mentally Disordered Offenders*, ACOP.

Allen H. (1987) *Justice Unbalanced: Gender, Psychiatry and Judicial Decisions*, Open University Press.

Austin C. *et al* (2003) 'Improving Psychiatric Information for Magistrates' Courts', *Justice of the Peace* 167, 6-7.

Barker M. and Swyer B. (1994) 'Communication and Collaboration in Community Care for Mentally Disordered Offenders', *Probation Journal* 41, 130-134.

Bean P. *et al* (1991) *Out of Harm's Way*, MIND Publications.

Bean P. and Nemitz T. (1994) *Out of Depth and Out of Sight*, MENCAP.

Birmingham L., Mason D. and Grubin D. (1996) 'Prevalence of Mental Disorder in Remand Prisoners', *BMJ* 313, 1521-24.

Blom-Cooper L. (Chair) (1992) *Report of Committee of Inquiry into Complaints about Ashworth Hospital*, HMSO.

Blom-Cooper L. *et al* (1995) *The Falling Shadow: One Patient's Mental Health Care 1978-93*, Duckworth Press.

Blumenthal S. and Wessely S. (1992) 'National Survey of Current Arrangements for Diversion from Custody in England and Wales', *BMJ* 305, 1322-1325 (summarising The Extent of Local Arrangements for the Diversion of the Mentally Abnormal Offender from Custody, Report to Department of Health, 1992).

Brooke D. *et al* (1996) 'Point Prevalence of Mental Disorder in Unconvicted Male Prisoners in England & Wales', *BMJ* 313, 1524-7.

Brown A. and Crisp D. (1992) 'Diverting Cases from Prosecution in the Public Interest', *Home Office Research Bulletin* No.32, 7-12.

Brown D. (1997) *PACE Ten Years On: A Review of the Research*, Research Study 155, Home Office.

Browne D. (1990) *Black People, Mental Health and the Courts*, NACRO, CRE and Afro-Caribbean Mental Health Association.

Bucke T. and Brown D. (1997) *In Police Custody: Police Powers and Suspects' Rights under the Revised PACE Codes of Practice*, Research Study 174, Home Office.

Butler, Lord (chair) (1975) *Report of the Committee on Mentally Abnormal Offenders*, Cmnd 6244, HMSO.

Chambers C. and Rix K. (1999) 'A Controlled Evaluation of Assessments by Doctors and Nurses in a Magistrates' Court Mental Health Assessment and Diversion Team', *Med.Sci.Law* 39, 38-48.

Children's Legal Centre (1994) *Mental Health Handbook: A Guide to the Law affecting Children and Young People* (2nd ed), CLC.

Chung M. *et al* (1998) 'A Description of a Forensic Diversion Service in one City in the UK', *Med.Sci.Law* 38, 242-49.

Chung M. *et al* (1999) 'A Follow-Up Study of Mentally Disordered Offenders after a Court Diversion Scheme: Six Month and One-Year Comparison', *Med.Sci.Law* 39, 31-37.

Clark J. *et al* (2002) 'Psychiatric Probation Orders: Failed Provision or Future Panacea?', *Med.Sci.Law* 42(1), 58-63.

Coid J. (1988) 'Mentally Abnormal Prisoners on Remand', *BMJ* 296, 1779-1782.

Coid J. (1991) 'Psychiatric Profiles of Difficult/Disruptive Prisoners' in Bottomley K. and Hay W. (eds), *Special Units for Difficult Prisoners*, Hull University Centre for Criminology and Criminal Justice.

Coid J. *et al* (2002) 'The National Survey of Psychiatric Morbidity among Prisoners and the Future of Prison Healthcare', *Med.Sci. Law* 42(3), 245-50.

Cooke A. *et al* (1994) 'Something to Lose: Case Management for Mentally Disordered Offenders, *Journal of Mental Health* 3, 59-67.

Cooke D. (1991) 'Psychological Treatment as an Alternative to Prosecution: A Form of Primary Diversion', *Howard Journal* 30(1), 53-65.

Crisp D. *et al* (1995) *Public Interest Case Assessment Schemes*, Research Study No.138, Home Office.

Dell S. (1984) *Murder into Manslaughter: The Diminished Responsibility Defence in Practice*, Oxford University Press.

Dell S. and Robertson G. (1988) *Sentenced to Hospital*, Oxford University Press.

Dell S. *et al* (1993) 'Remands and Psychiatric Assessments in Holloway Prison I: The Psychotic Population, II: The Non-Psychotic Population', *British Journal of Psychiatry* 163, 634-643.

Department of Health/Home Office (2000) *Reforming the Mental Health Act.*

Department of Health (2000) *Inpatients Formally Detained under MHA 1983 and other legislation, England: 1989-1990 to 1999-2000*, Statistical Bulletin 2000/19, DoH.

Department of Health/Home Office/Welsh Office (2001) *Changing the Outlook: A Strategy for Developing and Modernising Mental Health Services in Prisons*, DoH.

DHSS *et al* (1978) *Review of the Mental Health Act 1959*, Cmnd 7320, HMSO.

Dixon D. *et al* (1990) 'Safeguarding the Rights of Suspects in Police Custody', *Policing and Society* 1, 115-40.

Dolan M. and Campbell A. (1994) 'The Criminal Procedure (Insanity and Unfitness to Plead) Act 1991: A Case Report and Selected Review of the Legal Reforms', *Med.Sci.Law* 34, 155-160.

Dolan M. *et al* (1999) 'Health Status of Juvenile Offenders: A survey of young offenders appearing before the juvenile courts', *Journal of Adolescence* 22, 137-44.

Dooley E. (1990) 'Prison Suicide in England and Wales 1972-87', *British Journal of Psychiatry* 156, 40-45.

Eastman N. (1996) 'Hybrid Orders: an analysis of their likely effects on sentencing practice and on forensic psychiatric services', *Journal of Forensic Psychiatry* 7, 481-94.

Eastman N. and Peay J. (1998) 'Sentencing Psychopaths: Is the "Hospital and Limitation Direction" an Ill-Considered Hybrid?', *Crim LR* 93-108.

Exworthy T. and Parrott J. (1993) 'Evaluation of a Diversion Scheme at Magistrates' Court', *Journal of Forensic Psychiatry* 4, 497-505.

Exworthy T. and Parrott J. (1997) 'Comparative Evaluation of a Diversion from Custody Scheme', *Journal of Forensic Psychiatry* 8, 406-16.

Fallon P. *et al* (1999) Report of the Committee of Inquiry into the Personality Disorder Unit, Ashworth Special Hospital (Cm 4194), Department of Health.

Farrington D. and Jolliffe D. (2002) *A Feasibility Study into Using a Randomised Controlled Trial to Evaluate Treatment Pilots at HMP Whitemoor*, Online Report 14/02, Home Office.

Fazel S. *et al* (2001) 'Hidden Psychiatric Morbidity in Elderly Prisoners', *BJ Psychiatry* 179, 535-39.

Fryers T. *et al* (1998) 'Severe Mental Illness in Prisoners', *BMJ* 317, 1025-6.

Geelan S. *et al* (1998) 'A Profile of Residents at Elliott House', *Health Trends* 30(4), 101-5.

Geelan S. *et al* (2000) 'A Bail and Probation Hostel for Mentally Disordered Defendants', *Journal of Forensic Psychiatry* 11, 93-104.

Gordon D. and Hedderman C. (1993) 'Panel Assessment Schemes and other responses to mentally disordered offenders', *Home Office Research Bulletin* No.34, 9-12.

Gray N. *et al* (2001) 'Fitness to Plead: Implications from Case-Law arising from the Criminal Justice & Public Order Act 1994', *Journal of Forensic Psychiatry* 12, 52-62.

Greenberg N. *et al* (2002) 'A Prospective Survey of Section 136 in Rural England', *Med.Sci.Law* 42, 129-34.

Greenberg N. and Haines N. (2003) 'The Use of Section 136 in a Family of Rural English Police Forces', *Med.Sci.Law* 43, 75-78.

Greenhalgh N. *et al* (1996) 'Pilot Mental Health Assessment and Diversion Scheme for an English Metropolitan PSD', *Med.Sci.Law* 36, 52-58.

Griew E. (1988) 'The Future of "Diminished Responsibility"', *Crim LR* 75.

Grounds A. (1991) 'The Transfer of Sentenced Prisoners to Hospital 1960-83: Study in One Special Hospital', *BJ Crim.* 37, 544-51.

Grounds A. (2000) 'The Future of Prison Health Care', *Journal of Forensic Psychiatry* 11(2), 260-67.

Grubin D. (1993) 'What Constitutes Fitness to Plead?', *Crim LR* 748.

Grubin D. (1996) *Fitness to Plead in England & Wales*, Psychology Press.

Grubin D. (1996) 'Silence in Court: Psychiatry and the Criminal Justice & Public Order Act 1994', *Journal of Forensic Psychiatry* 7, 647-52.

Gudjonsson G. *et al* (1993) *Persons at Risk During Interviews in Police Custody: The Identification of Vulnerabilities*, RCCJ Research Study No.12, HMSO.

Gunn J. *et al* (1991) 'Treatment Needs of Prisoners with Psychiatric Disorders', *BMJ* 303, 338-341.

Harding J. and Cameron A. (1999) 'What the Probation Officer Expects from the Psychiatrist', *Advances in Psychiatric Treatment* 5, 463-70.

Haynes P. and Henfrey D. (1995) 'Making a Reality of Reed?', *Probation Journal* 42 (forthcoming).

Health Advisory Committee for the Prison Service (1997) *The Provision of Mental Health Care in Prisons*, Home Office.

Hedderman C. (1993) *Panel Assessment Schemes for Mentally Disordered Offenders*, Home Office Research and Planning Unit Paper No.76.

HM Inspectorate of Prisons (1996) *Patient or Prisoner?: a new strategy for health care in prisons*, Home Office.

HM Inspectorate of Prisons (2000) *Unjust Deserts: A Thematic Review*, Home Office.

HM Inspectorate of Probation (1993) *Probation Orders with Requirement for Psychiatric Treatment*, Home Office.

HM Prison Service and NHS Executive (1999) *The Future Organisation of Prison Health Care*, Home Office.

Hoggett B. (1996) *Mental Health Law* (4th ed), Sweet and Maxwell.

Holloway J. and Shaw J. (1992) 'Providing a Forensic Psychiatry Service to a Magistrates' Court', *Journal of Forensic Psychiatry* 3, 153-59.

Home Office (1995) *Appropriate Adults: Report of Review Group*, Home Office.

Home Office (1997) *Mentally Disordered Offenders: Survey of Inter-Agency Arrangements* (Circular MN97 1/71/1), Home Office

Home Office/Department of Health (1995) *Mentally Disordered Offenders: Inter-Agency Working*, HOC 12/1995, Home Office.

Home Office/Department of Health (1999) *Managing Dangerous People with Severe Personality Disorder: Proposals for Policy Development gramme*, Home Office/DoH.

Home Office, Department of Health and HM Prison Service (2002) *The Dangerous and Severe Personality Disorder Programme*, Factsheet, Home Office.

Hudson B. *et al* (1993) *Training for Work with Mentally Disordered Offenders*, CCETSW.

Hudson D. *et al* (1995a) *Psychiatric Court Liaison to Central London*, Riverside Mental Health.

Hudson D. *et al* (1995b) *Psychiatric Intervention at the Police Station*, Riverside Mental Health.

Humphries M., Kenney-Herbert J. and Gray C. (1998) 'Restricted Hospital Orders: A Survey of Forensic Psychiatrists' Practice and Attitudes to their Use', *Journal of Forensic Psychiatry* 9, 173-80.

Huws R. *et al* (1997) 'Prison Transfers to Special Hospitals since the Introduction of MHA 1983', *Journal of Forensic Psychiatry* 8, 74-84.

James A. (1996) *Life on the Edge: Diversion and the Mentally Disordered Offender*, Mental Health Foundation.

James D. (1999) 'Court Diversion at 10 Years: Can it work? Does it work? Has it a future?', *Journal of Forensic Psychiatry* 10, 503-20.

James D. (2000) 'Police Station Diversion Schemes: Role and Efficacy in Central London', *Journal of Forensic Psychiatry* 11, 532-55.

James D. *et al* (1997) 'A Court-Focused Model of Forensic Psychiatry: Abolishing Remands to Prison?', *Journal of Forensic Psychiatry* 8, 390-405.

James D. and Hamilton L. (1991) 'The Clerkenwell Scheme: assessing efficacy and cost of a psychiatric liaison service to a magistrates' court', *BMJ* 303, 282-285.

James D. and Hamilton L. (1992) 'Setting Up Psychiatric Liaison Schemes to Magistrates' Courts: Problems and Practicalities', *Med.Sci.Law* 32, 167-176.

James D. and Harlow P. (2000) 'Maximising the Efficacy of Court Diversion Schemes: Evaluation of a Supra-District Court Diversion Centre', *Med.Sci.Law* 40, 52-60.

James D. *et al* (2002) *Outcome of Psychiatric Admission Through the Courts*, RDS Occasional Paper No. 79, Home Office.

Johnson S. and Taylor R. (2002) *Statistics of Mentally Disordered Offenders 2002*, Statistical Bulletin 13/02, Home Office.

Jones R. (1999) *Mental Health Manual*, Sweet & Maxwell.

Joseph P. and Potter M. (1993) 'Diversion from Custody I:Psychiatric Assessment at the Magistrates' Court', *British Journal of Psychiatry* 162, 325-330 (summarising Joseph P. (1992) Psychiatric Assessment at the Magistrates' Court, Home Office and DoH).

Kaul A. (1994) 'Interim Hospital Orders: A Regional Secure Unit's Experience', *Med.Sci.Law* 34, 233-236.

Kennedy M. *et al* (1997) 'Supported Bail for Mentally Vulnerable Defendants', *Howard Journal* 36, 158-69.

Kershaw C. *et al* (1997) *Restricted Patients: Reconvictions and Recalls by the end of 1995*, Statistical Bulletin 1/97, Home Office.

Lader D. *et al* (2000) *Psychiatric Morbidity among Young Offenders in England and Wales*, Office of National Statistics, The Stationery Office.

Laing J. (1995) 'The Mentally Disordered Suspect at the Police Station', *Crim LR* 371-81.

Laing J. (1996) 'The Police Surgeon and Mentally Disordered Suspects: An Adequate Safeguard?', *Web Journal of Current Legal Issues* 1, 29-36.

Laing J. (1997) 'The Likely Impact of Mandatory and Minimum Sentences on the Disposal of Mentally Disordered Offenders', *Journal of Forensic Psychiatry* 9, 504-5.

Laing J. (1999) *Care or Custody?*, Oxford.

Lane Lord (Chair) (1993) *Report of the Committee on the Penalty for Homicide*, Prison Reform Trust.

Law Society Criminal Law Committee (1993) 'Police Station Advice', *Law Society Gazette* 90, 19 May 1993, 41-42.

Lee-Evans M. (1993) 'A View from the Private Sector' in Watson W. and Grounds A. (eds) *The Mentally Disordered Offender in an Era of Community Care*, Cambridge University Press.

Lewis P. (1980) *Psychiatric Probation Orders*, Cambridge Institute of Criminology.

Littlechild B. (1995) 'Reassessing the Role of the Appropriate Adult', *Crim LR* 540-45.

Lord Chancellor's Department Best Practice Advisory Group (1992) *Mentally Disordered Offenders*, LCD.

Mackay R. (1993) 'The Consequences of Killing Very Young Children' [1993] *Crim LR* 21-30.

Mackay R. (1995) *Mental Condition Defences in the Criminal Law*, Clarendon Press.

Mackay R. (1999) 'The Abnormality of Mind Factor in Diminished Responsibility', *Crim LR* 117-25.

Mackay R. and Kearns G. (1994) 'The Continued Underuse of Unfitness to Plead and the Insanity Defence' *Crim LR* 576-579.

Mackay R. and Kearns G. (1999) 'More Fact(s) about the Insanity Defence' [1994] *Crim LR* 714-25.

Mackay R. and Kearns G. (2000) 'An Upturn in Unfitness to Plead? Disability in Relation to the Trial under the 1991 Act', *Crim LR* 532-46.

Mackay R. and Machin M. (2000) 'The Operation of Section 48 of the Mental Health Act 1983' *BJ Criminology* 40, 727-45 (summarised in Mackay R. and Machin M. (1998) 'Transfers from Prison to Hospital: The Operation of Section 48 of the Mental Health Act 1983' *Research Findings No. 84*, Home Office).

Maden A., Swinton M. and Gunn J. (1994) 'A Criminological and Psychiatric Survey of Women Serving a Prison Sentence', *BJ Criminology* 34, 172-191.

Maden A. *et al* (1996) *Mental Disorder in Remand Prisoners*, Home Office.

Maier-Katkin D. and Ogle R. (1993) 'A Rationale for Infanticide Laws' [1993] *Crim LR* 903-914.

Mendelson E. (1992) 'A Survey of Practice at a Regional Forensic Service', *British Journal of Psychiatry* 160, 769-776.

Mental Health Foundation (1994) *Promoting Care and Justice*, Report of the Mental Health Foundation's Regional Conferences on Improving Services for Mentally Disordered Offenders, MHF.

Mitchison S. *et al* (1994) 'Recorded Psychiatric Morbidity in a Large Prison for Male Remanded and Sentenced Prisoners', *Med.Sci.Law* 34, 324-330.

NACRO (1993a) *Community Care and Mentally Disturbed Offenders*, Mental Health Advisory Committee Policy Paper 1, NACRO.

NACRO (1993b) *Diverting Mentally Disturbed Offenders from Prosecution*, Mental Health Advisory Committee Policy Paper 2, NACRO.

NACRO (1993c) *Mentally Disturbed Prisoners at Winson Green*, NACRO.

NACRO (1994) *Diverting Mentally Disturbed Offenders from Custodial Remands and Sentences*, Mental Health Advisory Committee Policy Paper 3, NACRO.

NACRO (2002) *Mentally Disordered Offender User Survey: Long Term Medium Secure Care – Patient Views on Quality of Life*, NACRO.

Nadkarni R. *et al* (2000) 'Partnership with Probation Hostels: A Step Forward in Community Psychiatry', *Psychiatric Bulletin* 24, 222-4.

National Schizophrenia Fellowship (2000) *The NSF National Diversion/Liaison Scheme Register September 1999-April 2000*, NSF.

Nemitz T. and Bean P. (1994) 'The Use of the Appropriate Adult Scheme: A Preliminary Report', *Med.Sci.Law* 34, 161-166.

Nemitz T. and Bean P. (1998) 'The Effectiveness of a Volunteer Appropriate Adult Scheme', *Med.Sci.Law* 38, 251-6.

Palmer C. (1996) 'The Appropriate Adult', *Legal Action*, May 1996, 6-7.

Parker C. (1992) *Confessions and the Mentally Vulnerable Suspect*, unpublished LL.M thesis.

Parsons S., Walker L. and Grubin D. (2001) 'Prevalence of Mental Disorder in Female Remand Prisoners', *Journal of Forensic Psychiatry* 12, 194-202.

Pearse J. and Gudjonsson G. (1996) 'How Appropriate are Appropriate Adults?', *Journal of Forensic Psychiatry* 7, 570-80.

Phillips C. and Brown D. (1998) *Enquiry into the Criminal Justice System: A Survey of Police Arrests and their Outcomes*, Research Study 185, Home Office.

Pierzchniak P. *et al* (1997) 'Liaison between Prison, Court and Psychiatric Services', *Health Trends* 29, 26-29.

Prins H. (1993) 'The People Nobody Owns' in Watson W. and Grounds A. *The Mentally Disturbed in an Era of Community Care: New Directions in Provision*, Cambridge University Press.

Prins H. (1996) 'Can the Law Serve as the Solution to Social Ills? The case of the Mental Health (Patients in the Community) Act 1995', *Med.Sci.Law* 36, 217-220.

Pritchard C. *et al* (1992) 'Mental Illness, Drug and Alcohol Abuse and HIV Risk Behaviour in 214 Young Adult Probation Clients', *Social Work and Social Sciences Review* 3, 227-242.

Purchase N. *et al* (1996) 'Evaluation of a Psychiatric Court Liaison Scheme in North London', *British Medical Journal* 313, 531-32.

Rawlings B. (1999) 'Therapeutic Communities in Prisons: A Research Review', *Therapeutic Communities* 20, 177-93.

Rawlings B. (2000) 'Therapeutic Communities in Prisons', *Prison Service Journal* 129, 19-22.

Reed J. (chair) (1992) *Review of Health and Social Services for Mentally Disordered Offenders and Others Requiring Similar Services*, Cm 2088, HMSO.

Reed J. and Lyne M. (1997) 'Inpatient Care of Mentally Ill People in Prison: Results of a Year's Programme of Semi-Structured Inspections, *BMJ* 320, 1031-4.

Reed J. and Lyne M. (2000) 'The Quality of Health Care in Prison: Results of a Year's Programme of Semi-Structured Inspections, *BMJ* 315, 1420-4.

Revolving Doors (1994) *The Management of People with Mental Health Problems by the Paddington Police*, Revolving Doors.

Richardson T. *et al* (2003) 'Probation Orders with Conditions of Psychiatric Treatment: A Descriptive Study', *Med.Sci.Law* 43, 80-84.

Riordan S. *et al* (2000) 'Diversion at the Point of Arrest: Mentally Disordered People and Contact with the Police', *Journal of Forensic Psychiatry* 11, 683-90.

Ritchie J. et al (1994) *The Report of the Enquiry into the Care and Treatment of Christopher Clunis*, HMSO.

Robertson G. (1992) *The Role of Police Surgeons*, RCCJ Study No.6, HMSO.

Robertson G. *et al* (1992) 'Mentally Disordered Remand Prisoners', Home Office Research Bulletin 32, 1-6 (summarising Grounds A. *et al* (1991) Mentally Disordered Remanded Prisoners, Report to the Home Office, Cambridge Institute of Criminology).

Robertson G. *et al* (1994) 'A Follow-Up of Remanded Mentally Ill Offenders given Hospital Orders', *Med.Sci.Law* 34, 61-66.

Robertson G. *et al* (1996) 'Police Interviewing and the Use of Appropriate Adults', *Journal of Forensic Psychiatry* 7, 297-309.

Robertson G., Pearson R. and Gibb R. (1996) 'The Entry of Mentally Disordered People to the CJS', *British Journal of Psychiatry* 169, 172-80.

Romilly C. *et al* (1997) 'Limited Duration Restriction Orders: What are they for?', *Journal of Forensic Psychiatry* 8, 562-72.

Rowlands R. *et al* (1996) 'Diverted to Where? What Happens to the Diverted Mentally Disordered Offender?', *Journal of Forensic Psychiatry* 7, 284-296.

Salem S. (1982) *The Psychiatric Remand Process in Magistrates' Courts*, Report to the Home Office (unpublished), Cambridge Institute of Criminology.

Samuels A. (1995) 'Hospital Orders without Conviction' [1995] *Crim LR* 220-222.

Scottish Office (1998) *Interviewing People who are Mentally Disordered: 'Appropriate Adults' Schemes*, Scottish Office.

Shaw J. *et al* (1999) 'Prevalence and Detection of Psychiatric Disorder in Defendants Attending Court', *Lancet* 353, 1053-6.

Shaw J. *et al* (2001) 'Loss of Contact with Psychiatric Services in People Diverted from the Criminal Justice System', *Journal of Forensic Psychiatry* 12, 203-10.

Singleton N. *et al* (1998) *Psychiatric Morbidity among Prisoners in England & Wales*, Stationery Office.

Smith J. and Donovan M. (1990) 'The Prosecution of Psychiatric In-Patients', *Journal of Forensic Psychiatry* 4, 661-664.

Snowden P., McKenna J. and Jasper A. (1999) 'Management of Conditionally Discharged Patients and others who present similar risks in the community: Integrated or Parallel?', *Journal of Forensic Psychiatry* 10, 583-96.

Spence S. and McPhillips M. (1995) 'Personality Disorder and Section 136 in Westminster', *Med.Sci.Law* 35, 48-52.

Staite C. and Martin N. (1993) 'What else can we do? New Initiatives in Diversion from Custody', *JP* 157, 280-81.

Staite C. *et al* (1994) *Diversion from Custody for Mentally Disordered Offenders*, Longman.

Stone N. (1997) *A Companion Guide to Life Sentences*, Shaw and Sons.

Stone N. (1999) *A Companion Guide to Enforcement* (3rd ed), Shaw and Sons.

Stone N. (2001) *A Companion Guide to Sentencing: Part Two*, Shaw & Sons.

Stone N. (forthcoming) *A Companion Guide to Life Sentences* (2nd ed), Shaw and Sons.

Street R. (1998) *The Restricted Hospital Order: from court to community*, Research Study 186, Home Office.

Sullivan (1994) 'Intoxicants and Diminished Responsibility', *Crim LR* 156.

Taylor J. and Parrott J. (1988) 'Elderly Offenders: a study of age-related factors among custodially remanded prisoners, *B. J. Psychiatry* 152, 340-56.

Taylor R. (2000) 'A Seven-Year Reconviction Study of HMP Grendon Therapeutic Community', *Research Findings No. 115*, Home Office.

Tully B. and Cahill D. (1984) *Police Interviewing of the Mentally Handicapped: An Experimental Study*, Police Foundation.

Vaughan P. and Badger D. (1995) *Working with the Mentally Disordered Offender in the Community*, Chapman and Hall.

Vaughan P., Kelly M. and Pullen N. (1999) 'Psychiatric Support to Mentally Disordered Offenders within the Prison System', *Probation* 46, 106-12.

Vaughan P., Pullen N. and Kelly M. (2000) 'Services for Mentally Disordered Offenders in Community Psychiatry Teams', *Journal of Forensic Psychiatry* 11, 571-86.

Vaughan P., Kelly M. and Pullen N. (2001) 'The Working Practices of the Police in relation to Mentally Disordered Offenders and Diversion Services', *Med.Sci.Law* 41, 13-18.

Vaughan P. and Stevenson S. (2002) 'An Opinion Survey of Mentally Disordered Offender Service Users', *British Journal of Forensic Practice* 4, 11-20.

Ward T. (1997) 'Magistrates, Insanity and the Law', *Crim LR* 796-804.

Weaver T. *et al* (1997) 'Impact of a Dedicated Service for Mentally Disordered Remand Prisoners in N.W. London: Retrospective Study', *BMJ* 314, 1244-45.

White C. (2002) 'Re-Assessing the Social Worker's Role as an Appropriate Adult', *J. Social Welfare and Family Law* 24(1), 55-65.

White S. (1991) 'Insanity Defences and Magistrates' Courts' [1991] *Crim LR* 501-8.

Wickham T. (1994) *A Psychiatric Liaison Service for the Criminal Courts*, Social Work Monographs, University of East Anglia.

Wilczynski A. and Morris A. (1993) 'Parents who Kill their Children' [1993] Crim LR 31-36.

Williams J. (2000) 'The Inappropriate Adult', *J. Social Welfare and Family Law* 22(1), 43-57.

Wix S. (1994) 'Keeping on the Straight and Narrow: Diversion of MDOs at the Point of Arrest', *Psychiatric Care* 1, 102-4.

INDEX